T0354758

The
CROSS
before the
CROWN

The
CROSS
before the
CROWN

*Charles Spurgeon on Christ's
Last Words on the Cross*

*[Christ] is the most magnanimous of captains.
There was never His like among the choicest of
princes. He is always to be found in the thickest
part of the battle. When the wind blows cold, He
always takes the bleak side of the hill. The heaviest
end of the cross lies ever on His shoulders. If
He bids us carry a burden, He carries it also.*

—A part of Charles Haddon Spurgeon's last words
at the Metropolitan Tabernacle, London

Ernest LeVos

THE CROSS BEFORE THE CROWN
CHARLES SPURGEON ON CHRIST'S LAST WORDS ON THE CROSS

iUniverse books may be ordered through booksellers or by contacting:

iUniverse
1663 Liberty Drive
Bloomington, IN 47403
www.iuniverse.com
1-800-Authors (1-800-288-4677)

Because of the dynamic nature of the Internet, any web addresses or links contained in this book may have changed since publication and may no longer be valid. The views expressed in this work are solely those of the author and do not necessarily reflect the views of the publisher, and the publisher hereby disclaims any responsibility for them.

Any people depicted in stock imagery provided by Thinkstock are models, and such images are being used for illustrative purposes only.
Certain stock imagery © Thinkstock.

ISBN: 978-1-5320-0099-7 (sc)
ISBN: 978-1-5320-0098-0 (e)

Library of Congress Control Number: 2016912388

Print information available on the last page.

iUniverse rev. date: 09/06/2016

CONTENTS

PREFACE

Charles Haddon Spurgeon (June 19, 1834–January 31, 1892) went from being labeled the "Boy Preacher" (the "young servant") to the "Prince of Preachers" in Victorian England in the nineteenth century. The subject of his ministry was "the person of Jesus Christ." Christ was Surgeon's passion, and preaching on the second person of the Godhead warmed his heart even during the years when he was afflicted, downcast, and suffering from depression. He had a gospel to preach "which is not exhausted," and he trusted in a Spirit "who never deserts those who confide in him."

On April 8, 1861, in his comments at the opening meeting at the Metropolitan Tabernacle, Newington, Spurgeon said that the providence of God led him to the Metropolitan Tabernacle. In 1879, on his pastoral silver anniversary, he remarked, "I care nothing about fine language, or about petty speculations of prophecy, or a hundred dainty things; but to break the heart and bind it, to lay hold on a sheep of Christ and bring it back to the fold, is the one thing I would live for." Spurgeon was confident that the ministry and membership of the Metropolitan Tabernacle would abound "in answer to earnest prayer, (and) the Spirit of God will be poured out yet more abundantly upon the minister and the people, and that we, being bound together yet more surely in ties of affection and in ties of hearty cooperation, may go from strength to strength in glorifying God and another."

Prayers were answered, and the devoted preacher also became a writer. The membership of the Metropolitan Tabernacle numbered 5,346 in 1878, and the tabernacle was more than a house for worship; it was a working church that reached out to the city of London, to other parts of England, and to "the utter most part of the earth."

Besides more than one hundred publications and more than thirty-five hundred sermons, Spurgeon in 1865 edited *The Sword and the Trowel: A Record of Combat with Sin and Labor for the Lord* with the purpose of reporting "the efforts of the Churches and Associations, which are more or less intimately connected with the Lord's work at the Metropolitan Tabernacle, and to advocate those views of doctrine and Church order which are most certainly received among us."

This current publication is a continuation of this author's devotional and academic interest that commenced in 1988 and 2008, respectively. In 2014, this author's work *C. H. Spurgeon and the Metropolitan Tabernacle: Addresses and Testimonials, 1854–1879* was published. Dr. Tom Nettles, author of *Living by Revealed Truth* (2013), wrote on the former publication, saying, "that the lovely volume of Spurgeon testimonials ... contain some of the most moving passages of humble appreciation and love between pastor and church to be found in literature anywhere."

From the Cross to the Crown contains some of the most powerful and inspiring sermons Spurgeon preached, commencing in 1856. This author sends this book out with a prayer that those who read it will (1) take the apostle Peter's words in 2 Peter 3:18 seriously ("but grow in the grace and knowledge of our Lord and Savior Jesus Christ") and (2) take equally seriously Spurgeon's assignment in his sermon "God Forsaking His Son?" to make a life study of that bitter but blessed question "Why have You forsaken Me?"

INTRODUCTION

Charles Spurgeon in his sermon entitled "A Remarkable Benediction" said, "If you would make *your last words* worth hearing, let your whole life be worth the seeing. It is graceful to be blessing, but let it be always consistent with the blessedness of our former life" ("A Remarkable Benediction," *MTP*, Sermon # 3540, v. 62–63, 1916–1917, p. 566; my emphasis supplied). The whole life and ministry of Christ is perfect and priceless. His life was and will continue to be a blessing to countless numbers of believers.

Spurgeon, as his sermons and expositions testify, treasured the last words of the Lord Jesus Christ on the cross. In his ministry, he made the whole life of Christ worth beholding: His life, death, and resurrection and His work as the heavenly Mediator. There is not an ounce of inconsistency in the life and work of Christ.

Spurgeon's last words in the Metropolitan Tabernacle speak eloquently of his commitment and dedication to his Master:

> If you wear the livery of Christ, you will find Him so meek and lowly of heart that you will find rest unto your soul. He is the most magnanimous of captains. There was never His like among the choicest of princes. He is always to be found in the thickest part of the battle. When the wind blows cold, He always takes the bleak side of the hill. The heaviest end of the cross lies ever on His shoulders. If He bids us carry a burden, He carries it also. If there is anything that is gracious, generous, kind and tender, yes lavish and superabundant in love, you will always find it in Him. His service is life, peace, and joy.

Spurgeon would not dispute that his publications are secondary sources, of second importance, compared to Christ the Word, the divine primary source. Spurgeon's ministry was to be the very person of Jesus Christ: Christ's divine nature, His human relationships, His finished work, His death and resurrection, His present glorious intercession, His second coming, and His eternal communion and fellowship.

In his sermons, with the effective ministration of the Holy Spirit (Spurgeon leaned very heavily on the aid of the Spirit), he constantly exalted the One greater than all the patriarchs, prophets, priests, and princesses. All of the inspired scripture spoke of "the things concerning [Christ]." After announcing his text for all the messages and sermons he delivered, Spurgeon darted to the cross. Then he placed his text and message in its context, and he labored diligently in offering his congregation, his listeners, practical and relevant applications.

Here is a sample of a sermon he delivered the morning of December 9, 1877, at the Metropolitan Tabernacle, Newington, entitled "Jesus Christ Himself," taking three words form Ephesians 2:20: "And are built upon the foundation of the apostles and prophets, *Jesus Christ himself* being the chief corner stone." He commenced his sermon with these words:

> 'Jesus Christ Himself' is to occupy all our thoughts this morning. What an ocean opens up before me. Here is room in the sea for the largest ship. In which direction shall I turn your thoughts? I am embarrassed with riches. I know not where to begin, and when I once begin, where shall I end? Assuredly we need not go abroad for joys this morning, for we have a feast at home! The words are few, but the meaning vast, 'Jesus Christ Himself.' Beloved, the religion of our Lord Jesus Christ contains in it nothing so wonderful as Himself. It is a mass of marvels, but He is THE miracle of it! The wonder of wonders is 'The Wonderful' Himself'!

In this sermon, Spurgeon opened up the following six points to his congregation: "Jesus Christ Himself is (1) 'The Essence of His Own

Work'; (2) 'The Substance of the Gospel'; (3) 'The Object of Our Love'; (4) 'The Source of All Our Joy'; (5) 'Jesus Christ is the Model of Our Life', and (6) 'He is the Lord of Our Soul.'"

On his second point, "The Substance of the Gospel," Surgeon said:

> Beloved, because Jesus is the sum of the Gospel, He must be our constant theme. 'God forbid that I should glory save in the Cross of our Lord Jesus Christ.' 'I determined not to know anything among you save Jesus Christ and Him crucified.' So spoke men of old and so say we. When we have done preaching Christ we had better have done preaching …. Put out the sun and light is gone, life is gone, all is gone. When Jesus is pushed into the background or left out of a minister's teaching, the darkness is darkness that might be felt and the people escape from it into Gospel light as soon as they can. A sermon without Jesus in it is savorless and worthless to God's tried saints—they soon seek other food. The more of Christ in our testimony, the more of light and life and power to save.

So, why continue focusing on the Spurgeon and his ministry? He is to this writer/editor a valuable pastor and teacher. His sermons are a precious mine of nuggets in practical applications, the principles of which are relevant today. He offers a preacher the appropriate ingredients for a sermon: doctrine (teachings of the Word), duty (offering encouragement and admonishing repentance and confession), devotion (beholding Christ's attributes and offices), and destiny (directing the believer's heart to heaven).

His publications are a rich secondary source on several theological subjects, although one may hold a different orientation and have a different perspective from Spurgeon. His daily readings in *The Cheque Book of the Bank of Faith* are a rich reservoir of biblical promises (do purchase the edition that includes the preface; see appendix B). His books are sources for prayer and study. He constantly makes one rush to the cross and especially, to the scriptures that speak of salvation, which is of the Sovereign Lord alone. Where the inspired scriptures are concerned, Spurgeon would exhort anyone, with the aid of the Holy Spirit, to read, hear, study, memorize, reflect, and meditate on the Word; yes, to inwardly digest the words of Christ and lace one's heart with what the Savior offers. The Lord Jesus Christ, who calls you just as you are (Matthew 11:28), will not allow you to remain just as you are.

He exhorted everyone who heard him preach to believe on the Great Substitute, His saving merits, and not to worship the accomplishments of man. Like the apostle Paul, Spurgeon would have asked, "Who then is Spurgeon?" With the aid of his elders, deacons, and various societies within the Metropolitan Tabernacle (the ministration of the Holy Spirit not excluded), Spurgeon planted and labored hard for his parishioners, "But God gave the increase" (1 Corinthians 3:4–6). He was a minister of the gospel, the good news, but Christ was his All-in-All.

A Guide to Reading *The Cross before the Crown*

Several of the publications of Spurgeon has been repackaged. This book falls into this category. (The editing of the sermons were kept to a minimum. Pronouns referring to deities, such as Jesus Christ, are capitalized, and the subtitles of sermons are capitalized and italicized. The emphasis supplied in bold and italics are mine.) *The book in your hands is intended to be a devotional.* It is divided into three parts, which include twenty-two sermons and six expositions by Spurgeon; one sermon by Octavius Winslow (1808–1878); and one selection by Matthew Henry (1662–1714) from his commentary, in place of a lack of a sermon by Spurgeon on John 19:25–28.

- Begin your reading with a prayerful reliance on the Holy Spirit. Your reading of Christ's last words can supplement your daily devotions. You may have a choice of your own devotionals. An excellent devotional supplement is Spurgeon's *Morning and Evening* (available from Christian Book Distributors, USA).

- Commence reading the two sermons in Part I: "The Scriptures of Hope and Christ's First Recorded Words." You may read and reflect on the whole sermon beginning with the *Focus* (a precis of the sermon) and the introduction; then move on to each part of the sermon (that varies from two to six parts), and end with the *Exhortation by responding to the appeal and questions.*
- Proceed to Part II, which constitutes the seven categories of the last words of Christ on the cross, and end with Part III, "From the Cross to His Glorious Appearance."
- Meditate upon and review the parts and texts of each sermon that are highlighted or are in italics.
- Consult the scriptural portions Spurgeon uses in his sermons (Spurgeon's sermons are a secondary source; the Bible is the divine primary source). You may want to keep a journal of reflective notes.

Further Reading

The following are a few sources you may desire to consult and read (besides what you may find on the Internet):

A. John Flavel, *The Works of John Flavel*, Volume I (The Banner of Truth Trust, Reprinted 2015). See Sermons 30–36, pp. 369–454. Flavel places John 19:27 as the verse for "the Second excellent Word of Christ upon the Cross" and the words of Christ to the dying thief in Luke 23:43 as "The Third of Christ's last Words upon the Cross."

B. Leslie Hardinge, *These Watched Him Die* (Washington, DC: Review and Herald Publishing Association, 1966). The following people watched Christ die: (1) Simon the Conscripted, the African farmer—"He bore the Cross"; (2) Herod the Crafty, the Edomite king—"That Fox"; (3) Caiaphas the Cynical, the high priest—"It is Expedient"; (4) Pilate the Cowardly, the

Roman judge—"I Am Innocent"; (5) Nicodemus the Cautious, the teacher of Israel—"How?"; (6) Peter the Craven, the chosen disciple—"I Know Him Not"; (7) Judas the Covetous, the smart follower—"How Much?"; (8) Centurion the Conscientious, the heathen executioner—"Truly This Was The Son of God"; (9) John the Confused, the foster brother—"Our Hands Have Handled"; (10) Thief the Converted, the lad who strayed— "Remember Me"; (11) Mary the Consecrated, the woman who fell—"Rabbani"; (12) Mary the Virgin, the woman who shared—"How May This Be?"

C. A. W. Pink, *Seven Sayings of the Saviour on the Cross: The Purpose of the Cross, Revealed* (Fearn, Ross-shire, Scotland: Christian Focus Publications, 1993, 2010). Pink includes an introduction and the seven sayings. There is ample devotional material in Pink's book. Do read chapter 3, "The Word of Affection," to complement the selection by Matthew Henry and the exposition by Spurgeon on John 19:25–28.

D. C. H. Spurgeon, *Sermons on Cries from the Cross* (Peabody, MA: Hendrickson Publishers, 2015). Nine of Spurgeon sermons on the seven last sayings of Christ in this publication are also included in the author's book. There are three sermons included in this publication a reader will desire to read: "The Miracles of Our Lord's Death" (#2059), "The Messages of Our Lord Love" (#2060), and "The Evidence of Our Lord's Wounds" (#2061), which are available from Spurgeon Gems. All sixty-three volumes of C. H. Spurgeon's sermons are available online: http://spurgeongems.org.

ACKNOWLEDGMENTS

Dedication, and in Remembrance

Thanks: to Emmett O'Donnell for the use of the sermons and expositions from Spurgeon Gems; to Pastor Ibrahim Ag Mohamed of the Metropolitan Tabernacle for suggesting A. W. Pink's book and the sermons delivered on the last words of Christ at the Metropolitan Tabernacle in 2013; to Chris Cooper, elder at the Metropolitan Tabernacle, and his wife for the encouraging question in 2015 as what I am doing to do next, after my first publication on Charles Haddon Spurgeon; to Jillian LeVos-Carlson for her questions on my Spurgeon projects; to Jonathan and Jody LeVos for their gift, purchased online from Christian Heritage Museum, of "an authentic hand corrected sermon note" that Spurgeon delivered February 12, 1888, entitled "The Lord and the Leper" and Jonathan's photo for the book cover; to Pastor Richard Rushing for his continued interest in Spurgeon and his encouragement to pursue future devotional projects on Spurgeon; to the editors of iUniverse for their editorial assistance. And, last but not least, to my wife Carey, for word-processing assistance and helping make this publication a reality.

This book is dedicated to my family. Let us rely on the saving merits of the Lord Jesus Christ abiding in His Grace alone.

In Remembrance

Dr. Leslie Hardinge (1912–2002),

my major professor in religion at

Pacific Union College (1966–1969), who

delivered a week of prayer lectures in 1965 on

"These Watched Him Die."

The students present, led by Rosalyn Morgan
Upshaw, sang the theme song:

"Were you there when they crucified my Lord?"

Were you there?

Were you there when they crucified my Lord? (Were you there?)
Were you there when they crucified my Lord?
O! Sometimes it causes me to tremble! tremble! tremble!
Were you there when they crucified my Lord?

Were you there when they nailed him to the cross? (Were you there?)
Were you there when they nailed him to the cross?
O! Sometimes it causes me to tremble! tremble! tremble!
Were you there when they nailed him to the cross?

Were you there when they pierced him in the side? (Were you there?)
Were you there when they pierced him in the side?
O! Sometimes it causes me to tremble! tremble! tremble!
Were you there when they pierced him in the side?

Were you there when the sun refused to shine? (Were you there?)
Were you there when the sun refused to shine?
O! Sometimes it causes me to tremble! tremble! tremble!
Were you there when the sun refused to shine?

Were you there when He rose up from the dead? (Were you there?)
Were you there when He rose up from the dead?
O! Sometimes I feel like shouting glory, glory, glory!
Were you there when He rose up from the dead?

[Negro spiritual, nineteenth century, first published in 1899. Words
and music unknown; last stanza credited to John Wesley Work II,
1872–1925. Other stanzas include: "Were you there when they laid Him
in the tomb?" and "Were you there when the stone was rolled away?"]

PART I

THE SCRIPTURES OF HOPE AND CHRIST'S FIRST RECORDED WORDS

A. Patience, Comfort and Hope from the Scriptures

"For whatever things were written before were
written for our learning, that we through the patience
and comfort of the Scriptures might have hope"
(Romans 15:4 NKJV).

FOCUS: **The Scriptures, the inspired word of God, offers us several examples and lessons of patience. The word of God also offers comfort and hope.**

THE apostle Paul was an inspired man when he wrote this epistle, so there was no necessity on the part of the Holy Spirit, when guiding his mind and pen, to employ words which had been used before in the Scriptures, for His language is unlimited. Yet Paul, inspired as he was, frequently quoted from the Old Testament and in the verse preceding our text he quotes from the Psalms: *"As it is written, the reproaches of them that reproached You fell on Me."* One special reason for quoting from the Old Testament was, doubtless, to put honor upon it, for the Holy Spirit foresaw that there would be some in these later days who would speak of it disparagingly. Not so did our Lord Jesus Christ. Not so did His apostles. Not so did any by whom the Holy Spirit spoke. The Old Testament is not to be regarded with one jot less of reverence and love than is the New Testament; they must remain bound together, for

1

they are the one Revelation of the mind and will of God and woe be to the man who shall attempt to rend asunder that seamless garment of Holy Scripture.

There are some who speak of the Old Testament as if it were worn out, but, indeed, it has about it all the freshness, the force and the dew of its youth and, in the additional light that the New Testament throws upon its histories, its prophecies and its promises, it has gathered force rather than lost any, so that we, probably, can appreciate the Old Testament Scripture far more highly, now that we also have the New Testament, than we could have done if we had not received both the early and the later Revelations.

Some have supposed that the light of the New Testament is so bright that it quite eclipses the light of the Old Testament, as the rising of the sun makes us forget the moon, but it is not so. **The Old Testament now shines with a brighter light than ever to those whose faith is fixed on Jesus Christ and whose eyes behold Him in the pages of the New Testament**. I confess that, sometimes, a type or an emblem which would have been dark or obscure but for the light that has been shed upon it by the New Testament, has seemed to me, if possible, to be clearer even than the New Testament itself. I have seemed to see the brightness of the glory of the Revelation concentrated and focused about some of the darker passages of the Old Testament so manifestly that, instead of the Old seeming to be outdone by the New, I have almost thought it to be the other way around, if such a thought might be tolerated for a moment. There is no need, however, to compare them, for they are both a part of all that Scripture which is God-breathed.

Nor has the authority of the Old Testament ceased. Of course the legal ceremonies of the Mosaic dispensation are done away with, for we are not under the Law, but under Grace, yet even in their passing away, they answer an important purpose. They often afford us instruction where they are not needed for direction. Still is it true ... concerning the entire Book that it was *"written for our learning."* And he is a learned man who knows much of Scripture. But he is unlearned and unstable in the things of God who knows a thousand other things, but does not know *"what things were written before,"* and who does not bend his soul, his heart, his intellect to the believing and the understanding of that which God has spoken of old times by His prophets and apostles.

Believing this most truly, as I am sure we do, let us think, for a little while, about Holy Scripture and that which grows out of it. **The text says, *"That we through the patience and comfort of the Scriptures might have hope."***

I shall take the liberty of reading the text not exactly as it is in our [KJV] version, but putting in the articles which our translators have left out. I never like to leave out the article where it is inserted by the original writer. So the passage runs thus, *"That we through the patience and the comfort of the Scriptures might have the hope."* That rendering conveys to us another shade of meaning and I am convinced that it is the true one. Grammatical construction requires that the meaning should be thus brought out by the use of the articles.

So, **first**, we will consider *THE PATIENCE OF THE SCRIPTURES*. **Second**, *THE COMFORT OF THE SCRIPTURES.* And then, third, though that may not be precisely according to the letter of the text, yet, I think perfectly consistent with the Truth of God: *THE HOPE OF THE SCIPTURES.*

A. *THE PATIENCE OF THE SCRIPTURES.*

You, know that we are saved by faith, and that by faith we find complete and immediate salvation in our Lord Jesus Christ. **But you must never forget that as soon as we are saved, we come under the discipline of Christ and a part of that discipline lies in the exercise of patience, patience in many senses, and "the patience of the Scriptures."**

First, there is the patience inculcated in the Scriptures of which I should say, first, that it signifies resignation to the Divine will. In the olden times, the Scriptures enjoined submission to the will of the Highest, whatever that submission might involve. Solomon *wrote, "My son, despise not the chastening of the Lord; neither be weary* *of His correction: for whom the Lord loves He corrects; even as a father, the son in whom he delights."* The Lord Himself said, by the mouth of His servant, the psalmist, *"Be still and know that I am God."* And the Holy Spirit said through the lips of the weeping Prophet Jeremiah, *"Why does a living man complain, a man for the punishment of his sins?"* The Old Testament, like the New, bids us be patient under the hand of God. So we must be. Submit yourselves unto God for this is an essential part of the life of faith. The man who will not yield himself up to the Divine will and meekly bear it, whatever it may be, is evidently rebellious against his God. How, then, can he be said to be trusting in the Lord? He has at least some unbelief still clinging to him, for, were he fully a Believer, he would resign himself to the Lord's will and humble himself under the mighty hand of God that he might exalt Him in due time.

This patience also includes a continuance in the good work and walk, though we may have to face human or even satanic opposition. The patience inculcated in the Scriptures is a patient perseverance in well-doing; it is the walking in the path of the just which *"shines more and more unto the perfect day."* It is the constant abiding in the fear of the Lord. Nowhere does either the Old or the New Testament speak of our being saved by a kind of temporary faith or a spasm of love, but herein is seen the patience of the saints, that although they are opposed by the seed of the serpent and by the old serpent, himself, they still hold on their way despite all opposition and persecution, even to the end, and so they are saved.

This patience of the saints also includes the bearing of our brother's burdens. It is in that connection that our text appears: *"We, then, that are strong, ought to bear the infirmities of the weak, and not to please ourselves."* And this is part of the patience inculcated in the Scriptures. The old Law taught men to love their neighbors as themselves. Now, we quickly make excuses for our own infirmities and it, therefore, behooves us to endure the infirmities of others, to put a kind construction on what might have been harshly condemned, to bear with the misconceptions of our conduct made by others in their mistake, or even misrepresentations made in their anger, to be gentle and tender as a nurse is with a child, never to be hard, harsh, or severe, for this is contrary to the Second Table of the Law which can be summed up in the brief expression, love to men. I would to God that we had more of this spirit in all our churches. Our Savior said to His disciples, *"A new commandment I give unto you, that you love one another; as I have loved you, that you also love one another."* But how often is that new commandment forgotten in the impatient way in which we show our petulance towards weak and, perhaps, provoking saints? God grant that in the future we may have more patience in this respect.

Patience in the Old Testament is often set forth in waiting for the fulfillment of the promises and the prophecies. The Patriarchs had to wait. Israel had to wait. We, also, are exhorted to wait on the Lord and to be of good courage, for He shall strengthen our heart. *"Though the vision tarry, wait for it; because it will surely come, it will not tarry."* So you see that the patience of the Scriptures, that is to say, the patience which the Scriptures inculcate, is that which we all need to exercise.

But it is also the patience which the Scriptures exhibit, for, when you turn to the grand old Book, you find that it gives us, in actual life, the exemplification of the precepts which were written upon the tablets of stone, or upon the ancient rolls of Scripture. *"You have heard of the patience of Job,"* says the apostle James. You may not have to sit among the ashes as he did, or to endure such trials as fell upon him, but, between here and Heaven, you may expect to have losses, crosses, bereavements and harsh words from those who ought to be your comforters. O Beloved, may you have, at such times, the patience of the Scriptures and be able to say with Job, *"The Lord gave, and the Lord has taken away; blessed be the name of the Lord."* Job is one of the earthly patterns of patience, though he was not perfect in it. May our patience at least come up to his standard.

We need, too, the patience of David. He held on his way though opposed by wicked men, and especially by Saul who hunted him like a partridge upon the mountains. Yet David behaved himself with discretion and would not lift up his hand to smite the Lord's anointed, even though the crown of Israel seemed again and again to be within his reach. You know how patiently he persevered, notwithstanding all the opposition which came to thrust him out of his course.

Then with regard to bearing the infirmities of our brethren, you know the patience of the Scriptures as set forth in the case of Joseph. How tender and kind he was to his brothers even when he seemed to be most severe to them. With what a generous heart did he forgive their cruelty to him. You remember how he framed excuses for them as he said, "*So now it was not you that sent me here, but God,*" though he knew right well that in their jealousy and malice they had sold him for a slave.

If I speak of **the patience that waits for the fulfillment of promises**, I may remind you that the Old Testament sets before you notable examples of this kind of waiting in Abraham, Isaac and Jacob. They waited long in the land of which they owned not so much as a single foot, except the field that contained Abraham's place of burial in the cave of Machpelah ["A field which contained a cave, and which Abraham bought for a burying place (Gen. 23:9, 17)" [*Bible Dictionary and Concordance*, 1996]. Dwelling in tents, they waited, sojourners with God and strangers in the land, until the time when the promise should be fulfilled. This is just how you, also, have to live, Believer. This world is not a place of rest for you, for it is polluted, so you are to live the separated life of a pilgrim and a stranger until the Lord shall bring you into the Heavenly Canaan and give you the "*inheritance, incorruptible and undefiled, and that fades not away,*" which is "*reserved in Heaven for you.*"

This patience is, however, most clearly set forth in the Scriptures in the life of our dear Lord and Master. You will find in Him patience in its highest perfection. He is the model of patient perseverance in the work His Father gave Him to do. He is the pattern of patient silence under the reproaches and sarcasms of wicked men, the image of patient suffering as He bowed His head unto death, even the death of the Cross. He it is, "*who for the joy that was set before Him endured the Cross,* *despising the shame."* This is part of the patience of the Scriptures and such patience as this we have, each one of us, to seek.

But, in addition to its being the patience inculcated and the patience exhibited, it is the patience produced by the Scriptures. Beloved, if you read the Scriptures diligently and meditate much upon them, if you drink in of their spirit, it will be with you as it is with certain insects which, when they feed upon a peculiar kind of flower, their silk is colored like that upon which they feed. You shall find that feeding upon the patience of the Scriptures in meditation and prayer, you will find reproduced in you the patience of the Scriptures.

[*Application*] **If you want to kill impatience turn to the Word of God, look up an appropriate text, ask to have it applied to your heart by the Holy Spirit and see whether the Grace of patience is not thus implanted within you.** Have you become weary in well-doing? Then stay yourselves upon a precious promise and your weariness will speedily depart. Do you seem as if you could not bear the continued opposition of ungodly men? Turn to the promises of your gracious Lord and Master and you shall learn to rejoice and be exceedingly glad, even when they persecute you and say all manner of evil against you falsely for His name's sake. The saints of God have long proved that the Scriptures produce patience. **There is no literature in the world that is comparable to the many Books that are put here into one library called the Bible.** There are no philosophical maxims under Heaven that can produce such patience as the Word of God produces when the Spirit of God comes riding in His own chariot of the Word into the soul of man. It is not the patience of a brute beast that cannot complain, or the patience of the stoic who refuses to feel; it is the patience of a child who believes in his father's love, the patience of a soldier who does not expect to conquer the enemy without stern fighting, the patience of a pilgrim who pushes on because he believes in the inheritance which he will ultimately reach. **This is the patience of the Scriptures.** May God, in His great mercy, work it in each one of us.

B. Then, in addition to the patience of the Scriptures, we are exhorted to seek to possess ***THE COMFORT OF THE SCRIPTURES.***

It is not right for us to be patient, yet miserable. I think I have seen some who professed to be Christians give themselves up to a mode of life which was not at all what it should be. They did not actually complain, but one could see that they were not happy. This is not the point to which the Spirit of God would bring us, He would have us get the comfort of the Scriptures. Well, now, what is the comfort of the Scriptures?

To go over the same heads again, I should say that it is, **first, the comfort which the Scriptures inculcate. You know how the Word of God abounds in injunctions and promises concerning comfort and consolation.** *"Comfort you, comfort you My people, says your God. Speak comfortably to Jerusalem."* There are many passages in the Old Testament in which we are plainly exhorted to be glad. And when you come to the New Testament, you have such messages as this. *"Let not your heart be troubled: you believe in God, believe also in Me."* Or this, *"Rejoice in the Lord always and again I say, Rejoice."* The Scripture bids us not merely to submit to tribulation, but to rejoice in it, not simply to be patient, but to glory in infirmities, to glory in trials, to glory in tribulations because then the Grace of God rests upon us all the more manifestly.

Then, ... we should have the comfort which the Scriptures exhibit. What a charming picture of a comfortable, happy frame of mind is that of Enoch, who walked with God for centuries together. *"Enoch walked with God, after he begat Methuselah, three hundred years."* How beautifully do we see the spirit of consolation exhibited in the character of Abraham, who, with all his troubles as a stranger in a strange land, walks among men as a king. Have you never envied that quiet dignity with which, believing in God, he seemed also to master all around him without any sign of agitation of mind? Oh, that you had such comfort as he had when he took his son, his only son, whom he loved, to offer him up for a sacrifice. You never have had such a test as that and, probably, you never will, but in all that time of testing, what solid comfort he had. There were no written Scriptures then, yet how grand is the consolation which the Scripture describes him as having. *"By faith Abraham, when he was tried, offered up Isaac: and he that had received the promises offered up his only begotten son, of whom it was said, that in Isaac shall your seed be called: accounting that God was able to raise him up, even from the dead; from hence also he received Him in a figure."* Therefore, he staggered not at the promise through unbelief.

Admire, too, the comfort that you often see in the case of David. His was a troubled life, but he stayed himself upon his God. As one remarkable instance of this, think of the time when he came back from the Philistines and found Ziklag burned. ["A city of the south of Judah, assigned to Simeon, where David heard of Saul's death." *BDC*]. All who were left in it were carried away captive and *"the people"*, his own followers, *"spoke of stoning him but David encouraged himself in the Lord his God."* All through the Psalms you get beautiful pictures of the comfort that David enjoyed even in his times of trouble. *"Why are you cast down, O my Soul? And why are you disquieted within me? Hope you in God, for I shall yet praise Him, who is the health of my countenance and my God."* Thus he talked to himself and admonished himself, and even when he sank in deep waters, he still cried unto the Lord and still hoped in His mercy. What a sweet song of hope he sings in the 23rd Psalm. *"Yea, though I walk through the valley of the shadow of death, I will fear no evil: for You are with me; Your rod and Your staff, they comfort me."*

So, be patient … but be comfortable, too. **Submit to the will of God, but do not do it like slaves who submit because they must, but like children who learn to rejoice in their father's will and who, though they cannot understand it, yet believe it to be good and right. If you want to exhibit the comfort of the Scriptures, do as Hezekiah did when Rabshakeh came with Sennacherib's letter full of filthiness and blasphemy. *"Hezekiah went up into the House of the Lord and spread it before the Lord."* This is the comfort of the Scriptures that we may go to the Lord in the worst time of trouble and spread the whole case before the eyes of Infinite**

Love, expecting and being sure that God will, in some way, work deliverance for us.

And, as I said about the patience of the Scriptures, so is it with the comfort. I have spoken of the comfort which the Scriptures inculcate and exhibit. Now, I want to speak of **the comfort which the Scriptures produce.** How sweetly do the Scriptures console and cheer the heart? I am only saying what many of you ... know as well as I do, and I know it in my very heart. There have been times in my life when all the words of men, however kindly they may have been spoken, have altogether failed to comfort me. But a promise, yes, I was about to say, half a promise from God has lifted my soul out of the depths of despair and made it rise like a lark, singing as it soared in the clear sunlight of Jehovah's Countenance. When the Spirit of God applies even the briefest portion of Scripture to our spirit, it is a balm for every care and the end of every difficulty. We are glad, then, in the worst of weathers, to take up our cross and go on our way rejoicing when the consolations of the Holy Scriptures are applied to us by the Holy Spirit. For, ... the Scriptures always exactly fit our case, whatever it may be.

Was there ever a book that was so much written for you as this Book is? I claim that it was written for me, yet I grant that it was also written for you, I mean, not merely for you all, as a whole congregation, but for each child of God. There are passages in the Bible which sometimes come to my heart with such force that it seems as if the Holy Spirit must have written them the very day I read them. He must have known all about my case, for He has put a little word into that verse which just exactly suits me. I know that it was written thousands of years ago, but what a marvelous prescience must have been there to foresee the peculiarity and specialty of my trouble. Have not you found it so, Beloved? Has not the comfort of the Scriptures been so suitable, so tender, so condescending, that you have enjoyed it and been made glad by it?

There is also this further comfort, that the Scriptures are so certain. When we have trusted in a praise of God, we have not relied upon a cunningly devised fable. When we rely upon a Covenant declaration, it is not a bruised reed which will break beneath our weight, but it is a strong, substantial column which will bear all the load that we can possibly put upon it, so that we may have the fullest consolation and good hope through Grace by this comfort of the Scriptures.

Let us just think of a few Old Testament passages and see if they do not give us great comfort. *"I know their sorrows."* That is a very old statement of God concerning the children of Israel in Egypt, but, it is just as true concerning all our sorrows, they are all known to God. *"The eternal God is your refuge, and underneath are the everlasting arms."* **That is part of the last message of Moses to the children of Israel. Does not that comfort of the Scriptures cheer you?** Here is another precious passage: *"Fear not, you worm Jacob, and you men of Israel; I will help you, says the Lord, and your Redeemer, the Holy One of Israel."* *"The mountains shall depart, and the hills be removed; but My kindness shall not depart from you, neither shall the Covenant of My peace be removed, says the Lord that has mercy on you."* *"I have loved you with an everlasting love: therefore, with loving kindness have I drawn you."* *"Can a woman forget her sucking child, that she should not have compassion on the son of her womb? Yes, they may forget, yet will I not forget you."*

"Weeping may endure for a night, but joy comes in the morning." *"Cast your burden upon the Lord, and He shall sustain you: He shall never suffer the righteous to be moved."* *"No good thing will He withhold from them that walk uprightly."* *"Trust in the Lord, and do good: so shall you dwell in the land, and verily you shall be fed."* *"As your days, so shall your strength be."* Do you want me to keep on quoting such precious promises as these? I might do so all night long, for these charming notes of the comfort of the Scriptures are practically without end. Oh, may the Divine Spirit lay some of them home to your troubled hearts, so that … you may not only have patience and comfort, but that you may have the patience and the comfort of the Scriptures.

C. Now I have to speak briefly on the last part of our subject, which is, **THE HOPE OF THE SCRIPTURES**, *"that we through the patience and the comfort of the Scriptures might have the hope."*

You have noticed, **I daresay, that the matters which concern our salvation are always spoken of as the objects of faith.** A man does not obtain the pardon of his sins by hoping for it; he is not regenerated because he hopes to be born-again. Justification is not given to him because he hopes for it. **All these things are matters of faith, not of hope. We are justified by faith. It is by faith that we receive the forgiveness of our sins. Faith has to do with the past, with what Christ has accomplished. But hope looks forward to the future. Hope is for those who are saved and hope comes to us and is strengthened in us by the patience and the comfort of the Scriptures.**

Well now, what is the hope which we get as God enables us to have the patience and the comfort of the Scriptures? Well, to go over the same three points again, it is such **a hope as the Scriptures** hold forth. For instance, they hold forth this hope: *"The righteous shall hold on his way, and he that has clean hands shall be stronger and stronger."* So, if you have **the patience and the comfort of the Scriptures,** you will be sure about **that great and glorious Doctrine of the Perseverance of the Saints.** Your hope will be very bright about that matter because you will feel sure that we shall be preserved, upheld, comforted and rendered triumphant even over the last enemy, which is death, for He has said, *"I will never leave you, nor forsake you."* That is one hope which the Scripture sets forth to us. Then there is the hope that after death will come the Resurrection and eternal life and Glory, for that is also part of the hope set forth in the Scriptures, as Job said, *"I know that my Redeemer lives and that He shall stand at the latter day upon the earth: and though after my skin, worms destroy this body, yet in my flesh shall I see God."* And David said, *"As for me, I will behold Your face in righteousness: I shall be satisfied, when I awake, with Your likeness."* And Isaiah said, *"Your dead men shall live, together with my dead body shall* *they arise."* Albeit that the Old Testament in itself has not the brightness of hope that there is in the New Testament, yet there is enough, even there, to make us very hopeful for the future. And if you read the whole of the Scriptures through, you will see that the man who, by the patience of the Scriptures is holding on his way, and by the comfort of the Scriptures is cheered, in so doing has the good hope of final perseverance and of eternal glory.

Then, also, **this hope is such as the Scriptures exhibit. We have a very beautiful picture of hope in the 11th Chapter of Hebrews where the apostle describes all those heroes of the faith** and then says, *"These all died in faith, not having received the promises, but having seen them afar off, and were persuaded of them, and embraced them."* They all died looking for what they had not seen, but of which they were so sure that they already embraced it. Over their mausoleum we may inscribe the words, "the children of the morning." They had not seen the full light of the day, but they were persuaded of its coming; they watched for it, spoke of it and lived and died in expectation of it. You are to have the same kind of hope that Abraham had, of whom our Lord said to the Jews, *"Your father Abraham rejoiced to see My day: and he saw it and was glad."* You are to have the same sort of hope that all the Patriarchs had when they remained far off from the country from which they had gone out because, like Abraham, they *"looked for a city who has foundations, whose Builder and Maker is God."* You are to have a hope like that of Joseph, who died in Egypt, yet gave commandment concerning his bones, that they were not to be left there, for he still claimed his portion, not with Pharaoh, but with his forefathers in the land of promise.

I have not time to go through the list of the hopeful spirits of the Old Testament, but I would just remind you that they never hoped to have the inheritance without patiently waiting on God's time for them to receive it, and they only hoped to have it through the comfort of the Scriptures which had promised it to them. It must be the same with us. Through believing in Christ Jesus our Lord, and relying upon **the promises of our faithful, Covenant-keeping God, we also,**

through the patience of the Scriptures, and the comfort of the Scriptures, shall inherit the hope which is set forth and exhibited in the Scriptures.

D. **Lastly, this is a hope such as the Scriptures always produce in those who believe them, obey them and follow them.** If you are patiently fighting the battles of the Lord, determined that nothing shall turn you aside from following the great Captain of your salvation, if you are resting in the precious blood of Jesus and the Holy Spirit has worked in you this determination that come what may, you will never turn aside from the King's highway of holiness, then I know that you will delight in and seek after all the comforts that are stored up for you in the Inspired Word of God. *You will prize your Lord's promises, you will observe your Lord's ordinances and, above all, you will esteem and love your blessed Lord, Himself, who is "the Consolation of Israel."* You will honor the Divine Spirit, who is the Comforter, who brings the comfort of which our text speaks. And when you have thus realized the patience and the comfort of the Scriptures, oh, what a hope you will have. You will share the hopes of all the saints, the hopes which stirred their spirits when they died, some of them in anguish at the stake or on the rack, or dragged at the heels of wild horses, or stoned, or sawn in two, or slain with the sword. You will have the hope with which your godly mother died. The hope with which all those who were in Christ have died. You will have the hope that when the Master comes, He will find you ready to welcome Him, the hope that when His Throne is set and His courtiers are gathered around it in the Great Day of Account, you will be there, and the hope that, forever, you will be with Him where He is, to behold His Glory, the Glory which the Father has given Him.

E. I could not, if I had the tongues of men and of angels, explain and expound all that is included in the hope of patient souls that are comforted by the Inspired Word of God. It is a hope full of immortality and of it the apostle Paul says, when writing to the Hebrews, *"which hope we have as an anchor of the soul, both sure and steadfast, and which enters into that within the veil; where the Forerunner is for us entered, even Jesus, made a High Priest forever after the order of Melchisedec."* ["The king of righteousness"]. This hope we would not part with for ten thousand worlds if we had them, do you not say so, Beloved? Oh, let your eyes sparkle at the very thought of this hope. Let your hearts dance even at the mere mention of it. Let your whole soul be invigorated and kept in tune by this hope, that when Jesus comes in His Glory, you shall be with Him and shall reign with Him forever and ever.

Now I must send you away with this mournful reflection that there are some of you who have no hope. Sometimes, we use the word, "hope," very incorrectly. A man dies without any faith in Christ and someone says, "Well, I hope it is all right with him." I dare not say that. I dare say, "I wish it had been all right with him. I desire that it might have been." But hope needs solid ground to rest upon if it is to be a good hope. An idle, vain hope is for idle and vain men. A foolish hope is only fit for fools. What right have some of you to hope that you will ever get to Heaven? If, when you go out of this [Metropolitan] Tabernacle, you were to turn to the left and go towards London Bridge [central London], it would be very absurd for you to say that you hoped that, in that way, you would get to Clapham [south-east London]. And when you turn your faces towards the world, towards self, towards sin, it is idle for you to say, "I hope we shall all meet in Heaven." I am sure I wish, with all my heart that we may and that means that I hope the Lord will turn your faces heavenward.

EXHORTATION: May the Holy Spirit bring you to repent of sin, to believe in Jesus, to cast yourselves wholly upon Him; may He, by His Grace, cut the links which now bind you to the world and enable you to give yourselves up wholly to Christ, that He may save you. May the Lord do this in His infinite mercy, for Christ's sake. Amen.

B. The First Recorded Words of Jesus

"So when they saw Him, they were amazed; and His
mother said to Him, Son, why have You done this to us?
Look, Your father and I have sought You anxiously. And
He said to them, 'Why did you seek Me? Did you not
know that I must be about My Father's business?'"
(Luke 2:48, 49 NJKV).

FOCUS: **The first recorded words of Jesus, views the perceptions of Jesus as a Holy Child. The sermon also considers His home, His occupation, and the lessons He teaches to any of us who may be seeking Him.**

THESE words are very interesting because they are the first recorded utterances of our Divine Lord. No doubt He said much that was very admirable while yet a Child, but the Holy Spirit has not seen fit to record anything except these two questions, as if to teach us that childhood should be retiring and modest, a stage of preparation rather than of observation. We hear little of a Holy Child, for modesty is a precious part of its character. We ought, therefore, to give all the more earnest heed to these words because they stand at the very forefront of our Lord's teaching and are, in some respects, the announcement of His whole life.

Spoken, as they were, at twelve years of age, we may regard them as the last words of His childhood and the first words of His youth. He is just passing away from the time in which He could be called a child into that in which He becomes, in the eastern clime, where men ripen faster than here, a young Man, a son of the Law, fit to sit among the doctors in the temple and to be instructed by them. The early days of youth are very perilous, for then it is that the rest of life is often shaped. Happy, indeed, is he who so early begins with God and chooses as his business the service of the Lord. If all our youth had the same mind which was in Christ Jesus, what evidence we should have that the Spirit of God had been working upon our children and was now about to speak through our youth.

I suppose that these words must have come into Luke's Gospel through Mary, herself. How, otherwise, could the evangelist have known that, *"they understood not the saying which He spoke unto them,"* or that Mary, *"kept all these sayings in her heart"*? Mary evidently narrates the words of the Holy Child, words which she had pondered again and again. **She treasured up for us the gems which dropped from Jesus' lips.** She tells us that this saying, simple though it seems to be, was not fully understood either by herself or by His reputed father, Joseph. And yet, mark you, we are told, expressly, that Mary, *"kept all these sayings in her heart."*

When you cannot put a Truth of God into your understandings, yet lay it up in your affections. If there is anything in God's Word which is exceedingly difficult, do not, therefore, reject it, but rather *preserve* it for future study. In a father's talk with his child there must be a good deal that the child cannot fully comprehend. If he is a wise child, he will seize upon the very thing he does not understand and treasure it for future use, expecting that light will spring out of it, by-and-by. Be not among those who say that they will limit their faith by their understanding. It is probable that you will have a narrow faith if it is so, or else you will have a wide conceit, for a proud conceit, alone, can make us believe that we are able to understand even one-tenth of what God has revealed.

No, I will go further. Although we may understand enough to be saved by the Truth, yet the full depth of the Truths of God are understood by no man and if, therefore, we make it the rule to limit our faith by our understanding, we shall have an extremely limited range of faith. No, let us treasure up these things. Let us highly prize these diamonds which can only be cut by diamonds. **Let us not put them aside because they are difficult, for it may be one index of their genuineness that they are so. We are grateful that the Spirit of God has given us this first word of our Lord Jesus and we love it none the less because it is a deep word.**

We are not surprised that even as a Child, the Son of God should give forth mysterious sayings. **Do you wonder that there should be much in Scripture which you cannot comprehend, when even the**

first words of Christ, when He is yet a boy, is not understood? No, not understood by those who had nursed Him, who had lived with Him the whole twelve years and, consequently, knew His mode of speech and the peculiarities of His youthful language. If even Mary and Joseph did not understand, who am I, that I should forever be saying, "I must understand this or I will not receive it"? **No, if we understand it not, yet will we keep all these sayings in our hearts, for we have this advantage that the Holy Spirit is now given, by whose teaching we understand things which were hidden from the wisest saints of old.**

Beloved Friends, how great and full of meaning was this first word which seems so simple. The longer you look into it, the more you will be astonished at its fullness. Only superficiality and ignorance will think it plain! The closest student will be the most astonished with the profundity of its meaning. [Rudolph D. D.] Stier, to whom I am much indebted for thoughts upon this subject [*The Words of Jesus*, 1869], calls this text, "the solitary flower out of the enclosed garden of thirty years." What fragrance it exhales. It is a bud, but how lovely. It is not the utterance of His ripe manhood, but the question of His youth, yet this half-opened bud discovers delicious sweets and delightful colors worthy of our admiring meditation.

We might call these questions of Jesus the prophecy of His Character, and the program of His life. In this, our text, He set before His mother all that He came into the world to do, revealing His high and lofty Nature and disclosing His glorious errand. This verse is one of those which [Martin] Luther would call His Little Bibles, with the whole Gospel compressed into it. What if I compare it to the perfume of roses, of which a single drop might suffice to perfume nations and ages? It would not be possible to overrate these "beautiful words! Wonderful words! Wonderful words of life!" Who, then, am I that I should venture to take such a text? I do not take it with any prospect of being able to unveil all its meaning, but merely to let you see how unfathomable it is. Emmanuel, God with Us, speaks divinely while yet in His youth. **The words of THE WORD surpass all others.** May the Spirit of God open them to us.

I shall handle the text thus: **First**, here is *THE HOLY CHILD'S PERCEPTION*. **Second**, *THE HOLY CHILD'S HOME*. *Third*, *THE HOLY CHILD'S OCCUPATION*, and **Fourth**, *THE HOLY CHILD'S LESSON* to any of us who may be seeking Him.

A. Here we see *THE HOLY CHILD'S PERCEPTION*. Notice, first, that He evidently perceived most clearly His high relationship. Mary said, *"Your father and I have sought You sorrowing."* The Child Jesus had been known to call Joseph His father, no doubt, and Joseph *was* His father in the common belief of those round about Him. We read in reference to our Lord even at thirty years of age these words "Being, as was supposed, the son of Joseph." The Holy Child does not deny it, but He looks over the head of Joseph and He brings before His mother's mind another Father. *"Know you not that I must be about My Father's business?"*

He does not explain this saying, but it is evident enough that He remembered, then, the wonderful relationship which existed between His Humanity and the great God, for He was not conceived after the ordinary manner, but He had come into the world in such a fashion that it was said to Mary, *"That Holy Thing which shall be born of you shall be called the Son of God."* In a still higher sense and as a Divine Being, He claimed filial relationship with the Highest, but here, no doubt, He speaks as a Man, and as a Man He calls God, "My Father," after a higher fashion than we can do because of His mysterious birth.

You notice that all through His Life He never calls God, "Our Father," although He bids *us* do so. We are children of the same family and when we pray we are to say, *"Our Father which art in Heaven,"* but our Lord Jesus has still a filial relationship more special than ours and, therefore, to God He says on His own account, "My Father." He expressly claims this personal relationship for Himself and I am sure we do not grudge Him that relationship, for upon it our own relationship to the Father depends. Because He is the Son of the Highest, therefore we enter into the filial relationship with the Eternal One according to our capacity. Jesus the Child perceived that He was the Son of the Highest and with all the simplicity of childhood He declared the secret to His mother who already knew how true it was.

This Holy Child's perception should be an instruction to us. Do you and I often enough and clearly enough perceive that God is *our* Father, too? Do we not often act upon the hypothesis that we are *not* related to Him, or that we are orphans and that our Father in Heaven is dead? Do you not catch yourselves, sometimes, departing from under the influence of the spirit of adoption and getting into the spirit of independence, and of waywardness and sin? This will never do. Let us learn from this Blessed One that as He early perceived His high and eminent relationship to the Father, so ought we, also, even though we may be nothing more than children in Grace. We ought to know and to value beyond all expression our sonship with the great Father who is in Heaven. In truth this Truth of God should override every other and we should live and move and act under the consciousness of our being the children of God. **O Holy Spirit, teach us this.**

This Holy Child, next, perceived the constraints of this relationship. He says, *"Know you not that I **must** be about My Father's business?"* Write that, **"MUST,"** in capital letters! It is the first appearing of an imperious, "must," which swayed the Savior all along. We find it written of Him that, *"He **must** go through Samaria,"* and He Himself said, *"I **must** preach the Kingdom of God."* And again to Zacchaeus, *"I **must** abide in your house,"* and again, *"I **must** work the works of Him that sent Me."* *"The Son of Man **must** suffer many things, and be rejected of the elders."* *"The Son of Man **must** be lifted up."* *"It behooved Christ to suffer."* As a Son, He must learn obedience by the things which He suffered. This First-Born among many brethren must feel all the drawings of His Sonship, the sacred instincts of the holy Nature and, therefore, He must be about His Father's business.

Now, I put this to you again, **for I need to be *PRACTICAL* all along:** Do you and I feel this Divine, "must," as we ought? Is necessity laid upon us, yes, *woe* laid upon us unless we serve our Divine Father? Do we ever feel a hungering and a thirsting after Him so that we must draw near to Him and must come to His House and approach His feet and must speak with Him and must hear His voice and must behold Him face to face? We are not truly subdued to the Son-Spirit unless it is so. But when our sonship shall have become our master idea, then shall this Divine necessity be felt by us, also, impelling us to seek our Father's face. As the sparks fly upward to the central fire, so must we draw near unto God, our Father and our All.

This Holy Child also perceived the forgetfulness of Mary and Joseph and He wondered. He sees that His mother and Joseph do not perceive His lofty birth and the necessities arising out of it, and He wonders. "How is it," He says, in a childlike way, *"How is it that you sought Me? Know you not that I must be about My Father's business?"* He is astonished that they do not recognize His Sonship; that they do not perceive that God is His Father. Does not Mary remember the angel's word at the Annunciation? Did she not know how He was born and remember His mysterious relationship to God? Of course she did. But she was a woman and as a woman she had nursed this Child, and she had brought Him up and, therefore, she began to forget the mystery which surrounded Him, in the sweet familiarities with which she had been indulged. And so she has to be reminded of it by her Child's wonder that she should have forgotten that He was the Son of the Highest.

Have you those perceptions, dear children of God? Do you not often wonder why men do not know that you are a child of God? Have you sometimes spoken and they have smiled at you as if you were idiotic or fanatical, and you have thought to yourself, "What? Do they not know how a child of God should speak and how a child of God should act?" "Therefore the world knows us not, because it knew Him not." *"'Tis no surprise thing/That we should be unknown! /The Jewish world know not Their King, /God's everlasting Son."*

The spiritual man is not understood, He is a wonder unto many. Marvel not, my Brothers and Sisters, if carnal men do not understand you. Yes, even your own Brothers and Sisters in Christ, those who love your Father, have, sometimes, been astonished at you when you have only been acting simply out of your own renewed heart.

Many Christians get so stilted that they are not like children at home. They act more like strangers or hired servants in the Father's house who have bread enough and to spare, but yet never can talk as the children do. Few let their hearts flow out with that holy fearlessness, that sweet familiarity which becomes a child of God. Why, if you and I went about the world under the full possession of this idea, *"Beloved, now are we the sons of God,"* I have no doubt we would act in such a way that the mass of professors would be amazed at us and we should be still more amazed at their amazement and astonished at their astonishment. If we only acted as our innermost nature would dictate to us, what manner of persons we would be.

So this Holy Child perceived His glorious Sonship, perceived the constraints of the Sonship working within Him and perceived that His parents did not comprehend His feelings. The Child Jesus began, also, to perceive that He, personally, had a work to do and so He said, *"Know you not that I must be about My Father's business?"* He had been twelve years silent, but now the shadow of the Cross began to fall upon Him and He felt a little of the burden of His lifework. He perceives that He has not come here merely to work in a carpenter's shop, or to be a peasant child at Nazareth. He has come here to vindicate the honor of God, to redeem His people, to save them from their sins and to lead an army of blood-washed ones up to the Throne of the great Father above and, therefore, He declares that He has a higher occupation than Mary and Joseph can understand.

Yet He must go back to the home at Nazareth and, for eighteen years He must do His Father's business by, as far as we read, doing nothing in the way of public ministry. He must do His Father's business by hearing the Father, in secret, so that when He comes out, He may say to His disciples, *"All things which I have heard of My Father I have made known unto you."* So great a lesson had He to teach that He must spend another eighteen years in learning it fully and God must open His ears and awaken Him morning by morning to hear as an instructed one, that afterwards He may come forth the Teacher of Israel, the Lord and Master of apostles and evangelists.

Beloved, I come back to the practical point again. **Have you, with your Sonship, obtained a vivid perception of your call and your work?** You have not redemption set before you to *accomplish*, but you have to make known that redemption far and wide. As God has given to Christ power over all flesh that He may give eternal life to as many as the Father has given Him, so has Jesus given *you* power over such-and-such flesh, and there are some in this world who never will receive eternal life except through you. It is appointed that from your lips they shall hear the Gospel! It is ordained in the Divine decree that through your instrumentality they shall be brought into the Kingdom of God! It is time that you and I, who perhaps have reached thirty, forty, fifty or sixty years, should now bestir ourselves and say, *"Know you not that I must be up and doing my Father's business?"*

David had to wait till he heard the sound of a going in the tops of the mulberry trees: do you not hear the sound of a going now? Are there not signs and indications that you must work the will of Him that sent you and must finish His work? The night comes wherein no man can work. Up, then, you children of God, and, following the Holy Child Jesus, begin to ask this question, *"Know you not that I must be about my Father's business?"* These were the perceptions of this Holy Child. Oh that they may come strong upon us in our own smaller way. May we perceive that we are born of God. May we perceive the Spirit within us whereby we cry, "Abba, Father!" May we have a wonderment that others do not understand the calls and urgencies of our condition and may we have such a sense of our high calling as to proceed at once to fulfill it as God, the Holy Spirit, shall help us.

B. We shall now think of *THE HOLY CHILD'S HOME*. Here I am obliged to amend our version and I am certain that the correction is, itself, correct. I am all the more strengthened in this opinion because the Revised Version endorses the alteration. This is how they read it, *"Know you not that I must be in My Father's house?"* That may not be verbally exact, but it is the true sense. It should run thus, "Know you not that I must be in My Father's?" There is no word for "house," But in almost all languages, "house," is understood. You know how we commonly say to one another, "I am going down to my father's," or, "I shall spend the evening at my brother's." Everybody knows that we mean "house," and that is just how the Greek, here, runs. *"Know you not that I must be in My Father's?"* It means, "house."

That must be the first and primary meaning of it. The text says nothing of business, unless we understand it to be included as a matter of course, since we may be sure that Jesus would not be idle in His Father's, for He said, "My Father works and I work." Observe that the question of Mary was, *"Why have You thus dealt with us? Behold Your father and I have sought You sorrowing."* The answer is, *"Know you not that I must be in My Father's house?"* That is plainly a complete answer and therein strikes you as more natural than a reference to business. If Jesus had only said, *"Know you not that I must be about My Father's business?"* it would not have been any guide to them as to where He would be, because all His Life He *was* about His Father's business.

But He was not always in the Temple. **He was about His Father's business when He sat by the well and talked to the woman of Samaria. And He was about His Father's business when He trod the waves of the Sea of Galilee. He might be anywhere and yet be about His Father's *business,* but the natural answer to the question was, "How is it that you sought Me? Know you not that I must be in My Father's house?"** Let us read the passage thus, and see the child's home. Where should Jesus be but in His Father's dwelling place? I doubt not that with desire He had desired to eat that Passover when He should get to be twelve years old and be old enough to go up to His Father's house. He looked upon the Temple as being, for the time, the residence of God where He manifested Himself in an unusual degree and so this Holy Child looked upon those walls and courts with delight as His Father's house.

It seemed most natural to Him that when He reached the place He should stay there. He had never really been at home before. **Nazareth**

was the place where He was brought up, but Jerusalem's Temple was on earth His true home. I picture to my mind how that blessed Child loved the place where His Father was worshipped! He would stand and gaze on the lambs and the bullocks that were slain in sacrifice, understanding much more about them, though a Child, than you or I do, though we are grown up. It must have been all wonderland to Him as a Child, I speak not of Him as God, it must have been all marvelous to Him and deeply interesting. When the Psalms went up, how He sang them with His sweet youthful voice. He said within Himself, *"I must sing praises unto My Father."* When the solemn prayers were uttered and He heard them, there were none as devout as He as He heard the people worship His Father in Heaven.

It is touching to think of Him, in His Father's palace, **He was greater than the Temple and yet a youth**. It was His Father's house in a special sense because in the Temple did everything speak of God's Glory and everything there was meant for God's worship. It was His Father's house, too, in the sense that there His Father's work went on. If it had not been for the sin which had turned aside the Rabbis and the priests from the faithful following of God, the Temple was the place out of which God's power went forth. *"Out of Zion, the perfection of beauty, God has shined."* There, too, His Father's Truth was proclaimed and His ordinances were celebrated. The Temple was the center of the great Husband-man's farm; it was the homestead from which all the workers went forth to till the fields of Christ's own Father.

It was there, especially, to Him that His Father's name was taught. **He speedily made His way away from the place of sacrifice to that of teaching,** *"sacrifice and offering You did not desire,"* but away He went to the doctors. This thoughtful, spiritual Child wanted to know about everything sacred and so He took His place among the learners and the teachers were astonished when this new, "Child of the Law," put to them questions which showed that He must have thought vastly more than any other person in the Temple. When these enquiries were answered, they were but the predecessors of a whole army of other questions, for He wanted to know more. They were amazed that such enquiries should come from a youthful mind. In return they put questions to the youth and He answered well, for He had a remarkable mind and His mother had taught Him the precious Word of God so that He had the Law and the Prophets at His finger-tips. **No doubt He quoted, in His answers, the sayings of Isaiah or of Jeremiah and utterly astounded the doctors as they perceived that He saw deep into the Holy Words.**

Now, to be practical again ... where should be our home as God's children but in our Father's house? Do you think we have enough of the child spirit about us to feel this? *"Know you not that I must be in my Father's house?"* **That house is His Church. Among the faithful He dwells. The saints of God are built together for a habitation of God through the Spirit.** Let me be often among His people, for I must be in my Father's house. Ought I not, must I not, shall I not, if I am, indeed, a child of God, love to be where God is worshipped? Will not **the hymns of God's house** charm me? Will not **the prayers of God's people** delight me? Shall I not be eager to be at the **Prayer Meetings of the saints**? Shall I not rejoice to join in their praise? Will not my soul be delighted to be at **the Table of communion** and everywhere else where God has appointed to be worshipped by His saints?

Shall I not love every place where God's work is going on? If I hear the Gospel preached, shall I not say, "Let me be there"? If there is tract distribution from house to house, shall I not say, "I, too, will take a district if I can"? If there is Sunday School work, shall I not cry, "Let me have a class according to my ability. **Let me take a share in this holy enterprise**"? "Know you not that I must be at my Father's? In my Father's work and in my Father's house engaged in all my Father's concerns?" Should not this compulsion, blessed and sweet and irresistible, continually be upon us? I must be where God is. If I am not with His people because I am detained by sickness, yet I must be in my Father's house! There are many mansions in that great house on earth as well as in Heaven, and we can be with God in the streets and in His house when working in the fields! But we *must* be in our Father's house, we cannot bear to be away from God. Loss of communion is loss of peace, loss of delight.

Oh, **crave fellowship with God! Be covetous of it.** Love everything that keeps you in. Hate everything that leads you from it. Rise early to commune with God, before the smoke of earth obscures the face of Heaven. Sit up late to commune with God while dews are falling all around. If you can do nothing else, deny yourself rest and wake in the night to commune with God your Father. Shall not a child love to speak with his Father and hear his Father speak to him? It must be so. It will be so. It cannot help being so with you if you feel the child-spirit strong within you as our blessed Lord and Master did when but twelve years of age.

C. Consider, thirdly, *THE HOLY CHILD'S OCCUPATION*. Although I object to its being the correct reading, "Know you not that I must be about My Father's *business?*" yet we know that this Holy Child would not be in His Father's house as an idler. He would be sure to be in the Father's house in the sense of being one of the workers in it. Our Father's house is a business house and, therefore, we must be in our Father's business when we are at our Father's. That is the word. Though the translation which mentions business may be a questionable one, yet it is abundantly lawful to say that this Holy Child's occupation was to be about His Father's matters.

What, then, did He do? **First, He spent His time in learning and enquiring.** "How I want to be doing good" says some young man. You are right, but you must not be impatient. Go among the teachers and learn a bit. You cannot *teach* yet, for you do not *know,* go and learn before you think of teaching! Hot spirits think that they are not serving God when they are learning, but in this they err. Beloved, Mary at Jesus' feet was commended rather than Martha, cumbered with much service. "But," says one, "we ought not to be always *hearing* sermons." No, I do not know that any of you are. "We ought to get to work at once," cries another. Certainly you ought, after you have first learned what the work is. If everybody that is converted begins to teach, we shall soon have a mess of heresies and many raw and undigested dogmas taught which will rather do damage than good.

Run, messenger, run! The King's business requires haste! No, rather pause a little. Have you any tidings to tell? **First learn your message and *then* run as fast as you please. There must be time for learning the message. If our blessed Lord waited thirty *years*, He is an example to eager persons who can scarcely wait thirty minutes.** See how fast light things will travel. How eager are those to speak who know nothing. How swift to speak what they do not know and to testify what they have never seen. This comes not of wisdom, but is the untimely fruit of folly. I have heard it said that Dissenters do not go to their chapels for worship, but for hearing sermons. It is not true. But if it were, I beg to say that hearing sermons may be one of the most God-pleasing forms of worship out of Heaven, for in hearing the Gospel as it should be heard, every sacred passion is brought into play and every power of our renewed manhood is made to bow before the Majesty on high.

Faith by embracing the Promise, love by rejoicing in it, hope by expecting its fulfillment, all are *worship* when the theme is some gracious Word of the Most High. Thought, memory, understanding, emotion are all exercised. I do not know that I have ever worshipped God better than when I have heard a humble, simple-minded man tell out the story of the Cross and of his own conversion. With the tears running down my eyes I have heard the Gospel and adored the living God who has sent it among men. I have so seldom the privilege of hearing a sermon that when I do, it occasions an intense delight which I can scarcely describe, I then draw nearer to God than in any other exercise. I suppose it is so with you, at any rate, it would be so if the preaching were what it ought to be. True preaching begets worship.

This Holy Child was about His Father's business when He was simply asking questions and learning of the appointed teachers. In fact, we need to do more of this kind of business. We are meager, lean and weak, because we are frothing at the mouth with talking too much before we have drunk in the Truth of God into our inmost souls. Remember, the good matter cannot come out of you if it has never gone *into* you, and if you have no time for receiving instruction, the matter which comes out of you will be of little worth. This Holy Child is about His Father's business, for He is engrossed in it. His whole heart is in the hearing and asking questions. There is a force, to my mind, in the Greek, which is lost in the translation, which drags in the word, "about." There is nothing parallel to it in the Greek, which is, *"Know you not that I must be in my Father's?"* **The way to worship God is to get heartily *into* it.** *"Blessed is the man whose strength is in You; in whose heart are Your ways."*

We say, sometimes, when preaching, "I felt that I got fairly into the subject," and you, yourselves, know when the preacher is really getting into it. Often he is paddling about on the shore of his text and possibly he wades into it up to his ankles. But, oh, when he plunges into the "rivers to swim in," then you have grand times. When the precious Truth of God has fairly carried him off his feet, you take a header, too, and swim likewise. Our Lord, when He went into the Temple, became engrossed with its worship and teaching, and that was His answer to Mary. He did as good as say, "Know you not that I was absorbed in My Father's? I did not know you were gone. I forgot all about you. Know you not that My soul was in My Father's? I was so taken up with what I was learning from the doctors and what I was seeing in the Temple that I could not but remain. Did you not know that? Did you not also become absorbed?"

He seems to think they might have been as interested as He and they *would* have been if they had borne the same relation to God as He did. It is natural that we should become engrossed in our worship. I should not wonder if, sometimes, we were a little rude to those who sat next to us, or moved about a little more than etiquette would suggest; or vented our feelings in involuntary expressions and became troublesome to those next us in the pews, so that they said, "What can be the matter with these people?" Friends, we have got into the holy engagement and we cannot quite govern ourselves! And we feel as if we could say to you, **"Know you not that I must be in my Father's work, worship and Truth?"** We cannot be half-hearted. We are too happy for that. We are carried clean away. Do you not know that we cannot be proper and calm, for we must be all taken up with our holy service"?

Besides, the Holy Child declares that He was under a necessity to be in it. *"Know you not that I must be in My Father's?"* He could not help Himself! Christ could never be a half-hearted pupil or a lukewarm worshipper. It was not possible for Him to be that. He must get absorbed in it; drawn right into the blessed whirlpool, He must be lost in it and give His whole thought and attention to it, and He tells His mother so. *"Know you not that I must be about My Father's business?"* Other things did not interest the Holy Child, but this thing *absorbed* Him. You know the story of Alexander, that when the Persian ambassadors came to his father's court, little Alexander asked them many questions, but they were not at all such as boys generally think of.

He did not ask them to describe to him the throne of ivory, nor the hanging gardens of Babylon, nor anything as to the gorgeous apparel of the king. He asked what weapons the Persians used in battle; in what form they marched and how far it was to their country, for the *boy* Alexander felt the *man* Alexander within him and he had presentiments that he was the man who would conquer Persia and show them another way of fighting that would make them turn their backs before him. It is a singular parallel to the case of the Child, Jesus, who is taken up with nothing but what is His Father's because it was for Him to do His Father's work and to live for His Father's Glory and to execute His Father's purpose even to the last.

D. Let us, lastly, learn **THIS HOLY CHILD'S SPECIAL LESSON TO THOSE OF US WHO ARE SEEKERS**. Do I address any children of God who have lost sight of Christ? It does happen at times that we miss the Holy Child and it happens most often when we are happy in company and so are taken off from Him. Mary and Joseph were, no doubt, delighted with the festival and so they forgot Jesus. **You and I, when in God's house, may forget the Lord of the House. Did you ever lose Him at His Own Table? Did you ever lose Him while engaged in His work? Have you ever missed Him even while you were busy with holy things? When you do, perhaps you will say to Him, "Lord, I have sought You long; I**

have been among Your kinsfolk; I have been to dear saints of God and spoken to them and have said, 'Have you seen Him whom my soul loves, for I have lost Him?'"

His answer is, "Why have you sought Me?" He is not lost to those who long for Him. Cannot you trust Him when He is away? He is all right even when you see Him not! Though He does not always smile, He loves us to the end. If you are not walking in the light of His Countenance, yet you are living in the love of His heart. Jesus sees you when you do not see Him; He has reasons for hiding Himself which are founded in wisdom. Mark, dearly beloved ones, if you and I need to find our Lord, we know where He is. Do we not? He is at His Father's. Let us go unto His Father's; let us go to our Father and His Father and let us speak with God and ask *Him* where Jesus is if we have lost His company. We may be sure that He is in His Father's work. We are sure of that.

Let us go to work for Him again. Do not let us say, "I feel so dull I cannot pray." Now is the time in which we must pray. "But I do not feel as if I could praise Him." Now is the time when you *must* praise Him and the praise will come while you are praising. At times we have no heart for holy exercises and the devil says, "Do not go." My dear Friend, be sure to go up to the assembly, go to get the heart for going! Have you begun not to care about Prayer Meetings? Are you going to stay away till you *do* care about them? Then you will die in indifference. Come and have another turn at them. Those who are most at them, love them best. Does Satan say, with regard to private prayer, "You have not the spirit of prayer. You must not pray"? Tell the devil you are going to pray for the spirit of prayer and that you will plead till you get it! It is a sign of sickness when you cannot pray and surely, then, you should go to the Physician.

If there is ever a time when a man should pray more than usual, it is when he feels dead and cold in the holy engagement, go and seek Jesus at the Father's and seek Him in the Father's work, and those of you who have lost communion with Him will find it again.

31

When you take the Sunday school class, again, that you left because you said you had had enough of it. When you go again and preach at the street corner, you have not done that lately. When you begin, again, to **be active in the Lord's service**, then you will again meet with this Blessed One who is about His Father's business, whether you are or not.

One more word and that is to sinners who are seeking Christ. I would not say a word to discourage any who are seeking Jesus, but I should like to get them far beyond the stage of seeking. Perhaps the Holy Spirit will help them to do so if I read Christ's words to them. *"How is it that you sought ME?"* Dear, dear! That is, indeed, a turning of things upside down. Our Lord Jesus has come into the world to seek and to save the lost; is it not an odd thing when those who are lost get to seeking Him? That is a reversal of all order! "How is it," He says, "that you sought Me?" Now, if I, this morning, am a poor, lost sinner and can honestly say I am seeking Christ, there must be some blunder somewhere! How can this be? How shall I make heads or tails of it? Here is a sheep seeking the shepherd! A lost piece of silver seeking its owner! How can this be?

It will all come right if you will just think of this, first, that Jesus Christ is not far away. He is in the Father's house. "Where is the Father's house?" Why, all around us. The great Father's house covers the whole world and all the stars. He lives everywhere. He dwells not in temples made with hands, like this Tabernacle, or yonder cathedral, the Lord God is outside in the fields, in the streets, wherever you seek Him. Say not, who shall climb to Heaven to find, Him, or dive into the deeps to bring Him up? "The Word is near you." Here is Christ in the midst of us. What are you looking for, man? Are you seeking for some spirit of the night, or specter of darkness? Jesus is near! Believe in Him.

EXHORTATION: Remember another thing, that Christ must be about His Father's business. And what is His Father's business? Why, to save sinners. This is His Great Father's delight. He is glad to bring His prodigals home. Are you seeking Jesus as if He could not be found, as if it were hard to make Him hear and difficult to win

His help? Why, He is busy in saving sinners. Jesus sits on Zion's hill He still receives poor sinners. Be encouraged and do not go about among your kinsfolk seeking Him, nor with bitter tears and cries of despair look for Him as if He were hiding from you. He is not far from any one of us. He stands before you and He bids you trust Him.

Look to Him and be saved! Do you look? You are saved! Go on your way rejoicing! God bless you. Amen.

PART II

THE LAST WORDS OF JESUS CHRIST FROM THE CROSS

A. Words of Forgiveness

1. The Unknown Depths of Sin and the Heights [of Mercy]

"Then Jesus said, 'Father, forgive them,
or they do not know what they do'"
(Luke 23: 34 NKJV).

FOCUS: **There is a great depth to this text. There are two things, [to keep in mind] the unknown depths of human iniquity [sin],** *"They know not what they do,"* **and the unknown heights of mercy, as manifested in Christ's dying plea,** *"Father, forgive them."*

HE breathes a prayer, *"Father, forgive them,"* My murderers, the *rough men who have stripped Me, the cruel men who have nailed My hands and pierced My feet, "Father, forgive them; for they know not what they do."* **The sayings of Christ upon the Cross have a deeper meaning than that which appears upon the surface.** They were texts of which His eternal life should be the sermon; they were no common words. **As no Word of Scripture is of private interpretation, no Word of the Savior upon the Cross loses its force and significance in later**

times. What He said then, He is saying now. What He said then was but the utterance of a sentence which shall roll through the ages and which shall prevail with God through time and throughout eternity. *"Father, forgive them,"* was the prayer of a dying Man, but it was not a dying prayer. *"They know not what they do,"* was the plea of lips that were about to be closed, but it was no plea which was doomed to silence; it is heard in Heaven today, as much as when Jesus first offered it on Calvary from His Cross.

A. It appears from the text that *THERE ARE UNKNOWN DEPTHS IN HUMAN INIQUITY. "They know not what they do."*

Perhaps, Christ applied this remark to His murderers who did not know that He was the Son of God, for if they had known Him to be the Messiah, and *"they would not have crucified the Lord of Glory."* And it might have been said to them, "You did it ignorantly in unbelief." I grant you that this was the immediate meaning of Christ's words, but I think, to return to what I have already affirmed, this saying is true of the entire human family, whenever any of us sin, we know not what we do.

Do not misunderstand me. There is no man in the world who has not enough perception left to teach him the difference between right and wrong. Even upon the natural conscience of man there is engraved so much of the Law of God that his conscience either accuses or excuses him. I can scarcely think that there is any race of bushmen, or that there is a single tribe of aboriginal savages who have altogether lost that *"candle of the Lord which searches all the inward parts of the belly."* They know enough to leave them without excuse, so that if they perish, they perish through willful sin. Yet I must admit, at the outset, that it is possible for the conscience to become so blind through prevailing customs, so seared through lengthened habit and so preserved through absolute ignorance, that men may sin and yet know not what they do.

There may be some in whom the judgment has left its seat, they have become maniacs so far as any moral judgment is concerned. They sin with both their hands and, perhaps, write down that very sin as being righteousness, and their obscenity as being a sacrifice acceptable to God. There are none such, however, here. I think in a land like this [England], with an open Bible, with a preached Gospel, with the Presence of the Spirit of God, I need not address such an assembly as this as not knowing what they do in that sense. If you sin, my Hearers, you sin against light and knowledge. You sin knowing that you do wrong. You put out your hand to touch the accursed thing knowing that it is accursed. You sin willingly and many shall be your stripes, seeing that you know your Master's will and do it not. But still, of the whole human race it is nevertheless true that when they sin, *"they know not what they do."* Let me show you, as briefly and forcibly as I can, how this is the fact.

1. ***Who among us knows, to the full, the real meaning and nature of sin?* I can give some description** to you of what sin is, but I question, whether even the most enlightened of us know the whole of the exceeding sinfulness of sin. Sinner, I address myself pointedly to you. **Do you know that when you sin, you call God a fool?** You say that His Law is not the best thing for you, that He has made a mistake and has asked you to do that which would not conduce to your happiness. You call God a fool, is that nothing? Do you know that when you sin, you **call God a liar?** He tells you that sin is a bitter and an evil thing. You say, "No, it is sweet. It is pleasant. At any rate, I will taste it." You give the lie to the Eternal God! Is that nothing? **Whenever you sin, you call God a tyrant**. You do, in fact, avow that He has given Laws which are hard and arbitrary, which He ought not to have given and which you are determined to break because you feel that they are not for your happiness, they do not promote your comfort. And is this nothing? **Is this nothing, to call the all-wise God a fool, the truthful God a liar and the good and generous God a tyrant?**

But there is more than this in your sin. Every time a man sins, he aims a blow at the crown of God. He refuses to let God be the King but puts his hand, his wicked hand, upon the diadem of Deity and would dash the crown from God's head if he could. No, more. He aims a blow at God's very existence. The language of sin is, "No God!" And every time a sinner sins, he tries to get rid of God, and his aim and drift is to stop the Eternal One and to put the King of kings out of His own universe. Is this nothing? Is this nothing? Does not even this, feeble though the explanation is, make sin to be exceedingly sinful? Verily, when we sin, we know not what we do! I can hardly believe that there is a man or woman in this assembly who would, in cold blood, stand up and say, "I defy God! I will do my best to drive Him from His throne. Yes, and to drive Him from existence!" And yet, Sinner, every time you curse, or lie, or swear, or break God's Law in any way whatever, you do, in fact, do all these things and I think I may say you know not what you do.

Let us now shift the kaleidoscope and get another view of this great and solemn Truth of God.

2. ***Some of us know what we do if we judge of sin by its loathsomeness in God's sight.*** There is no man living who knows how much God hates and abhors sin. You may detest the loathsome toad. You may give way to a wicked disposition and hate some enemy till you cannot live till that enemy is slain. But you cannot loathe the toad, you cannot hate your foe as thoroughly as God abhors and hates sin. Wherever sin is, there is God's utmost hate, anger and ire. He cannot endure it. His eyes cannot light upon it without burning it up and His hand is always longing to smite it to the death.

Why, God had a choice archangel, a glorious being whose wings were like the beams of the rising sun, whose stature was like a great snow-clad mountain and whose beauty was as a fair field girt with flowers. He sinned and God spared neither him nor the angels that followed him in his rebellion, but cast them down to Hell and reserved them *"in everlasting chains under darkness unto the judgment of the great day."* Angelhood could not save an angel; angelic stature, a seraphic voice and a cherubic flight could not save Satan and his hosts when the stain of sin had fallen on them! How much, then, must God hate sin?

When God had made the world, He smiled and said, "It is good." The morning stars sang together and all the sons of God shouted for joy, for the world was very good and God's own heart was glad at the sight of the new-made world. But when Adam sinned, God did not spare Eden, with all its perfections of beauty. And later, when the iniquity of man was fully ripe, He did not spare the round world itself, but bade the floods leap up from their cavernous darkness and bade the clouds burst their swaddling bands, and the earth was covered with a flood, for "it repented the Lord that He had made man on the earth, and it grieved Him at His heart."

No, **if we still want to see more clearly how God hates sin, let us see how sin came upon His own Son, His only-begotten, His well-beloved Son**. It came there, not by any deed of His own, but because He took our iniquities upon Himself and, therefore, was numbered with the transgressors. And did His Father spare Him? Far from it. He smote Him with the rod, He scourged Him with the lash, and He pierced Him to the heart with His sword. He gave up His darling to the power of the dog, and "Lama Sabachthani?" was a sorrowful proof that God hates and loathes sin, let it be wherever it may. Now, Sirs, would you go and press to your bosom and dandle and pamper and pet that thing which God loathes and hates? I think not. If we ever had, before our eyes, God's hatred of sin and this were revealed to our heart by the Holy Spirit, we would long to be rid of it and, therefore, I say that when we take hold of it and embrace it, we know not what we do.

3. *Again, what man among us knows sin in its awful consequences?* Is there a mother here who would go home tonight and ask herself the quickest way to damn her child's soul? Is there a father here who would take counsel with his own wickedness as to the readiest method of sending his son to Hell? I think not. And yet, when the father is a drunk or a

swearer, what does he do but do his worst to ruin his child? And when the mother is prayerless, Godless, Christless, does she not do her utmost to murder her child's soul? Verily, we in our relationships, when we go into sin, know not what we do. What master could sit down wantonly to undermine the spiritual health of his workmen? What citizen would wish to become the deadly Upas tree [in tropical Africa and Asia] dropping poison from all its branches? What man of influence would wish to be the basilisk [legendary reptile] whose eyes should tempt men to their destruction? Not one. And yet when you commit iniquity, and especially those of you who occupy the responsible position of parents, or masters, or ministers, or employers in any way, you do your best to destroy the souls of others. So I can truly say, "Surely you know not what you do."

Do you know, Sinner, that every time you sin, your sin affects the whole world? Let me not stagger you. It is only our finite vision which prevents us seeing the effect of even one thought upon the entire universe. The word I am speaking, just now, sets in motion a wave in the air which reaches your ears. It will abide in your memory, to a certain degree, throughout eternity. In limiting the sphere of my voice to your ears, I have set eternity pulsating, you shall think these things over either in the waves of fiery Hell, or in the fields of glorious Heaven. Eternity has been affected by the speech of a man. And so it is with what you do, there is an effect produced on earth, in Heaven, in Hell by whispered blasphemy or by an unseen lust, you cannot sin alone. You are part of a universe; you cannot disentangle yourself from the meshes of the net of society. You are in the ship of the universe and you cannot get out of it. You cannot even be thrown out of it, as Jonah was cast out of the ship into the sea. Your sin is dragging other men down to Hell, or else the Grace that is in you is helping to lift up others towards God and Heaven. Mind that when you sin, for from this day on I think that you will hardly be able to say as, perhaps, you may have done before, and that you know not what you do.

4. ***But Sinner, let me speak to you solemnly, to you, about
   something in which no imagination is needed.*** Do you see
   that man yonder? What is he doing? I see a pearly gate within
   which I mark the splendors of unutterable bliss and hear the
   hymns of the Paradise of God. What is that man doing? He is
   putting bolts and bars upon that gate to shut himself out. Do
   you call him a madman? Sinner, that madman is you. Your
   sins are shutting you out of Heaven. Do you see yonder man?
   He is carrying wood on his weary shoulders and stooping to
   the very ground as he bears his burden. For what purpose
   is he carrying that fuel? It is to make a bed of fire on which
   he shall lie and swelter in flames forever. Do you call him
   a madman? Sinner, that madman is yourself. What is Hell
   but the laying on upon your back of a whip whose knots you
   have yourself tied? What is it but the drinking of a cup of
   gall, every drop of which was distilled from your own sin?
   These are awful things to say, but I feel that when I look at
   what Hell is, in all its horrors, and what the loss of Heaven
   is, with all its dreadful darkness, I must say to you when you
   sin, surely you know not what you do. The man who puts
   himself to death with the halter, or drives the knife into his
   heart, or throws himself into his watery grave may have some
   present griefs which may, to him, though not to us, seem to
   be an excuse for fleeing from them. But you, when you sin,
   are a suicide without excuse because you flee from good that
   stands before you to an evil that has no mixture of benefit or
   mercy. You leap into the fire yourself, a fire which you have
   yourself kindled and which your own blasphemous breath has
   fanned. May God teach us, when we sin, what we have really
   done, that we may not do it again and that, by His Grace, we
   may be led to the precious blood of Christ to have the guilt of
   it washed away! *"There is a fountain filled with blood, / Drawn
   from Emmanuel's veins. /And sinners plunged beneath that flood/
   Lose all their guilty stains".*

But have I some here who say that they do know what they are doing? They have been so faithfully warned, so affectionately dealt with, so earnestly prayed for that when they sinned, they sinned willfully, knowing what they did. O my dear [Readers], that is true of some of you! I have often felt, when I have come out of the pulpit that you would be without excuse in the Day of Judgment. God knows that I have not shunned to declare unto you the whole counsel of God: Divine Sovereignty in all its absoluteness and the sinner's responsibility in all its fullness. I have preached to you the Doctrines of Grace, but I have not, therefore, kept back the demands of God upon you. And I know that should you perish, it will neither be for want of preaching, nor of weeping. Well, Sirs, if you do perish with the Gospel preached in your ears, you perish fearfully indeed.

God have mercy upon you, my [Readers]. May His Sovereign Grace be extended toward you. May the lines of His election embrace you, the blood of Christ's redemption wash you, the voice of His effectual calling awaken you and the power of His Grace preserve you.

I have thus tried, in all simplicity, as God's servant, to expound Christ's plea, "Father, forgive them; for they know not what they do."

B. Now, very briefly, but oh, may God grant that it may be with the unction of the Holy One, let me speak upon *THE UNKNOWN HEIGHTS OF GRACE.*

1. **If there were any men in all the world who under the Covenant of Works, or under that mingle-mangle covenant which some preach, which is half Law and half works, and neither Law nor works, if there were any men who should have been excluded from the Election of Grace it was those men who nailed the Savior to the Cross.** And yet, mark this, while Christ did not mention by name the best of the Pharisees, He did mention, before God, particularly and personally, those degraded men who with many an addition of cruel mockery, nailed Him to the Cross. "Father, forgive them." He did not say,

"Father, forgive Pontius Pilate, for he sinned unwillingly." He did not say, "Father, forgive Judas, for he repented and cast down his ill-gotten gain in the Temple." But He said, "Father, forgive them." There they are the mark of the nails has not yet gone out of their hands, there is the print of the head of the nails in the center of their palm even now. Look, the blood of Jesus is on their clothes, the very blood which spurted forth from the Redeemer's hands when they drove the nails through them. Yet He prays, "Father, forgive them." There they are, they are grinning at their ghastly work and saying, "Aha! Aha!" and joining with the ribald crew and thrusting their tongues into their checks, saying, "He saved others, Himself He could not save." And yet there is heard, above the clamor of their iniquity which appeals to God for justice, the cry of the Savior, "Father, forgive them."

2. **There is no consciousness of need of forgiveness in them. Their hearts are hard as nether millstones.** They laugh at the prayer itself. "Forgive?" they say, "we have done many a worse piece of work than this! We need not be forgiven." They are as cold as ice and stern as steel and hard as the granite rock. And yet Jesus prays, "Father, forgive them." There are no past good works to recommend them, they never did a good thing in their lives, they are soldiers who have slain, every man, perhaps his hundred men. They have learned to split a little infant on the blade of their swords. They know how to rip up, and tear, and cut off a head and gouge out eyes, they are men whose deeds of blood must be written in fire, but whose deeds of goodness have never yet come to light! And yet Jesus cries, "Father, forgive them."

They are men who if the Gospel were preached to them, would reject it. If Christ were offered to them, they would refuse Him. If they were moved by some qualms of conscience, they would stifle them. If they were wept over by the minister, they would ridicule his tears. If they were pleaded for by the Church, they would laugh at the pleas and yet the Savior says, "Father, forgive them." Amid such splendors of

Grace, where shall I find words to fitly describe them? Language, you are a dull, cold thing in such a case as this! Words, you have not strength enough to carry the mighty meaning of my soul just now. Was there ever Grace like this, except, when Jesus prayed for me and said, "Father, forgive him"? And when He prayed for you, my Brother, and you, my Sister, and said, "Father, forgive them"?

3. O my [Readers], **when Jesus pleads for us, it is not because there is anything in us why He should plead. It is not because we flee to Him that He pleads for us.** It is not because we long for mercy and value it that He pleads for us. He prays for us long before we pray to Him. He died for us before we knew anything about our death in sin. And He lived and pleaded before His Father's Throne when we were cursing, blaspheming and defying Him. Ah, Souls, I would that you could get rid, once and for all, of any idea that Jesus Christ needs anything in you to move His heart of compassion towards you. Where He loves, He loves for His own sake, not because of the worthiness of the object of His love. The source of Grace is in the God of Grace, not in the receiver of Grace. The reason for pardon is not in the penitent, but in the Pardoner.

4. **The ground of acceptance is not in our faith, but in Christ, the Author and Finisher of that faith** and hence it is that the Gospel is adapted to the worst of sinners, to the scum, the chaff, the off-scouring, the parings, the filth, the vileness, the rottenness, the stench, the offal of the world. Oh, if we had a Gospel that was half Grace and half human goodness, then the good, the upright, the educated, the refined, the moral would have some degree of hope. But the poor outcast would have none. But now, tonight, I preach a Gospel which comes right down to you, just where you are, in the bog, the mire, the slough, next door to Hell, lying at Hell's gate, not like Lazarus when the dogs licked his sores at the rich man's gate, but lying at the gate of Hell while Hell hounds lick your wounds, cast out from

God, abhorred, detested, abhorrent to yourself, obnoxious to your own conscience, such a sinner that you wish you had never been born, or that you had been a viper, a snake, a toad rather than have been a man. Yet can God's Grace reach even you and *"unto you is the word of this salvation sent."* I do believe that over such sinners as you Jesus pleads tonight, "Father, forgive them."

And now, ..., is there something in you which seems to say, "Unite in that prayer"? Does the Spirit of God whisper in your soul, "[This] is the hour of mercy? Jesus Christ is passing by; He is interceding for the transgressors"? Then I pray you say, "Father, forgive me." What? Shall my Master say, "Father, forgive them," and will not you pray for yourself? The adamant might melt, the steel dissolve and will not you melt? Spirit of God, bring the fire and melt the heart. And now, poor Soul, say, "Father, forgive me. I did not know the full guilt of my sin, but I knew enough to make me so guilty that I deserve Your wrath. I have no merits, Lord. I have no righteousness. If You slay me, You are just. If You curse me, I deserve it. But Father, forgive me." Do not use Christ's plea, that is His, not yours. He could say, "Father, forgive them; for they know not what they do." You must use another plea. "Father, forgive me through Your Son's precious blood."

Oh, I think my soul would be ready to leap from earth to Heaven if I could but be sure that there was someone here who was saying in his heart, *"Father, I have sinned against Heaven, and am no worthier to be called Your son."* Or if some heart were saying, "By His agony and bloody sweat, by His Cross and passion, by His precious death and burial, by His Glorious Resurrection and Ascension, Father, forgive me!" Soul, your prayer is heard, "go, and sin no more. Your sins, which are many, are all forgiven you."

EXHORTATION: Go home and tell your friends and your kinsfolk what God has done for your soul and, by-and-by, come here and tell us what God has done for you, and then come to this Communion Table and spiritually eat with us of His flesh and drink of His blood, "for His flesh is meat, indeed, and His blood is drink, indeed."
May the Lord add His blessing, for Jesus' sake. Amen.

2. [His] First Cry from the Cross

"Then said Jesus, 'Father, forgive them,
for they do not know what they do'"
(Luke 23:34 NKJV).

FOCUS: The text is illustrative of our Savior's intercession; it is also instructive of the work of the church and offers suggestions to the unconverted.

OUR Lord was at that moment enduring the first pains of Crucifixion; the executioners had just then driven the nails through His hands and feet; He must have been greatly depressed, and brought into a condition of extreme weakness by the agony of the night in Gethsemane, and by the scourging and cruel mocking which He had endured all through the morning from Caiaphas, Pilate, Herod, and the Praetorian guards. Yet neither the weakness of the past, nor the pain of the present could prevent Him from continuing in prayer.

The Lamb of God was silent to men, but He was not silent to God. Dumb as a sheep before her shearers, He had not a word to say in His own defense to man, but He continues in His heart crying unto His Father, and no pain, and no weakness can silence His Holy Supplications. **Beloved, what an example our Lord here presents to us; let us continue in prayer as long as our heart beats; let no excess of suffering drive us away from the Throne of Grace, but rather let it drive us closer to it:** *"Long as they live should Christians pray, / For only while they pray they live."*

To cease from prayer is to renounce the consolations which our case requires. Under all distractions of spirit and overwhelming of heart, great God, help us still to pray, and never from the Mercy Seat may our footsteps be driven by despair. Our blessed Redeemer persevered in prayer even when the cruel iron tore His tender nerves, and blow after blow of the hammer jarred His whole frame with anguish; and this perseverance may be accounted for by the fact that **He was so**

in the habit of prayer, that He could not cease from it; He had acquired a mighty velocity of Intercession which forbade Him to pause. Those long nights upon the cold mountainside; those many days which had been spent in solitude, those perpetual arrows of prayer which He would dart up to Heaven, all these had formed in Him a habit so powerful, that the severest torments could not slow its force.

Yet it was more than habit. **Our Lord was baptized in the spirit of prayer; He lived in it, it lived in Him; it had come to be an element of His Nature.** He was like that precious spice which being bruised, does not cease to give forth its perfume, but rather yields it all the more abundantly; because of the blows to the pestle, its fragrance is no outward and superficial quality, but an inward virtue essential to its nature, which the pounding does but fetch from it, causing it to reveal its secret soul of sweetness. So Jesus prays, even as a bundle of myrrh gives forth its smell, or as birds sing because they cannot do otherwise; prayer wrapped His very soul as with a garment, and His heart went forth in much array. I repeat it, let this be our example, never, under any circumstances, however severe the trial, or depressing the difficulty, let us cease from prayer.

Observe further that our Lord, in the prayer before us, remains in the vigor of faith as to His Sonship. The extreme trial to which He now submitted Himself could not prevent His holding fast His Sonship; His prayer begins, "Father." **It was not without meaning that He taught us when we pray to say "Our Father," for our prevalence in prayer will much depend upon our confidence in our relationship to God.** Under great losses and crosses, one is apt to think that God is not dealing with us as a father with a child, but rather as a severe judge with a condemned criminal; but the cry of Christ, when He is brought to an extremity which we shall never reach, betrays no faltering in the spirit of Sonship, and in Gethsemane, when the bloody sweat fell fast upon the ground, His most bitter cry commenced with, "My *Father,*" asking that if it were possible the cup of gall might pass from Him. He pleaded with the Lord as His Father, even as He over and over again had called Him on that dark and doleful night.

Here again, in this, **the first of His seven expiring cries, it is "Father." O that the Spirit that makes us cry, "Abba, Father," may never cease His operations!** May we never be brought into spiritual bondage by the suggestion, *"If you are the Son of God";* or if the Tempter should so assail us, may we triumph as Jesus did in the hungry wilderness! May the Spirit which cries, "Abba, Father," repel each unbelieving fear when we are chastened, as we must be (for what son is there whom his father chastens not?) may we be in loving subjection to the Father of our spirits and live; but never may we become captives to the spirit of bondage, so as to doubt the Love of our gracious Father, or our share in His Adoption. More remarkable, however, is the fact that our Lord's prayer to His Father was not for Himself; He continued on the Cross to pray for Himself, it is true, and His lamentable cry, *"My God, My God, why have You forsaken Me?"* **shows the personality of His prayer, but the first of the seven great cries on the Cross has scarcely even an indirect reference to Himself. It is, *"Father, forgive them."***

The petition is altogether for others, and though there is an allusion to the cruelties which they were exercising upon Him, yet it is remote. And you will observe He does not say, "I forgive them," that is taken for granted; He seems to lose sight of the fact that they were doing any wrong to Him; it is the wrong which they were doing to the *Father* that is on His mind. The insult which they are paying to the Father, in the Person of the Son, He thinks not of Himself at all; the cry "Father, forgive them," is altogether unselfish. He is in the prayer, as though He were not; so complete is His self-annihilation that He loses sight of Himself and His woes. ... If there had ever been a time in the life of the Son of Man when He might have rigidly confined His prayer to Himself without anyone complaining, surely it was when He was beginning His death throes.

We would not marvel if any man here were fastened to the stake, or fixed to a cross, if his first, and even his last, and *all* his prayers were for support under so arduous a trial; but see, **the Lord Jesus began His prayer by pleading for others.** Can't you see what a great heart is revealed here; what a soul of compassion was in the Crucified; how

Godlike, how Divine? Was there ever such a one before Him who, even in the very pangs of death, offers as his first prayer an intercession for others? Let this unselfish spirit be in *you* also…. Look not every man upon his own things, but every man also, on the things of others; love your neighbors as yourselves, and as Christ has set before you this paragon of unselfishness, seek to follow Him, treading in His steps. There is however a crowning jewel in this diadem of glorious Love. The Sun of Righteousness sets upon Calvary in a wondrous splendor, but among the bright colors which glorify His departure, there is this one; the prayer was not alone for others, but it was for His cruelest enemies.

His enemies, did I say? **There is more than that to be considered; it was not a prayer for enemies who had done Him an ill deed, years before, but for those who were then and there murdering Him.** Not in cold blood did the Savior pray, after He had forgotten the injury, and could the more easily forgive it, but while the first red drops of blood were spurting on the hands which drove the nails; while yet the hammer was stained with crimson gore, His blessed mouth poured out the fresh warm prayer, *"Father, forgive them, for they know not what they do."* I say not that that prayer was confined only to His immediate executioners; **I believe that it was a far-reaching prayer, which included Scribes and Pharisees, Pilate and Herod, Jews and Gentiles, yes, the whole human race, in a certain sense, since we were all partakers in that murder, but certainly the immediate persons upon whom that prayer was poured like precious nard *were* those who then and there were committing the brutal act of fastening Him to the accursed tree.** How sublime is this prayer if viewed in such a light! It stands alone upon a mountain of solitary Glory.

No other had prayer had been prayed like it before; it is true, Abraham, and, and the Prophets had prayed for the wicked, but not for wicked men who had pierced their hands and feet. It is true that Christians have since that day offered the same prayer, even as **Stephen cried, "Lay not this sin to their charge,"** and many a martyr has made his last words at the stake words of pitying intercession for his persecutors, but you know where they learned this.

Let me ask you, where did He learn it? Was not Jesus the Divine Original? He learned it nowhere; it leaped up from His Own Godlike Nature; a Compassion peculiar to Himself dictated this originality of prayer; the inward Royalty of His Love suggested to Him so memorable an intercession, which may serve us for a pattern, but of which no pattern had existed before. I feel as though I could better kneel before my Lord's Cross at this moment than stand in this pulpit to talk to you. I need to adore Him. I worship Him in heart for that prayer. If I knew nothing else of Him but this one prayer, I must adore Him, for that one matchless plea for Mercy convinces me most overwhelmingly of the Deity of Him who offered it, and fills my heart with reverent affection. Thus have I introduced to you our Lord's first vocal prayer upon the Cross; I shall now, if we are helped by God's Holy Spirit, make some use of it.

A. First ... let us look at this very wonderful text as *ILLUSTRATION OF OUR LORD'S INTERCESSION.*

He prayed for His enemies then; He is praying for His enemies now. The past on the Cross was an earnest of the present on the Throne; He is in a higher place, and in a nobler condition, but His occupation is the same. He still continues before the Eternal Throne to present pleas on the behalf of guilty men, crying, "Father, O forgive them." All His Intercession is in a measure, like the Intercession on Calvary, and Calvary's cries may help us to guess the character of the whole of His Intercession above.

(1) **The first point in which we may see the character of His Intercession is this, it is *most gracious.*** Those for whom our Lord prayed, according to the text, did not deserve His prayer; they had done nothing which could call forth from Him a benediction as a reward for their endeavors in His service. On the contrary, they were most undeserving persons who had conspired to put Him to death; they had crucified Him;

Crucified Him wantonly and malignantly; they were even then taking away His Innocent Life. His clients were persons, who, so far from being meritorious, were utterly undeserving of a single good wish from the Savior's heart; they certainly never asked Him to pray for them, it was the last thought in their minds to say, "Intercede for us, You dying King; offer petitions on our behalf, You Son of God!"

I will venture to believe the prayer itself, when they heard it, was either disregarded, and passed over with contemptuous indifference, or perhaps it was caught at as a theme for jest. I admit that it seems to be too severe upon humanity to suppose it possible that such a prayer could have been the theme for laughter, and yet there were other things enacted around the Cross which were quite as brutal, and I can imagine that this also might have happened.

Yet our Savior not only prayed for persons who did not deserve the prayer, but on the contrary, merited a *curse;* persons who did not ask for the prayer, and even scoffed at it when they heard it. **Even so in Heaven there stands the great High Priest who pleads for guilty men, for *guilty* men, my Hearers.** There are none on earth who deserve His Intercession; He pleads for none on the supposition that they deserve it, but He stands there to plead as the Just One on the behalf of the unjust. Not if any man is *righteous,* but *"if any man sins, we have an Advocate with the Father."* Remember too that our great Intercessor pleads for such as never asked Him to plead for them. His Elect, while yet dead in trespasses and sins, are the objects of His Intercessions, and while they even scoff at His Gospel, His heart of Love is entreating the favor of Heaven on their behalf.

See, then, Beloved, if such is the Truth of God, how sure you are to find favor with God who earnestly asks the Lord Jesus Christ to plead for you. Some of you with many tears and much earnestness, have been beseeching the Savior to be your Advocate. Will He refuse you? Stands it to reason that He can? He pleads for those who *reject* His pleadings, much more for you who prize them beyond gold. Remember, my dear

Hearer, if there is nothing good in you, and if there is everything conceivable that is malignant and bad, yet none of these things can be any barrier to prevent **Christ's exercising the Office of Intercessor** for you. Even for *you* He will plead. Come, put your case into His hands; for you He will find pleas which you cannot discover for yourselves, and He will put the case to God for you as for His murderers, "Father, forgive them."

(2)   **A second quality of His Intercession is this:** *its careful spirit.* You notice in the prayer, *"Father, forgive them, for they know not what they do,"* our Savior did as it were, look His enemies through and through to find something in them that He could urge in their favor; but He could see nothing until His wisely affectionate eyes lit upon their ignorance, "they know not what they do." How carefully He surveyed the circumstances, and the characters of those for whom He prayed. Just so it is with Him in Heaven. Christ is no careless Advocate for His people; He knows your precise condition at this moment, and the exact state of your heart with regard to the temptation through which you are passing; more than that, He foresees the temptation which is awaiting you, and in His Intercession He takes note of the future event which His Prescient eyes behold. *"Satan has desired to have you that he may sift you as wheat; but I have prayed for you that your faith fail not."* Oh, the condescending tenderness of our Great High Priest. He knows us better than we know ourselves. He understands every secret grief and groan. You need not trouble yourself about the wording of your prayer, He will put the wording right, and even the understanding as to the exact petition, if you should fail in it, He cannot, for as He knows what is the mind of God, so He knows what is your mind also. He can spy out some reason for His Mercy in you which you cannot detect in yourselves, and when it is so dark and cloudy with your soul that you cannot discern a foothold

for a plea, that you may urge with Heaven, the Lord Jesus has the pleas ready-framed, and petitions ready drawn up, and He can present them acceptable before the Mercy Seat. His Intercession then, you will observe, is very gracious, and in the next place it is very thoughtful.

(3) **We must next note its *earnestness*.** No one doubts who reads these words, *"Father, forgive them, for they know not what they do,"* that they were Heaven-piercing in their fervor. Brethren, you are certain, even without a thought, that Christ was terribly in earnest in that prayer; but there is an argument to prove that. Earnest people are usually witty and quick of understanding to discover anything which may serve their turn; if you are pleading for life, and an argument for your being spared is asked of you, I will guarantee you that you will think of one when no one else might. Now, Jesus was so in earnest for the Salvation of His enemies that He struck upon an argument for Mercy which a less anxious spirit would not have thought of, *"They know not what they do."* Why, Sirs, that was in strictest justice but a scant reason for mercy. And indeed, ignorance, if it is willful, does not extenuate sin, and yet the ignorance of many who surrounded the Cross *was* a willful ignorance. They should have known that He was the Lord of Glory; was not Moses plain enough; had not Elijah been very bold in his speech; were not the signs and tokens such that one might as well doubt which is the sun in the firmament as the claims of Jesus to be the Messiah? Yet, for all that, the Savior, with marvelous earnestness, and consequent dexterity, turns what might not have been a plea, into a plea, and puts it thus, *"Father, forgive them, for they know not what they do."* Oh, how mighty are His pleas in Heaven, then, in their earnestness. Do not suppose that He is less quick of understanding there, or less intense in the vehemence of His entreaties; no, my Brothers and Sisters, the heart of

Christ still labors with the Eternal God; He is no slumbering Intercessor, but for Zion's sake He does not hold His peace, and for Jerusalem's sake He does not cease nor will He, till her Righteousness goes forth as brightness, and her Salvation as a lamp that burns.

(4) It is interesting to note ... **that the prayer here offered helps us to judge of His Intercession in Heaven as to its continuance, perseverance, and perpetuity.** As I remarked before, if our Savior might have paused from intercessory prayer, it was surely when they fastened Him to the tree; when they were guilty of direct acts of deadly violence to His Divine Person. He might then have ceased to present petitions on their behalf, but sin cannot tie the tongue of our interceding Friend. Oh, what comfort is here. You have sinned, Believer; you have grieved His Spirit; but you have not stopped that potent tongue which pleads for you! Perhaps my Brother you have been unfruitful, and like the barren tree you deserve to be cut down, but your lack of fruitfulness has not withdrawn the Intercessor from His place. He interposes at this moment, crying, "Spare it yet another year." Sinner, you have provoked God by long rejecting His Mercy, and going from bad to worse, but neither blasphemy, nor unrighteousness, nor infidelity shall stop the Christ of God from urging the suit of the very chief of sinners. **He lives, and while He lives, He pleads; and while there is a sinner upon earth to be saved, there shall be an Intercessor in Heaven to plead for him.**

These are but fragments of thought, but I hope they will help you, to realize the Intercession of your great High Priest.

(5) **Think yet again, this prayer of our Lord on earth is like His prayer in Heaven because of its *Wisdom*.** He seeks the best thing, and that which His clients most need, "Father,

forgive them." That was the great point in hand; they needed most of all, then and there, *forgiveness* from God. He does not say, "Father, enlighten them, for they know not what they do," for mere *enlightenment* would but have created torture of conscience and hastened on their Hell. No, He cries, "Father, forgive." And while He used His Voice, the precious drops of blood which were then distilling from the nail wounds were also pleading, and God heard and doubtless did forgive. The first Mercy which is necessary to guilty sinners is forgiven sin; Christ wisely prays for the blessing most needed. It is so in Heaven, He pleads wisely and prudently. Let Him alone, He knows what to ask for at the Divine hand. Go to the Mercy Seat, and pour out your desires as best you can, but when you have done, always put it thus, "O my Lord Jesus, answer no desire of mine if it is not according to Your Judgment, and if in anything that I have asked I have failed to seek for what I need, amend my pleas, for You are Infinitely Wiser than I." Oh, it is sweet to have a Friend at court to perfect our petitions for us before they come unto the Great King. I believe that there is never presented to God anything but a perfect prayer; I mean that before the Great Father of us all, no prayer of His people ever comes up imperfect. There is nothing left out, and there is nothing to be erased, and this, not because their prayers were originally perfect in themselves, **but because the Mediator** *makes them perfect* **through His Infinite Wisdom, and they come up before the Mercy Seat molded according to the Mind of God Himself, and He is sure to grant such prayers.**

(6) **Once more, this memorable prayer of our Crucified Lord was like His Universal Intercession in the matter of its prevalence.** Those for whom He prayed were, many of them, forgiven; do you remember that He said to His disciples when He bade them preach, "beginning at Jerusalem"; and on

that day when Peter stood up with the Eleven, and charged the people that with wicked hands they had crucified and slain the Savior, 3,000 of these persons who were thus justly accused of His Crucifixion became Believers in Him, and were baptized in His name. That was an answer to Jesus' prayer. The priests were at the bottom of our Lord's murder; they were the most guilty, and it is said, "a great company, also, of the priests believed." Here was another answer to the prayer. Since all men had their share representatively, Gentiles as well as Jews, in the death of Jesus, the Gospel was soon preached to the Jews, and within a short time it was preached to the Gentiles also. Was not this prayer, "Father, forgive them," like a stone cast into a lake, forming at first a narrow circle, and then a wider ring, and soon a larger sphere, until the whole lake is covered with circling waves? Such a prayer as this, cast into the whole world, first created a little ring of Jewish converts and of priests, and then a wider circle of such as were beneath the Roman sway; and today its circumference is as wide as the globe itself, so that tens of thousands are saved through the prevalence of this one Intercession, "Father, forgive them." It is certainly so with Him in Heaven; He never pleads in vain; with bleeding hands He yet won the day; with feet fastened to the wood, He was yet victorious; forsaken of God, and despised of the people, He was yet triumphant in His pleas. How much more so now the tiara is about His brow; how much more so now His hand grasps the universal scepter, and His feet are shod with silver sandals, and He is crowned King of kings, and Lord of lords? If tears and cries out of weakness were Omnipotent, even more mighty, if possible, must be that sacred Authority which, as the risen Priest, He claims when He stands before the Father's Throne to mention the Covenant which the Father made with Him! O you trembling Believers, trust Him with your concerns.

Come ..., you guilty, and ask him to plead for you. O you that cannot pray, come, ask Him to intercede for you. Broken hearts and weary heads, and disconsolate bosoms, come to Him who into the golden censer will put *His* Merits, and then place *your prayers* with them so that they shall come up as the smoke of perfume, even as a fragrant cloud into the nostrils of the Lord God of Hosts, who will smell a sweet savor and accept you and your prayers in the Beloved. We have now opened up more than enough room for your meditations at home ..., therefore, we leave this first point. We have had an illustration in the prayer of Christ on the Cross of what His prayers always are in Heaven.

B.   Second, the text is *INSTRUCTIVE OF THE CHURCH'S WORK*.

1.   **As Christ was, so His Church is to be in this world. Christ came into this world not to be ministered unto, but to minister; not to be honored, but to save others.** His Church, when she understands her work, will perceive that she is not here to gather to herself wealth or honor, or to seek any temporal aggrandizement and position; she is here *unselfishly* to live, and if necessary, unselfishly to *die* for the deliverance of the lost sheep, the Salvation of lost men. Brothers and Sisters, Christ's prayer on the Cross, I told you, was altogether an unselfish one; He does not remember Himself in it, and such ought to be the Church's life-prayer, the Church's active interposition on the behalf of sinners. She ought to never live for her ministers, or for herself, but always for the lost sons of men. Do you imagine that churches are formed to maintain ministers; do you conceive that the church exists in this land merely that so much salary may be given to bishops, deans and curates, and I know not what? ... It were well if the whole thing were abolished if that were its only aim. The aim of the church is not to provide backdoor relief for the younger sons of the nobility when they have not brains enough to win their livelihood any other way; churches are not made so that men of ready speech may stand up on Sundays

and talk, and so win daily bread from their admirers. No, there is another end and aim from this; these places of worship are not built that you may sit here comfortably, and hear something that shall make you pass away your Sundays with pleasure; a church in London which does not exist to do good in the slums, and dens, and kennels of the city is a church that has no reason to justify its existence any longer. A church that does not exist to reclaim heathenism, to fight with evil, to destroy error, to put down falsehood; a church that does not exist to take the side of the poor, to denounce injustice, and to hold up righteousness, is a church that has no right to be. Not for yourself, O Church, do you exist, any more than Christ existed for Himself. His Glory was that He *laid aside* His Glory, and the glory of the church is when she lays aside her respectability and her dignity, and counts it to be her glory to gather together the outcasts, and her highest honor to seek amid the foulest mire the priceless jewels for which Jesus shed His blood. To rescue souls from Hell, and lead them to God, to hope, to Heaven, this is her heavenly occupation. O that the Church would always feel this. Let her have her bishops and her preachers, and let them be supported, and let everything be done for Christ's sake decently and in order, but let the end be looked to, namely, the *conversion* of the wandering, the *teaching* of the ignorant, the help of the *poor*, the maintenance of the *right*, the putting down of the wrong, and the upholding at all hazards of the Crown and Kingdom of our Lord Jesus Christ.

2. **Now the prayer of Christ had a great spirituality of aim.** You notice that nothing is sought for these people but that which concerns their souls, "Father *forgive* them." And I believe the Church will do well when she remembers that she wrestles not with flesh and blood, nor with principalities and powers, but with *spiritual* wickedness, and that what she has to dispense is not the law and order by which magistrates may be upheld, or tyrannies pulled down, but the *spiritual* government by which

hearts are conquered to Christ, and judgments are brought into subjection to His Truth. I believe that the more the Church of God strains after, before God, the forgiveness of sinners, and the more she seeks in her life prayer to teach sinners what sin is, and what the blood of Christ is, and what the Hell that must follow if sin is not washed out, and what the Heaven is which will be ensured to all those who are cleansed from sin, the more she keeps to this, the better. Press forward as one man, my Brothers, to secure the root of the matter in the forgiveness of sinners. As to all the evils that afflict humanity, by all means take your share in battling with them; let temperance be maintained; let education be supported; let reforms, political and ecclesiastical, be pushed forward as far as you have the time and effort to spare, **but the *first* business of every Christian man and woman is with the hearts and consciences of men as they stand before the Everlasting God**. Let nothing turn you aside from your Divine errand of mercy to undying souls; this is your one business; tell sinners that sin will damn them; that Christ, alone, can take away sins, and make this the one passion of your souls, "Father, forgive them; forgive them. Let them know how to be forgiven; let them be actually forgiven, and let me never rest except as I am the means of bringing sinners to be forgiven, even the guiltiest of them."

3. **Our Savior's prayer teaches the Church that while her spirit should be unselfish, and her aim should be spiritual, the range of her mission is to be unlimited**. Christ prayed for the wicked; what if I say the most wicked of the wicked, that ribald crew that had surrounded His Cross? He prayed for the ignorant; does He not say, "They know not what they do"? He prayed for His persecutors; the very persons who were most at enmity with Him lay nearest to His heart. Church of God, your mission is not to the respectable few who will gather about your ministers to listen respectfully to their words; your mission is not to the *elite* and the eclectic, the intelligent who will criticize

59

your words and pass judgment upon every syllable of your teaching; your mission is not to those who treat you kindly, generously, affectionately; not to these, I mean, alone, though certainly to these as among the rest, but your great errand is to the harlot, to the thief, to the swearer, and the drunkard, to the most depraved, and debauched. If no one else cares for these, the Church always must, and if there are any who are first in her prayers, it should be these who, alas, are generally last in our thoughts. The ignorant we ought diligently to consider; it is not enough for the preacher that he preaches so that those instructed from their youth up can understand him; he must think of those to whom the most common phrases of theological truth are as meaningless as the jargon of an unknown tongue; he must preach so as to reach the meanest comprehension, and if in the ignorant, many come not to hear him, he must use such means as best he may to *induce* them, no, *compel* them to hear the Good News. The Gospel is also meant for those who persecute religion; it aims its arrows of God's Love against the hearts of its foes; if there are any whom we should first seek to bring to Jesus, it should be just these who are the farthest off, and most opposed to the Gospel of Christ. "*Father,* forgive *them;* if You pardon none besides, yet be pleased to forgive *them.*" So, too, the Church should be *earnest* as Christ was, and if she is so, she will be quick to notice any ground of hope in those she deals with; she will be quick to observe any plea that she may use with God for their Salvation. She must be *hopeful,* too, and surely no church ever had a more hopeful sphere than the church of this present age. If ignorance is a plea with God, look on the heathens at this day, millions of them never heard Messiah's name. Forgive them, great God, indeed they know not what they do.

My time has been much too short for so vast a subject as I have undertaken, but I wish I could speak words that were as loud as thunder, with a sense and earnestness as mighty as the lightning. I would gladly excite every Christian here, and kindle in him a right idea of what his work is as a part of Christ's Church. My Brothers and Sisters, you must not live to yourselves. The accumulation of money, the bringing up of your children, the building of houses, the earning of your daily bread; all this you may do, but there must be a greater objective than this if you are to be Christ-like, as you should be, since you are bought with Jesus' blood.

Begin to live for others. Make it apparent unto all men that you are not yourselves the end-all, and be-all of your own existence, but that you are spending and being spent; that through the good you do to men God may be glorified, and Christ may see in you His Own Image, and be satisfied.

C. Time fails me, but the last point was to be a word *SUGGESTIVE TO THE UNCOVETED.*

Listen attentively to these sentences; I will make them as terse and condensed as possible. Some of you here [October 24, 1869] are not saved; now some of you have been very ignorant, and when you sinned you did not know what you did; you knew you were sinners, you knew *that*, but you did not know the far-reaching *guilt* of sin. You have not been attending the House of Prayer long; you have not read your Bible; you have not Christian parents. Now you are beginning to be anxious about your souls; remember your ignorance does not excuse you, or else Christ would not say, "Forgive them." They must be *forgiven*, even those who know not what they do, and therefore they are individually guilty. But still that ignorance of yours gives you just a little gleam of hope; the times of your ignorance God winked at, but now commands all men everywhere to repent. Bring forth, therefore, fruits meet for Repentance. The God whom you have ignorantly forgotten is willing to pardon, and ready to forgive; the Gospel is just this, trust Jesus Christ who died for the *guilty,* and you shall be saved. O may God help you to do so this very morning, and you will become new men and new women; a change will take place in you equal to a new birth, you will be new creatures in Christ Jesus. But ah, my Friends, there are some here for whom even

Christ Himself could not pray this prayer, in the widest sense at any rate, "Father, forgive them, for they know not what they do," for you *have* known what you did, and every sermon you hear, and especially every impression that is made upon your understanding and conscience by the Gospel adds to your responsibility, and takes away from you the excuse of not knowing what you do.

EXHORTATION: You know that there is the world and Christ, and that you cannot have both; you know that there is sin and God, and that you cannot serve both; you know that there are the pleasures of evil and the pleasures of Heaven, and that you cannot have both. In the light which God has given you, may His Spirit also come, and help you to choose that which true wisdom would make you choose. Decide today for God, for Christ, for Heaven. The Lord decide You for His name's sake. Amen.

3.   [Christ's] Plea from the Cross

"Then Jesus said, 'Father, forgive them for they do not know what they do'"
(Luke 23:34 NKJV).

FOCUS: The Savior's plea from the Cross shows His love and what he asks of us; the text informs us for whom Christ offered this petition and the admonition this prayer offers to the unrepentant.

TO the godly heart there is a brighter light on Calvary than anywhere else beneath the sun. He who often resorts to Golgotha, if his spirit is right, must be wise. It is the University of Saints. He who would know sin, its heinousness, its penalty, must see the Son of God making Expiation for it by His death on the accursed tree. He who would know love, the love which many waters cannot quench, and which the floods cannot drown, must read it in the Savior's face or, if you will, written in crimson lines in the Savior's heart, pierced with the spear. He who would know how he may get his sin forgiven, must resort to the Cross. There, and there only, is seen the way by which sin can be pardoned and the sinner accepted with God! And he who, finding pardon there, would seek to be useful to his fellow men and bring them into the same condition, must, himself, keep near that Cross, that he may speak much of it and, in the power of it, may be able to persuade and to prevail with the sons of men. **Abide at the Cross, Beloved, there is no air as healthy and quickening as that which is breathed there. There was the birthplace of your hope. There its native air. There must be on earth, the climax of your joy. Live upon a Crucified Savior as you live by a Crucified Savior.**

And now **this word which we hear at Calvary, the first word of our Savior after He had been fastened to the Cross,** this word I shall not attempt to fathom, or go into the depths of it, but shall rather touch the surface of it, skimming it, and uttering a few such sentences, as it were, one after the other that have arisen to my mind while listening to the voice of our Lord in this, His plaintive cry, "Father, forgive them, for they know not what they do." I will suppose that I have many here, and I fear I need not make it a supposition, who as yet are unpardoned, unreconciled to God. Will you come with me and make a pilgrimage to Calvary? Will you look at your Savior? He has just come up the hill of doom! They have thrown Him upon His back. There is the Cross, the executioners have stretched out His hands and His feet, they have taken the nails, they have driven them through His hands and feet. He is fastened to the wood, and now as they are lifting Him up, before it jars into the ground, you hear Him cry, "Father, forgive them, for they know not what they do." I want you to learn a few lessons out of this. And the first shall be, see here:

A. *THE SAVIOR'S LOVE TO SINNERS.*

It is His last hour, but He thinks of them. He had searched for them in His health and strength. He went about doing good. He

came to seek and to save the rebellious and He had spent His active life in their service. He is about to die, but the ruling passion is strong in death. He is still seeking sinners and if He can preach no more, yet He can pray. And if He will not speak to them, yet He can speak to God for them, and so He continues to show which way His heart runs, by the prayer for those that nailed Him to the wood, "Father, forgive them, for they know not what they do." He had been thirty years in their midst and His holy soul had been much vexed by them. He had endured the contradiction of sinners against Himself, but you see He has not cast them off, He has not turned His love to wrath. He is not weary of them, but He still pleads, "Father, oh, forgive them." What love is this. One would suppose that the pain which He then felt might have distracted His mind from others, and His prayer might have been for Himself, that patience might be given, that strength might be sustained. But no, oblivious of Himself, His only care is still for those He seeks the sinful sons of men. Just as an arrow from a bow shot forth with such force that it speeds onward to its target, His whole strength and soul speeds onward to the mark of the salvation of the sons of men. One thing, one thing only, does He do, He seeks their good. And I say again, if not now by active ministering to them, yet by ministering for them, He prays "Father, forgive them."

It is one thing to love persons at a distance and to have philanthropic desires for their good. it is quite another thing to live with them and still have the same fondness towards them. And it is quite another thing by far to receive bad treatment from them, contumely, scorn and a worse thing even than that, to be about to receive your death from them and still to pray for them. But such is the perseverance of Jesus' love that it cannot be turned aside.

They have spit into His face, but still He prays for them. They have **scourged Him** with their cruel lashes. They have **hounded Him** along the streets. They have, at last, **pierced His hands and feet, and stripped Him**. And they now hang Him up upon the Cross between Heaven and earth, but still nothing can diminish the flame of His love, nor turn aside His heart's desire from them, it is still for them He lives, for them He dies. "Father, oh, forgive them," is the sign and proof that He is still holding to the one great work He undertook. Now I would, O Sinner, I would that you would learn this lesson. Herein is love, behold what love. Will you not come and share in it? What keeps you back? Can you hold your heart from Immanuel? Can you refuse to love such a dear lover of the sons of men? I think if our hearts were not adamant or worse, they would melt at the sight of the pleading love of Jesus upon the Cross. Come, Soul, have done with your hardness, let a drop of Christ's blood melt that heart of yours. Have done with your carelessness, let a spark of love set your heart on fire towards Him. Are you afraid to come, afraid of Him who died for sinners, afraid of love, terrified at mercy? Oh, be not so, but come and welcome. Put your trust in Him who, with His dying breath, proves the strength of His Almighty love by pleading for His foes. Let that stand for the first remark. **Here is the strong love of Christ.** Here, next, we see:

B. *HOW LOVE SHOWS ITSELF.*

How did Jesus prove His love in this last great moment? It was by prayer! Love shows itself in prayer. Prayer, alone, would not be a sufficient proof of love, but He who dies and prays, whose life is a prayer, and whose death is a prayer, proves His love by adding to His life and death the vocal utterance of both in this cry, "Father, forgive them." If Jesus Christ would prove His love to you, He does it by praying for you. Observe, then, the extreme value of prayer. It is a ripe fruit of the Cross. It is, if I may call it so, a golden apple of the Cross, intercessory prayer. See, then, Sinner, the need there is for you to pray. If Jesus prays and proves His love by prayer, and if the saints on earth who love you pray for you, depend upon it, prayer is no light thing. **Bend those knees of yours, lift your eyes to Heaven and let a prayer go up from the depths of your spirit, "Father, forgive me! Your Son has prayed, so pray I. He says, 'Father, forgive them,' and I pray, 'Father, forgive me.'" Ought not this to bring every sinner to his knees?** Would it not, if men were in their senses? Would not the sight of a dying Christ pleading for the guilty make the guilty plead? Oh, who can restrain prayer for himself when Jesus leads the way? When He says, "Forgive them," will you not say, "Amen"? Oh, deserve you not right well to perish if you cannot join your assent to the Divine Intercession of the pleading Savior. Sinner, I beseech you now, in the secret of your soul, to pray, *"Father, forgive me."* *"God, be merciful to me, a sinner."* Is there no woman, is there no man that could pray that now? You need not speak, let but your lips move. But, oh, since Jesus Christ tonight is set forth before you in the delightful attitude of an Intercessor praying for the guilty, I implore you pray for yourselves and may God send you, this night, an answer of peace, may your pardon be signed and sealed to the comfort of your spirit.

And now leaving that observation, we pass to the next. We saw the love of Jesus. We saw how that love shows itself in prayer. See next:

C. *WHAT IT IS THE SAVIOR ASKS.*

He asks forgiveness, "Father, forgive them." If the Savior should pray for all of us here present, He need not amend that prayer. It was suitable to those who nailed Him to the tree. They needed pardon for the murder of their Savior. It was suitable to the clamoring multitude, who had said, *"Crucify Him, and crucify Him."* They needed forgiveness for that blood which they then brought upon themselves, but it is equally suitable to each one here present, "Forgive them." May I ask you to look back upon your past lives? Have you been kept from grosser sins? Thank God for it, but your sins of heart, of mind, of tongue, your sins of omission. What? Are these nothing? God grant you may feel them to be something and may you feel, tonight, that what you need is even as if you had been an open offender, you need forgiveness and if, perchance, there are some here who have gone into open sin with a high hand and an outstretched arm, yet, my Brother, yet my Sister, this prayer needs no enlargement to suit you, "Father, forgive them." "Father, forgive them," forgiveness covers all. A man receipts a bill. He puts his name at the bottom. If that bill were for ten thousand pounds or ten pence, it is the same, the receipt has covered all and Jesus' hand, when

He puts it with the bloody red nail prints upon the great record of our sins, draws a red line down the page and blots out the whole and leaves not a single sin on the page. "Though your sins are as scarlet, they shall be as wool; though they are red like crimson, they shall be whiter than snow." Oh, the greatness of that word, "forgiven."

Blessed be the Lord Jesus for praying such a prayer as that. Do you know, I do not think it need be altered for the best man and the best woman here, for even our best things need forgiveness. When you have prayed the best prayer you ever prayed, you might well ask God to forgive it. **If you have preached the best sermon you ever preached, you may ask to be forgiven it, for some sin has mingled with your holiest action, so forgiveness is needed at best, and always needed at the worst, needed today, tomorrow and all through life, and needed when the breath leaves the body, always needed that blessed prayer that sweeps the compass of mortal existence that comprehends so much, "Father, forgive them."** This is the great thing love asks, for the forgiveness of those for whom she pleads. But passing on you will observe:

D. *FOR WHOM IT IS THAT OUR SAVIOR, IN THIS CASE, OFFERED THE PETITION.*

"Father, forgive them, for they know not what they do." **Now that little word, "them," is a great word because it is so little. "Father, forgive them." The Savior is explicit, He does not mention the names of the four soldiers who pierced His hands and feet. No. He meant them, but He meant more.** He does not mention the names of these in the crowd who were gazing upon Him with insolent stare, He meant them. He does not mention those that had cried, *"Crucify Him, crucify Him,"* He had meant them. He does not say, "Father, forgive them, for they knew not what they did," for that would look as if He only prayed for sins that had already been committed. He does not say, "Father, forgive them, for they know not what they shall do," for that would look as if He only prayed for sins that would be committed. But He says, "Father forgive them, for they know not what they do." And

putting it thus in the present, it seems as though the petition had one hand to reach out to the past sins of mankind before He died, and another hand to the sins to come of mankind after He had offered the Sacrifice. "They know not what they do." It is put so indefinitely, the, "them," and the, "do," the tense of the verb and the pronoun, they are so indefinite that I bless God for the wide extent of their range. "Father, forgive them, for they know not what they do." Who, then, is included in that word, "them"? I venture to say every man that is willing to be included, every man that feels he is included. Did you slay Christ? Have your sins caused Him to die? Do you know, tonight, that your sins fastened Him to the cruel tree? Could you join in the hymn we sung just now? Then, when Jesus said, "Father, forgive them, for they know not what they do," He included you in that prayer, and me in that prayer, and tens of thousands besides in that word, "them."

Yet, you will observe in that word He put it specially. He does not exclude any, but He does include some more peculiarly than others, for His prayer is for those who knew not what they did. Can I get in there? I think I can. I believe that most here present can. I do not think all the sons of men can, Judas, for instance, I fear he did know what he did, and deliberately sold his Lord and Master. I am half afraid that Pilate, to a great extent, knew what he did, and there are some of whom it is written, "There is a sin unto death; I do not say that you shall pray for it." A great Doctrine, but it is in the Word, a terrible Doctrine, but there it stands. You know how Peter put it in that first sermon. He said, "I know, my brethren that through ignorance you did it, as did also your rulers," as if he felt that had they known what they did, their sin had been unpardonable. And the apostle Paul, himself, speaking of his own persecution, said, "Because I did it ignorantly, in unbelief." There is a deliberate Crucifixion of Christ as Christ, knowing what you are doing, doing it out of sheer malice to the Christ of God, out of intense hatred to Him, to Him personally, which is unpardonable, for this reason, that the man who commits it never repents. Could he repent, the pardon was sure, but the capacity to do that argues incapacity to ever be made penitent. The man is given over, hardened, he perishes in his sin.

But the Lord Jesus in this prayer felt that those around Him did not know what they were doing, the most of them did not know He was God's Son. They would not have crucified Him had they known; they would not have crucified the Lord of Glory. They did know, most of them knew, that He was a righteous Man and they must have felt they were doing very wrong in putting Him to death, but they did not recognize Him as the Messiah and as the Son of God, otherwise the most of them would have held back their hand. Now, though I have sinned against light and knowledge, and you have done the same, my Brothers and Sisters, yet in our past sin we did not deliberately intend to put Christ to death. We did not, like Satan of *malice propense*, [premeditated and deliberate] desire to overthrow the Kingdom of God and Christ. Blessed be God, He saved us from that. We went far, very far, horribly far, but restraining Grace kept us back from that, and the Savior puts it there, makes such the object of His prayer. I do not say He excludes those who did it knowingly, but He does include peculiarly those who did not know what they did, whose sin, to a great extent, as to its far-reaching heinousness was wrapped in ignorance. He says, "Father, forgive them, for they know not what they do." Then the prayer of love is offered for a vast company of sinners in darkness and ignorance, who have sinned, but who have not been allowed utterly, knowingly, willfully, viciously to crucify the Son of God and put Him to an open shame.

Now I want you to **notice what this prayer of love admits**. There is something in it that ought never to be forgotten. "Father, forgive them, for they know not what they do." You see, then, this prayer, even of a patient, loving, gentle Savior, who wishes to plead all He can on the behalf of those for whom He prays, this prayer admits that they need to be forgiven who have sinned ignorantly. Some people have thought, "If I did not know it to be sin to the full extent, then it was not sin." Ah, not so. It was sin, for Christ asks to have it forgiven. If I, doing what I did not fully understand, yet did wrong, I am not excused the wrong because I did not know to the fullest extent how wrong it was. I am just as guilty as if I did know, from some points of view, though not from others, but from any point of view, I still need to be forgiven. Ignorance of the law does not prevent the guilt of him who breaks it. As you know, my Brothers and Sisters, human law, the law of the land, for instance, never takes ignorance of the law as a complete excuse for the breach of the law. The laws of England always assume that every man knows the law. The law is made; it is a public law and he who breaks it cannot go before the Magistrate and say, "I did not know it was the law; you must discharge me." The Magistrate may, as a man, say, "Well, if you did not know it was law, there is some excuse for you." As a Magistrate, he must not say that, for the law judges the man on its own self as publicly known, and does not allow for the excuse of not knowing the law.

If the Savior, in His infinite mercy, said, "Father, forgive them, for they know not what they do," it was a plea, of course, but not a plea of law. Sinai has no room for that excuse, for Sinai says, "If you don't know, you ought to have known." And in this particular case, especially, if they did not know Christ to be God, they ought to have known it. The prophecies were so clear. The Person of Christ so exactly fitted in to every type and every prophetic declaration, that it was "a willful blindness that had happened unto Israel." They ought to have known it. One sin is never an excuse for another sin. It was a sin for them not to know. That sin, therefore, did not excuse them for committing the other. It is only Sovereign Grace that brought that in as a plea, it is not justice, nor is it law, it the heart of mercy that pleads that.

What I want you to notice, now, then, is though I did not know when I sinned as child and as a young man all that was meant by sin, though I especially did not know that I was crucifying Christ, yet the guilt is just the same as before God, and I need to be forgiven for it, or else it will be laid to my charge, and I shall be punished as surely as God's Law stands fast. Do you think the Savior would say, "Father, forgive them," if it were not a wrong? He never prayed a superfluous prayer. The prayer, "Forgive," is a sentence in itself, teaching us that sins of ignorance are sins. Oh, my dear Hearers, there are none of us who know to the full extent the sin of our sin. The most tender heart here does not know the blackness of its sin. I have sometimes talked with persons under conviction who have told me what dreadful sinners they were, and they have looked a little surprised when I have said, "But you are ten times worse than you think you are." No, they scarcely thought that could be possible, yet I would venture to say that to the most tender-hearted penitent that ever lived, you have no idea, my Friend, of the aggravation of your sin, nor is it possible you should have, nor do I know that it is desirable. So long as you know enough of your sin to hate it, and to flee to Christ for the pardon of it, that will suffice. But, oh, the scholarship that would be needed to understand all the depths of sin, it were the scholarship of the Cross over again, you would have need to die like Christ to know what sin means in its infinite, its boundless guilt. Do not ask to know that, but do pray that the Lord would search you and forgive you your sins. You did not know of pardoned sins you have committed, manifold sins that have passed by your notice, that you have not observed and, consequently, could not have confessed in particular. Beseech the Savior, whose cry is, "Father, forgive them, for they know not what they do," to pray for unknown mercy by His unknown agony for your unknown sin. It is a wondrous prayer, this, but we cannot stay much longer on it.

We make yet another remark, "Father forgive them for they know not what they do."

E. *THIS PRAYER WARNS US.*

I have felt intense pleasure in thinking it over, but at the same time that pleasure has been mingled with great bitterness. **There is such a warning there, "Father, forgive them, for they know not what they do" It does not say, as I have already said, that if they did know, Christ would not pray for them, but it does seem to hint that. In the background I see a something, not that every sin committed against light is unpardonable, God be thanked that is not so, but some sins committed against light and knowledge so harden the heart that the man never repents.**

He never will, he will go to Hell hardened like steel. And I am afraid some of you are in great likelihood of committing it. Those who have not heard the Gospel cannot very readily commit this, unless their conscience has been desperately violated, but some of you who have been hearers often, and perhaps were once professors who have knowingly chosen the wrong path and have deliberately sacrificed your character for drink or gain or lust, I will not say that you have passed that boundary, but I do tremble as I hear the booming of that text, "There is a *sin unto death;* I do not say that you shall pray for it," even as I hear the Master's words, "Father, forgive them, for they know not what they do." But these persons knew what they did, did it deliberately, did it over again and again, and again, perhaps went to the Lord's Table and deliberately went to their uncleanness, stood up in public, it may be, and then deliberately went to their filthiness. Or they listened to the sermon on Sunday and they said, "I'll do better" and then deliberately went on Monday to their drunken companions again. Oh, Man, you may have stood in the street, perhaps, and said to yourself, "Now, which shall it be? I feel as if I were called to serve God, but yet how can I give up such-and-such a darling lust?" There is a point in men's lives wherein if they deliberately choose the wrong, knowing it is wrong, with the Light of God shining on their eyeballs, yet they deliberately give up Christ, Heaven, pardon and they choose Hell and their own delusions, I fear that with many from that hour the wax is cooled upon their death warrant and it will never be reversed, for this text, though it gently flows from the Savior's lips and drops like dew, has about it the lightning flash and thunderbolt that startles, "Father, forgive them, they know not what they do."

But there are some who know what they do and take the hammer and nail Christ up to the Cross. They take a spear and pierce His side and do it knowing what they are doing! And all the while they are glibly talking of religion, taking the Bible to make jokes out of it, taking the very ministers they once professed to love and scoffing them, taking the Doctrines of the Gospel and making these a cloak for their sins, these men, what will I say of them? God have mercy upon them, but I fear, I fear, that He never will, for they will never seek it, and He will never grant it. Could they seek it; He would give it. While a man can seek, he shall find. While a heart can melt, God will pity. There is never a contrite soul but what God looks with love upon it. But here is the mischief, for these men, who know what they do, repent not, but are seared as with a hot iron, they become wandering stars, for whom is reserved the blackness of darkness forever.

But I must close here. This shall be a closing word. At the same time, you see the text woos. It warns, but it woos. How it woos the ignorant, especially. "Father, forgive them, for they know not what they do." Oh, some of you have dropped in here tonight who, perhaps, don't often listen to the Gospel. You have been living a life of sin. You knew it was sin, You knew it was sin, but you did not know that you were nailing Christ to the Cross. You sought your own pleasure, you sought your own gratifications. You have been very guilty. You have lived a careless, Godless, Christless life, but still you did not mean to sin against God so as to crucify Christ. You see you have done so, now you feel you are guilty of it, but before, you had not that Light of God that you now have. Then Jesus says, "Come to Me, come to Me. My prayer goes up to Heaven for you, you ignorant one." Sinful, but without light, Jesus intercedes. Join your prayer with the prayer of Jesus, and say, "Father, forgive Your ignorant child, Your sinful, wayward child. I do not plead, 'I knew not what I did,' but Christ pleads it for me. I plead that Jesus died. Oh, for His sake, have pity. Hear His blood as it drops from His hands and feet; hear it and plead for me, 'Father, forgive them.'"

EXHORTATION: If you will seek the Lord, you shall have Him. If you will but turn your eyes to Him upon the Cross, you shall live. Whoever among you in this house will but trust Him, shall find Him able and willing to save to the uttermost them that come unto God by Him. Oh, come and welcome, come and welcome. And may God grant that you may come tonight: "But if your ears refuse /The language of His Grace, /And hearts grow gross like stubborn Jews, /That unbelieving race. /The Lord in vengeance dressed /Will lift His hand and swear / 'You that despised My promised rest /Shall have no portion there." God bless you. Amen.

4.   Exposition on Matthew 27:32–49

Verse 32. *And as they came out, they found a man of Cyrene, Simon by name: him they compelled to bear His Cross.*

Perhaps they were afraid that Christ would die from exhaustion, so they compelled Simon to bear His Cross. Any one of Christ's followers might have wished to have been this man of Cyrene, but we need not envy him, for there is a cross for each of us to carry. Oh, that we were as willing to bear Christ's Cross as Christ was to bear our sins on His Cross. If anything happens to us by way of persecution or ridicule for our Lord's sake, and the Gospel's, let us cheerfully endure it. As knights are made by a stroke from the sovereign's sword, so shall we become princes in Christ's realm as He lays His Cross on our shoulders.

33, 34. *And when they were come unto a place called Golgotha, that is to say, a place of a skull, they gave Him vinegar to drink mingled with gall: and when He had tasted thereof, He would not drink.*

Golgotha was the common place of execution for malefactors, the … Old Bailey [the central criminal court in England] of Jerusalem, outside the gate of the city. There was a special symbolical reason for Christ's suffering outside the gate, and His followers are bid to "go forth unto Him outside the camp, bearing His reproach" (Hebrews 13:11-13). A stupefying draught was given to the condemned, to take away something of the agony of crucifixion, but our Lord came to suffer, and He would not take anything that would at all impair His faculties. He did not forbid His fellow sufferers drinking the vinegar mingled with gall ("wine mingled with myrrh," Mark 15:23), but He would not drink thereof. Jesus did not refuse this draught because of its bitterness, for He was prepared to drink even to the last dreadful dregs the bitter cup of wrath which was His people's due.

35. *And they crucified Him, and parted His garments, casting lots: that it might be fulfilled which was spoken by the Prophet, they parted My garments among them, and upon My vesture did they cast lots.*

There is a world of meaning in that short sentence, "and they crucified Him," driving their bolts of iron through His blessed hands and feet, fastening Him to the Cross and lifting Him up to hang there upon some gallows reserved for felons. We can scarcely realize all that the Crucifixion meant to our dear Lord, but we can join in Faber's prayer: *"Lord Jesus! May we love and weep, /Since You, for us, are crucified."*

Then was fulfilled all that our Lord had foretold in Chapter 20:17–19, except His Resurrection, the time for which had not arrived.

The criminals' clothes were the executioners' profits. The Roman soldiers who crucified Christ had no thought of fulfilling the Scriptures when they parted His garments, casting lots, yet their action was exactly that which had been foretold in Psalm 22:18. The seamless robe would have been spoiled if it had been torn, so the soldiers raffled for the vesture, while they shared the other garments of our Lord. The dice would be almost stained with the blood of Christ, yet the gamblers played on beneath the shadow of His Cross. Gambling is the most hardening of all vices. Beware of it in any form. No games of chance should be played by Christians, for the blood of Christ seems to have bespattered them all.

36. *And sitting down they watched Him there.*

Some watched Him from curiosity, some to make sure that He really did die, some even cruel eyes with His sufferings, and there were some, hard by the Cross, who wept and bewailed, a sword passing through their own hearts while the Son of Man was agonizing even unto death.

37. *And set up over His head His accusation written, THIS IS JESUS, THE KING OF THE JEWS.*

What a marvelous Providence it was that moved Pilate's pen. The representative of the Roman Emperor was little likely to concede kingship to any man, yet he deliberately wrote, "This is Jesus, the King of the Jews," and nothing would induce him to alter what he had written. Even on His Cross, Christ was proclaimed King, in the sacerdotal Hebrew, the classical Greek, and the common Latin, so that everybody in the crowd could read the inscription. When will the Jews admit Jesus as their King? They will do so one day, looking on Him whom they pierced. Perhaps they will think more of Christ when Christians think more of them when our hardness of heart towards them has gone, possibly their hardness of heart towards Christ may also disappear.

38. *Then were there two thieves crucified with Him, one on the right hand, and another on the left.*

As if to show that they regarded Christ as the worst of the three criminals, they put Him between the two thieves, giving Him the place of dishonor. Thus was the prophecy fulfilled, "He was numbered with the transgressors." The two malefactors deserved to die, as one of them admitted (Luke 23:40, 41), but a greater load of guilt vested upon Christ, for, "He bore the sin of many," and, therefore, He was rightly distinguished as the King of Sufferers, who could truly ask, "Was ever grief like Mine?"

Verses 39, 40. *And they that passed by reviled Him, wagging their heads, and saying, You who destroys the temple, and builds it in three days, save Yourself. If You are the Son of God, come down from the Cross.*

Nothing torments a man when in pain more than mockery. When Jesus Christ most needed words of pity and looks of kindness, they who passed by, reviled Him, wagging their heads. Perhaps the most painful part of ridicule is to have one's most solemn sayings turned to scorn, as were our Lord's words about the temple of His body, "You who destroys the temple, and builds it in three days, save Yourself." He might have saved Himself, He might have "come down from the Cross," but if He had done so, we could never have become the sons of God. It was because He was the Son of God that He did not come down from the Cross, but hung there until He had completed the Sacrifice for His people's sin. Christ's Cross is the Jacob's ladder by which we mount up to Heaven. This is the cry of the Socinian today, "Come down from the Cross. Give up the atoning Sacrifice and we will be Christians." **Many are willing to believe in Christ, but not in Christ Crucified.** They admit that He was a good Man and a great Teacher, but by rejecting His Vicarious Atonement, they practically unChrist the Christ, as these mockers at Golgotha did.

41–43. *Likewise, also the chief priests mocking Him, with the scribes and elders, said, He saved others; Himself He cannot save. If He is the King of Israel, let Him now come down from the Cross and we will believe Him. He trusted in God: let Him deliver Him now, if He will have Him: for He said, I am the Son of God.*

The chief priests, with the scribes and elders, forgetting their high station and rank, joined the ribald crew in mocking Jesus in His death pangs. Every word was emphatic, every syllable cut and pierced our Lord to the heart. They mocked Him as a Savior, "He saved others; Himself He cannot save." They mocked Him as a King, "If He is the King of Israel, let Him now come down from the Cross, and we will believe Him." They mocked Him as a Believer, "He trusted in God; let Him deliver Him now, if He will have Him." They mocked Him as the Son of God, "For He said, I am the Son of God." Those who say that Christ was a good Man, virtually admit His Deity, for He claimed to be the Son of God. If He was not what He professed to be, He was an impostor. Notice the testimony that Christ's bitterest enemies bore even as they reviled Him. "He saved others." "He is the King of Israel" (RV) "He trusted in God."

44. *The thieves, also, who were crucified with Him, cast the same in His teeth.*

The sharers of His misery, the wretches who were crucified with Him, joined in reviling Jesus. Nothing was lacking to fill up His cup of suffering and shame. The conversion of the penitent thief was all the more remarkable because he had but a little while before been among the mockers of his Savior. What a trophy of Divine Grace he became.

45. *Now from the sixth hour there was darkness over all the land unto the ninth hour.*

Some have thought that this darkness covered the whole world, and so caused even a heathen to exclaim, "Either the world is about to expire, or the God who made the world is in anguish." This darkness was supernatural; it was not an eclipse. The sun could no longer look upon its Maker surrounded by these who mocked Him. He covered his face and traveled on in tenfold night, in very shame that the great Sun of Righteousness should, Himself, be in such terrible darkness.

46. *And about the ninth hour Jesus cried with a loud voice, saying, Eli, Eli, lama Sabachthani? That is to say, My God, My God, why have You forsaken Me?*

In order that the Sacrifice of Christ might be complete, it pleased the Father to forsake His Well-beloved Son. Sin was laid on Christ, so God must turn away His face from the Sin-Bearer. To be deserted of His God was the climax of Christ's grief, the quintessence of His sorrow. See here the distinction between the martyrs and their Lord, in their dying agonies they have been Divinely sustained, but Jesus, suffering as the Substitute for sinners, was forsaken of God. The saints who have known what it is to have their Father's face hidden from them, even for a brief space, can scarcely imagine the suffering that wrung from our Savior the agonizing cry, "My God, My God, why have You forsaken Me?"

47. *Some of them that stood there, when they heard that, said, This Man calls for Elijah.*

They knew better, yet they jested at the Savior's prayer. Wickedly, willfully and scornfully, they turned His death shriek into ridicule.

48, 49. *And straightway one of them ran and took a sponge, and filled it with vinegar, and put it on a reed, and gave Him to drink. The rest said, Let Him be, let us see whether Elijah will come to save Him.*

A person in such agony as Jesus was suffering might have mentioned many pangs that He was enduring, but it was necessary for Him to say, "I thirst," in order that another Scripture might be fulfilled. One of them, more compassionate than his companions, ran, and took a sponge, and filled it with vinegar, from the vessel probably brought by the soldiers for their own use, and put it on a reed, and gave Him to drink. It always seems to me very remarkable that the sponge, which is the very lowest form of animal life, should have been brought into contact with Christ, who is at the top of all life. In His death the whole circle of Creation was completed. As the sponge brought refreshment to the lips of our dying Lord, so may the least of God's living ones help to refresh Him, now that He has ascended from the Cross to the Throne.

5. [The Son's Plea to the Father for] Ignorant Sinners

"Then Jesus said, 'Father, forgive them for
they do not know what they do'"
(Luke 23:34 NKJV).

FOCUS: **These last words of Jesus will be handled by way of experience rather than by exposition. There are four lines of thought: First, we are in a measure ignorant. Second, we are to confess that this ignorance is of no excuse. Third, we are to bless** our Lord for pleading for us. Fourth, we can rejoice in the pardon we have obtained. "May the Holy Spirit graciously help us in our meditation."

WHAT tenderness we have here; what self-forgetfulness; what almighty love. Jesus did not say to those who crucified Him, "Be gone." One such word and they would have all fled. When they came to take Him in the garden, they went backward and fell to the ground when He spoke but a short sentence. And now that He is on the Cross, a single syllable would have made the whole company fall to the ground, or flee away in fright.

Jesus says not a word in His own defense. When He prayed to His Father, He might justly have said, "Father, note what they do to Your Beloved Son. Judge them for the wrong they do to Him who loves them and who has done all He can for them." But there is no prayer against them in the words that Jesus utters. It was written of old, by the Prophet Isaiah, *"He made intercession for the transgressors,"* and here it is fulfilled. He pleads for His murderers, *"Father, forgive them."*

He does not utter a single word of upbraiding. He does not say, "Why do you do this? Why pierce the hands that fed you? Why nail the feet that followed after you in mercy? Why mock the Man who loved to bless you?" No, not a word, even, of gentle upbraiding, much less anything like a curse. "Father, forgive them." You notice Jesus does not say, "I forgive them," but you may read that between the lines. He says that all the more because He does not say it in words. But He had laid aside His majesty and is fastened to the Cross and, therefore, He takes the humble position of a suppliant, rather than the loftier place of One who had power to forgive. How often, when men say, "I forgive you," is there a kind of selfishness about it? At any rate, self is asserted in the very act of forgiving. Jesus takes the place of a *pleader*, a pleader for those who were committing murder upon Himself. Blessed be His name.

This word on the Cross we shall use, tonight, and we shall see if we cannot gather something from it for our instruction, for, though we were not there and we did not actually put Jesus to death, yet we really caused His death, we, too, crucified the Lord of Glory and His prayer for us was, "Father, forgive them; for they know not what they do."

A. Looking back upon our past experience, let me say, first, that **WE WERE, IN A MEASURE, IGNORANT.** We who have been forgiven, we who have been washed in the blood of the Lamb, we once sinned in a great measure through ignorance. Jesus says, "*They know not what they do.*" Now, I shall appeal to you, Brothers and Sisters, when you lived under the dominion of Satan and served yourselves and sin, was there not a measure of ignorance in it? You can truly say, as we said in the hymn we sang just now, "*Alas! I knew not what I did.*"

It is true, first, that we were ignorant **of the awful meaning of sin.** We began to sin as children, we knew that it was wrong, but we did not know all that sin meant. We went on to sin as young men, perhaps we plunged into much wickedness. We knew it was wrong, but we did not see the end from the beginning. It did not appear to us as rebellion against *God.* We did not think that we were presumptuously defying God, setting at nothing His wisdom, defying His power, deriding His love, spurning His holiness, yet we were. There is an abysmal depth in sin. You cannot see the bottom of it. When we rolled sin under our tongue as a sweet morsel, we did not know all the terrible ingredients compounded in that deadly bittersweet. We were, in a measure, ignorant of the tremendous crime we committed when we dared to live in rebellion against God. So far, I think, you are with me.

We did not know, at that time, God's great love for us. I did not know that He had chosen me from before the foundation of the world. I never dreamed of that. I did not know that Christ stood for me as my Substitute, to redeem me from among men. I did not know the love of Christ, did not understand it. You did not know that you were sinning against eternal Love, against infinite compassion, against a distinguishing Love such as God had fixed on you from eternity. So far, we knew not what we did.

I think, too, that **we did not know all that we were doing in our rejection of Christ and putting Him to grief.** He came to us in our youth and, impressed by a sermon, we began to tremble and to seek His face. But we were decoyed back to the world and we refused Christ. Our mother's tears, our father's prayers, our teacher's admonitions often moved us, but we were very stubborn and we rejected Christ. We did not know that, in that rejection, we were virtually putting Him away and crucifying Him. We were denying His Godhead, or else we would have worshipped Him. We were denying His love, or else we would have yielded to Him. We were practically, in every act of sin, taking the hammer and the nails and fastening Christ to the Cross, but we did not know it. Perhaps, if we had known it, we would not have crucified the Lord of Glory. We knew we were doing wrong, but we did not know all the wrong that we were doing.

Nor did we know fully the meaning of our delays. We hesitated, we were on the verge of conversion, but we went back and turned, again, to our old follies. We were hardened, Christless, still prayerless, and each of us said, "Oh, I am only waiting a little while till I have fulfilled my present engagements, till I am a little older, till I have seen a little more of the world." The fact is, we were refusing Christ and choosing the pleasures of sin instead of Him, and every hour of delay was an hour of crucifying Christ, grieving His Spirit and choosing this harlot world in the place of the lovely and ever-blessed Christ. We did not know that.

I think we may add one thing more. **We did not know the meaning of our self-righteousness.** We used to think, some of us, that we had a righteousness of our own. We had been to Church regularly, or we had been to the Meeting House whenever it was open. We were christened; we were confirmed, or, perhaps, we rejoiced that we never had either of those things done to us. Thus, we put our confidence in ceremonies, or the *absence* of ceremonies. We said our prayers; we read a chapter in the Bible night and morning. We did, I do not know what we did *not* do. But there we rested, we were righteous in our own esteem. We had not any particular sin to confess, nor any reason to lie in the dust before the Throne of God's majesty. We were about as good as we could be and we did not know that we were, even, then, perpetrating the highest insult upon Christ, for, if we were not sinners, why did Christ die? And, if we had a righteousness of our own which was good enough, why did Christ come here to work out a righteousness for us?

We made Christ to be a superfluity, by considering that we were good enough without resting in His Atoning Sacrifice. But we did not think we were doing that. We thought we were pleasing God by our religiousness, by our outward performances, by our ecclesiastical correctness. *But all the while we were setting up antichrist in the place of Christ. We were making out that Christ was not needed. We were robbing Him of His office and glory.* Alas, Christ would say of us with regard to all these things, *"They know not what they do."* I want you to look quietly at the time past wherein you served sin and see whether there was not a darkness upon your mind, a blindness in your spirit, so that you did not know what you did.

B. Well now, secondly, *WE CONFESS THAT THIS IGNORANCE IS NO EXCUSE.* Our Lord might urge it as a plea, but *we* never could. We did not know what we did and so we were not guilty to the fullest possible extent, but we were guilty enough, therefore let us acknowledge it.

For first, remember, **the law never allows this as a plea.** In our own English law, a man is supposed to know what the law is. If he breaks it, it is no excuse to plead that he did not know it. It may be regarded by a judge as some extenuation, but the law allows nothing of the kind. God gives us the Law and we are bound to keep it. If I erred through not knowing the Law, still it was a sin. **Under the Mosaic Law there were sins of ignorance and for these there were special offerings. The ignorance did not blot out the sin.** That is clear in my text, for, if ignorance rendered an action no longer sinful, they why would Christ say, "Father, forgive them"? But He does, He asks for mercy for what is *sin,* even though the ignorance, in some measure, is supposed to mitigate the criminality of it.

But, dear Friends, **we might have known.** If we did not know, it was because we *would* not know. There was the preaching of the Word, but we did not care to hear it. There was this blessed Book, but we did not care to read it. If you and I had sat down and looked at our conduct by the light of the Holy Scripture, we might have known much more of the evil of sin, much more of the love of Christ, much more of the ingratitude which is possible in refusing Christ and not coming to Him.

In addition to that, **we did not think.** "Oh, but," you say, "young people never think!" But young people *should* think. If there is anybody who need not think, it is the old man whose day is nearly over. If he thinks, he has but a very short time in which to improve, but the young have all their lives before them. If I were a carpenter and had to make a box, I would not think about it *after* I had made the box. I would think, before I began to cut my timber, what sort of box it was to be. In every action, a man thinks before he begins or else he is a fool. A young man ought to think more than anybody else, for now he is, as it were, making his box. He is beginning his life-plan; he should be the most thoughtful of all men. Many of us, who are now Christ's people, would have known much more about our Lord if we had given Him more careful consideration in our earlier days. A man will consider about taking a wife. He will consider about making a business. He will consider about buying a horse or a cow, but he will not consider about **the claims of Christ and the claims of the Most High God.** And this renders his ignorance willful and inexcusable.

Besides that, dear Friends, although we have confessed to ignorance, **in many sins we did not know a great deal.** Come, let me quicken your memories. There were times when you knew that such an action was wrong when you began it. You looked at the gain it would bring you, and you sold your soul for that price and deliberately did what you were well aware was wrong. Are there not some here, saved by Christ, who must confess that, at times, they did violence to their conscience? They did despite to the Spirit of God, quenched the Light of Heaven, and drove the Spirit away from them, distinctly knowing what they were doing. Let us bow before God in the silence of our hearts and acknowledge to all of this. We hear the Master say, "Father, forgive them; for they know not what they do." Let us add our own tears as we say, "And forgive us, also, because in some things we *did* know. In *all* things we *might* have known, but we were ignorant for lack of thought, which thought was a solemn duty which we ought to have rendered to God."

One more thing I will say on this head. When a man is ignorant and does not know what he ought to do, what should he do? Well, he should do nothing till he does know. **But here is the mischief of it, when we did not know, yet we chose to do the wrong thing. If we did not know, why did we not choose the *right* thing?** But, being in the dark, we never turned to the right, but always blundered to the left from sin to sin. Does not this show us how depraved our hearts are? Though we are seeking to be right, when we are left alone, we go wrong of ourselves. Leave a child alone. Leave a man alone. Leave a *tribe* alone without teaching and instruction, what comes of it? Why, the same as when you leave a field alone. It never, by any chance, produces wheat or barley. Leave it alone and there are rank weeds, thorns and briars showing that the natural set of the soil is towards producing that which is worthless.

O Friends, confess the innate evil of your hearts as well as the evil of your lives, in that, when you did not know, yet, having a perverse instinct, you chose the evil and refused the good and, when you did not know enough of Christ and did not think enough of Him to know whether you ought to have Him or not, you would not have come to Him that you might have life. You needed light but you shut your eyes to the sun. You were thirsty but you would not drink of the living spring and so, your ignorance, though it was there, was a *criminal* ignorance which you must confess before the Lord. Oh, come to the Cross, you who have been there, before, and have lost your burden there. Come and confess your guilt, again, and clasp that Cross afresh. Come and look to Him who bled upon it and praise His dear name that He once prayed for you, "Father forgive them; for they know not what they do."

Now, I am going a step further. We were, in a measure, ignorant, **but we confess that that measurable ignorance was no excuse.**

C. Now, thirdly, ***WE BLESS OUR LORD FOR PLEADING FOR US.***

Do you notice *when* it was that Jesus pleaded? **It was while they were crucifying Him.** They had not just driven in the nails, they had lifted up the Cross and dished it down into its socket and dislocated all His bones so that He could say, "I am poured out like water, and all My bones are out of joint." Ah, dear Friends, it was *then* that, instead of a cry or groan, this dear Son of God said, "Father, forgive them; for they know not what they do." They did not ask for forgiveness for themselves, Jesus asks forgiveness for them. Their hands were stained with His blood and it was then, even then, that He prayed for them. Let us think of the great love with which He loved us, even while we were yet sinners, when we were rioting in sin, when we drank it down as the ox drinks down water. Even *then* **He prayed for us.** *"While we were yet without strength, in due time Christ died for the ungodly."* **Bless His name tonight. He prayed for you when you did not pray for yourself. He prayed for you when you were crucifying Him.**

Then think of His plea, **He pleads His Sonship.** He says, *"Father,* forgive them." He was the Son of God and He put His Divine Sonship into the scale on our behalf. He seems to say, "Father, as I am Your Son, grant Me this request and pardon these rebels. Father, forgive them." The filial rights of Christ were very great. He was the Son of the Highest. "Light of Light, very God of very God," the second Person in the Divine Trinity and He puts that Sonship here before God and says, "Father, Father, forgive them." Oh, the power of that Word from the Son's lips when He is wounded, when He is in agony, when He is dying. He says, "Father, Father, grant My one request. O Father, forgive them; for they know not what they do." And the great Father bows His awful head in token that the petition is granted.

Then notice **that Jesus here, silently, but really pleads His sufferings.** The attitude of Christ when He prayed this prayer is very noteworthy. His hands were stretched upon the transverse beam. His feet were fastened to the upright tree and there He pleaded. Silently His hands and feet were pleading and His agonized body from the very sinew and muscle pleaded with God! His Sacrifice was presented complete and so it is His Cross that takes up the plea, "Father, forgive them." O blessed Christ. It is thus that we have been forgiven, for His Sonship and His Cross have pleaded with God and have prevailed on our behalf.

I love this prayer, also, **because of the indistinctness of it.** It is, "Father, forgive them." He does not say, "Father, forgive the soldiers who have nailed Me here." He includes them. Neither does He say, "Father, forgive sinners in ages to come who will sin against Me." But He means them. Jesus does not mention them by any accusing name, "Father, forgive My enemies. Father, forgive My murderers." No, there is no word of accusation upon those dear lips. "Father, forgive *them*." Now into that pronoun, "them," I feel that I can crawl. Can you get in there? Oh, by a humble faith, appropriate the Cross of Christ by trusting in it and get into that big little word, "*them*." It seems like a chariot of mercy that has come down to earth into which a man may step, and it shall bear him up to Heaven. "Father, forgive them."

Notice, also, what it was that Jesus asked for, to omit that would be to leave out the very essence of His prayer. **He asked for full absolution for His enemies,** "Father, forgive them. Do not punish them. Forgive them. Do not remember their sin. Forgive it, blot it out, and throw it into the depths of the sea. Remember it not, My Father. Mention it not against them any more forever. Father, forgive them." Oh, blessed prayer, for the forgiveness of God is broad and deep! **When man forgives, he leaves the remembrance of the wrong behind. But when God pardons, He says, "I will forgive their iniquity and I will remember their sin no more." It is *this* that Christ asked for you and me long before we had any repentance, or any faith, and in answer to that prayer we were brought to feel our sin. We were brought to confess it and to believe in Him. And now, glory be to His name, we can bless Him for having pleaded for us and obtained the forgiveness of all our sins.**

D. I come now to my last remark, which is this: **WE NOW REJOICE IN THE PARDON WE HAVE OBTAINED.** Have you obtained pardon? Is this your song? *"Now, oh joy. My sins are pardoned, /Now I can, and do believe."*

I have a letter, in my pocket, from a man of education and standing, who has been an agnostic. He says that he was a sarcastic agnostic and he writes praising God and invoking every blessing upon my head for bringing him to the Savior's feet. He says, "I was without happiness for this life and without hope for the next." I believe that that is a truthful description of many an unbeliever. What hope is there for the world to come apart from the Cross of Christ? … I do not know of any religion but that of Christ Jesus which tells us of sin pardoned, absolutely pardoned.

Now, listen. Our teaching is not that, when you come to die, you *may, perhaps,* find out that it is all right, but, *"Beloved, now we are the sons of God." "He that believes on the Son has everlasting life."* He has it now and he knows it, and he rejoices in it. So I come back to the last head of my discourse: we rejoice in the pardon Christ has obtained for us. We are pardoned. I hope that the larger portion of this audience can say, **"By the Grace of God, we know that we are washed in the blood of the Lamb."**

Pardon has come to us through Christ's plea. Our hope lies in the plea of Christ and especially in His death. If Jesus paid my debt, and He did it if I am a believer in Him, then I am out of debt. If Jesus bore the penalty of my sin, and He did it if I am a Believer, then there is no penalty for me to pay, for we can say to Him: *"Complete Atonement You have made, /And to the utmost farthing paid /Whatever Your people owed. / Nor can His wrath on me take place, / If sheltered in Your Righteousness, /And sprinkled with Your blood. /If You have my discharge procured, /And freely in my place endured /The whole of wrath Divine— /Payment God can't twice demand, / First of my bleeding Surety's hand, / And then, again, at mine."*

If Christ has borne my punishment, I shall never bear it. Oh, what joy there is in this blessed assurance. Your hope that you are pardoned lies in this, that Jesus died. Those dear wounds of His bled for you.

We praise Him for our pardon because *we do know, now, what we did.* I know not how much we ought to love Christ because we sinned against Him so grievously. Now we know that sin is, "exceedingly sinful." Now we know that sin crucified Christ. Now we know that we stabbed our heavenly Lover to His heart! We slew, with ignominious death, our best and dearest Friend and Benefactor. We know that, now, and we could almost weep tears of blood to think that we ever treated Him as we did. But, it is all forgiven, all gone. Oh, let us bless that dear Son of God who has put away even such sins as ours. We feel them more, now, than ever before. We know they are forgiven and our grief is because of the pain that the purchase of our forgiveness cost our Savior. We never knew what our sins really were till we saw Him in a bloody sweat. We never knew the crimson hue of our sins till we read our pardon written in crimson lines with His precious blood. Now we see our sin and yet we do not see it, for God has pardoned it, blotted it out, cast it behind His back forever.

From now on *ignorance,* **such as we have described,** *shall be hateful to us.* Ignorance of Christ and eternal things shall be hateful to us. If, through ignorance, we have sinned, we will have done with that ignorance. We will be students of His Word. We will study that masterpiece of all the sciences, the knowledge of Christ Crucified. **We will ask the Holy Spirit to drive far from us the ignorance that genders sin.** God grant that we may not fall into sins of ignorance any more, but we may be able to say, *"I know whom I have believed and, henceforth I will seek more knowledge till I comprehend, with all saints, what are the heights, and depths, and lengths, and breadths of the love of Christ, and know the love of God, which passes knowledge."*

I put in a practical word here. If you rejoice that you are pardoned, **show** *your gratitude by your imitation of Christ.* There was never before such a plea as this, "Father, forgive them; for they know not what they do." Plead like that for others. Has anybody been injuring you? Are there persons who slander you? Pray, tonight, "Father, forgive them; for they know not what they do." **Let us always render good for evil, blessing for cursing, and when we are called to suffer through the wrong-doing of others, let us believe that they would not act** as they do if it were not because of their ignorance. Let us pray for them and make their very ignorance the plea for their forgiveness, *"Father, forgive them; for they know not what they do."*

I see *reason for hope in the very ignorance that surrounds us.* I see hope for this poor city of ours [London], hope for this poor country [England], hope for Africa, China and India. "They know not what they do." Here is a strong argument in their favor, for they are more ignorant than we were. They know less of the evil of sin and less of the hope. Send up this fiery shaft of prayer, straight to the heart of God, while Jesus, from His Throne, shall add His prevalent intercession, "Father, forgive them; for they know not what they do."

EXHORTATION: If there are any unconverted people here, and I know that there are some, we will mention them in our private devotion, as well as in the public assembly. And we will pray for them in words like these, "Father, forgive them; for they know not what they do." May God bless you all, for Jesus Christ's sake. Amen.

6. Exposition on Luke 23:33–46

We have often read the story of our Savior's sufferings, but we cannot read it too often. Let us, therefore, once again repair to "the place which is called Calvary." As we just now sang: *"Come, let us stand beneath the Cross, / So may the blood from out His side /Fall gently on us, drop by drop. / Jesus, our Lord is crucified."*

We will read, first, Luke's account of our Lord's crucifixion and death.

Luke 23:33. *And when they were come to the place which is called Calvary, there they crucified Him, and the malefactors, one on the right hand, and the other on the left.*

They gave Jesus the place of dishonor. Reckoning Him to be the worst criminal of the three, they put Him between the other two.

They heaped upon Him the utmost scorn which they could give to a malefactor, and in so doing they unconsciously honored Him. Jesus always deserves the chief place wherever He is. In all things He must have the pre-eminence. He is King of sufferers as well as King of saints.

34. *Then said Jesus, Father, forgive them; for they know not what they do.*

How startled they must have been to hear such words from One who was about to be put to death for a supposed crime. The men that drove the nails, the men that lifted up the tree must have been started back with amazement when they heard Jesus talk to God as His Father, and pray for them, "Father, forgive them; for they know not what they do." Did ever Roman legionary hear such words before? I should say not. They were so distinctly and diametrically opposed to the whole spirit of Rome. There it was, blow for blow, only in the case of Jesus, they gave blows where none had been received. The crushing cruelty of the Romans must have been startled, indeed, at such words as these, "Father, forgive them; for they know not what they do."

34, 35. *And they parted His raiment, and cast lots. And the people stood beholding.*

The gambling soldiers little dreamed that they were fulfilling the 22nd Psalm, which so fully sets forth our Savior's sufferings and which He probably repeated while He hung on the tree. David wrote, *"They parted My garments among them, and cast lots upon My vesture."* "And the people stood beholding," gazing, looking on the cruel spectacle. You and I would not have done that there is a public sentiment which has trained us to hate the sight of cruelty, especially of deadly cruelty to one of our own race, but these people thought that they did no harm when they "stood beholding." They also were thus fulfilling the Scriptures, for the 17th verse of the 22nd Psalm says, "They look and stare upon Me."

35. *And the rulers also with them derided Him.*

Laughed at Him, made Him the object of course jests.

35, 36. *Saying, He saved others; let Him save Himself, if He is Christ, the Chosen of God. And the soldiers also mocked Him, coming to Him, and offering Him vinegar.*

In mockery, not *giving* it to Him, as they did later in mercy, but in mockery, pretending to present Him with weak wine, such as they drank.

37. *And saying, If You are the King of the Jews, save Yourself.*

I fancy the scorn that they threw into their taunt, "If You are the King of the Jews, "that was a bit of their own. "Save yourself," that they borrowed from the rulers. Sometimes a scoffer or a mocker cannot exhibit all the bitterness that is in his heart except by using borrowed terms, as these soldiers did.

38. *And a superscription also was written over Him in the letters of Greek, Latin and Hebrew, THIS IS THE KING OF THE JEWS.*

John tells us that Pilate wrote this title and that the chief priests tried in vain to get him to alter it. It was written in the three current languages of the time, so that the Greek, the Roman and the Jew might, alike, understand who He was who was thus put to death. Pilate did not know as much about Christ as we do, or He might have written, ***THIS IS THE KING OF THE JEWS AND OF THE GENTILES, TOO.***

39. *And one of the malefactors which were hanged railed at Him, saying, If You are Christ, save Yourself and us.*

He, too, borrows this speech from the rulers who derided Christ, only putting the words, "and us," as a bit of originality. "If You are the Christ, save Yourself and us."

40, 41. *But the other answering rebuked him saying, do you not fear God, seeing you are in the same condemnation? And we, indeed, justly, for we receive the reward of our deeds: but this Man has done nothing amiss.*

A fine testimony to Christ, "This Man has done nothing amiss," nothing unbecoming, nothing out of order, nothing criminal, certainly, but nothing even, "amiss." This testimony was well spoken by this dying thief.

42–46. And *he said unto Jesus, Lord, remember me when You come into Your Kingdom. And Jesus said unto him, Verily, I say unto you, today shall you be with Me in Paradise. And it was about the sixth hour, and there was a darkness over all the earth until the ninth hour. And the sun was darkened, and the veil of the Temple was rent in the midst. And when Jesus had cried with a loud voice, He said, Father, into Your hands I commend My spirit: and having said thus, He gave up His ghost.*

He yielded His life. He did not die, as we have to do, because our appointed time has come, but willingly the great Sacrifice parted with His life, "He gave up the ghost." He was a willing Sacrifice for guilty men. Now let us see what John says concerning these hours of agony, these hours of triumph.

B. Words of Remembrance and Salvation

1. The Believing Thief [on the Cross]

*"Then he said to Jesus, 'Lord, remember me when You come
into Your kingdom.'" And Jesus said to him, "'Assuredly,
I say to you, today you will be with Me in Paradise'"
(Luke 23:42, 43 NKJV).*

FOCUS: **The thief on the cross was our Lord Jesus Christ last companion on earth and the first at the gate of paradise as the sermon explains. These words spoken to us from the cross is an act of divine grace.**

SOME time ago I preached upon the whole story of the dying thief. I do not propose to do the same today but only to look at it from one particular point of view. **The story of the salvation of the dying thief is a standing instance of the power of Christ to save and of His abundant willingness to receive all that come to Him in whatever plight they may be.** I cannot regard this act of Divine Grace as a solitary instance any more than the salvation of Zacchaeus, the restoration of Peter, or the call of Saul, the persecutor. Every conversion is, in a sense, singular, no two is exactly alike and yet any one conversion is a type of others.

The case of the dying thief is much more similar to our conversion than it is dissimilar. In point of fact his case may be regarded as typical rather than as an extraordinary incident. So I shall use it at this time. May the Holy Spirit speak through it to the encouragement of those who are ready to despair.

Remember, beloved Friends that our Lord Jesus at the time He saved this malefactor was at His lowest. His Glory had been ebbing out in Gethsemane and before Caiaphas and Herod and Pilate. But it had now reached the utmost low water mark. Stripped of His garments and nailed to the Cross, our Lord was mocked by a ribald crowd and was dying in agony, then was He *"numbered with the transgressors,"* and made as the off scouring of all things. Yet while in that condition He achieved this marvelous deed of Divine Grace. Behold the wonder worked by the Savior when emptied of all His Glory and a spectacle of shame upon the brink of death!

How certain is it that He can do great wonders of mercy *now*, seeing that He has returned unto His Glory and sits upon the Throne of light? *"He is able to save them to the uttermost that come unto God by Him, seeing He ever lives to make intercession for them."* **If a dying Savior saved the thief, <u>my argument</u> is that He can do even more, now that He lives and reigns. All power is given unto Him in Heaven and in earth, can anything at this present time surpass the power of His Grace?**

It is not only the weakness of our Lord which makes the salvation of the penitent thief memorable. It is the fact that the dying malefactor saw it before his very eyes. Can you put yourself into his place and suppose yourself to be looking upon one who hangs in agony upon a cross? Could you readily believe Him to be the Lord of Glory who would soon come to His kingdom? That was no mean faith which, at such a moment, could believe in Jesus as Lord and King. If the apostle Paul were here and wanted to add a New Testament chapter to the eleventh of Hebrews, he might certainly commence his instances of remarkable faith with this thief.

He believed in a crucified, derided, and dying Christ and cried to Him as to one whose kingdom would surely come. The thief's faith was the more remarkable because he was, himself, in great pain and bound to die. It is not easy to exercise confidence when you are tortured with deadly anguish. Our own rest of mind has at times been greatly hindered by pain of body. When we are the subjects of acute suffering it is not easy to exhibit that faith which we fancy we possess at other times. This man, suffering as he did and seeing the Savior in so sad a state, nevertheless believed unto life eternal. Herein was such faith as is seldom seen.

Remember also, that he was surrounded by scoffers. It is easy to swim with the current and hard to go against the stream. This man heard the priests, in their pride, ridicule the Lord. The great multitude of the common people, with one consent, joined in the scorning, even his comrade caught the spirit of the hour and also mocked Jesus. And perhaps he did the same for a while. **But through the Grace of God he was changed and believed in the Lord Jesus in the teeth of all the scorn. His faith was not affected by his surroundings.**

But he, dying thief as he was, proclaimed his confidence. Like a jutting rock standing out in the midst of a torrent, he declared the innocence of the Christ whom others blasphemed. His faith is worthy of our imitation in its fruits. He had no member that was free except his tongue, and he used that member wisely to rebuke his brother malefactor, and defend *his Lord*. His faith brought forth a brave testimony and a bold confession.

I am not going to praise the thief or his faith. **I am going to extol the glory of that Divine Grace which gave the thief such faith and then freely saved him by its means.** I am anxious to show how glorious is the Savior, that Savior to the uttermost, who at such a time could save such a man and give him so great a faith and so perfectly and speedily prepare him for eternal bliss. Behold the power of that Divine Spirit who could produce such faith on soil so unlikely and in a climate so unfavorable.

A. *Carefully note THAT THE CRUCIFIED THIEF WAS OUR LORD'S LAST COMPANION ON EARTH.* What sorry company our Lord selected when He was here. He did not consort with the religious Pharisees or the philosophic Sadducees, He was known as "the friend of publicans and sinners." How I rejoice at this. It gives me assurance that He will not refuse to associate with me. When the Lord Jesus made a friend of me He certainly did not make a choice which brought Him credit. Do you think He gained any honor when He made a friend of you? Has He ever gained anything by befriending us?

No, my Brethren. If Jesus had not stooped very low, He would not have come to me. And if He did not seek the most unworthy He might not have come to you. You feel it so and you are thankful that He came "not to call the righteous, but sinners, to repentance." **As the great Physician, our Lord was much with the sick, He went where there was room for Him to exercise His healing art**. The whole have no need of a Physician, they cannot appreciate Him, and therefore He did not frequent their abodes. But after all, our Lord did make a good choice when He saved you and me. For in us He has found abundant room for His mercy and Grace. There has been plenty of elbow room for His love to work within the awful emptiness of our necessities and sins. And therein He has done great things for us, and we are glad.

Lest any here should be despairing and say, "He will never look on me," I want you to notice that the last companion of Christ on earth was a sinner and no ordinary sinner. He had broken even the laws of man, for he was a robber. One calls him "a brigand," [a bandit] and I suppose it is likely to have been the case. The brigands of those days mixed murder with their robberies, he was probably a freebooter in arms against the Roman government, making this a pretext for plundering as he had opportunity. At last he was arrested and was condemned by a Roman tribunal, which, on the whole, was usually just, and in this case was certainly just.

He himself confessed the justice of his condemnation. The malefactor who believed upon the cross was a convict who had lain in the condemned cell and was then undergoing execution for his crimes. **A convicted felon was the person with whom our Lord last consorted upon earth. What a lover of the souls of guilty men is Jesus. How He stoops to the very lowest of mankind. To this most unworthy of men the Lord of Glory, before He gave up His life, spoke with matchless grace. He spoke to him such wondrous words as never can be excelled if you search the Scriptures through: *"Today shall you be with Me in Paradise."***

I do not suppose that anywhere in this [Metropolitan] Tabernacle [1889] there will be found a man who has been convicted before the Law or who is even chargeable with a crime against common honesty. But if there should be such a person among my hearers, I would invite him to find pardon and change of heart though our Lord Jesus Christ. You may come to Him whoever you may be. For this man did. Here is a specimen of one who had gone to the extremes of guilt and who acknowledged that he had done so. He made no excuse and sought no cloak for his sin. He was in the hands of justice, confronted with execution, and yet he believed in Jesus and breathed a humble prayer to Him, and he was saved upon the spot.

As is the sample, such is the bulk. Jesus saves others of like kind. Let me, therefore, put it very plainly here so that no one may misunderstand me, none of you are excluded from the infinite mercy of Christ. **However, great your iniquity, if you believe in Jesus, He will save you.**

This man was not only a sinner, he was a sinner newly awakened. I do not suppose that he had seriously thought of the Lord Jesus before. According to the other Evangelists he appears to have joined with his fellow thief in scoffing at Jesus. If he did not actually himself use [scornful] words he was so far consenting that the Evangelist did him no injustice when he said, "The thieves also, which were crucified with Him, cast the same in His teeth." But, now, suddenly, he wakes up to the conviction that the Man who is dying at his side is something more than a man. He reads the title over His head and believes it to be true, *"This is Jesus the King of the Jews."*

Thus believing, he makes his appeal to the Messiah, whom he had so newly found, and commits himself to His hands. My [Reader], do you see this Truth of God that the *moment* a man knows Jesus to be the Christ of God he may at once put his trust in Him and be saved? A certain preacher, whose Gospel was very doubtful, said, "Do you, who have been living in sin for fifty years believe that you can in a moment be made clean through the blood of Jesus?" I answer, "Yes, we do believe that in one moment, through the precious blood of Jesus, the blackest soul can be made white. We believe that in a single instant the sins of sixty or seventy years can be absolutely forgiven and that the old nature which has gone on growing worse and worse can receive its death wound and eternal life may be implanted in the soul at once."

It was so with this man. He had reached the end of his tether, but all of a sudden he woke up to the assured conviction that the Messiah was at his side, and believing, he looked to Him and lived. So now, my Brothers and Sisters, if you have never in your life before been the subject of any religious conviction, if you have lived up till now an utterly ungodly life, if now you will believe that God's dear Son has come into the world to save men from sin and will sincerely confess your sin and trust in Him, you shall be immediately saved. Yes, while I speak the word, **the deed of Divine Grace may be accomplished by that glorious One who has gone up into Heaven with omnipotent power to save.**

I desire to put this case very plainly, **this man who was the last companion of Christ upon earth was a sinner in misery.** His sins had found him out, he was now enduring the reward of his deeds. I constantly meet with persons in this condition; they have lived a life of wantonness, excess and carelessness and they begin to feel the fire-flakes of the tempest of wrath falling upon their flesh. They dwell in an earthly Hell, a prelude of eternal woe. Remorse, like an asp, has stung them and set their blood on fire, they cannot rest, they are troubled day and night. *"Be sure your sin will find you out."* It has found them out and arrested them and they feel the strong grip of conviction.

This man was in that horrible condition, what is more, he was in the absolutely extreme. He could not live long; the crucifixion was sure to be fatal. In a short time, his legs would be broken to end his wretched existence. He, poor soul, had but a short time to live, only the space between noon and sundown. But it was long enough for the Savior, who is mighty to save. Some are very much afraid that people will put off coming to Christ if we state this. I cannot help what wicked men do with the Truth of God but I shall state it all the same. If you are now within an hour of death, believe in the Lord Jesus Christ and you shall be saved. If you never reach your homes again but drop dead on the road, if you will *now* believe in the Lord Jesus you shall be saved, saved now, on the spot.

Looking and trusting to Jesus, He will give you a new heart and a right spirit and blot out your sins. This is the glory of Christ's

Grace. How I wish I could extol it in proper language. He was last seen on earth before His death in company with a convicted felon to whom He spoke most lovingly. Come, O you guilty and He will receive you graciously.

Once more, **this thief whom Christ saved at last was a man who could do no good works.** If salvation had been by good works, he could not have been saved. For he was fastened hand and foot to the tree of doom. It was all over with him as to any act or deed of righteousness. He could say a good word or two but that was all. He could perform no acts. And if his salvation had depended on an active life of usefulness, certainly he never could have been saved. He was also a sinner who could not exhibit a long-enduring repentance for sin for he had so short a time to live. He could not have experienced bitter convictions lasting over months and years, for his time was measured by moments and he was on the borders of the grave.

His end was very near, and yet the Savior could save him and did save him so perfectly that the sun went not down till he was in Paradise with Christ. This sinner, whom I have painted to you in colors none too black, was one who believed in Jesus and confessed his faith. He did trust the Lord. Jesus was a man and he called Him so. **But he knew that He was also Lord and he called Him so and said, "Lord, remember me." He had such confidence in Jesus that he knew if He would but only think of him, if Jesus would only remember him when He came into His kingdom that would be all that he would ask of Him.**

… The trouble with some of you is that you know all about my Lord and yet you do not trust Him. **Trust is the saving act.** Years ago you were on the verge of really trusting Jesus but you are just as far off from it now as you were then. This man did not hesitate, he grasped the one hope for himself. He did not keep his persuasion of our Lord's Messiahship in his mind as a dry, dead belief. No, he turned it into trust and prayer, **"Lord, remember me when You come into Your kingdom."** Oh, that in His infinite mercy many of you would trust my Lord this morning. You shall be saved; I am sure you shall, if you are not saved when you trust, I must myself also renounce all hope.

This is all that we have done, we looked and we lived and we continue to live because we look to the living Savior. **Oh, that this morning, feeling your sin, you would look to Jesus, trust Him and confess that trust. Owning that He is Lord to the Glory of God the Father, you must and shall be saved.** In consequence of having this faith which saved him, this poor man breathed the humble, but fitting prayer, *"Lord, remember me."* This does not seem too much to ask. But as he understood it, it meant all that an anxious heart could desire. As he thought of the kingdom he had such clear ideas of the glory of the Savior that he felt that if the Lord would *think* of him, his eternal state would be safe.

Joseph, in prison, asked the chief butler to remember him when he was restored to power. But he forgot him. *Our Joseph never forgets a sinner who cried to Him in the low dungeon.* **In His Kingdom He remembers the moans and groans of poor sinners who are burdened with a sense of sin. Can you not pray this morning and thus secure a place in the memory of the Lord Jesus?**

Thus, **I have tried to describe the thief. And after having done my best I shall fail of my objective unless I make you see that whatever this thief was, he is a picture of what *you* are.** Especially if you have been a great offender and if you have been living long without caring for eternal things. And yet you, even you, may do as that thief did. You may believe that Jesus is the Christ, and commit your souls into His hands and He will save you as surely as He saved the condemned brigand. Jesus graciously says, *"Him that comes to me I will in no wise cast out."* This means that if you come and trust Him, whoever you may be, He will for no reason and on no ground and under no circumstances ever cast you out. Do you catch that thought? Do you feel that it belongs to you and that if you come to Him you shall find eternal life? I rejoice if you so far perceive the Truth.

Few persons have so much contact with desponding and despairing souls as I have. Poor, cast down ones, write to me continually. I scarcely know why. I have no especial gift of consolation, but I gladly lay myself out to comfort the distressed and they seem to know it. What joy I have when I see a despairing one find peace. I have had this joy several times during the week just ended. How much I desire that any of you who are breaking your hearts because you cannot find forgiveness, would come to my Lord and trust Him and enter into rest! Has He not said, *"Come unto Me, all you that labor and are heavy laden and I will give you rest"?* **Come and try Him and that rest shall be yours.**

B. In the second place, note that *THIS MAN WAS OUR LORD'S COMPANION AT THE GATE OF PARADISE.* I am not going into any speculations as to where our Lord went when He quit the Body which hung on the Cross. It would seem from some Scriptures that He descended into the lower parts of the earth, that He might fulfill all things. But He very rapidly traversed the regions of the dead. Remember that He died perhaps an hour or two before the thief and during that time the eternal glory flamed through the underworld and was flashing through the gates of Paradise just when the pardoned thief was entering the eternal world.

Who is this that enters the pearly gate at the same moment as the King of Glory? Who is this favored companion of the Redeemer? Is it some honored martyr? Is it a faithful apostle? Is it a patriarch like Abraham? Or a prince like David? It is none of these. Behold and be amazed at Sovereign Grace. He that goes in at the gate of Paradise with the King of Glory is a *thief* who was saved in the article of death. He is saved in no inferior way and received into bliss in no secondary style. Verily there are last which shall be first.

Here I would have you notice the condescension of our Lord's choice. The comrade of the Lord of Glory for whom the cherub turns aside his sword of fire is no great one, but a newly-converted malefactor. And why? I think the Savior took him with Him as a specimen of what He meant to do. He seemed to say to all the heavenly powers, "I bring a sinner with Me. He is a sample of the rest." Have you ever heard of him who dreamed that he stood without the gate of Heaven and while there he heard sweet music from a band of venerable persons who were on their way to God enquiring "What are these?" he was told that they were the goodly fellowship of the Prophets. He sighed and said, "Alas, I am not one of those." He waited a while and another band of shining ones drew near, who also entered Heaven with hallelujahs and when he enquired, "Who are these and from where they came?" the answer was, "These are the glorious company of the apostles." Again he sighed and said, "I cannot enter with them." Then came another body of men, white-robed and bearing palms in their hands who marched amid great acclamation into the golden city. These he learned were the noble army of martyrs. And again he wept and said, "I cannot enter with these."

In the end he heard the voices of much people and saw a greater multitude advancing among whom he perceived Rahab and Mary Magdalene, David and Peter, Manasseh and Saul of Tarsus and he espied especially the thief who died at the right hand of Jesus. These all entered in a strange company. Then he eagerly enquired, "Who are these?" and they answered, "This is the host of sinners saved by Divine Grace." Then was he exceeding glad and said, "I can go in with these." But he thought there would be no shouting at the approach of this company and that they would enter Heaven without song. Instead of which, there seemed to rise a seven-fold hallelujah of praise unto the Lord of Love. **For there is joy in the presence of the angels of God over sinners that repent.**

I invite any poor soul here that can neither aspire to serve Christ, nor to suffer for Him as yet, nevertheless to come in with other believing sinners, in the company of Jesus who now sets before us an open door. While we are handling this text, note well the blessedness of the place to which the Lord called this penitent. Jesus said, "*Today* shall you be with Me in Paradise." Paradise means a garden, a garden filled with delights. The garden of Eden is the type of Heaven. We know that Paradise means Heaven, for the apostle speaks of such a man caught up into Paradise and he calls it the third Heaven. Our Savior took this dying thief into the Paradise of infinite delight, and this is where He will take all of us sinners who believe in Him. If we are trusting Him, we shall ultimately be with Him in Paradise.

The next word is better still. Note the glory of the society to which this sinner is introduced, "Today shall you be with Me in Paradise." If the Lord said, "Today shall you be with Me," we should not need Him to add another word. Where He is, is Heaven to us. He added the word, "Paradise," because otherwise none could have guessed where He was going. Think of it, you uncomely soul. **You are to dwell with the Altogether Lovely One forever.** You poor and needy ones, you are to be with Him in His Glory, in His bliss, in His perfection. Where He is and as He is, you shall be. The Lord looks into those weeping eyes of yours this morning and He says, "Poor Sinner, you shall one day be with Me." I think I hear you say, "Lord, that is bliss too great for such a sinner as I am." But He replies, I have loved you with an everlasting love, therefore with loving kindness will I draw you, till you shall be with Me where I am....

In those few hours the beggar was lifted from the dunghill and set among princes. "Today shall you be with Me in Paradise." Can you measure the change from that sinner, loathsome in his iniquity when the sun was at high noon, to that same sinner clothed in pure white and accepted in the Beloved, in the Paradise of God, when the sun went down? O glorious Savior, what marvels You can work. How rapidly can You work them.

Please notice, also, the majesty of the Lord's Grace in this text. The Savior said to him, "Verily I say unto you, today shall you be with Me in Paradise." Our Lord gives His own will as the reason for saving this man. "*I* say." He says it, who claims the right thus to speak. It is He who will have mercy on whom He will have mercy and will have compassion on whom He will have compassion. He speaks royally, "Verily I say unto you." Are they not imperial words? The Lord is a King in whose Word there is power. What He says none can deny. He that has the keys of Hell and of death says, "I say unto you, today shall you be with Me in Paradise." Who shall prevent the fulfillment of His Word?

Notice the certainty of it. He says, "Verily." Our blessed Lord on the Cross returned to His old majestic manner as He painfully turned His head and looked on His convert. He was likely to begin His preaching with," Verily, verily, I say unto you." And now that He is dying He uses His favorite manner and says, "Verily." Our Lord took no oath, His strongest asseveration was, "Verily, verily." **To give the penitent the plainest assurance, He says, "Verily I say unto you, today shall you be with Me in Paradise."** In this the thief had an absolutely indisputable assurance that though he must die, yet he would live and find himself in Paradise with his Lord.

I have thus shown you that our Lord passed within the pearly gate in company with one to whom He had pledged Himself. **Why should not you and I pass through that pearly gate in due time, clothed in His merit, washed in His blood and resting on His power?** One of these days' angels will say of you and of me, "Who is this that comes up from the wilderness, leaning upon her Beloved?" The shining ones will be amazed to see some of us coming. If you have lived a life of sin until now, and yet shall repent and enter Heaven; what an amazement there will be in every golden street to think that you have come there. In the early Christian Church, Marcus Caius Victorinus was converted [philosopher, theologian converted before 361 A.D.]. But he had reached so great an age and had been so gross a sinner that the pastor and Church doubted him.

He gave, however, clear proof of having undergone the Divine change, and then there were great acclamations and many shouts of, "Victorinus has become a Christian!" Oh, that some of you big sinners might be saved! How gladly would we rejoice over you! Why not? Would it not glorify God? The salvation of this convicted highwayman has made our Lord illustrious for mercy even unto this day; would not your case do the same? Would not saints cry, "Hallelujah! Hallelujah!" if they heard that some of you had been turned from darkness to marvelous light? Why should it not be? Believe in Jesus and it is so.

C. Now I come to my third and most practical point: Note *THE LORD'S SERMON TO US FROM ALL THIS.* The devil wants to preach this morning a bit. Yes, Satan asks to come to the front and preach to you. But he cannot be allowed. Out of here, you deceiver.

Yet I should not wonder if he gets at some of you when the sermon is over and whispers, "You see, you can be saved at the very last. Put off repentance and faith. You may be forgiven on your deathbed." Sirs, you know who it is that would ruin you by this suggestion. Abhor his deceitful teaching! Do not be ungrateful because God is kind. Do not provoke the Lord because He is patient.

Such conduct would be unworthy and ungrateful. Do not run an awful risk because one escaped the tremendous peril. The Lord will accept all who repent. But how do you know that you will repent? It is true that one thief was saved, but the other thief was lost. One is saved and we may not despair. The other is lost and we may not presume. Dear Friends, I trust you are not made of such diabolical stuff as to fetch from the mercy of God an argument for continuing in sin. If you do, I can only say of you, that your damnation will be just. You will have brought it upon yourselves.

Consider now the teaching of our Lord, see the glory of Christ in salvation. He is ready to save at the last moment. He was just passing away; His foot was on the doorstep of the Father's house. Up comes this poor sinner, the last thing at night, at the eleventh hour, and the Savior smiles and declares that He Himself will not enter except with this belated wanderer. At the very gate He declares that this seeking soul shall enter with Him. There was plenty of time for him to have come before, you know how apt we are to say, "You have waited to the last moment. I am just going off, and I cannot attend to you now." Our Lord had His dying pangs upon Him and yet He attends to the perishing criminal and permits him to pass through the heavenly portal in His company.

Jesus easily saves the sinners for whom He painfully died. Jesus loves to rescue sinners from going down into the pit. You will be very happy if you are saved but you will not be one half as happy as He will be when He saves you. See how gentle He is: *"His hand no thunder bears, /No terror clothes His brow; /No bolts to drive our guilty souls /To fiercer flames below."*

He comes to us full of tenderness with tears in His eyes, mercy in His hands and love in His heart. Believe Him to be a great Savior of great sinners. I have heard of one who had received great mercy who went about saying, **"He is a great forgiver."** And I would have you say the same. You shall find your transgressions put away and your sins pardoned once and for all if you trust Him now.

The next doctrine Christ preaches from this wonderful story is **faith in its permitted attachment.** This man believed that Jesus was the Christ. **The next thing he did was to appropriate that Christ. He said, "Lord, remember me."** Jesus might have said, "What have I to do with you and what have you to do with me? What has a thief to do with the perfect One?" Many of you good people try to get as far away as you can from the erring and fallen. They might infect your innocence. Society claims that we should not be familiar with people who have offended against its laws. We must not be seen associating with them, for it might discredit us. Infamous bosh!

Can anything discredit sinners such as we are by nature and by practice? If we know ourselves before God, are we not degraded enough in and of ourselves? Is there anybody, after all, who is worse than we are when we see ourselves in the faithful glass of the Word? As soon as ever a man believes that Jesus is the Christ, let him hook himself on to Him. The moment you believe Jesus to be the Savior, seize upon Him as *your* Savior. If I remember rightly, Augustine called this man, *"Latro laudabilis et mirabilis," **a thief to be praised and wondered at,** who dared, as it were, to seize the Savior for his own.*

In this he is to be imitated. Take the Lord to be yours and you have Him. Jesus is the common property of all sinners who are bold enough to take Him. Every sinner who has the will to do so may take the Lord home with Him. He came into the world to save the sinful. Take Him by force as robbers take their prey. The kingdom of Heaven suffers the violence of daring faith. Get Him and He will never get Himself away from you. If you trust Him, He must save you. Next, notice the doctrine of faith in its immediate power: *"The moment a sinner believes, /And trusts in his crucified God, /His pardon at once he receives, / Redemption in full through His blood."*

"Today shall you be with Me in Paradise." **He has no sooner believed than Christ gives him the seal of his believing in the full assurance that he shall be with Him forever in His Glory.** O dear Hearts, if you believe this morning, you shall be saved this morning. God grant that you, by His rich Grace, may be brought into salvation here on the spot and at once.

The next thing is the nearness of eternal things. Think of that a minute. Heaven and Hell are not places far away. You may be in Heaven before the clock ticks again. Could we but rend that veil which parts us from the unseen. It is all there and all near. "Today," said the Lord. Within three or four hours at the longest, "shall you be with Me in Paradise." It is so near. A statesman has given us the expression of being "within measurable distance." We are all within measurable distance of Heaven or Hell. If there is any difficulty in measuring the distance, it lies in its brevity rather than in its length: *One gentle sigh the fetter breaks, /We scarce can say, 'He's gone,' /Before the ransomed spirit takes / Its mansion near the Throne."*

Oh, that we, instead of trifling about such things because they seem so far away, would solemnly realize them, since they are really so very near. This very day, before the sun goes down, some Hearer now sitting in this place may see in his own spirit the realities of Heaven or Hell. It has frequently happened in this large congregation, someone in our audience has died before the next Sabbath has come round may happen this week. Think of that, and let eternal things impress you all the more because they lie so near.

Furthermore, know that if you have believed in Jesus you are prepared for Heaven. It may be that you will have to live on earth twenty, or thirty, or forty years to glorify Christ. And if so, be thankful for the privilege. But if you do not live another hour, your instantaneous death would not alter the fact that he that believes in the Son of God is meet for Heaven. Surely, if anything beyond faith is needed to make us fit to enter Paradise, the thief would have been kept a little longer here. But no, he is in the morning in the state of nature, at noon he enters the state of Divine Grace, and by sunset he is in the state of Glory.

The question never is, whether a deathbed repentance is accepted if it is sincere, the question is, is it sincere? If it is, if the man dies five minutes after his first act of faith, he is as safe as if he had served the Lord for fifty years. If your faith is true, if you die one moment after you have believed in Christ you will be admitted into Paradise, even if you shall have enjoyed no time in which to produce good works and other evidences of Divine Grace. He that reads the heart will read your faith written on its fleshy tablets and He will accept you through Jesus Christ, even though no act of Divine Grace has been visible to the eye of man.

I conclude by again saying that this is not an exceptional case. I began with that and I want to finish with it. So many demi-semi-gospelers are so terribly afraid of preaching Free Grace too fully. I read somewhere and I think it is true, that some ministers preach the Gospel in the same way as donkeys eat thistles, namely, very, very cautiously. On the contrary, I will preach it boldly. I have not the slightest alarm about the matter. If any of you misuse Free Grace teaching, I cannot help it. He that will be damned can as well ruin himself by perverting the Gospel as by anything else. I cannot help what base hearts may invent.

But mine it is to set forth the Gospel in all its fullness of grace and I will do it. If the thief was an exceptional case, and our Lord does not usually act in such a way, there would have been a hint given of so important a fact. A hedge would have been set about this exception to all rules. Would not the Savior have whispered quietly to the dying man, "You are the only one I am going to treat in this way"? Whenever I have to do an exceptional favor to a person I have to say, "Do not mention this, or I shall have so many besieging me."

If the Savior had meant this to be a solitary case, He would have faintly said to him, "Do not let anybody know. But you shall today be in the kingdom with Me." No! Our Lord spoke openly and those about Him heard what He said. Moreover, the inspired penman has recorded it. If it had been an exceptional case it would not have been written in the Word of God. Men will not publish their actions in the newspapers if they feel that the record might lead others to expect from them what they cannot give. The Savior had this wonder of Divine Grace reported in the daily news of the Gospel because He means to repeat the marvel every day.

EXHORTATION: The bulk shall be equal to the sample, and therefore He sets the sample before you all. He is able to save to the uttermost, for He saved the dying thief. The case would not have been put there to encourage hopes which He cannot fulfill. Whatsoever things were written aforetime were written for our learning and not for our disappointing. I pray you, therefore, if any of you have not yet trusted in my Lord Jesus come and trust in Him now. Trust Him wholly. Trust Him only. Trust Him at once. Then will you sing with me: "The dying thief rejoiced to see / That fountain in his day, / And there have I, though vile as he, / Washed all my sins away." Amen.

2. The Witness of Christ on the Cross

"Then one of the criminals who were hanged blasphemed Him, saying, 'If You are the Christ, save Yourself and us.' But the other, answering, rebuked him, saying, 'Do you not even fear God, seeing you are under the same condemnation? And we indeed justly, for we receive the due reward of our deeds; but this Man has done nothing wrong.' Then he said to Jesus, 'Lord, remember me when You come into Your kingdom.' And Jesus said to him, 'Assuredly, I say to you, today you will be with Me in Paradise'"
(Luke 23:39–43 NKJV).

FOCUS: We come close up to the dying thief and look at his faith, at the confession and prayers of his faith, and the answer of faith. The Holy Spirit will help us consider the words of this dying malefactor.

THE dying thief was certainly a very great wonder of Divine
Grace. He has generally been looked upon from one point of view only,
as a sinner called at the eleventh hour and, therefore, an instance of
special mercy because he was so near to death. Enough has been made
of that circumstance by others. To my mind, it is by no means the
most important point in the narrative. Had the thief been predestined
to come down from the Cross and live for half a century longer, his
conversion would have been neither more nor less than it was. **The
work of Grace which enabled him to die in peace would, if it had
been the Lord's will, have enabled him to live in holiness.** We may
well admire Divine Grace when it so speedily makes a man fit for
the bliss of Heaven. But it is equally to be adored when it makes him
ready for the battle of earth. **To bear a saved sinner away from all
further conflict is great Grace.** But the power and love of God are,
if anything, even more conspicuous when, like a sheep surrounded by
wolves, or a spark in the midst of the sea, a Believer is enabled to live on
in the teeth of an ungodly world and maintain his integrity to the end.
Dear Friend, whether you die as soon as you are born-again, or remain
on earth for many years is comparatively a small matter, and will not
materially alter your indebtedness to Divine Grace. In the one case the
great Husbandman will show how He can bring His flowers speedily to
perfection. And in the other He will prove how He can preserve them
in blooming beauty despite the frosts and snows of earth's cruel winter.
In either case your experience will reveal the same love and power.

There are other things, it seems to me, to be seen in the conversion
of the thief besides the one single matter of his being brought to know
the Lord when near to death's door.

**Observe the singular fact that our Lord Jesus Christ should die
in the company of two malefactors.** It was probably planned in order
to bring Him shame and it was regarded by those who cried, "Crucify
Him! Crucify Him!" as an additional ignominy. Their malice decreed
that He should die as a criminal and with criminals, and in the center,
between two, to show that they thought Him the worst of the three. But
God, in His own way, baffled the malice of the foe and turned it to the

triumph and Glory of His Dear Son, for had there been no dying thief hanging at His side, then one of the most illustrious trophies of His love would not have been gained. And we would not have been able to sing to His praise: *"The dying thief rejoiced to see / That fountain in his day; / And there have I, though vile as he, / Washed all my sins away!"*

His enemies gave our Lord Jesus an opportunity for still continuing the seeking, as well as the saving of the lost! They found Him an occasion for manifesting His conquering Grace when they supposed they were heaping scorn upon Him. How truly did the Prophet in the Psalm say, *"He that sits in the heavens shall laugh. The Lord shall have them in derision,"* for that which was meant to increase His misery revealed His majesty. Moreover, though it was intended to add an ingredient of bitterness to His cup, I do not doubt that it supplied Him with a draught of comfort. **Nothing could so well have cheered the heart of Jesus and taken His mind off, for just an instant, His own hitter pangs, as having an object of pity before Him, upon whom He could pour His mercy. The thief's confession of faith and expiring prayer must have been music to his Savior's ears, the only music which could in any degree delight Him amid His terrible agonies. To hear and to answer the prayer, "Lord, remember me when You come into Your Kingdom," afforded our Lord a precious solace.** An angel strengthened Him in the Garden, but here it was a man, nailed up at His side, who ministered consolation by the indirect, but very effective method of seeking help at His hands.

Furthermore, the long-continued testimony and witness for Christ among men was at that time exceedingly feeble and ready to expire, but the thief's confession maintained it. The apostles, where were they? They had fled. Those disciples who ventured near enough to see the Lord, scarcely remained within speaking distance. They were poor confessors of Christ, scarcely worthy of the name. Was the chain of testimony to be broken? Would none declare His Sovereign Power? No, **the Lord will never let that testimony cease, and lo, He raises up a witness where least you would expect it on a cross. One just ready to die bears witness to the Redeemer's innocence and to His assured** coming to a Kingdom. As many of the boldest testimonies to Christ have come from the stake, so here was one that came from a cross and gained for the witness the honor of being the last testifier to Christ before He died.

Let us always expect, then, dear Friends, that God will overrule the machinations of the foes of Christ so as to get honor from them. *At all times of the world's history, when things appear to have gone to pieces and Satan seems to rule the hour, do not let us despair, but be quite sure that, somehow or other, the Light of God will come out of darkness and good out of evil.*

A. *HIS FAITH.*

It was of the operation of the Spirit of God and there was nothing in his previous character to lead up to it. How came that thief to be a Believer in Jesus? You who carefully read the Gospels will have noticed that Matthew says (Matt 27:44), "*The thieves also, which were crucified with Him, cast the same in His teeth.*" Mark also says, "*They that were crucified with Him reviled Him.*" These two Evangelists plainly speak of both thieves as reviling our Lord. How are we to understand this? Would it be right to say that those two writers speak in broad terms of the thieves as a class because one of them so acted, just as we in common conversation speak of a company of persons doing such-and-such, when, in fact, the whole matter was the deed of one man of the party? Was it a loose way of speaking? I think not. I do not like the look of suppositions of error in the Inspired volume. Would it not be more reverent to the Word of God to believe that the thieves did both revile Jesus? May it not be true that, at the first, they both joined in saying, "If you are the Christ, save Yourself and us," but that afterwards, one, by a miracle of Sovereign Grace, was led to a change of mind and became a Believer? Or would this third theory meet the case, that at the first the thief who afterwards became a penitent, having no thought upon the matter, by his silence gave consent to his fellow's reviling so as fairly to come under the charge of being an accomplice therein, but when it gradually dawned upon his mind that he was under error as to this Jesus of Nazareth, it pleased God in Infinite Mercy to change his mind so that he became a confessor of the Truth of God, though he had at first silently assented to the blasphemy of his companion? **It would be idle to dogmatize, but we will gather this lesson from it, that faith may enter the mind, notwithstanding the sinful state in which the man is found. Grace can transform a reviling thief into a penitent Believer.**

Neither do we know the outward means which led to this man's conversion. We can only suppose that he was affected by seeing the Lord's patient demeanor, or, perhaps, by hearing that prayer, "Father, forgive them, for they know not what they do." Surely there was enough in the sight of the Crucified Lord with the blessing of God's Spirit to turn a heart of stone into flesh. Possibly the inscription over the head of our Lord may have helped him, "Jesus of Nazareth, the King of the Jews." Being a Jew, he knew something of the Scriptures, and putting all the facts together, may he not have seen in the prophecies a light which gathered around the head of the Sufferer and revealed Him as the true Messiah? Possibly the malefactor remembered Isaiah's words, *"He is despised and rejected of men; a Man of Sorrows, and acquainted with grief: and we hid, as it were, our faces from Him; He was despised, and we esteemed Him not."* Or, perhaps, the saying of David, in the 22nd Psalm rushed upon his memory, *"They pierced My hands and My feet."* Other texts which he had learned in his youth at his mother's knee may have come before his mind, and putting all these together, he may have argued, "It may be. Perhaps it is. It is. It must be. I am sure it is. It is the Messiah, led as a lamb to the slaughter." All this is but our supposition and it leads me to remark that there is much faith in this world which comes, "not with observation," but is worked in men by unknown instrumentalities. And so long as it really exists, it matters very little how it entered the heart, for in every case it is the work of the Holy Spirit. The history of faith is of small importance compared with the *quality* of faith.

We do not know the origin of this man's faith, but we do know that **it was amazing faith under the circumstances.** I very gravely question whether there was ever greater faith in this world than the faith of this thief, for he, beyond all others, realized the painful and shameful death of the Lord Jesus and yet believed. We hear of our Lord's dying upon the Cross, but we do not realize the circumstances and, indeed, even if we were to think upon that death very long and intently, we shall never realize the shame, weakness and misery which surrounded our Lord as that dying thief did, for he was suffering the pangs of crucifixion at the Savior's side and, therefore, to him it was no fiction, but a vivid reality. Before him was the Christ in all His nakedness and ignominy surrounded by the mocking multitude, and dying in pain and weakness, and yet he believed Him to be Lord and King. What do you think, Sirs? Some of you say you find it hard to believe in Jesus, though you know that He is exalted in the highest heavens. But had you seen Him on the Cross. Had you seen His marred countenance and emaciated body, could you then have believed on Him and said, "Lord remember me when you come into Your Kingdom"? Yes, you could have done so if the Spirit of God had created faith in you like that of the thief! But it would have been faith of the first order, a jewel of priceless value! As I said before, so I say again, the vivid sympathy of the thief with the shame and suffering of the Lord rendered his faith remarkable in the highest degree.

This man's faith, moreover, was singularly clear and decided. *He rolled his whole salvation upon the Lord Jesus and said, "Lord, remember me when You come into Your Kingdom."* He did not offer a single plea fetched from his works, his present feelings, or his sufferings, he cast himself upon the generous heart of Christ. "You have a Kingdom, You are going to it. Lord, remember me when You come into it." That was all. I wish that some who have been professors for years had as clear a faith as the thief, but they are too often confused between Law and Gospel, works and Grace, while this poor felon trusted in nothing but the Savior and His mercy. Blessed be God for clear faith. I rejoice to see it in such a case as this, so suddenly worked and yet so perfect, so outspoken, so intelligent, so thoroughly restful.

That word, "restful," reminds me of a lovely characteristic of his faith, namely, its deep peace-giving power. There is a world of rest in Jesus in the thief's prayer, "Lord, remember me when You come into Your Kingdom." **A thought from Christ is all he needed!** And after the Lord said, "Today shall you be with Me in Paradise," we never read that the petitioner said another word. I did think that, perhaps, he would have said, "Blessed be the name of the Lord for that sweet assurance. Now I can die in peace." But his gratitude was too deep for words and his peace so perfect that calm silence seemed most in harmony with it. Silence is the thaw of the soul, though it is the frost of the mouth, and when the soul flows most freely, it feels the inadequacy of the narrow channel of the lips for its great water floods: "Come, then, expressive silence, muse His praise." He asked no alleviation of pain, but in perfect satisfaction died as calmly as saints do in their beds.

B. *CONFESSION OF FAITH.*

He had faith and he confessed it. He could neither be baptized nor sit at the Communion Table, nor unite with the Church below. He could not do any of those things which are most right and proper on the part of other Christians, but he did the best he could under the circumstances to confess his Lord.

He confessed Christ, first of all, almost of necessity, because a holy indignation made him speak out. He listened for a while to his brother thief, but while he was musing, the fire burned and then spoke he with his tongue, for he could no longer bear to hear the innocent Sufferer reviled. He said, "Do not you fear God, seeing you are in the same condemnation? And we, indeed, justly, for we receive the due reward of our deeds: but this Man has done nothing amiss." Did this poor thief speak out so bravely and can some of you silent Christians go up and down the streets and hear men curse and blaspheme the name of Christ, and not feel stirred in spirit to defend His cause? While men are so loud in their reviling, can you be quiet? The stones you tread on may well cry out against you. If all were Christians and the world teemed with Jesus' praise, we might, perhaps, afford to be silent. But, amidst abounding superstition and loud-mouthed infidelity, we are bound to show our colors and avow ourselves on Christ's side. We doubt not that the penitent thief would have owned his Lord apart from the railing of his comrade, but as it happened, that reviling was the provoking cause. Does no such cause arouse you? Can you play the coward at such a time as this?

Observe next, **that he made a confession to an unsympathetic ear.** The other thief does not seem to have made any kind of reply to him, but it is feared that he died in sullen unbelief. The believing thief made his confession where he could not expect to gain approbation, yet he made it none the less clearly. How is it that some dear friends who love the Lord have never confessed their faith even to their Christian Brothers and Sisters? You know how glad we would be to hear of what the Lord has done for you, but yet we have not heard it. There is a mother who would be so happy if she did but know that her boy was saved, or that her girl was converted, and you have refused her that joy by your silence. This poor thief spoke for Jesus to one who did not enter into his religious experience, and you have not even told yours to those who would have communed with you and rewarded you with comfort and instruction.

I cannot understand cowardly lovers of Christ. How you manage to smother your love so long, I cannot tell. Love is usually like a cough, which speaks for itself, or a candle which must be seen, or a sweet perfume which is its own revealer. How is it that you have been able to conceal the day which has dawned in your hearts? What can be your motive for coming to Jesus only by night? I cannot understand your riddle and I hope you will explain it away. Do confess Jesus if you love Him, for He bids you do it and says, *"He that confesses Me before men, him will I confess before My Father which is in Heaven."*

Observe well that this poor thief's confession of faith was attended with a confession of sin. Though he was dying a most horrible death by crucifixion, yet he confessed that he was suffering justly. "We indeed justly." He made his confession not only to God, but to men, justifying the law of his country under which he was then suffering. **True faith confesses Christ and, at the same time, confesses its sin.** There must be repentance of sin and acknowledgment of it before God if faith is to give proof of its authenticity. A faith that never had a tear in its eye, or a blush on its cheek, is not the faith of God's elect. He who never felt the burden of sin, never felt the sweetness of being delivered from it. This poor thief is as clear in the avowal of his own guilt as in his witness to the Redeemer's innocence. Reader, could we say the same of you?

The thief's confession of faith was exceedingly honoring to the Lord Jesus Christ. He confessed that Jesus of Nazareth had done nothing amiss, when the crowd around the Cross were condemning Him with speech and gesture. He honored Christ by calling Him, Lord, while others mocked Him. He honored Christ by believing in His Kingdom even while Jesus was dying on the Cross and by entreating Him to remember him though he was in the agonies of death. Do you say that this was not much? Well, I will make bold to ask many a professor whether he could honestly say that throughout the whole of his life he has done as much to honor Christ as this poor thief did in those few minutes. Some of you certainly have not, for you have never confessed Him at all! And others have confessed Him in such a formal manner that there was nothing in it. Oh, there have been times when, had you played the man and said right straight out, in the midst of a ribald crew, "I do believe in Him whom you scoff and I know the sweetness of that dear name which you trample under foot," you might have been the means of saving many souls, but you were silent and whispered to yourself that prudence was the better part of valor and so you allowed the honor of your Master to be trailed in the mire. Oh, had you, my Sister, taken your stand in the family, had you said, "You may do what you will, but as for me, I will serve the Lord," you might have honored God far more than you have done, for I fear you have been living in a halting, hesitating style, giving way to a great deal which you knew was wrong, not bearing your protest, not rebuking your brother in his iniquity, but studying your own peace and comfort instead of seeking the Redeemer's Glory. We have heard people talk about this dying thief as if he never did anything for his Master, but let me ask the Christian Church if it has not members in its midst, gray-haired members, too, who have never, through fifty years of profession, borne one such bravely honest and explicit testimony for Christ as this man did while he was agonizing on a cross? Remember, the man's hands and feet were tortured and he was suffering from that natural fever which attends upon crucifixion. His spirit must have melted within him with his dying grief, and yet he was as bold in rebuke, as composed in prayer, and as calm in spirit as if he were suffering nothing. And thus he reflected much Glory upon his Lord.

One other point about this man's confession is worthy of notice, namely, **that he was evidently anxious to change the mind of his companion.** He rebuked him and he reasoned with him. Dear Friends, I must again put a personal question. Are there not many professing Christians who have never manifested a tithe as much anxiety for the souls of others as this thief felt? You have been a Church member ten years, but did you ever say as much to your brother as this dying thief said to the one who was hanging near him? Well, you have meant to do so. Yes, but did you ever do it? You reply that you have been very glad to join others in a meeting. I know that, too, and so far so good. But did you ever personally say as much to another as this dying man did to his old companion? I fear that some of you cannot say so. I, for my part, bless and magnify the Grace of God which gave this man one of the sweet fruits of the Spirit, namely, holy charity towards the soul of another so soon after he, himself, had come to believe in Jesus. May we, all of us, have it yet more and more! So much for the confession of his faith. Now a little, in the third place, about:

C. *HIS PRAYER OF FAITH.*

"Lord, remember me when You come into Your Kingdom." **He addressed the dying Savior as Divine.** Wonderful faith this, **to call Him Lord** who was "a worm and no man," and was hanging there upon the Cross to die. What shall we say of those who, now that He is exalted in the highest heavens, yet refuse to acknowledge His Deity?

This man had a clearer knowledge of Christ than they have. The Lord take the scales from their eyes and make them pray to Jesus as Divine.

He prayed to Him, also, as having a kingdom. That needed faith, did it not? He saw a dying Man in the hands of His foes nailed to the Cross, and yet he believed that He would come into a kingdom! He knew that Jesus would die before long, the marks of the death-agony were upon Him, and yet he believed that He would come to a kingdom. O glorious faith! Dear Friend, do you believe in Christ's Kingdom? Do you believe that He reigns in Heaven and that He will come a second time to rule over all the earth? Do you believe in Christ as King of kings and Lord of lords? Then pray to Him as such, "Lord, remember me when You come into Your Kingdom." May God give you the faith which set this thief a praying in so excellent a fashion.

Observe **that his prayer was for a spiritual blessing only.** The other thief said, "Save Yourself and us!" He meant, "Save us from this cross. Deliver us from the death which now threatens us!" He sought temporal benefits, but this man asked only to be remembered by Christ in His Kingdom. Do your prayers run that way, dear Friends? Then I bless the Lord that He has taught you to seek eternal, rather than temporal blessings! If a sick man cares more for pardon than for health, it is a good sign. Soul mercies will be prized above all others where faith is in active exercise.

Observe **how humbly he prays.** He did not ask for a place at Christ's right hand. He did not, in fact, ask the Lord to do anything for him, but only to "remember" him. Yet that, "remember," is a great word and he meant much by it. "Do give a thought to Your poor companion who now confesses his faith in You. Do in Your Glory dart one recollection of Your love upon poor me and think on me for good." It was a very humble prayer and all the sweeter for its lowliness. It showed his great faith in Jesus, far he believed that even to be remembered by Him would be enough. "Give me but the crumbs that fall from Your table, and they shall suffice me. But a thought, Lord Jesus, but one thought from Your loving mind, and that shall satisfy my soul."

Did not his prayer drip with faith as a honeycomb with honey? It seems to me as if it laid soaking in his faith till it was saturated through and through with it, for he prays so powerfully, albeit so humbly. Consider what his character had been, and yet he says, "Lord, remember me when You come into Your Kingdom." **Note well that it is a thief, an outcast, a criminal on the gallows who thus prays!** He is an outcast by his country's laws and yet he turns to the King of Heaven and asks to be remembered! Bad as he is, he believes that the Lord Jesus will have mercy upon him! Oh, brave faith.

We see how strong that faith was because he had no invitation to pray. I do not know that he had ever heard Christ preach. No apostle had said to him, "Come to Christ and you will find mercy," and yet he came to Jesus! **Here comes an uninvited guest in the sweet bravery of holy confidence in Christ's majestic love, he comes boldly and pleads, "Lord, remember me." It was strong faith which thus pleaded.** Remember, too, that he was upon the verge of death. He knew that he could not live very long and probably expected the Roman bone-breaker to give him, very soon, the final blow. But in the very hour and article of death he cried, "Lord, remember me," with the strong confidence of a mighty faith.

Glory be to God who worked such a faith in such a man as this. We have done when we have mentioned, in the fourth place:

D. *THE ANSWER TO HIS FAITH.*

We will only say that **his faith brought him to Paradise**. We had a Paradise, once, and the first Adam lost it. Paradise has been regained by the Second Adam, and He has prepared for Believers an Eden above, fairer than that first Garden of delights below. Faith led the dying thief to be with Christ in Paradise which was best of all! "Today shall you be with Me in Paradise." Whatever the joy of Christ, and the Glory of Christ, the thief was there to see it and to share it as soon as Christ Himself.

And it brought him Paradise that very day. Sometimes a crucified man will be two or three days a-dying. Jesus, therefore, assures him that he shall not have long to suffer and confirms it with a, "verily," which was our Lord's strong word of asseveration, "Verily I say unto you, today shall you be with Me in Paradise." Such a portion will faith win for each of us, not today, perhaps, but one day. **If we believe in Jesus Christ, who died for our sins, we shall be with Him in the delights and happiness of the spirit world and with Him in the Paradise of everlasting Glory.** If we commenced to believe at once and were to die immediately, we would be with Christ at once, as surely as if we had been converted fifty years ago. You cannot tell how short your life will be, but it is well to be ready. A friend was here last Lord's-Day of whom I heard this morning that he was ill, and in another hour that he was dead. It was short work. He was struck down and gone at once. That may be the lot of any one of you. And if it should be, you will have no cause whatever to fear it if you now, like the thief, trust yourself wholly in Jesus' hands, crying, "Lord, remember me when You come into Your Kingdom."

The lesson of our text is not merely that Christ can save in our last extremity, though that is true, but that now, at this moment, Jesus is able to save us, and that, if saved at all, salvation must be an immediate and complete act, so that, come life or come death, we are perfectly saved. It will not take the Lord long to raise the dead, in a moment, in the twinkling of an eye, the dead shall be raised incorruptible, and the Lord takes no time in regenerating a soul. Dead souls live in an instant when the breath of the Spirit quickens them. Faith brings instantaneous pardon. There is no course of probation to go through. There are no attainments to be sought after and no protracted efforts to be made in order to be saved. You are saved if you believe in Jesus. The finished work of Christ is yours. You are God's beloved, accepted, forgiven, adopted child! Saved you are, and saved you shall be forever and ever if you believe.

EXHORTATION: Instantaneous salvation. Immediate salvation. This, the Spirit of God gives to those who trust in Jesus. You need not wait till tomorrow's sun has dawned. Talk not of a more convenient season. Sitting where you are, the Almighty Grace of God can come upon you and save you, and this shall be a sign unto you that Christ is born in your heart, the hope of Glory, when you believe in Him as your Pardon, Righteousness, and All–in–All, you shall have peace. If you do but trust yourself in Jesus' hands, you are a saved soul and the angels in Heaven are singing high praises to God and the Lamb on your account. Amen.

C.   Words of Affection and Love

1.   The Care Jesus Took of His Poor Mother by Matthew Henry

"When Jesus therefore saw His mother, and the disciple whom He loved standing by, He said to His mother, 'Woman, behold your son!' Then He said to the disciple, 'Behold your mother!' And from that hour that disciple took her to his own home"
(John 19: 26–27 NKJV).

FOCUS: Mary, the mother of Jesus attended her son, the Lord Jesus Christ at His death. In turn, the Lord tenderly attends to His mother at His death. He calls her woman, not mother. He directs her to look upon John her son: "Behold him as thy son, who stands there by thee and be as a mother to him, and as a mother to him." See first, an instance of divine goodness to be observed for our encouragement; second, an instance of filial duty, to be observe for our imitation, and third, the confidence he reposed in the beloved disciple.

A.   **His mother attended her Son to His death.** *There stood by the cross,* as near as they could get, his mother, and some of his relations and friends with her. At first, they stood near, as it is said here: but afterwards it is probable, the soldiers forced them to stand afar off, as it is said in Matthew and Mark, or they themselves removed out of the ground.

1. See how the tender affection of these pious women to our Lord Jesus in his sufferings. When all His disciples, except John, has forsaken Him, they continued their attendance on Him. Thus they were as feeble as David (*In that day shall the LORD defend the inhabitants of Jerusalem; and he that is feeble among them at that day shall be as David; and the house of David shall be as God, as the angel of the Lord before them.* Zech. 12:8). They were not deterred by the fury of the enemy nor the horror of the sight. They could not rescue Him nor relieve Him, yet they attended Him, to show their good will ....

2. We may easily suppose what an affliction it was to these poor women to see Him thus abused, especially to the blessed virgin. Now was fulfilled Simeon's word, *"A sword shall pierce through thy own soul,"* Luke 2:35. His torments were her tortures. She was upon the rack, while He was upon the cross and her heart bled with His wounds and *the reproaches wherewith they reproached Him* fell on those who attended Him.

3. We might justly admire the power of divine grace in supporting these women, especially the virgin Mary under this heavy trial. We do not find His mother wringing her hands, or tearing her hair, or rending her clothes, or making an outcry, but with a wonderful composure, standing by the cross, and her friends with her. Surely she and they were strengthened by a divine power to this degree of patience and surely the virgin Mary had a fuller expectation of His resurrection than the rest had, which supported her thus. We know not what we can bear till we are tired, and then we know who had said, *My grace is sufficient for thee.*

B. **He tenderly provides for His mother at His death.** It is probable that Joseph, her husband, was long since dead, and that her son

Jesus had supported her, and her relation to him had been her maintenance, and now that He was dying what would become of her? He saw her standing by and knew her cares and griefs. [Besides,] He saw John standing not far off, and so He settled a new relation between His beloved and His beloved disciple .... He said to her, "*Woman, behold thy son,* for whom hence forward thou must have a motherly affection," and said to him, "*Behold thy mother,* to whom thou must pay a filial duty." And so from that hour, that hour never to be forgotten, *that disciple took her to his own home.*

C. See here, **the care Christ took care of His dear mother.** He was not so much taken up with a sense of His sufferings as to forget His friends, all whose concerns He bore upon His heart. His mother, perhaps, was so taken up with His sufferings that she thought not of what would become of her, but He admitted that thought. *Silver and Gold He had none* to leave, no estate, real or personal. His clothes the soldiers had seized, and we hear no more of the bag since Judas, who had carried it, hanged himself. He had therefore no other way to provide for His mother than by His interest in a friend, which he does here.

1. He calls her woman, not mother, not only of any disrespect to her, but because mother would have been a cutting word to her that was already wounded to the heart with grief, like Isaac saying to Abraham, *My father.* He speaks as one that was *now no more in the world,* but was already dead to those in it that were dearest to him. His speaking in this seemingly slight manner to his mother, as he had done formerly, was designed to obviate and give a check to the undue honors which he foresaw would be given to her in the Ravish church as if she was a joint purchaser with Him in the honors of the Redeemer.

2. He directs her to look upon John her son: "Behold him as thy son, who stands there by thee and be as a mother to him,' and as a mother to him." See her *first,* **an instance of divine goodness**

to be observed for our encouragement. Sometimes, when God removes one comfort from us, He raises up another for us, perhaps where we looked not for it. We read of children which the church shall have after she had lost the other, Isa. 49:21 [*The shalt thou say in thine heart, who hath begotten me these, seeing I have lost my children, and am desolate, a captive, and removing to and fro? And who hath brought up these? Behold, I was left alone; these, where they had been?*] Let none therefore reckon all gone with one cistern dried up, for from the same fountain another may be filled. *Secondly*, **an instance of filial duty, to be observe for our imitation**. Christ has taught children to provide, to the utmost of their power, for the comfort of their aged parents. When David was in Distress, he took care of his parents, and found a shelter for them [*And David went thence to Mizpeh of Moab: and he said unto the King of Moab, Let my father and my mother, I pray thee, come forth, and be with you, till I know what God will do for me.* 1 Sam. 22:3]; so the Son of David here. Children at their death, according to their ability, should provide for their parents, if they survive them, and need their kindness.

D. **The confidence he reposed in the beloved disciple**. It is to him He says, *Behold thy mother*, that is, I recommend her to thy care, be thou as a son to her to guide her [*There is none to guide her among all the sons whom she hath brought forth; neither is there any that taketh her by the hand of all the sons that she hath brought up.* Isa. 51:18]; and *forsake her not when she is old*, [*Hearken unto thy father that begat thee, and despise not thy mother when she is old.*] Prov. 23:22. Now, [*first*], this was an honor put upon John, and a testimony, both to his prudence and his fidelity. If he who knows all things had not known that John loved Him, he would not have made him His mother guardian. It is a great honor to be employed for Christ, and to be entrusted with any of His interest in the world. But, [*second*], it would be a care and some charge to John, but he cheerfully accepted it, *and took her to his own home,* not objecting the trouble nor expense, nor his obligations to his own family, nor the ill-will he might contract by it.

EXHORTATION: Those that truly love Christ, and are beloved of him, will be glad of an opportunity to do any service to Him or His. Amen.

2. Exposition on John 19:25–28

John 19:25. *Now there stood by the Cross of Jesus His mother, and His mother's sister, Mary, the wife of Cleophas, and Mary Magdalene.*

Last at the Cross, first at the sepulcher. No woman's lips betrayed her Lord; no woman's hands ever smote Him; their eyes wept for Him; they gazed upon Him with pitying awe and love. God bless the Marys! When we see so many of them about the Cross, we feel that we honor the very name of Mary.

26. *When Jesus therefore saw His mother, and the Disciple standing by, whom He loved, He said unto His mother, Woman, behold your son!*

Sad, sad spectacle. Now was fulfilled the word of Simeon, "Yes, a sword shall pierce through your own soul, also, that the thoughts of many hearts may be revealed." Did the Savior mean, as He gave a glance to John, "Woman, you are losing one Son, but yonder stands another who will be a son to you in My absence"? "Woman, behold your son!"

27. *Then said He to the Disciple, Behold your mother!*

"Take her as your mother, stand in My place, and care for her as I have cared for her." Those who love Christ best shall have the honor of taking care of His Church and of His poor. Never say of any poor relative or friend, the widow or the fatherless, "They are a great burden to me." Oh, no! Say, "They are a great honor to me, my Lord has entrusted them to my care." John thought so, let us think so. Jesus selected the Disciple He loved best to take His mother under his care. He selects those whom He loves best, today, and puts His poor people under their wings. Take them gladly and treat them well.

28. *And from that hour that Disciple took her into his own home.*

You expected him to do it, did you not? He loved his Lord.

D.   Words of Anguish

1.   [His Cries] from the Cross

*"My God, why have You forsaken Me? Why are You so far
from helping Me, And from the words of My groaning"?
(Psalm 22:1 NKJV).*

FOCUS: Our attention is called to three questions: "My God, why have You forsaken Me? Why are You so far from helping Me, and from the words of My groaning"? We will answer the three questions. Finally, a word of earnest expostulation and affectionate warning is given.
WE here behold the Savior in the depths of His agonies and sorrows. No other place so well shows the griefs of Christ as Calvary and no other moment at Calvary is so full of agony as that in which this cry rends the air, **"My God, My God, why have You forsaken Me?"** At this moment, physical weakness brought upon Him by fasting and scourging, was united with the acute mental torture which He endured from the shame and ignominy through which He had to pass and, as the

culmination of His grief, He suffered spiritual agony which surpasses all expression on account of the departure of His Father from Him. This was the blackness and darkness of His horror. Then it was that He penetrated the depths of the caverns of suffering.

"My God, My God, why have You forsaken Me?" There is something in these words of our Savior always calculated to benefit us. When we behold the sufferings of men, they afflict and appall us, but the sufferings of our Savior, while they move us to grief, have about them something sweet and full of consolation. Here, even here, in this black spot of grief, we find our Heaven while gazing upon the Cross. This, which might be thought a frightful sight, makes the Christian glad and joyous. If he laments the cause, yet he rejoices in the consequences.

A. **First,** in our text, there are *THREE QUESTIONS to which I shall call your attention.*

The first is, *"My God, My God, why have You forsaken Me?"* By these words we are to understand that our blessed Lord and Savior was, at that moment, forsaken by God in such a manner as He had never been before. He had battled with the enemy in the desert, but thrice He overcame him and cast him to the earth. He had striven with that foe all His life long and even in the garden He had wrestled with him till His soul was "exceedingly sorrowful." It is not till now that He experiences a depth of sorrow which He never felt before. It was necessary that He should suffer, in the place of sinners, what sinners ought to have suffered. It would be difficult to conceive of punishment for sin apart from the frown of Deity. **With crime we always associate anger, so that when Christ died,** *"the Just for the unjust, that He might bring us to God,"* **when our blessed Savior became our Substitute,** He became, for the time, the victim of His Father's righteous wrath, seeing that our sins had been imputed to Him in order that His righteousness might be imputed to us. It was necessary that He should feel the loss of His Father's smile, for the condemned in Hell must have tasted of that bitterness and therefore the Father closed the eyes of His love, put the hand of justice before the smile of His face and left His Son to cry, "My God, My God, why have You forsaken Me?"

There is no man living who can tell the full meaning of these words, not one in Heaven or on earth. I had almost said, in Hell there is not a man who can spell these words out with all their depth of misery. Some of us think, at times, that we could cry, "My God, my God, why have You forsaken me?" **There are seasons when the brightness of our Father's smile is eclipsed by clouds and darkness. But let us remember that God never really forsakes us.** It is only a seeming forsaking with us, but in Christ's case it was a real forsaking. God only knows how much we grieve, sometimes, at a little withdrawal of our Father's love, but the real turning away of God's face from His Son who shall calculate how deep the agony which it caused Him when He cried, "My God, My God, why have You forsaken Me?"

In our case, this is the cry of unbelief. In His case it was the utterance of a fact, for God had really turned away from Him for a time. O you poor, distressed Soul who once lived in the sunshine of God's face, but are now in darkness, you who are walking in the Valley of the Shadow of Death, you hear noises and you are afraid! Your soul is startled within you; you are stricken with terror if you think that God has forsaken you! Remember that He has not really forsaken you, for *"Mountains when in darkness shrouded, /Are as real as in day."*

God in the clouds is as much our God as when He shines forth in all the luster of His benevolence. But since even the thought that He has forsaken us gives us agony, what must the agony of the Savior have been when He cried, "My God, My God, why have You forsaken Me?"

The next question is, *"Why are You so far from helping Me?"* Up to now, God had helped His Son, but now He must tread the winepress alone, even His own Father cannot be with Him. Have you not felt, sometimes, that God has brought you to do some duty and yet has apparently not given you the strength to do it? Have you ever felt that sadness of heart which makes you cry, "Why are You so far from helping me?" But remember, if God means you to do anything, you can do it, for He will give you the power! Perhaps your brain reels, but God has ordained that you must do it and you shall do it! Have you not felt as if you must go on, even while every step you took, you were afraid to put your foot down for fear you should not get a firm foothold? If you have had any experience of Divine things, it must have been so with you. We can scarcely guess what it was that our Savior felt when He said, "Why are You so far from helping Me?" His work is one which none but a Divine Person could have accomplished, yet His Father's eyes were turned away from Him! With more than Herculean labors before Him, but with none of His Father's might given to Him, what must have been the strain upon Him? Truly, as Hart says, He *"Bore all Incarnate God could bear, /With strength enough, and none to spare."*

The third enquiry is, "Why are You so far from the words of My roaring?" The word here translated, "roaring," means, in the original Hebrew, that deep, solemn groan which is caused by serious sickness and which suffering men utter. Christ compares His prayers to those roars and complains that God is so far from Him that He does not hear Him. Beloved, many of us can sympathize with Christ, here. How often have we, on our knees, asked some favor of God and we thought we asked in faith, yet it never came? Down we went upon our knees again. There is something which withholds the answer and, with tears in our eyes, we have wrestled with God some more, we have pleaded, for Jesus' sake, but the heavens have seemed like brass! In the bitterness of our spirit we have cried, "Can there be a God?" And we have turned round and said, "'My God, my God, why have You forsaken me? Why are You so far from the words of my roaring?' Is this like You? Do You ever spurn a sinner? Have You not said, 'Knock, and it shall be opened unto you?' Are You reluctant to be kind? Do You withhold Your promise?"

And when we have been almost ready to give up, with everything apparently against us, have we not groaned and said, *"Why are You so far from the words of my roaring?"* Though we know something, it is not much that we can truly understand of those direful sorrows and agonies which our blessed Lord endured when He asked these three questions: "My God, My God, why have You forsaken Me? Why are You so far from helping Me, and from the words of My roaring?"

B. Let as now, in the **second** place, *ANSWER THESE THREE QUESTIONS.*

The answer to the first question I have given before. I think I hear the Father say to Christ, *"My Son, I forsake You because You stand in the sinner's place.* As You are holy, just and true, I never would forsake You. I would never turn away from You, for, even as a Man, You have been holy, harmless, undefiled and separate from sinners, but on Your head rests the guilt of every penitent, transferred from him to You and You must expiate it by Your blood. Because You stand in the sinner's place, I will not look at You till You have borne the full weight of My vengeance. Then, I will exalt You on high, far above all principalities and powers."

O Christian, **pause here and reflect! Christ was punished in this way for you!** Oh, look at that Countenance so wrung with horror, those horrors gather there for you! Perhaps in your own esteem you are the most worthless of the family, certainly the most insignificant, but the meanest lamb of Christ's flock is as much the object of purchase as any other. Yes, when that black darkness gathered round His brow and when He cried out, "Eloi, Eloi," in the words of our text, for the Lord Omnipotent to help Him. When He uttered that awfully solemn cry it was because He loved you, because He gave Himself for you that you might be sanctified here and dwell with Him hereafter. God forsook Him, therefore, first, because He was the sinner's Substitute.

The answer to the second question is, "Because I would have You get all the honor to Yourself; therefore, I will not help You lest I should have to divide the spoil with You." **The Lord Jesus Christ lived to glorify His Father, but He died to glorify Himself in the redemption of His chosen people.** God says, "No, My Son, You shall do it alone, for You must wear the crown alone. And upon Yourself shall all the regalia of Your Sovereignty be found. I will give You all the praise and. therefore. You shall perform all the labor." He was to tread the winepress alone and to get the victory and glory alone to Himself.

The answer to the third question is essentially the same as the answer to the first. *To have heard Christ's prayers at that time would*

have been inappropriate. This turning away of the Divine Father from hearing His Son's prayer is just in keeping with His condition as the sinner's Surety. His prayer must not be heard. As the sinner's Surety, He could say, "Now that I am here, dying in the sinner's place, You seal Your ears against My prayer." God did not hear His Son because He knew His Son was dying to bring us near to God. And the Son, therefore, cried, "My God, My God, why have You forsaken Me?"

C. In conclusion I shall offer you *A WORD OF EARNEST EXPOSTULATION AND OF AFFECTIONATE WARNING.*

Is it nothing to some of you that Jesus should die? You hear the tale of Calvary but, alas, you have dry eyes. You never weep concerning it. Is the death of Jesus nothing to you? Alas! It seems to be so with many. Your hearts have never throbbed in sympathy with Him. O Friends, how many of you can look on Christ, thus agonizing and groaning, and say, "He is my Ransom, my Redeemer"? Could you say, with Christ, "My God"? Or is God another's and not yours? Oh, if you are out of Christ, hear me speak one word, it is a word of warning. **Remember, to be out of Christ is to be without hope. If you die unsprinkled with His blood, you are lost.**

And what is it to be lost? I shall not try to tell you the meaning of that dreadful word, "lost." Some of you may know it before another sun has risen. God grant that you may not! Do you desire to know how you may be saved? Listen to me. *"God so loved the world that He gave His only-begotten Son, that whoever believes in Him should not perish, but have everlasting life." "He that believes and is baptized shall be saved."* To be baptized is to be buried in water in the name of the Father, and of the Son, and of the Holy Spirit. Have you believed in Christ? Have you professed faith in Christ? Faith is the Divine Grace which rests alone on Christ. Whoever will be saved, before all things it is necessary that he should feel himself to be lost that he should know himself to be a ruined sinner and then he should believe this: *"It is a faithful saying, and worthy of all acceptation, that Christ Jesus came into the world to save sinners,"* even the very chief of sinners. You need no mediator between yourselves and Christ! You may come to Christ just as you are, guilty, wicked, poor, Christ will take you just as you are. There is no necessity for washing beforehand. You need no riches, in Him you have all you require, will you bring anything to, "all"? You need no garments, for in Christ you have a seamless robe which will amply suffice to cover even the biggest sinner on earth, as well as the least.

Come, then, to Jesus at once. Do you say you do not know how to come? Come just as you are. Do not wait to do anything. What you need is to leave off doing and let Christ do all for you. What do you need to do when He has done all? **All the labor of your hands can never fulfill what God commands. Christ died for sinners and you must say,** "Sink or swim, I will have no other Savior but Christ." Cast yourself wholly upon Him: *"And when your eye of faith is dim, /Still trust in Jesus, sink or swim! /Still at His footstool humbly, bow, / O Sinner! Sinner! Prostrate now!"*

EXHORTATION: He is able to pardon you at this moment. There are some of you who know you are guilty and groan concerning it. Sinner, why do you wait? "Come, and welcome!" is My Master's message to you. If you feel you are lost and ruined, there is not a barrier between you and Heaven, Christ has broken it down. If you know your own lost estate, Christ has died for you.

Believe, and come. Come, and welcome, Sinner, come! O Sinner, come. Come. Come. Jesus bids you come and as His ambassador to you, I bid you come as one who would die to save your souls if it were necessary, as one who knows how to groan over you and to weep over you, one who loves you even as you love yourself. I, as His minister, say to you, in God's name and in Christ's place, "Be you reconciled to God." What do you say? Has God made you willing? Then rejoice. Rejoice, for He has not made you willing without giving you the power to do what He has made you willing to do. Come. Come. This moment you may be as sure of Heaven as if you were there, if you cast yourself upon Christ and have nothing but Jesus for your soul's reliance. Amen.

2. [The Lord Jesus Christ's] Solemn Inquiry

"And about the ninth hour Jesus cried out with a loud
voice, saying, 'Eli, Eli, lama sabachthani?' that is,
'My God, My God, why have You forsaken Me?'"
(Matthew 27: 46 NKJV).

FOCUS: **There are five lessons for the believer to the question our Lord Jesus Christ asks which He received a glorious answer to, first, under desertion of soul, the Lord Jesus still turns to God; second, though under a sense of desertion of desertion, our Master does not relax His hold on His God; third, although our Lord uttered this deep and bitter cry of pain, yet we are to learn from His silence; fourth, our Lord, when He does cry, cries with the inquiring voice of a loving child and fifth, Christ though He was forsaken of God, still pursued His Father's work, the work He came to do.**

IF any one of us, lovers of the Lord Jesus Christ, had been anywhere near the Cross when He uttered those words, I am sure our hearts would have burst with anguish, and one thing is certain, we would have heard the tones of that dying cry as long as we ever lived. There is no doubt that at certain times they would come to us again, ringing shrill and clear through the thick darkness. We would remember just how they were uttered and where the emphasis was placed. And I have no doubt we would turn that text over, and over, and over in our minds. But there is one thing, I think, we would never have done if we had heard it, therefore, I am not going to do it, we would never preach from it. It would have been too painful a recollection for us to ever have used it as a text.

No, we would have said, "It is enough to hear it." Fully understand it, who can? And to expound it, since some measure of understanding might be necessary to the exposition, that surely were a futile attempt. We would have laid that by. We would have put those words away as too sacred, too solemn, except for silent reflection and quiet, reverent adoration. I felt when I read these words again, as I have often read them, that they seemed to say to me, "You cannot preach from us," and, on the other hand, felt as Moses did when he took off his shoes in the Presence of the burning bush, because the place where he stood was holy ground.

Beloved, there is another reason why we should not venture to preach from this text, namely, that it is probably an expression out of the lowest depths of our Savior's sufferings. With Him into the seas of grief we can descend some part of the way, but when He comes where all God's waves and billows go over Him, we cannot go there. We may, indeed, drink of His cup and be baptized with His Baptism, but never to the full extent and, therefore, where our fellowship with Christ cannot conduct us to the full, though it may in a measure, we shall not venture, not beyond where our fellowship with Him would lead us aright, lest we blunder by speculation and "darken counsel by words without knowledge."

Moreover, it comes forcibly upon my mind that though every word here is emphatic, we would be pretty sure to put the emphasis somewhere or other, too little. I do not suppose we would be likely to put it anywhere too much. It has been well said that every word in this memorable cry deserves to have an emphasis laid upon it. If you read it, *"My God, My God, why have You forsaken Me? I marvel not that My disciples should, but why have You gone, My Father God? How could You leave Me?"* There is a wondrous meaning there. Then take it thus, *"My God, My God, why have You forsaken Me? I know why You have smitten Me. I can understand why You chasten Me, but why have You forsaken Me? Will You allow Me no ray of love from the brightness of Your eyes, no sense of Your Presence whatever?"*

This was the worm-wood and the gall of all the Savior's bitter cup. Then God forsook Him in His direst need. Or if you take it thus, "My God, My God, why have You forsaken Me?" there comes another meaning. *"Me, Your Well-Beloved, Your eternal Well-Beloved, Your innocent, Your harmless, Your afflicted Son, why have You forsaken Me?"* Then, indeed, it is a marvel of marvels not that God should forsake His saints, or appear to do so, or that He should utterly forsake sinners, but that He should forsake His Only Son. Then, again, we might with great propriety throw the whole force of the verse upon the particle of interrogation, *"Why." "My God, My God, why, ah, why have You forsaken Me? What is Your reason? What Your motive? What compels You to this, You Lord of Love? The sun is eclipsed, but why is the Son of Your love eclipsed? You have taken away the lives of men for sin, but why do You take away Your love, which is My life, from Me who has no sin? Why, oh why, do You act thus?"* Now, as I have said, every word requires more emphasis than I can throw into it, and some part of the text would be quite sure to be left and not dealt with as it should be. Therefore, we will not think of preaching upon it, but instead, thereof, we will sit down and commune with it.

You must know that the words of our text are not only the language of Christ, but they are the language of David. You who are acquainted with the Psalms know that the 22nd Psalm begins with just these words, so that David said what Jesus said and I gather from this that many a child of God has had to say precisely what the Lord Jesus, the First-Born of the family, uttered upon the Cross. Now as God's children are brought into the same circumstances as Christ, and Christ is considered the Exemplar, my objective tonight will be simply this, not to expound the words, but to say to Believers who come into a similar plight, Do as Jesus did. If you come into His condition, lift up your hearts to God that you may act as He did in that condition! So we shall make the Savior now not a study for our learning, but an example for reproduction. The first one of these points in which, I think, we should imitate Him is this:

A. **First, *UNDER DESERTION OF SOUL, THE LORD JESUS STILL TURNS TO GOD.***

At that time when He uttered these words, God had left Him to His enemies. No angel appeared to interpose and destroy the power of Roman or Jew. He seemed utterly given up. The people might mock Him and they might put Him to what pain they pleased. At the same time, a sense of God's love to Him as Man was taken from Him. The comfortable Presence of God, which had all His life long sustained Him, began to withdraw from Him in the garden and appeared to be quite gone when He was just in the article of death upon the Cross. And meanwhile the waves of God's wrath on account of sin began to break over His spirit and He was in the condition of a soul deserted by God.

Now sometimes Believers come into the same condition, not to the same extent, but in a measure. Yesterday they were full of joy, for the love of God was shed abroad in their hearts, but today that sense of love is gone. They droop. They feel heavy. Now the temptation will be at such times for them to sit down and look into their own hearts. And if they do, they will grow more wretched every moment, until they will come well near to despair, for there is no comfort to be found within, when there is no light from above! Our signs and tokens within are like sundials. We can tell what time it is by the sundial when the sun shines, but if it does not, what is the use of the sundial? And so, marks of evidence may help us when God's love is shed abroad in the soul, but when that is done, marks of evidence stand us in very little stead.

Now observe our Lord. **He is deserted of God, but instead of looking in, and saying, "My Soul, why are You this?** Why are You that? Why are You cast down? Why do You mourn?" **He looks straight away from that dried-up well that is within, to those eternal waters that never can be stayed, and which are always full of refreshment. He cries, "My God." He knows which way to look, and I say to every Christian here, it is a temptation of the devil, when you are desponding and when you are not enjoying your religion as you did, to begin peering and searching about in the dunghill of your own corruptions and stirring over all that you are feeling, and all you ought to feel, and all you do not feel, and all that. Instead of that look from within, look above. Look to your God, again, for the light will come from Him.**

And you will notice that **our Lord did not at this time look to any of His friends.** In the beginning of His Sufferings He appeared to seek consolation from His disciples, but He found them sleeping for sorrow. Therefore, on this occasion He did not look to them in any measure. He had lost the Light of God's Countenance, but He does not look down in the darkness and say, "John, dear faithful John, are you there? Have you not a word for Him whose bosom was a pillow for your head? Mother Mary, are you there? Can you not say one soft word to your dying Son to let Him know there is still a heart that does not forget Him?" No, Beloved, our Lord did not look to the creature. Man as He was, and we must regard Him as such in uttering this cry, yet He does not look to friend or brother, helper or human arm. But though God is angry, as it were, yet He cries, "My God." Oh, it is the only cry that befits a Believer's lips. Even if God seems to forsake you, keep on crying to Him.

Do not begin to look in a pet and a jealous humor to creatures, but look to your God. Depend upon it, He will come to you sooner or later. He cannot fail you. He must help you. Like a child, if its mother strikes it, still, if it is in pain, it cries for its mother, it knows her love, it knows its deep need of her, and that she, alone, can supply its need. Oh, Beloved, do the same. **Is there one in this house who has lately lost his comforts and Satan has said, "Don't pray"? Beloved, pray more than ever you did. If the devil says, "God is angry, what is the use of praying to Him?" He might have said the same to Christ, "Why do You pray to One who forsakes You?" But Christ did pray, "My God" still, though He says, "Why do You forsake Me?" Perhaps Satan tells you not to read the Bible again. It has not comforted you of late, the promises have not come to your soul.**

Dear Brother, Sister, read and read more, read twice as much as you ever did. Do not think that, because there is no light coming to you, the wisest way is to get away from the light. No, stay where the light is. And perhaps Satan even says to you, "Don't attend the House of God, again. Don't go to the Communion Table. Why, surely you won't wish to commune with God when He hides His face from you." I say the words of wisdom, for I speak according to the example of Christ, come still to your God in private and in public worship, and come still, dear Brothers and Sisters, to the Table of fellowship with Jesus, saying,

"Though He slays me, yet will I trust in Him," for I have none else to trust. And though He hides His face from me, yet will I cry after Him, and my cry shall not be, "My friends," but, "My God!" And my eyes shall not look to my soul, my friends, or my feelings, but I will look to my God and to Him, alone. That is the first lesson, not an easy one to learn, mark you, easier to hear than you will find it to practice, but *"the Spirit helps our infirmities."* The second lesson is this, observe that:

B. Second, *THOUGH UNDER A SENSE OF DESERTION, OUR MASTER DOES NOT RELAX HIS HOLD OF HIS GOD.*

Observe it, "My God," it is one hand He grips Him with. "My God," it is the other hand He grasps Him with. Both united in the cry, "My God." **He believes that God is still His God.** He uses the possessive particle twice, "My God, My God."

Now it is easy to believe that God is ours when He smiles upon us and when we have the sweet fellowship of His love in our hearts, **but the point for faith to attend to is to hold to God when He gives hard words, when His Providence frowns upon you, and when even His Spirit seems to be withdrawn from you.** Oh, let go of everything, but do not let go of your God. If the ship is tossed and ready to sink, and the tempest rages exceedingly, cast out the ingots, let the gold go! Throw out the wheat, as Paul's companions did. Let even necessities go, but oh, always hold to your God. Give not up your God. Still say, notwithstanding all, "In the teeth of all my feelings, doubts and suspicions, I hold Him yet. He is my God, by His Grace I will not let Him go."

You know that in the text our Lord calls God in the original, His "Strong One," "Eli, Eli," "My Strong One, My Mighty One." **So let the Christian, when God turns away the brightness of His Presence, still believe that all his strength lies in God and that, moreover, God's power is on his side.** Though it seems to crush him, yet faith says, "It is a power that will not crush me. If he smites me, what will I do? I will lay hold upon His arm and He will put strength in me! I will deal with God as Jacob did with the angel. If He wrestles with me, I will borrow strength from Him and I will wrestle with Him until I get the blessing from Him." Beloved, we must neither let go of God, nor let go of our sense of His power to save us! We must hold to our possession of Him and hold to the belief that He is worth possessing, that He is God, All-Sufficient, and that He is still our God.

Now I would like to put this personally to any tried child of God here. Are you going to let go of your God because you have lost His smile? Then I ask you, did you base your faith upon His smile? For if you did, you mistook the true ground of faith! The ground of a Believer's confidence is not God's smile, but God's promises! It is not His temporary sunshine of His love, but His deep eternal love, itself, as it reveals itself in the Covenant and in the promises. **Now the present smile of God may leave you, but God's promises do not, and if you believe upon God's promises, they are just as true when God frowns as when He smiles!** If you are resting upon the Covenant, that Covenant is as true in the dark as in the light. It stands as good when your soul is without a single gleam of consolation as when your heart is flooded with sacred bliss. Oh, come, then, to this, the promises are as good as ever. Christ is the same as ever. His blood is as great a plea as ever and the oath of God is as Immutable as ever. We must get away from all building upon our apprehensions of God's love. It is the love, itself, we must build on, not on our enjoyment of His Presence, but on His faithfulness and on His truth. Therefore, be not cast down, but still call Him, "My God."

Moreover, I may put it to you, if, because God frowns, you give Him up, what else do you mean to do? Why, is it not better to trust in an angry God than not to trust in God at all? Suppose you leave off the walk of faith, what will you do? The carnal man never knew what faith was and, therefore, gets on pretty fairly in his own blind, dead way. But you have been quickened and made alive, enlightened. And if you give up your faith, what is to become of you? Oh, hold to Him then: "*For if your eye of faith is dim, /Still hold on to Jesus, sink or swim! /Still at His footstool bow the knee/And Israel's God your strength shall be.*"

Don't give Him up!

Moreover, if your faith gives up her God because He frowns, what sort of a faith was it? Can you not believe in a frowning God? What? Have you a friend who did, the other day, but give you a rough word, and you said, "At one time I could die for that man." But because he gives you one rough word, are you going to give him up? Is this your kindness to your friends? Is this your confidence in your God? But how Job played the man. Did he turn against his God when He took away is comforts? No! He said, "*The Lord gave, and the Lord has taken away, and blessed be the name of the Lord.*" And do you not remember how he put it best of all when he said, "*Though He slays me, yet will I trust in Him*"? Yes, if your faith is only a fair weather faith. If you can only walk with God when He sandals you in silver, and smoothes the path beneath your feet, what faith is this? Where did you get it? The faith that can foot it with the Lord through Nebuchadnezzar's furnace of fire and that can go walking with Him through the valley of the shadow of death, this is the faith to be had and sought after. May God grant it to us, for that was the faith that was in the heart of Christ when forsaken of God. He yet says, "My God."

We have learned two lessons. Now that we have learned them, (**we have gone over them, but have we learned them?), may we practice them and turn to God in ill times, and not relinquish our hold.**

C. **The third lesson is this:** *ALTHOUGH OUR LORD UTTERED THIS DEEP AND BITTER CRY OF PAIN, YET LEARN FROM HIS SILENCE.*

[Christ] **never uttered a single syllable of murmuring, or brought any accusation against His God.** "My God, why have You forsaken Me?" There! Look at those words. Can you see any blots in them? I cannot. They are crystallized sorrow, but there is no defilement of sin. It was just (I was about to say) what an angel could have said, if he could have suffered. It is what the Son of God did say when He was suffering,

He who was purer than angels. Listen to Job, and we must not condemn Job, for we could not have been half as good as he, I daresay, but he does let his spirit utter itself, sometimes, in bitterness. He curses the day of his birth and so on. But the Lord Jesus does not do that. There is not a syllable about "cursed be the day in which I was born in Bethlehem, and in which I came among such a rebellious race as this," no, not a word, not a word! And even the best of men, when in sorrow, have at least wished that things were not just so.

David, when he had lost Absalom, wished that he had died instead of Absalom. But Christ does not appear to want things altered. He does not say, "Lord, this is a mistake. Would God I had died by the hands of Herod when He sought My life, or had perished when they tried to throw Me down the hill of Capernaum!" No! Nothing of the kind. There is grief, but there is no complaining. There is sorrow, but there is no rebellion. Now this is the point, Beloved, I want to bring to you. If you should extremely suffer and it should ever come to that terrible pinch that even God's Love and the enjoyment of it appears to be gone, put your finger to your lips and keep it there! "I was dumb with silence. I opened not My mouth because You did it." Believe that He is still a good God! **Know that assuredly He is working for your good, even now, and let not a syllable escape you by way of murmuring, or if it does, repent of it and recall it. You have a right to speak to God, but not to murmur against Him, and if you would be like your Lord, you would say just this, "Why have you forsaken me?" But you will say no more and there you will leave it. And if there comes no answer to your question, you will be content to be without an answer.**

Now again, I say, this is a lesson I can teach, but I do not know if I can practice it and I do not know that you can. Only, again, "the Spirit helps our infirmities," and He will enable us when we come to, "lama Sabachthani," to come so far, but not to go farther, to stop there with our Lord.

D. **The fourth, *OUR LORD, WHEN HE DOES CRY, CRIES WITH THE INQUIRING VOICE OF A LOVING CHILD.***

"My God, why, ah, why have You forsaken Me?" He asks a question not in curiosity, but in love. Loving, sorrowful complaints He brings. "Why, My God? Why? Why?" Now this is a lesson to us, because we ought to endeavor to find out why it is that God hides Himself from us. **No Christian ought to be content to live without full assurance of faith. No Believer ought to be satisfied to live a moment without knowing to a certainty that Christ is His.** And if he does not know it, and assurance is gone, what ought he to do? Why, he should never be content until he has gone to God with the question, "Why have I not this assurance? Why have I not Your Presence? Why is it that I cannot live once as I did in the light of Your Countenance?" And, Beloved, the answer to this question in our case will sometimes be, "I have forsaken you, My child, because you have forsaken Me. You have grown cold of heart by slow degrees. Gray hairs have come upon you, and you did not know. And I have made you know it to make you see your backsliding and sorrowfully repent of it." Sometimes the answer will be, "My child, I have forsaken you because you have set up an idol in your heart. You love your child too much, your gold too much, your trade too much. And I will not come into your soul unless I am your Lord, your Love, your Bridegroom and your All." Oh, we shall be glad to know these answers, because the moment we know them our heart will say: *"The dearest idol I have known, / Whatever that idol be?/Help me to tear it from its throne, / And worship only Thee."*

Sometimes the Lord's answer will be, "My child, I have gone from you for a little to try you, to see if you love Me." A true lover will love on under frowns. It is only the superficial professor that needs sweetmeats every day, and only loves his God for what he gets out of Him. But the genuine Believer loves Him when He smites him, when He bruises him with the bruises of a cruel one! Why then, we will say, *"O God, if this is why You forsake us, we will love You still, and prove to You that Your Grace has made our souls to hunger and thirst for You."* Depend upon it, the best way to get away from trouble, or to get great help under it, is to run close in to God! In one of [Francis] Quarles's poems, he has the picture of a man striking another with a great flail. Now the further off the other is, the heavier it strikes him. So the man whom God is smiting runs close in and he cannot be hurt at all! O my God, my God, when away from You, affliction stuns me, but I will close with You, and then even my affliction I will take to be a cause of glory, and glory in tribulations, also, so that Your blast shall not sorely wound my spirit.

Well, I leave this point with the very same remark I made before. To cry to God with the enquiry of a child is the fourth lesson of the text. Oh, **learn it well. Practice it when you are in much trouble**. If you are in such a condition at this time, practice it now, and in the pew say, "*Show me why You contend with me. Search me and try me, and see if there is any wicked way in me, and lead me in the way everlasting.*" Now the fifth observation is one to be treasured up:

E. ***THAT OUR LORD, THOUGH HE WAS FORSAKEN OF GOD, STILL PURSUED HIS FATHER'S WORK***, the work He came to do. "My God, why have You forsaken Me?" But, mark you, He does not leave the Cross. He does not unloose the nails as He might have done with His will. He did not leap down amidst the assembled mockers and scorn them in return, and chase them far away. He kept on bleeding, suffering, even until He could say, "It is finished," and He did not give up the ghost till it was finished.

Now, Beloved, I find it, and I daresay you do, a very easy and pleasant thing to go on serving God when I have got a full sense of His love and Christ shining in my face, when every text brings joy to my heart and when I see souls converted and know that God is going with the Word to bless it. That is very easy. **But to keep on serving God when you get nothing for it but blows, when there is no success and when your own heart is in deep darkness of spirit, I know the temptation.** Perhaps you are under it. Because you have not the joy you once had. You say, "I must give up preaching. I must give up that

Sunday school. If I have not the light of God's Countenance, how can I do it? I must give it up." Beloved, you must do no such thing! Suppose there were a loyal subject in a nation and he had done something or other which grieved the king, and the king, on a certain day, turned his face from him? Do you think that loyal subject would go away and neglect his duty because the king frowned? No, I think he would say to himself, "I do not know why the king seems to deal harshly with me. He is a good king and I know he is good. If he does not see any good in me, I will work for him more than ever. I will prove to him that my loyalty does not depend upon his smiles. I am his loyal subject, and will still stand to him." What would you say to your child if you had to chasten him for doing wrong and if he were to go away and say, "I shall not attend to the errand that Father has sent me upon, and I shall do no more in the house that Father has commanded me to do because Father has beaten me this morning"? Ah, what a disobedient child! If the scourging had its fit effect upon him, he would say, "I will wrong you no more, Father, lest you smite me again." So let it be with us.

Besides, should not our gratitude compel us to go on working for God? Has not He saved us from Hell? Then we may say, with the old heathen, "Strike, so long as You forgive!" Yes, if God forgives, He may strike if He will. Suppose a judge should forgive a malefactor condemned to die, but he should say to him, "Though you are not to be executed as you deserve, yet, for all that, you must be put in prison for some years"? He would say, "Ah, my Lord, I will take this lesser chastisement, so long as my life is saved." And oh, **if our God has saved us from going down to the pit by putting His Own Son to death on our behalf, we will love Him for that if we never have anything more.** If, between here and Heaven, we should have to say, like the elder brother, "You never gave me a kid that I might make merry with my friends, we will love Him, still". And if He never does anything to us between here and Glory but lay us on a sick bed, and torture us there, yet we will still praise and bless Him, for He has saved us from going down to the Pit. Therefore, we will love Him as long as we live. Oh, if you think of God as you ought to, you will not be at ups and downs with Him, but you will serve

Him with all your heart, soul and might, whether you are enjoying the light of His Countenance or not! Now to close. Our Lord is an Example for us in one other matter. He is to us our type of what shall happen to us, for whereas He said, "Why have You forsaken Me?"

F. *HE HAS RECEIVED A GLORIOUS ANSWER.*

And so shall every man that, in the same spirit in the hour of darkness, asks the same question! Our Lord died. No answer had He to the question, but the question went on ringing through earth, and Heaven, and Hell. **Three days He slept in the grave and after a while He went into Heaven, and my imagination, I think, may be allowed if I say that as He entered there the echo of His words, "Why have You forsaken Me?" just died away, and then the Father gave Him the practical answer to the question, for there, all along the golden streets, stood white-robed bands, all of them singing their Redeemer's praise!** All of them chanting the name of Jehovah and the Lamb, and this was a part of the answer to His question! God had forsaken Christ that these chosen spirits might live through Him. They were the reward for the travail of His soul. They were the answer to His question. And ever since then, between Heaven and earth, there has been constant commerce. If your eyes were opened that you could see, you would perceive in the sky not falling stars, shooting downwards, but stars rising upward from England, many every hour from America, from all countries where the Gospel is believed and from heathen lands where the Truth of God is preached and God is acknowledged, for you would see every now and then down on earth a dying bed, but upwards through the skies, mounting among the stars, another spirit shot upward to complete the constellations of the glorified! **And as these bright ones, all redeemed by His sufferings, enter Heaven, they bring to Christ fresh answers to that question, "Why have You forsaken Me?"** And if stooping from His Throne in Glory, the Prince of Life takes view of the sons of men who are lingering here, even in this present assembly, He will see tonight a vast number of us met together around this Table, I hope the most, if not all of us, are redeemed by His blood and rejoicing in His salvation! And the Father points down tonight to this [Metropolitan] Tabernacle, and to thousands of similar scenes where Believers cluster around the Table of fellowship with their Lord, and He seems to say to the Savior, "There is My answer to Your question, 'Why have You forsaken Me?'"

Now, Beloved, we shall have an answer to our question something like that. When we get to Heaven, perhaps not until then, God will tell us why He forsook us. When I tossed upon my bed three months ago in weary pain that robbed me of my night's rest and my day's rest, too, I asked why it was I was there, but I have realized since the reason, for God helped me afterwards so to preach that many souls were gathered in. **Often you will find that God deserts you that He may be with you after a nobler sort, hides the light, that afterwards the light of seven suns at once may break in upon your spirit and there you shall learn that it was for His Glory that He left you, for His Glory that He tried your faith.** Only mind you stand to that! Still cry to Him, and still call Him God, and never complain, but ask Him why, and still pursue His work under all difficulties and so being like Christ on earth, you shall be like Christ above, as to the answer.

I cannot sit down without saying just this word.

EXHORTATION: God will never forsake His people forever. But as many of you as are not His people, if you have not believed in Him, He will forsake you forever, and forever, and forever. And if you ask, "Why have You forsaken me?" you will get your answer in the echo of your words, "You have forsaken Me." "How shall you escape if you neglect so great a salvation?" "Believe in the Lord Jesus Christ and you shall be saved."

"But if your ears refuse/The language of His Grace, /And hearts grow hard like stubborn Jews, /That unbelieving race. / The Lord in vengeance/Shall lift His hand and swear, /'You that despised My promised rest/Shall have no portion there.'" God grant it may never be so with you, for Christ's sake.

Amen.

3.   [His] Saddest Cry

"And about the ninth hour Jesus cried out with a loud
voice, saying, 'Eli, Eli, lama sabachthani?' that is,
'My God, My God, why have You forsaken Me?'"
(Matthew 27:46 NKJV).

FOCUS: Some thoughts about this 'strange question' "My God, My God, why have You forsaken Me?" will be offered and explained. Next, some lessons will be drawn from the question. We may find many practical uses for things which are beyond the grasp of our minds, and this saying of our Lord may be of great service to us even though we cannot comprehend it.

DURING the time that *"Moses kept the flock of Jethro, his father-in-law,"* he, *"came to the mountain of God, even to Horeb,"* and there he saw a strange sight, a bush that burned with fire and yet was not consumed. Then Moses, apparently overtaken by curiosity, was drawing near in order to examine this phenomenon when he heard God's voice say to him, *"Draw not near here: take off your shoes from your feet, for the place where on you stand is holy ground."* We also may well feel, as we think of our Lord Jesus in His agony, that the voice of God speaks to us from the Cross and says, "Curiosity, bold, daring, prying intellect, draw not near here. Take off your shoes from your feet, for the place where on you stand is the very Holy of Holies unto which no man may come except as the Spirit of God shall conduct him."

I think I can understand the words, "My God, my God, why have You forsaken me?" as they are written by David in the 22nd Psalm, but the same words, "My God, My God, why have You forsaken Me?" when uttered by Jesus on the Cross, I cannot comprehend, so I shall not pretend to be able to explain them.

There is no plummet that can fathom this deep. There is no eagle's eye that can penetrate the mystery that surrounds this strange question. I have read that once upon a time **Martin Luther** sat down in his study to consider this text. Hour after hour, that mighty man of God sat still and those who waited on him came into the room, again and again, and he was so absorbed in his meditation that they almost thought he was a corpse. He moved neither hand nor foot, and neither ate nor drank, but sat with his eyes wide open, like one in a trance, thinking over these wondrous words, "My God, My God, why have You forsaken Me?" And when, after many long hours, in which he seemed to be utterly lost to everything that went on around him, he rose from his chair, someone heard him say, *"God forsaking God! No man can understand that."* And so he went his way. Though that is hardly the correct expression to use, I should hesitate to endorse it, yet I do not marvel that our text presented itself to the mind of Luther in that light. It is said that he looked like a man who had been down a deep mine and who had come up again to the light. **I feel more like one who has not been down the mine, but who has looked into it or like one who has been part of the way down and shuddered as he passed through the murky darkness but who would not dare to go much lower, for this cry, "Eli, Eli, lama Sabachthani?" is a tremendous deep; <u>no man will ever be able to fathom it.</u>**

A. **First**, then, let me utter *SOME THOUGHTS ABOUT THIS STRANGE QUESTION:* "My God, My God, why have You forsaken Me?"

Jesus was accustomed to address God as His Father. If you turn to His many prayers, you will find Him almost invariably, if not invariably, speaking to God as His Father. And, truly, He stands in that relationship both as God and as Man. Yet, in this instance, He does not say, "Father," but, "My God, My God." Was it that He had any doubt about His Sonship? Assuredly not! Satan had assailed Him in the wilderness with the insinuation, "If You are the Son of God," but Christ had put him to the rout and I feel persuaded that Satan had not gained any advantage over Him, even on the Cross, which could have made Him doubt whether He was the Son of God or not.

I think that our Savior was then speaking as Man and that this is the reason why He cried, "My God, My God," rather than, "My Father." I think He must have been speaking as Man, as I can scarcely bring my mind to the point of conceiving that God the Son could say to God the Father, "My God, My God." **There is such a wonderful blending of the Human and the Divine in the Person of the Lord Jesus Christ that, though it may not be absolutely accurate to ascribe to the Deity some things in the life of Christ, yet is He so completely God and Man that, often, Scripture does speak of things that must belong to the Humanity only as if they belonged to the Godhead.** For instance, in his charge to the Ephesian elders, the apostle Paul said, *"Feed the Church of God, which He has purchased with His own blood,"* an incorrect expression, if judged according to the rule of the logician but accurate enough according to the Scriptural method of using words in their proper sense. Yet I do think that we must draw a distinction between the Divinity and the Humanity here. As the Lord Jesus said, "My God, My God," it was because it was His Humanity that was mainly to be considered just then.

My Brothers and Sisters, does it not show us *what a real Man the Christ of God was, that He could be forsaken of His God?* We might have supposed that Christ being Emmanuel, God with Us, the Godhead and the Manhood being indissolubly united in one Person, it would have been impossible for Him to be forsaken of God. We might also have inferred, for the same reason, that it would have been impossible for Him to have been scourged, spit upon and especially that it would not have been possible for Him to die. Yet all these things were made not only possible, but also sacredly certain. **In order to complete the redemption of His chosen people, it was necessary for Him to be both God's well-beloved Son and to be forsaken of His Father.** He could truly say, as His saints also have sometimes had to say, "My God, My God, why have You forsaken Me?" Persecuted and forsaken Believer, behold your Brother in adversity! Behold the One who has gone wherever you may have to go, who has suffered more than you can ever suffer and who has taken His part in the direst calamity that ever happened to human nature so that He had to cry out, in the agony of His soul, "My God, My God, why have You forsaken Me?"

What was this forsaking? We are trying to come a little closer to this burning yet unconsumed bush, with our shoes off our feet, I hope, all the while and in this spirit we ask, "What was this forsaking?" A devout writer says that it was *horror at the sight of human misery*. He affirms what is quite true, that our Lord Jesus Christ saw all that man had to suffer because of sin that He perceived the total sum of the miseries brought by sin upon all the past, present and future generations of the human race and that He must have had a holy horror as He thought of all the woes of man, caused by sin, in this life and in that which is to come, and being completely one with man, He spoke in the name of man and said, "My God, My God, why have You forsaken Me?" That is all true, **yet that explanation will not suffice, my Brothers and Sisters because our Savior did not say, "My God, My God, why have You forsaken MAN?" but, "Why have You forsaken Me?" This forsaking was something personal to Himself.**

Others have said that it was *a dreadful shrinking in His soul on account of human sin*. I have read of a child who had done wrong and whose father had faithfully rebuked and punished him. But the boy remained callous and sullen. He sat in the same room with his father, yet he refused to confess that he had done wrong. At last the father, under a sense of his child's great wickedness, burst into tears and sobbed and sighed. Then the boy came to his father and asked him why he sorrowed so, and he answered, "Because of my child's hardness of heart." **It is true that our Lord Jesus Christ did feel as that father felt, only far more acutely, but our text cannot be fully explained by any such illustration as that.** That would be only explaining it away, for Christ did not say, "My God, My God, why has man forsaken You, and why have You so completely left men in their sin?" No, His cry was, "Why have You forsaken Me?" It was not so much the God of man to whom He appealed, but, "My God, My God." It was a *personal grief* that wrung from Him *the personal cry*, "My God, My God, why have You forsaken *Me*?" For this forsaking, by His Father in whom He trusted, related peculiarly to Himself.

What was this forsaking? Was it physical weakness? Some of you may know that when the body is in a low condition, the soul also sinks. Quite involuntarily, unhappiness of mind, depression of spirit and sorrow of heart will come upon you. You may be without any real reason for grief and yet may be among the unhappiest of men because, for the time, your body has conquered your soul. But, my Brothers and Sisters, this explanation is not supposable in the case of Christ, for it was not many moments after this that He shouted, "with a loud voice," His conquering cry, "It is finished," and so passed from the conflict to His coronation. **His brave spirit overcame His physical weakness and though He was brought into the dust of death," and plunged into the deepest depths of depression of spirit, yet, still, the cry, "My God, My God," which also was uttered, "with a loud voice," proves that there was still a considerable amount of mental strength, notwithstanding His physical weakness, so that mere depression of spirit caused by physical reasons could not account for this agonizing cry.**

And, certainly, my Brothers and Sisters, *this cry was not occasioned by unbelief.* You know that, sometimes, a child of God in sore trial and with many inward struggles, cries out, "My God, my God, why have You forsaken me?" when, all the while, the Lord has been remembering the tried soul and dealing graciously with it. As long ago as Isaiah's day, *"Zion said, The Lord has forsaken me, and my Lord has forgotten me."* But the Lord's reply was, *"Can a woman forget her sucking child, that she should not have compassion on the son of her womb? Yes, they may forget, yet will I not forget you. Behold, I have engraved you upon the palms of My hand."* **Unbelief often makes us talk about God forgetting us when He does nothing of the kind, but our Lord Jesus Christ was a stranger to unbelief. It was impossible for Him to cherish any doubt about the faithfulness and loving kindness of His Father, so His cry did not arise from that cause.**

And, another thing, *it did not arise from a mistake.* I have known Believers, in sore trouble, make great blunders concerning what God was doing with them. They have thought that He had forsaken them, for they misinterpreted certain signs and dealings of God, and they said, "All these things are against us. The hand of God has gone out against us to destroy us." But Christ made no mistake about this matter, for God *had* forsaken Him. It was really so. When He said, "Why have You forsaken Me?" **He spoke Infallible Truth of God and His mind was under no cloud whatever! He knew what He was saying and He was right in what He said, for His Father had forsaken Him for the time.**

What, then, can this expression mean? *Does it mean that God did not love His Son?* O Beloved, let us, with the utmost detestation, fling away any suspicion of the kind that we may have harbored. God did forsake His Son but He loved Him as much when He forsook Him as at any other period. I even venture to say that if it had been possible for God's love towards His Son to be increased, He would have delighted in Him more when He was standing as the suffering Representative of His chosen people than He had ever delighted in Him before. We do not indulge, for a single moment, the thought that God was angry with Him personally, or looked upon Him as unworthy of His love, or regarded Him as one upon whom He could not smile because of anything displeasing in Himself. Yet, the fact remains that God had forsaken Him, for Christ was under no mistake about that matter. **He rightly felt that His Father had withdrawn the comfortable Light of His Countenance, that He had, for the time being, lost the sense of His Father's favor, not the favor, itself, but the consciousness of that Divine aid and succor which He had formerly enjoyed, so He felt Himself like a Man left all alone and He was not only left all alone by His friends, but also by His God.**

Can we at all imagine the state of mind in which our Lord was when He cried, "My God, My God, why have You forsaken Me?" No, that is not possible, yet **I will try to help you to understand it.** Can you imagine the misery of a lost soul in Hell, one who is forsaken of God and who cries, in bitterest agony, "God will never look upon me in mercy, or delight, or favor," can you picture that sad state? Well, if you can, you will not, even then, have got anywhere near the position of Christ because that soul in Hell does not want God's favor and does not seek it, or ask for it. That lost soul is so hardened in sin that it never troubles about whether God would receive it if it repented, the truth is that it does not want to repent! The misery that men will suffer in the world to come will be self-created misery arising out of the fact that they loved sin so much that they brought eternal sorrow upon themselves. It must be an awful thing for a soul, in the next world, to be without God, but, as far as its own consciousness is concerned, it will be so hardened that it will abide without God, yet not realizing all that it has lost because it is, itself, incapable of knowing the beauty of holiness and the perfection of the God from whom it is separated forever. **Yet how different was the case of our Lord Jesus Christ when upon the Cross! He knew, as no mere man could ever know, what separation from God meant.**

Think of a case of another kind. King Saul, when the witch of Endor brought up the spirit of Samuel, said to him, "God is departed from me, and answers me no more." You recollect the state of mind that he was in when the evil spirit was upon him and he needed David's harp to charm it away. But at last, even *that* failed, and I know of no unhappier character than Saul when God had departed from him. But, somehow, there was not the anguish in the soul of Saul that there would have been if he had ever really known the Lord. I do not think that he ever really did, in his inmost soul, know the Lord. After Samuel anointed him, he was "turned into another man," but He never became a new man and the sense of God's Presence that he had was not, for a moment, comparable to that Presence of God which a true saint enjoys and which Christ always enjoyed, except when He was on the Cross. So, when Saul lost the consciousness of that Presence, he did not suffer so great a loss and, consequently, so great an anguish as afterwards happened to our Lord.

Coming nearer to our own circumstances, I remind you that there are some of God's people who do really love Him and who have walked in the Light of His Countenance, yet, for some reason or other, they have lost the comfortable enjoyment of God's love. If any of you, dear Friends, know what that sad experience is, you are getting a faint impression of the meaning of this cry, "My God, My God, why have You forsaken Me." Oh, what anguish it is, what heart-break, to think that one is forsaken of God! I have heard of people dying of broken hearts, but I believe that the man who has been made to utter this cry has gone as near to dying of a broken heart as anyone might well do without actually dying. To be without God is to be without life. And we who love Him, can say with Dr. [Isaac] Watts: *"My God, my Life, my Love, /To You, to You I call! /I cannot live, if You remove, /For You are my All-in-All."*

But, my dear Brothers and Sisters, you have not got the whole truth yet, *for **no saint knows the Presence of God as Christ knew it.** **No saint has, to the fullest, enjoyed the love of God as Christ enjoyed it*** and, consequently, if he does lose it, he only seems to lose the moonlight whereas Christ lost the sunlight when, for a time, the face of His Father was withdrawn from Him. Only think what must have been the anguish of the Savior, especially as contrasted with His former enjoyment. Never did any mere human being know so much and enjoy so much of the love of God as Christ had done. He had lived in it, basked in it, there had never been any interruption to it. "I do always those things that please Him," He said, concerning His Father. And His Father twice said, concerning Him, "This is My Beloved Son, in whom I am well pleased." Now, as our Lord Jesus Christ had enjoyed the love of God to the very fullest, think what it must have been for Him to lose the conscious enjoyment of it. You know that you may go into a room and blow out the candle, but the blind people will not miss it. They miss the light most who have enjoyed it most, and **Christ missed the Light of God's Countenance most because He had enjoyed it most. Then, _reflect upon His intense love to God_. Jesus Christ, the Man Christ Jesus, loved God with all His heart, mind, soul and strength, as you and I have never yet been able to do. The love of Christ towards His Father was boundless. Well, then, for a frown to be upon His Father's face, or for the Light of that Father's face to be taken away from Him must have made it correspondingly dark and terrible to Him.**

Remember, too, the absolute purity of Christ's Nature. In Him there was no taint of sin, nor anything approaching to it. Now, holiness delights in God. God is the very sea in which holiness swims, the air which holiness breathes. Only think, then, of the perfectly Holy One, fully agreed with His Father in everything, finding out that the Father had, for good and sufficient reasons, turned His face away from Him. In proportion as you are holy; the absence of the Light of God's Countenance will be grief to you. And as Jesus was perfectly holy, it was the utmost anguish to Him to have to cry to His Father, "Why have You forsaken Me."

After all, Beloved, the only solution of the mystery is this, *Jesus Christ was forsaken of God because we deserved to be forsaken of God.* He was there, on the Cross, in our place. And as the sinner, by reason of his sin deserves not to enjoy the favor of God, so Jesus Christ, standing in the place of the sinner and enduring that which would vindicate the justice of God, had to come under the cloud, as the sinner must have come if Christ had not taken his place. But, then, since He has come under it, let us recollect that He was thus left of God that you and I, who believe in Him, might never be left of God. Since He, for a little while, was separated from His Father, we may boldly cry, "*Who shall separate us from the love of Christ?*" And, with the apostle Paul, we may confidently affirm that nothing in the whole universe "*shall be able to separate us from the love of God, which is in Christ Jesus our Lord.*"

Before I leave this point, let me say that *the Doctrine of Substitution is the key to all the sufferings of Christ.* I do not know how many theories have been invented to explain away the death of Christ. **The modern doctrine of the apostles of "culture" is that Jesus Christ did something or other, which, in some way or other, was, in some degree or other, connected with our salvation.** But it is my firm belief that every theory concerning the death of Christ, which can only be understood by the highly-cultured, must be false. "That is strong language," says someone. Perhaps it is, but it is true. I am quite sure that the religion of Jesus Christ was never intended only for the highly cultured, or even for them in particular. Christ's testimony concerning His own ministry was, "The poor have the Gospel preached to them," so if you bring me a Gospel which can only be understood by gentlemen who have passed through Oxford or Cambridge University, I know that it cannot be the Gospel of Christ. He meant the good news of salvation to be proclaimed to the poorest of the poor. In fact, the Gospel is intended for humanity in general, so, if you cannot make me understand it, or if, when I do understand it, it does not tell me how to deliver its message in such plain language that the poorest man can comprehend it, I tell you, Sirs, that your newfangled gospel is a lie. I will stick to the old one, which a man, only a little above an idiot in intellect, can understand. **I cling to the old Gospel for this, among many other reasons, that all the modern gospels that leave out the great central Truth of Substitution, prevent the message from being of any use to the great mass of mankind.**

If those other gospels which are not really gospels, please your taste and fancy, and suit the readers of Quarterly Reviews, and eloquent orators and lecturers, there are still the poor people in our streets and the millions of working men, the vast multitudes who cannot comprehend anything that is highly metaphysical, and you cannot convince me that our Lord Jesus Christ sent, as His message to the whole world, a metaphysical mystery that would need volume upon volume before it could even be stated. I am persuaded that He gave us a rough and ready Gospel like this, *"The Son of Man is come to seek and to save that which was lost."* Or this, "With His stripes we are healed." Or this, "The chastisement of our peace was upon Him." Or this, "He died, the Just for the unjust, to bring us to God." Do not try to go beyond this Gospel, Brothers and Sisters, you will get into the mud if you do. But it is safe standing here. And standing here, I can comprehend **how our Lord Jesus took the sinner's place and, passing under the sentence which the sinner deserved, or under a sentence which was tantamount thereto, could cry, "My God, My God, why have You forsaken Me?"**

B. Now, in closing, I am going to draw *A FEW LESSONS FROM THIS UTTERANCE OF CHRIST.*

The first lesson is, *Behold how He loved us.* When Christ stood and wept at the grave of Lazarus, the Jews said, *"Behold how He loved him!"* **But on the Cross He did not weep, He bled. And He not**

merely bled, He died and, before He died, His spirit sank within Him, for He was forsaken of His God. Was there ever any other love like this, that the Prince of Life and Glory should condescend to this shame and death?

Then, next, Brothers and Sisters, as He suffered so much for us, *let us be ready to suffer anything for His sake.* Let us be willing even to lose all the joy of religion if that would glorify God. I do not know that it would, but I think the Spirit of Christ ought to carry us even as far as Moses went when he pleaded for the guilty nation of Israel and was willing to have his own name blotted out of the Book of Life rather than that God's name should be dishonored. We have never had to go as far as that and we never shall, yet let us be willing to part with our last penny, for Christ's name's sake, if He requires it. Let us be willing to lose our reputation. Ah, it is a difficult timing to give that up! Some of us, when we first came into public notice and found our words picked to pieces, and our character slandered, felt it rather difficult. We have got used to it, now, but it was very trying at first. But, oh, if one had to be called a devil, if one had to go through this world and to be spat upon by every passer-by, still, if it were endured for Christ's sake, remembering how He was forsaken of God for us, we ought to take up even that cross with thankfulness that we were permitted to bear it.

Another lesson is that if ever you and I should feel that we are forsaken of God, *if we should get into this state in any way, remember that we are only where Christ has been before us.* If ever, in our direst extremity, we should be compelled to cry, "My God, my God, why have You forsaken me?" we shall have gone down no deeper than Christ Himself went! He knows that feeling and that state of heart, for He has felt the same. This fact should tend greatly to cheer you. Your deep depression is not a proof of reprobation that is evident, for Christ Himself endured even more! A man may say, "I cannot be a child of God, or else I should not feel as I do." Ah, you do not know what true children of God may feel. Strange thoughts pass through their minds in times of storm and doubt. A Puritan preacher was standing by the deathbed of one of his members who had been for thirty years in gloom of soul. The good old minister expected that the man would get peace at last, for he had been an eminent Christian and had greatly rejoiced in his Savior but, for thirty years or more, he had fallen into deep gloom. The minister was trying to speak a word of comfort to him, but the man said, "Ah, Sir! What can you say to a man who is dying and yet who feels that God has forsaken him?" The pastor replied, **"But what became of that Man who died, whom God really did forsake? Where is HE now?"** The dying man caught at that, and said, "He is in Glory and I shall be with Him! I shall be with Him where He is.

And so the Light of God came to the dying man who had been so long in the dark. He saw that Christ had been just where he was and that he should be where Christ was, even at the right hand of the Father. I hope, Brothers and Sisters, that you will never get down so low as that, but I beseech you, if you ever meet with any others who are there, do not be rough with them. Some strong-minded people are very apt to be hard upon nervous folk and to say, "They should not get into that state." And we are liable to speak harshly to people who are very depressed in spirit and say to them, "Really, you ought to rouse yourself out of such a state." I hope none of you will ever have such an experience of this depression of spirit as I have had, yet I have learned from it to be very tender with all fellow sufferers. The Lord have mercy on them and help them out of the Slough of Despond, for, if He does not, they will sink in deep mire where there is no standing.

I pray God specially to bless this inference from our text. *There is hope for you, if you are in this condition.* Christ came through it and He will be with you in it. And, after all, you are not forsaken as He was, you can be sure of that. With you, the forsaking is only in the apprehension that is bad enough but it is not a matter of fact, for, "the Lord will not forsake His people," nor cast away even one of those whom He has chosen.

I will tell you what is a much more awful thing even than crying out, "My God, my God, why have You forsaken me?" If you are afraid that God has left you and the sweat stands on your brow in very terror and if your soul seems to long for death rather than life, even in such a state as that, you are not in the worst possible condition. "Really," you ask, **"is there anything worse than that?" Yes, I will tell you what is much worse than that that is to be without God and not to care about it,** to be living, like some whom I am now addressing, without God and without hope, yet that never concerns them at all. I can pity the agony of the man who cannot bear to be without his God, but, at the same time, I can bless the Lord that he feels such agony as that, for that proves to me that his soul will never perish.

But those, whom I look upon with fear and trembling are the men who make a profession of religion, yet who never have any communion with God and, all the while are quite happy about it. Or backsliders who have gone away from God and yet seem perfectly at ease. You worldlings who are quite satisfied with the things of this world and have no longings for the world that is to come, I wish you had got as far as to be unhappy. I wish you had got as far as to be in an agony, for that is the road to heavenly joy. It was thus that Christ won it for us and it is by such a path as this that many a soul is first led into the experience of His saving power. Brothers and Sisters, weep not for those of us who sometimes have to cry out in anguish of soul! Mourn not for us who are cast down because we cannot live without Christ. You see, our Lord has made us covet the highest blessings. Our heads have been so often on His bosom that if they are not always there, we keep on crying till we get back to that blessed position again. This is a sweet sorrow; may we have more and more of it! But, oh, **I pray you, pity those who never ate the Bread of Heaven, never drank of the Water of Life, never knew the sweetness of the kisses of Christ's mouth, and never knew what it was to have a Heaven begun below in the enjoyment of fellowship with Him! In such cases, your pity is indeed required.**

EXHORTATION: I have finished when I have just said this, as you come to the Table of your Lord, come, Brothers and Sisters, with this cry of Christ ringing in your ears to make you love Him more than ever and, as you eat the bread and drink the wine, do it all out of fervent love to Him. And the Lord bless you, for His name's sake. Amen.

4. The Three Hours of Darkness

"Now from the sixth hour until the ninth hour
there was darkness over all the land"
(Matthew 27:45 NKJV).

FOCUS: Spurgeon writes: "I am going to speak of [the text] in four ways, as the Holy Spirit may help me. First, let us bow our spirits in the presence of a miracle which amazes us. Second, let us regard this darkness as a veil which conceals. Third, as a symbol which instructs. And fourth, as a display of sympathy which forewarns us by the prophecies which it implies."

FROM nine till noon the usual degree of light was present, so that there was time enough for our Lord's adversaries to behold and insult His sufferings. There could be no mistake about the fact that He was really nailed to the Cross, for He was crucified in broad daylight. We are fully assured that it was Jesus of Nazareth, for both friends and foes were eye-witnesses of His agonies, for three long hours the Jews sat down and watched Him on the Cross, making jests of His miseries. I feel thankful for those three hours of light, for otherwise the enemies of our faith would have questioned whether, in very deed, the blessed body of our Master was nailed to the tree and would have started false rumors as many as the bats and owls which haunt the darkness. Where would have been the witnesses of this solemn scene if the sun had been hidden from morn till night? As three hours of light gave opportunity for inspection and witness-bearing, we see the wisdom which did not allow it to close too soon.

Never forget that this miracle of the closing of the eye of day at high noon was performed by our Lord in His weakness. He had walked the sea, raised the dead and healed the sick in the days of His strength, but now He has come to His lowest, the fever is on Him, He is faint and thirsty. He hangs on the borders of dissolution. Yet He has power to darken the sun at noon! He is still very God of very God: *"Behold, a purple torrent runs/Down from His hands and head!/The crimson tide puts out the sun!/His groans awake the dead!*"

If He can do this in His weakness, what is He *not* able to do in His strength? Fail not to remember that this power was displayed in a sphere in which He did not usually put forth His might. The sphere of Christ is that of goodness and benevolence and, consequently, of light. When He enters the sphere of making darkness and of working judgement, He engages in what He calls His strange work. Wonders of terror are His left-handed deeds. It is but now and then that He causes the sun to go down at noon and darkens the earth in the clear day (Amos 8:9). **If our Lord can make darkness at will as He *dies*, what Glory may we not expect now that He lives to be the Light of the city of God forever?** The Lamb is the Light and what a Light. The heavens bear the impress of His dying power and lose their brightness. Shall not the new heavens and the new earth attest the power of the risen Lord? The thick darkness around the dying Christ is the robe of the Omnipotent, He lives again. All power is in His hands and all that power He will put forth to bless His chosen.

What a call must that mid-day midnight have been to the careless sons of men. They knew not that the Son of God was among them nor that He was working out human redemption. **The grandest hour in all history seemed likely to pass by unheeded, when, suddenly, *night* hastened from her chambers and usurped the day!** Everyone asked his companion, "What does this darkness mean?" Business stood still. The plow stayed in mid-furrow and the axe paused uplifted. It was the middle of the day, when men are busiest, but they made a general pause. Not only on Calvary, but on every hill and in every valley, the gloom settled down. There was a halt in the caravan of life. None could move unless they groped their way like the blind. The master of the house called for a light at noon and his servant tremblingly obeyed the unusual summons. Other lights were twinkling and Jerusalem was as a city by night, only men were not in their beds. How startled were mankind.

Around the great deathbed an appropriate quiet was secured. I doubt not that a shuddering awe came over the masses of the people and the thoughtful foresaw terrible things. **Those who had stood about the Cross and had dared to insult the majesty of Jesus, were paralyzed with fear.** They ceased their ribaldry and, with it, their cruel exultation. They were cowed though not convinced, even the basest of them. While the better sort "smote their breasts and returned," as many as could do so, no doubt, stumbled to their chambers and endeavored to hide themselves for fear of awful judgments which they feared were near. I do not wonder that there should be traditions of strange things that were said during the hush of that darkness. Those whispers of the past may or may not be true, they have been the subject of learned controversy, but the labor of the dispute was energy ill spent. Yet we could not have wondered if one did say, as he is reported to have done, "God is suffering, or the world is perishing." Nor should I drive from my beliefs the poetic legend that an Egyptian pilot passing down the river heard among the reed banks a voice out of the rustling rushes, whispering, "The great Pan is dead." Truly, the God of Nature was expiring and things less tender than the reeds by the river might well tremble at the sound.

We are told that this darkness was over all the land. And Luke puts it, *over all the earth."* That portion of our globe which was then veiled in natural night was not affected, but to all men awake and at their employment, it was the advertisement of a great and solemn event. It was strange beyond all experience and all men marveled, for when the light should have been brightest, all things were obscured for the space of three hours.

There must be great teaching in this darkness, for when we come so near the Cross, which is the center of history, every event is full of meaning. Light will come out of this darkness. I love to feel the solemnity of the three hours of death-shade and to sit down in it and meditate with no companion but the august Sufferer, around whom that darkness lowered.

A. **First, let us view this darkness as** *A MIRACLE WHICH AMAZES US.*

It may seem a trite observation that this darkness was altogether out of the natural course of things. Since the world began, was it ever heard that at high noon there should be darkness over all the land? It was altogether out of the order of Nature. Some deny miracles and, if they also deny God, I will not, at this time, deal with them. But it is very strange that anyone who believes in God should doubt the possibility of miracles. **It seems to me that, granted the Being of a God, miracles are to be expected as an occasional declaration of His independent and active will.** He may make certain rules for His actions and it may be His wisdom to keep them, but surely He must reserve to Himself the liberty to depart from His own laws, or else He has, in a measure, laid aside His Personal Godhead, deified law and set it up above Himself. It would not increase our idea of the Glory of His Godhead if we could be assured that He had made Himself subject to rule and tied His own hands from ever acting except in a certain manner. From the self-existence and freedom of will which enters into our very conception of God, we are led to expect that sometimes He should not keep to the methods which He follows as His general rule. This has led to the universal conviction that miracles are a proof of Godhead.

The general works of Creation and Providence are, to my mind, the best proofs, but the common heart of our race, for some reason or other, looks to *miracles* **as surer evidence, thus proving that miracles are expected of God.** Although the Lord makes it His order that there shall be day and night, He, in this case, with abundant reason, interposes three hours of night in the center of a day! Behold the reason. The unusual in lower Nature is made to consort with the unusual in the dealings of Nature's Lord. Certainly this miracle was most congruous with that greater miracle which was happening in the death of Christ. Was not the Lord, Himself, departing from all common ways? Was He not doing that which had never been done from the beginning and would never be done again? That man should die is so common a thing as to be deemed inevitable? We are not startled at the sound of a funeral knell; we have become familiar with the grave. As the companions of our youth die at our side, we are not seized with amazement, for death is everywhere about us and within us. But that the Son of God should die, this is beyond all expectation and not only above Nature, but contrary to it. He who is equal with God deigns to hang upon the Cross and die. I know of nothing that seems more out of rule and beyond expectation than this. **The sun darkening at noon is a fit accompaniment of the death of Jesus.** Is it not so?

Further, this miracle was not only out of the order of Nature, but it was one which *would have been pronounced impossible.* It is not possible that there should be an eclipse of the sun at the time of the full moon. The moon, at the time when she is in her full, is not in a position in which she could possibly cast her shadow upon the earth. The Passover was at the time of the full moon and, therefore, it was not possible that the *sun* should then undergo an eclipse. This darkening of the sun was not strictly an astronomical eclipse, the darkness was doubtless produced in some other way, yet to those who were present, it did seem to be a total eclipse of the sun, a thing impossible.

When we come to deal with man and the Fall, and sin, and God, and Christ, and the Atonement, we are at home with impossibilities! We have now reached a region where prodigies, marvels and surprises are the order of the day, sublimities become commonplace when we come within the circle of Eternal Love. Yes, more, we have now left the solid land of the possible and have put out to sea, where we see the works of the Lord and His wonders in the deep. When we think of impossibilities in other spheres, we start back. But the way of the Cross is ablaze with the Divine and we soon perceive that "with God, all things are possible."

See, then, in the death of Jesus, the possibility of the impossible. Behold, here, how the Son of God can die. We sometimes pause when we meet with an expression in a hymn which implies that God can suffer or die. We think that the poet has used too great a license, yet it behooves us to refrain from hypercriticism since, in Holy Writ, there are words like it. We even read (Acts 20:28) of *"the Church of God which*

He has purchased with His own blood," the blood of God. Ah well. I am not careful to defend the language of the Holy Spirit, but in its presence I take liberty to justify the words which we sang just now: *"Well might the sun in darkness hide, /And shut his glories in, /When God, the mighty Maker, died/For man, the creature's sin."*

I will not venture to explain the death of the Incarnate God. I am content to believe it and to rest my hope upon it. How should the Holy One have sin laid upon Him? That, also, I do not know. A wise man has told us, as if it were an axiom, that the imputation or the non-imputation of sin is an impossibility. Be it so, we have become familiar with such things since we have beheld the Cross. Things which men call absurdities have become foundational Truths of God to us. The Doctrine of the Cross is, to them that perish, foolishness. **We know that in our Lord was no sin and yet He bore our sins in His own body on the Cross.** We do not know how the innocent Son of God could be permitted to suffer for sins that were not His own. It amazes us that Justice should permit one so perfectly Holy to be forsaken of His God and to cry out, "Eloi, Eloi, lama Sabachthani?" But it was so and it was so by the decree of the highest Justice, and we rejoice in it! As it was so, that the sun was eclipsed when it was impossible that it should be eclipsed, so has Jesus performed, on our behalf, in the agonies of His death, things which, in the ordinary judgment of men, must be set down as utterly impossible. Our faith is at home in wonderland where the Lord's thoughts are seen to be as high above our thoughts as the heavens are above the earth.

Concerning this miracle, I have also further to remark that *this darkening of the sun surpassed all ordinary and natural eclipses.* It lasted longer than an ordinary eclipse and it came in a different manner. According to Luke, the darkness all over the land came first and the sun was darkened afterwards, the darkness did not *begin* with the sun, but *mastered* the sun. It was unique and supernatural. Now, among all grief, no grief is comparable to the grief of Jesus, of all woes, none can parallel the woes of our great Substitute. As strongest light casts deepest shade, so has the surprising love of Jesus cost Him a death such as falls not to the common lot of men. Others die, but this Man is *"obedient unto death."* Others drink the fatal draught, yet reckon not of its wormwood and gall, but my Master *"tasted death."* "He poured out His soul unto death." Every part of His Being was darkened with that extraordinary death-shade, and the natural darkness outside of Him did but shroud a special death which was entirely by itself.

And now, when I come to think of it, **this darkness appears to have been most natural and fitting.** If we had to write out the story of our Lord's death, we could not omit the darkness without neglecting a most important item. The darkness seems a part of the natural furniture of that great transaction. Read the story through and you are not at all startled with the darkness. After once familiarizing your mind with the thought that this is the Son of God and that He stretches His hands to the cruel death of the Cross, you do not wonder at the rending of the veil of the Temple. You are not astonished at the earthquake or at the rising of certain of the dead. These are proper attendants of our Lord's passion and so is the darkness. It drops into its place; it seems as if it could not have been otherwise: *"That Sacrifice! —the death of Him—/ The high and ever Holy One! /Well may the conscious Heaven grow dim, / And blacken the beholding sun."*

For a moment think again. Has it not appeared as if the death which that darkness shrouded was also a natural part of the great whole? We have grown, at last, to feel as if the death of the Christ of God were an integral part of human history. You cannot take it out of man's chronicles, can you? Introduce the Fall and see Paradise Lost and you cannot make the poem complete till you have introduced that greater Man who did redeem us, and by His death gave us our Paradise Regained. It is a singular characteristic of all true miracles, that though your wonder never ceases, they never appear to be unnatural, they are marvelous, but never monstrous! **The miracles of Christ dovetail into the general run of human history.** We cannot see how the Lord could be on earth and Lazarus not be raised from the dead when the grief of Martha and Mary had told its tale. We cannot see how the disciples could have been tempest-tossed on the Lake of Galilee and the Christ not walk on the water to deliver them! Wonders of power are expected parts of the narrative where Jesus is! **Everything fits into its place with surrounding facts.**

But the miracles of *Jesus*, this of the darkness among them, are essential to human history and especially is this so in the case of His death and this great darkness which shrouded it. **All things in human story converge to the Cross which seems not to be an afterthought nor an expedient, but the fit and foreordained channel through which Love should run to guilty men.**

I cannot say more from lack of voice, though I had many more things to say. Sit down and let the thick darkness cover you till you cannot even see the Cross and only know that out of reach of mortal eyes your Lord worked out the redemption of His people. He worked in silence, a miracle of patience and of love by which the Light of God has come to those who sit in darkness and in the valley of the shadow of death.

B. **Secondly, I desire you to regard this darkness as *A VEIL WHICH CONCEALS.*** The Christ is hanging on yonder tree. I see the dreadful Cross. I can see the thieves on either side. I look around and I sorrowfully mark that motley group of citizens from Jerusalem, along with scribes, priests and strangers from different countries, mingled with Roman soldiers. They turn their eyes on Him and, for the most part, gaze with cruel scorn upon the Holy One who is in the center. In truth it is an awful sight. Mark those dogs of the common sort and those bulls of Bashan of more notable rank who all unite to dishonor the Meek and Lowly One. **I must confess I never read the story of the Master's death, knowing what I do of the pain of crucifixion, without deep anguish, crucifixion was a death worthy to have been invented by devils. The pain which it involved was immeasurable.** I will not torture you by describing it. I know dear hearts that cannot read of it without tears and without lying awake for nights afterwards.

But there was more than anguish upon Calvary, ridicule and contempt embittered all. Those jests, those cruel gibes, those mockeries, those thrusting out of the tongues, what shall we say of these? At times I have felt some little sympathy with the French Prince who cried, "If I had been there with my guards, I would soon have swept those wretches away." It was too terrible a sight, the pain of the Victim was grievous enough, but the abominable wickedness of the mockers, who could bear it? Let us thank God that in the middle of the crime there came down a darkness which rendered it impossible for them to go further with it! Jesus must die. For His pains there must be no alleviation and from death there must be for Him no deliverance, but the scoffers must be silenced. Most effectually their mouths were closed by the dense darkness which shut them in.

What I see in that veil is, first of all, that it was *a concealment for those guilty enemies.* Did you ever think of that? It is as if God, Himself, said, "I cannot bear it. I will not see this infamy! Descend, O veil." Down fell the heavy shades: *"I asked the heavens, / 'What foe to God has done/This unexampled deed?' The heavens exclaim, / 'Twas man! And we, in horror, snatched the sun/From such a spectacle of guilt and shame.'"*

Thank God, the Cross is a hiding place. It furnishes for guilty men a shelter from the all-seeing eyes, so that justice need not see and strike. When God lifts up His Son and makes Him visible, He hides the sin of men. He says that *"the times of their ignorance He winks at."* Even the greatness of their sin He casts behind His back, so that He need not see it, but may indulge His long-suffering and permit His pity to endure their provocations. It must have grieved the heart of the Eternal God to see such wanton cruelty of men towards Him who went about doing good and healing all manner of diseases. It was horrible to see the teachers of the people rejecting Him with scorn, the seed of Israel, who ought to have accepted Him as their Messiah, casting Him out as a thing despised and abhorred! I therefore feel gratitude to God for bidding that darkness covers all the land and end that shameful scene! I would say to any guilty ones here, **Thank God that the Lord Jesus has made it possible for your sins to be hidden more completely than by**

thick darkness! Thank God that in Christ He does not see you with that stern eye of Justice which would involve your destruction. Had not Jesus interposed, whose death you have despised, you had worked out in your own death the result of your own sin long ago. But for your Lord's sake you are allowed to live as if God did not see you. This long-suffering is meant to bring you to repentance. Will you not come?

But, further, that darkness **was** *a sacred concealment for the blessed Person of our Divine Lord.* So to speak, the angels found for their King a pavilion of thick clouds in which His Majesty might be sheltered in its hour of misery. It was too much for wicked eyes to gaze so rudely on that Immaculate Person. Had not His enemies stripped Him naked and cast lots for His garments? Therefore, it was meet that the holy Manhood should, at length, find suitable concealment. It was not fit that brutal eyes should see the lines made upon that blessed form by the engraving tool of sorrow. It was not meet that revelers should see the contortions of that sacred frame, indwelt with Deity, while He was being broken beneath the iron rod of Divine Wrath on our behalf. It was meet that God should cover Him so that none should see all He did and all He bore when He was made sin for us. I devoutly bless God for thus hiding my Lord away; thus was He screened from eyes which were not fit to see the sun much less to look upon the Sun of Righteousness. This darkness also warns *us*, even we who are most reverent.

This darkness tells us all that the *Passion is a great mystery into which we cannot pry.* I try to explain it as substitution and I feel that where the language of Scripture is explicit, I may and must be explicit, too. But yet I feel that the idea of substitution does not cover the whole of the matter and that no human conception can completely grasp the whole of the dread mystery. It was worked in darkness because the full, far-reaching meaning and result cannot be beheld of finite mind. Tell me the death of the Lord Jesus was a grand example of self-sacrifice, I can see *that* and much more. Tell me it was a wondrous obedience to the will of God, I can see *that* and much more. Tell me it was the bearing of what ought to have been borne by myriads of sinners of the human race, as the chastisement of their sin, I can see *that* and found my best hope upon it. But do not tell me that this is all that is in the Cross. No, great as this would be, there is much more in our Redeemer's death. God only knows the love of God, Christ only knows all that He accomplished when He bowed His head and gave up the ghost. There are common mysteries of Nature into which it were irreverence to pry, but this is a Divine mystery before which we take our shoes off, for the place called Calvary is holy ground. **God veiled the Cross in darkness and in darkness much of its deeper meaning lies, not because God would not reveal it, but because we have not capacity enough to discern it all. God was manifest in the flesh and in that human flesh He put away sin by His Own Sacrifice, this we all know.** But *"without controversy great is the mystery of godliness."*

Once again, this veil of darkness also pictures to me the way in which **the powers of darkness will always endeavor to conceal the Cross of Christ.** We fight with darkness when we try to preach the Cross. "This is your hour and the power of darkness," said Christ, and I doubt not that the infernal hosts made, in that hour, a fierce assault upon the spirit of our Lord. Thus much we also know, that if the Prince of Darkness is anywhere in force, it is sure to be where Christ is lifted up. To becloud the Cross is the grand objective of the enemy of souls. Did you ever notice it? These fellows who hate the Gospel will let every other doctrine pass muster, but if the Atonement is preached and the Truths of God which grow out of it, straightaway they are awakened. Nothing provokes the devil like the Cross. **Modern theology has for its main goal the obscuration of the Doctrine of the Atonement.** [These modern theologians] make out sin to be a trifle and the punishment of it to be a temporary business, and thus they degrade the remedy by underrating the disease. We are not ignorant of their devices. Expect, my Brothers, that the clouds of darkness will gather as to a center around the Cross, that they may hide it from the sinner's view. But expect this, also, that there darkness shall meet its end. Light springs out of that darkness, the eternal Light of the undying Son of God, who, having risen from the dead, lives forever to scatter the darkness of evil.

C. **Now we pass on to speak of this darkness as** *A SYMBOL WHICH INSTRUCTS.* The veil falls down and conceals, but at the same time, as an emblem, it reveals. It seems to say, "Attempt not to search within, but learn from the veil, itself, it has cherub work upon it." This darkness teaches us what Jesus suffered. It aids us to guess at the griefs which we may not actually see.

The darkness is the symbol of *the wrath of God which fell on those who slew His only begotten Son.* God was angry and His frown removed the light of day. Well might He be angry, when sin was murdering His Only Son, when the Jewish farmers were saying, *"This is the heir; come, let us kill Him, and let us seize His inheritance."* This is God's wrath towards all mankind, for practically all men concurred in the death of Jesus. That wrath has brought men into darkness, they are ignorant, blinded, bewildered. They have come to love darkness better than light because their deeds are evil. In that darkness they do not repent, but go on to reject the Christ of God. Into this darkness God cannot look upon them in complacency, but He views them as children of darkness and heirs of wrath, for whom is reserved the blackness of darkness forever.

The symbol also tells us *what our Lord Jesus Christ endured.* The darkness outside of Him was the figure of the darkness that was within Him. In Gethsemane a thick darkness fell upon our Lord's spirit. He was *"exceedingly sorrowful, even unto death."* His joy was communion with God, that joy was gone and He was in the dark. His day was the light of His Father's face that face was hidden and a terrible night gathered around Him. Brothers, I should sin against that veil if I were to pretend that I could tell you what the sorrow was which oppressed the Savior's soul, only so far can I speak as it has been given me to have fellowship with Him in His sufferings. Have you ever felt a deep and overwhelming horror of sin, your own sin and the sins of others? Have you ever seen sin in the light of God's love? Has it ever darkly hovered over your sensitive conscience? Has an unknown sense of wrath crept over you like midnight gloom and has it been about you, around you, above you, and within you? Have you felt shut up in your feebleness and yet shut out from God? Have you looked around and found no help, no comfort, even, in God, no hope, no peace? In all this you have sipped a little of that salt sea into which our Lord was cast. If, like Abraham, you have felt a horror of great darkness creep over you, then you have had a taste of what your Divine Lord suffered when it pleased the Father to bruise Him and to put Him to grief.

This it was that made Him sweat great drops of blood falling to the ground, and this it was which, on the Cross, made Him utter that appalling cry, "My God, My God, why have You forsaken Me?" **It was not the crown of thorns, or the scourge, or the Cross which made Him cry, it was the darkness, the awful darkness of desertion which oppressed His mind and made Him feel like one distraught. All that could comfort Him was withdrawn and all that could distress Him was piled upon Him.** *"The spirit of a man will sustain his infirmity; but a wounded spirit who can bear?"* Our Savior's spirit was wounded and He cried, *"My heart is like wax, it is melted in the midst of My heart."* He was bereft of all natural and spiritual comfort and His distress was utter and entire. The darkness of Calvary did not, like an ordinary night, reveal the stars, but it darkened every lamp of Heaven. His strong crying and tears denoted the deep sorrow of His soul. He bore all it was possible for His capacious mind to bear, though enlarged and invigorated by union with the Godhead. He bore the equivalent of Hell, no, not that, only, but He bore that which stood instead of 10,000 Hells, so far as the vindication of the Law is concerned! Our Lord rendered, in His death agony, a homage to Justice far greater than if a world had been doomed to destruction. When I have said that, what more can I say? Well may I tell you that this unutterable darkness, this hiding of the Divine Face, expresses more of the woes of Jesus than words can ever tell.

Again, I think I see in that darkness, also, *what it was that Jesus was battling*, for we must never forget that the Cross was a battlefield to Him, wherein He triumphed gloriously. He was fighting, then, with darkness, with the *powers of darkness* of which Satan is the head, with the darkness of human ignorance, depravity and falsehood. The battle thus apparent at Golgotha has been raging ever since. Then was the conflict at its height, for the chiefs of the two great armies met in personal conflict. **The present battle in which you and I take our little share is as nothing compared with that wherein all the powers of darkness in their dense battalions hurled themselves against the Almighty Son of God. He bore their onset, endured the tremendous shock of their assault and, in the end, with shout of victory, He led captivity captive. He, by His power and Godhead, turned midnight into day, again, and brought back to this world a reign of light which, blessed be God, shall never come to a close. Come to battle again, you host of darkness, if you dare. The Cross *has* defeated you, the Cross *shall* defeat you. Hallelujah.** The Cross is the ensign of victory; its light is the death of darkness. The Cross is the lighthouse which guides poor weather-beaten humanity into the harbor of peace, this is the lamp which shines over the door of the great Father's house to lead His prodigals home.

Let us not be afraid of all the darkness which besets us on our way Home, since Jesus is the light which conquers it all. The darkness never came to an end till the Lord Jesus broke the silence. All had been still and the darkness had grown terrible. At last He spoke and His voice uttered a Psalm. It was the 22nd Psalm. "My God," He said, "My God, why have You forsaken Me?" Each repeated, "Eloi," flashed morning upon the scene! By the time He had uttered the cry, "Why have you forsaken Me?" men had begun to see, again, and some even ventured to misinterpret His words, more in terror than in ignorance. They said, "He calls Elijah!" They may have meant to mock, but I think not. At any rate, there was no heart in what they said, nor in the reply of their companions. Yet the light had come by which they could see to dip the sponge in vinegar. Brothers and Sisters, **no light will ever come to dark hearts unless Jesus shall speak and the light will not be clear until we hear the voice of His sorrows on our behalf as He cries, "Why have you forsaken Me?" His voice of grief must be the end of our grief. His cry out of the darkness must cheer away our gloom and bring the heavenly morning to our minds.**

You see how much there is in my text. It is a joy to speak on such a theme when one is in good health and full of vigor, then are we as Naphtali, a hind let loose, then we give goodly words. But this day I am in pain as to my body and my mind seems frozen. Nevertheless, the Lord can bless my feeble words and make you see that in this darkness there is a deep and wide meaning which none of us should neglect. If God shall help your meditations, this darkness will be light about you.

D. I come to my fourth point and my closing words will deal with **THE SYMPATHY WHICH PROPHESIES.** Do you see the sympathy of Nature with her Lord, the sympathy of the sun in the heavens with the Sun of Righteousness? It was not possible for Him by whom all things were made to be in darkness and for Nature to remain in the light.

The first sympathetic fact I see is this, all lights are dim when Christ shines not. All is dark when He does not shine. In the Church, if Jesus is not there, what is there? The sun, itself, could not yield us light if Jesus were withdrawn. **The seven golden lamps are ready to go out unless He walks among them and trims them with the holy oil. Brothers, you soon grow heavy, your spirits faint and your hands are weary if the Christ is not with you. If Jesus Christ is not fully preached. If He is not with us by His Spirit, then everything is in darkness. Obscure the Cross and you have obscured all spiritual teachings.** You cannot say, "We will be clear in every other point and clear upon every other doctrine, but we will shun the Atonement since so many quibble with it." No, Sirs! If that candle is put under a bushel, the whole house is dark. **All theology sympathizes with the Cross and is colored and tinctured by it. Your pious service, your books, your public worship must all be in sympathy with the Cross, one way or another. If the Cross is in the dark, so will all your work be:** *"What do you think of Christ? is the test/To try both your work and your scheme; /You cannot be right in the rest/Unless you think rightly of Him."*

Conjure up your doubts; fabricate your philosophies and compose your theories, there will be no Light of God in them if the Cross is left out. Vain are the sparks of your own making, you shall lie down in sorrow. All our work and travail shall end in vanity unless the work and travail of Christ is our first and only hope. **If you are dark upon that point, which alone is Light, how great is your darkness.**

Next, **see the dependence of all creation upon Christ, as evidenced by its darkness when He withdraws.** It was not meet that He who made all worlds should die and yet all worlds should go on just as they had done. If He suffers eclipse, they must suffer eclipse, too. If the Sun of Righteousness is made to set in blood, the natural sun must keep touch with Him. I believe, my Friends, that there is a much more wonderful sympathy between Christ and the world of Nature than any of us have ever dreamed. The whole creation groans and travails in pain together until now because Christ, in the Church, is in His travail pangs. Christ in His mystical body is in travail and so the whole creation must wait for the manifestation of the Son of God.

We are waiting for the coming of the Lord from Heaven and there is no hill or dale, there is no mountain or sea but what is in perfect harmony with the waiting Church. Wonder not that there should be earthquakes in many places, blazing volcanoes, terrible tempests, and sore spreading of deadly disease! Marvel not when you hear of dire portents and things that make one's heart to quail, for such things must be till the end shall come! Until the Great Shepherd shall make His crook into a scepter and shall begin His suffering reign, this poor earth must bleed at every vein! There must be darkness till these days of delay are ended. You that expect placid history till Christ shall come expect you know not what! You that think that generous politics shall create order and contentment and that the extension of free-trade shall breathe universal peace over the nations, look for the living among the dead. Till the Lord shall come, the word has gone out, "Overturn, overturn, overturn," and overturned all things must be, not only in other kingdoms, but in this also, till Jesus comes. All that can be shaken shall be shaken and only His immovable Throne and Truth shall abide.

Now is the time of the Lord's battle with darkness and we may not hope, as yet, for unbroken light.

Dear Friends, the sin which darkened Christ and made Him die in the dark, darkens the whole world. The sin that darkened Christ and made Him hang upon the Cross in the dark is darkening you who do not believe in Him, and you will live in the dark and die in the dark unless you get to Him, only, who is the Light of the World and can give light to you. There is no light for any man except in Christ. And until you believe in Him, thick darkness shall blind you and you shall stumble in it and perish! That is the lesson I would have you learn.

Another practical lesson is this, **if we are in the dark at this time; if our spirits are sunk in gloom, let us not despair, for the Lord Christ, Himself, was there**. If I have fallen into misery on account of sin, let me not give up all hope, for the Father's Well-Beloved passed through denser darkness than mine. O believing Soul, if you are in the dark, you are near the King's cellars and there are wines on the lees well refined lying there. You have gotten into the pavilion of the Lord and now may you speak with Him. You will not find Christ in the gaudy tents of pride, nor in the foul haunts of wickedness. You will not find Him where the viol and the dance and the flowing bowl inflame the lusts of men. But in the house of mourning you will meet the Man of Sorrows. He is not where Herodias dances, nor where Bernice displays her charms. He is where the woman of a sorrowful spirit moves her lips in prayer. He is never absent where penitence sits in darkness and bewails her faults: *"Yes, Lord, in hours of gloom, /When shadows fill my room/When pain breathes forth its groans, And grief its sighs and moans, Then You are near."*

If you are under a cloud, feel for your Lord, if haply you may find Him. Stand still in your black sorrow and say, "O Lord, the preacher tells me that Your Cross once stood in such darkness as this, O Jesus hear me." He will respond to you, the Lord will look out of the pillar of cloud and shed a light upon you. "I know their sorrows," He says. He is no stranger to heart-break. Christ also once suffered for sin. Trust Him

178

and He will cause His light to shine upon you. **Lean upon Him and He will bring you up out of the gloomy wilderness into the land of rest. God help you to do so.**

Last Monday, I was cheered beyond all I can tell you by a letter from a Brother who had been restored to life, light, and liberty by the discourse of last Sabbath morning [Refer to *Love Abounding, Love Complaining, Love Abiding,* Sermon No. 1895]. I know no greater joy than to be useful to your souls. For this reason, I have tried to preach, this morning, though I am physically quite unfit for it. Oh, I do pray I may hear more news from saved ones. Oh that some spirit that has wandered out into the dark moorland may spy the candle in my window and find its way home.

EXHORTATION: If you have found my Lord, I charge you, never let Him go, but cleave to Him till the day breaks and the shadows flee away. God help you so to do for Jesus' sake. Amen.

5. [God Forsaking His Son], "Why have you forsaken me?"

"And about the ninth hour Jesus cried out with a loud voice, saying, 'Eli, Eli, lama sabachthani?' that is, 'My God, My God, why have You forsaken Me?'"
(Matthew 27:46 NKJV).

FOCUS: **"Our first subject of thought will be the fact, or what He suffered, God had forsaken Him; second, we will note the inquiry, or why He suffered, this word, "why," is the edge of the text. "Why have You forsaken Me?" Then, third, we will consider the answer, or what came to His suffering. The answer flowed softly into the soul of the Lord Jesus without the need of words, for He ceased from His anguish with the triumphant shout of, "It is finished." His work was finished and His bearing of desertion was a chief part of the work He had undertaken for our sake."**

"THERE was darkness over all the land unto the ninth hour," this cry came out of that darkness. Expect not to see through its every word, as though it came from on high as a beam from the unclouded Sun of Righteousness. There is light in it, bright, flashing light, but there is a center of impenetrable gloom where the soul is ready to faint because of the terrible darkness. **Our Lord was then in the darkest part of His way. He had trodden the winepress now for hours and the work was almost finished.** He had reached the culminating point of His anguish. This is His dolorous lament from the lowest pit of misery, "My God, My God, why have You forsaken Me?"

I do not think that the records of time, or even of eternity, contain a sentence fuller of anguish. Here the wormwood, the gall and all the other bitterness are outdone. Here you may look as into a vast abyss, and though you strain your eyes and gaze till sight fails you, yet you perceive no bottom, it is measureless, unfathomable, and inconceivable. **This anguish of the Savior on your behalf and mine is no more to be measured and weighed than the sin which needed it, or the love which endured it. We will adore where we cannot comprehend.**

I have chosen this subject that it may help the children of God to understand a little of their infinite obligations to their redeeming Lord. You shall measure the height of His love, if it can be measured, by the depth of His grief, if that can ever be known. See with what a price He has redeemed us from the curse of the Law. As you see this, say to yourselves, What manner of people ought we to be? What measure of love ought we to return to One who bore the utmost penalty that we might be delivered from the wrath to come? I do not profess that I can dive *into* this deep, I will only venture to the edge of the precipice and bid you look down and pray the Spirit of God to concentrate your mind upon this lamentation of our dying Lord as it rises up through the thick darkness, "My God, My God, why have You forsaken Me?"

A. *By the help of the Holy Spirit let us first dwell upon, THE FACT or what our Lord suffered. God had forsaken Him.* Grief of mind is harder to bear than pain of body. You can pluck up courage and endure the pang of sickness and pain so long as the spirit is hale and brave. But if the soul itself is touched and the mind becomes diseased with anguish, then every pain is increased in severity and there is nothing with which to sustain it. Spiritual sorrows are the worst of mental miseries.

A man may bear great depression of spirit about worldly matters if he feels that he has his God to go to. He is cast down, but not in despair. Like David he dialogues with himself and he inquires, "Why are you cast down, O my Soul? And why are you disquieted in me? Hope you in God: for I shall yet praise Him." But if the Lord is once withdrawn, if the comfortable light of His Presence is shadowed even for an *hour*, there is a torment within the breast which I can only liken to the prelude of Hell. **This is the greatest of all weights that can press upon the heart.** This made the Psalmist plead, "Hide not Your face from me! Put not Your servant away in anger."

We can bear a bleeding body and even a wounded spirit **but a soul conscious of desertion by God is beyond conception unendurable!** When He holds back the face of His Throne and spreads His cloud upon it, who can endure the darkness? This voice out of "the belly of Hell" marks the lowest depth of the Savior's grief. *The desertion was real.* Though under some aspects our Lord could say, "The Father is with Me," yet was it solemnly true that God did forsake Him. **It was not a failure of faith on His part which led Him to imagine what not actual fact was.** Our faith fails us and then we think that God has forsaken us, but our Lord's faith did not, for a moment, falter, for He says twice, "*My* God, *My* God."

Oh, the mighty double grip of His unhesitating faith! He seems to say, "Even if You have forsaken Me, I have not forsaken You." Faith triumphs and there is no sign of any faintness of heart towards the living God. Yet, strong as is His faith, He feels that God has withdrawn His comfortable fellowship and He shivers under the terrible deprivation. It was no fancy or delirium of mind caused by His weakness of body, the heat of the fever, the depression of His spirit or the near approach of death. He was clear of mind even to this last. **He bore up under pain, loss of blood, scorn, thirst and desolation, making no complaint of the Cross, the nails or the scoffing.**

We read not in the Gospels of anything more than the natural cry of weakness, "I thirst." All the tortures of His Body He endured in silence. But when it came to being forsaken of God, *then* His great heart burst out into its "Lama Sabachthani?" His one moan is concerning His God! It is not, "Why has Peter forsaken Me? Why has Judas betrayed Me?" These were sharp griefs, but this is the sharpest. **This stroke has cut Him to the quick, "My God, My God, why have *You* forsaken Me?"**

It was no phantom of the gloom; it was a real absence which He mourned. **This was *a very remarkable desertion*. It is not the way of God to leave either His sons or His servants.** His saints, when they come to die in their great weakness and pain, find Him near. They are made to sing because of the Presence of God "Yes, though I walk through the valley of the shadow of death, I will fear no evil: for You are with me." Dying saints have clear visions of the living God. **Our observation has taught us that if the Lord is away at other times, He is *never* absent from His people in the article of death or in the furnace of affliction.**

Concerning the three holy children we do not read that the Lord was ever visibly with them till they walked the fires of Nebuchadnezzar's furnace, but then and there the Lord met with them. Yes, Beloved, **it is God's way and habit to keep company with His afflicted people.** And yet He forsook His Son in the hour of His tribulation. How usual it is to see the Lord with His faithful witnesses when resisting even unto blood. Read the Book of Martyrs and I care not whether you study the former or the later persecutions, you will find them all lit up with the evident Presence of the Lord with His witnesses.

Did the Lord ever fail to support a martyr at the stake? Did He ever forsake one of His testifiers upon the scaffold? **The testimony of the Church has always been that while the Lord has permitted His saints to suffer in body He has so divinely sustained their spirits** that they have been more than conquerors and have treated their sufferings as light afflictions! The fire has not been a "bed of roses," but it has been a chariot of victory. The sword is sharp and death is bitter, but the love of Christ is sweet and to die for Him has been turned into glory. No, it is not God's way to forsake His champions nor to leave even the least of His children in their hour of trial.

As to our Lord, this forsaking was *singular*. Did His Father ever leave Him before? Will you read the four Evangelists through and find any previous instance in which He complains of His Father for having forsaken Him? No. He said, "I know that you hear Me always." **He lived in constant touch with God. His fellowship with the Father was always near and dear and clear**. But now, for the first time, He cries, "Why have You forsaken Me?" It was very remarkable. It was a riddle only to be solved by the fact that He loved us and gave Himself for us and in the execution of His loving purpose came even unto this sorrow of mourning the absence of His God.

This forsaking was *very terrible*. Who can fully tell what it is to be forsaken of God? We can only form a guess by what we have ourselves felt under temporary and partial desertion. **God has never left us altogether, for He has expressly said, "I will never leave you, nor forsake you."** Yet we have sometimes felt as if He had cast us off. We have cried, "Oh, that I knew where I might find Him." The clear shining rays of His love have been withdrawn. Thus we are able to form some little idea of how the Savior felt when His God had forsaken Him.

The mind of Jesus was left to dwell upon one dark subject and no cheering theme consoled Him. **It was the hour in which He was made to stand before God as consciously the Sin-Bearer according to that ancient prophecy**, *"He shall bear their iniquities."* Then was it true, *"He has made Him to be sin for us."* Peter puts it, *"He His own self bore our sins in His own body on the tree."* Sin, sin, sin was everywhere around and about Christ. He had no sin of His own but the Lord had "laid on Him the iniquity of us all." He had no strength given Him from on high, no secret oil and wine poured into His wounds, He was made to appear in the lone Character of the Lamb of God which takes away the sin of the world, and therefore He must feel the weight of sin and the turning away of that sacred face which cannot look thereon.

His Father, at that time, gave Him no open acknowledgment. On certain other occasions a voice had been heard, saying, *"This is My Beloved Son, in whom I am well pleased."* But now, when such a testimony seemed most of all required, the oracle was not there. He was hung up as an accursed Thing upon the Cross, for He was *"made a curse for us, as it is written, Cursed is everyone that hangs on a tree."*

And the Lord His God did not own Him before men. If it had pleased the Father He might have sent Him twelve legions of angels, but not an angel came after Christ had left Gethsemane. His despisers might spit in His face but no swift seraph came to avenge the indignity. They might bind Him and scourge Him, but none of all the heavenly host would interpose to screen His shoulders from the lash. They might fasten him to the tree with nails and lift Him up and scoff at Him, but no cohort of ministering spirits hastened to drive back the rabble and release the Prince of Life. **No, He appeared to be forsaken, "smitten of God and afflicted," delivered into the hands of cruel men whose wicked hands worked Him misery without stint.** Well might He ask, "My God, My God, why have You forsaken Me?"

But this was not all. His Father now dried up that sacred stream of peaceful communion and loving fellowship which had flowed, up to now, throughout His whole earthly life. He said, Himself, as you remember, *"You shall be scattered, every man to His own, and shall leave Me alone: and yet I am not alone, because the Father is with Me."* Here was His constant comfort, but all comfort from this Source was to be withdrawn. The Divine Spirit did not minister to His human spirit. No communications with His Father's love poured into His heart. It was not possible that the Judge should smile upon One who represented the prisoner at the bar.

Our Lord's *faith* did not fail Him, as I have already shown you, for He said, "My God, My God," yet no sensible supports were given to His heart and no comforts were poured into His mind. One writer declares that Jesus did not taste of Divine wrath but only suffered a withdrawal of Divine fellowship. What is the difference? Whether God withdraws heat or creates cold is all the same. He was not smiled upon, nor allowed to feel that He was near to God, and this, to His tender spirit, was grief of the keenest order.

A certain saint once said that in his sorrow he had from God, "that which was meet, but not that which was sweet." Our Lord suffered to the extreme point of deprivation. He had not the light which makes existence to be life and life to be a blessing. You who know, in your degree, what it is to lose the conscious Presence and love of God, you can faintly guess what the sorrow of the Savior was now that He felt He had been forsaken of His God. "If the foundations are removed, what can the righteous do?" To our Lord, the Father's love was the foundation of *everything,* and when that was gone, all was gone. Nothing remained, within, without, above, when His Own God, the God of His entire confidence, turned from Him.

Yes, God in very deed forsook our Savior. **To be forsaken of God was *much more a source of anguish to Jesus than it would be to us.*** "Oh," you say, "how is that?" I answer because He was perfectly holy. A rupture between a perfectly holy Being and the thrice holy God must be in the highest degree strange, abnormal, perplexing and painful. If any man here who is not at peace with God could only know His true condition, he would swoon with fright. If your unforgiven ones only knew where you are and what you are at this moment, in the sight of God, you would never smile again till you were reconciled to Him. Alas, we are insensible, hardened by the deceitfulness of sin and therefore we do not feel our true condition.

His perfect holiness made it to our Lord a dreadful calamity to be forsaken of the thrice holy God. I remember, also, that our blessed Lord had lived in unbroken fellowship with God and to be forsaken was a new grief to Him. He had never known what the dark was till then, His life had been lived in the light of God. Think, dear child of God, if you had always dwelt in full communion with God, your days would have been as the days of Heaven upon earth! And how cold it would strike your heart to find yourself in the darkness of desertion. If you can conceive such a thing as happening to a *perfect* man, you can see why, to our Well-Beloved, it was a special trial.

Remember, He had enjoyed fellowship with God more richly, as well as more constantly, than any of us. **His fellowship with the Father was of the highest, deepest, fullest order and what must the loss of it have been?** We lose but drops when we lose our joyful experience of heavenly fellowship, and yet the loss is killing. But to our Lord Jesus Christ the sea was dried up, I mean His sea of fellowship with the Infinite God. Do not forget that He was such a One that to Him to be without God must have been an overwhelming calamity. In every part He was perfect and in every part fitted for communion with God to a supreme degree.

A sinful man has an awful need of God, but he does not know it and therefore he does not feel that hunger and thirst after God which would come upon a perfect man could he be deprived of God. The very perfection of his nature renders it inevitable that the holy man must either be in communion with God or be desolate. Imagine a stray angel, a seraph who has lost His God. Conceive him to be perfect in holiness and yet to have fallen into a condition in which he cannot find His God. I cannot picture him. Perhaps Milton might have done so. He is sinless and trustful and yet he has an overpowering feeling that God is absent from him.

He has drifted into the nowhere, the unimaginable region behind the back of God. I think I hear the wailing of the cherub, "My God, my God, my God, where are You?" What a sorrow for one of the sons of the morning. But here we have the lament of a Being far more capable of fellowship with the Godhead. In proportion as He is more fitted to receive the love of the great Father, in that proportion is His pining after it the more intense. **As a Son, He is abler to commune with God than ever a servant angel could be, and now that He is forsaken of God, the void within is greater and the anguish more bitter.**

Our Lord's heart and all His Nature were, morally and spiritually, so delicately formed, so sensitive, so tender, that to be without God was to Him a grief which could not be weighed. I see

Him in the text bearing desertion and yet I perceive that He cannot bear it. I know not how to express my meaning except by such a paradox. He cannot endure to be without God. He had surrendered Himself to be left of God, as the representative of sinners must be, but His pure and holy Nature, after three hours of silence, finds the position unendurable to love and purity. And breaking forth from it, now that the hour was over, He exclaims, "Why have You forsaken Me?"

He quarrels not with the suffering, but He cannot abide in the position which caused it. He seems as if He must end the ordeal, not because of the pain, but because of the moral shock. We have here the repetition after His passion of that loathing which He felt before it, when He cried, *"If it is possible let this cup pass from Me: nevertheless, not as I will, but as You will." "My God, My God, why have You forsaken Me?"* is the holiness of Christ amazed at the position of Substitute for guilty men.

There, Friends. I have done my best, but I seem to myself to have been prattling like a little child talking about something infinitely above me. So I leave the solemn fact that our Lord Jesus was on the Cross forsaken of His God.

B. This brings us to consider **THE INQUIRY**, or *why* He suffered. Note carefully this cry, "My God, My God, why have You forsaken Me?" It is pure anguish, undiluted agony, which cries like this, but it is the agony of a godly soul, for only a man of that order would have used such an expression.

Let us let from it useful lessons. This cry is taken from "the Book." Does it not show our Lord's love of the sacred volume, that when He felt His sharpest grief, He turned to the Scripture to find a fit utterance for it? Here we have the opening sentence of the 22nd Psalm. Oh that we may so **love the inspired Word** that we may not only sing to its score but even weep to its music. Note, again, that our Lord's lament is an address to *God*. The godly, in their anguish, turn to the hand which smites them.

The Savior's outcry is not *against* God, but *to* God. "My God, My God": He makes a double effort to draw near. True Sonship is here! The child in the dark is crying after His Father, "My God, My God." Both the Bible and prayer were dear to Jesus in His agony. Still, observe it is a faith-cry, for though it asks, "Why have You forsaken Me?" it first says, twice, "My God, My God." The grip of appropriation is in the word "My." But the reverence of humility is in the word, "God." It is, "My *God*, My *God*, You are ever God to Me, and I a poor creature. I do not quarrel with You. Your rights are unquestioned, for You are My God. You can do as You will and I yield to Your sacred sovereignty. I kiss the hand that smites Me, and with all My heart I cry, 'My God, My God.'"

When you are delirious with pain, think of your Bible when your mind wonders, let it roam towards the Mercy Seat, and when your heart and your flesh fail, still live by faith and still cry, "My God, my God." Let us come close to the inquiry. It looked to me, at first sight, like a question as of one distraught, driven from the balance of His mind, not unreasonable, but too much reasoning and therefore tossed about. "Why have You forsaken Me?" Did not Jesus know? Did He not know why He was forsaken? He knew it most distinctly and yet His *Manhood*, while it was being crushed, pounded and dissolved, seemed as though it could not understand the reason for so great a grief.

He must be forsaken, but could there be a sufficient cause for so sickening a sorrow? The cup must be bitter, but why this most nauseous of ingredients? I tremble lest I say what I ought not to say. I have said it and I think there is truth, the Man of Sorrows was overborne with horror. At that moment the finite soul of the Man Christ Jesus came into awful contact with the infinite Justice of God. The one Mediator between God and man, the Man Christ Jesus, beheld the holiness of God in arms against the sin of man whose nature He had espoused.

God was for Him and with Him in a certain unquestionable sense, but for the time, so far as His feelings went, God was against Him and necessarily withdrawn from Him. It is not surprising that the holy Soul of Christ should shudder at finding itself brought into painful contact with the infinite Justice of God, even though its design was only to vindicate that Justice and glorify the Law-Giver. Our Lord could now say, "All Your waves and Your billows are gone over Me," and therefore He uses language which is all too hot with anguish to be dissected by the cold hand of a logical criticism.

Grief has small regard for the laws of the grammarian. Even the holiest, when in extreme agony, though they cannot speak otherwise than according to purity and truth, yet use a language of their own which only the ear of sympathy can fully receive. I see not all that is here, but what I can see I am not able to put in words for you. *I think I see in the expression, submission and resolve.* Our Lord does not draw back. There is a forward movement in the question, they who quit a business ask no more questions about it. He does not ask that the forsaking may end prematurely, He would only understand anew its meaning. He does not shrink, but dedicates Himself anew to God by the words, "My God, My God," and by seeking to review the ground and reason of that anguish which He is resolute to bear even to the bitter end.

He would gladly feel anew the motive which has sustained Him and must sustain Him to the end. The cry sounds to me like deep submission and strong resolve, pleading with God. Do you not think that *the amazement of our Lord, when He was "made sin for us"* (2 Cor. 5:21), led Him thus to cry out? **For such a sacred and pure Being to be made a Sin-Offering was an amazing experience! Sin was laid on Him and He was treated as if He had been guilty, though He had personally** *never sinned*.

And now the infinite horror of rebellion against the most holy God fills His Holy Soul, the unrighteousness of sin breaks His heart and He starts back from it, crying, "My God, My God, why have You forsaken *Me?*" Why must I bear the dread result of conduct I so much abhor? Do you not see, moreover, *there was here a glance at His eternal purpose and at His Secret Source of joy?* That "why" is the silver lining of the dark cloud and our Lord looked wishfully at it. He knew that the desertion was necessary in order that He might save the guilty and He had an eye to that salvation as His comfort.

He is not forsaken needlessly, nor without a worthy design. The design is in itself so dear to His heart that He yields to the passing evil, even though that evil is like death to Him. He looks at that "why," and through that narrow window the light of Heaven comes streaming into His darkened life. "My God, My God, why have You forsaken Me?" Surely our Lord dwelt on that, "why," *that we might also turn our eyes that way*. He would have us see the why and the why of His grief. He would have us mark the gracious motive for its endurance. Think much of all your Lord suffered, but do not overlook the *reason* for it. If you cannot always understand how this or that grief worked toward the great end of the whole passion, yet believe that it has its share in the grand, "why." ***Make a life-study of that bitter but blessed question, "Why have You forsaken Me?"***

Thus the Savior raises an inquiry not so much for Himself as for *us* and not so much because of any despair within *His* heart as because of a hope and a joy set before Him which were wells of comfort to Him in His wilderness of woe. Think, for a moment, that the Lord God, in the broadest and most unreserved sense, could never, in very deed, have forsaken His most obedient Son. **He was ever with Him in the grand design of salvation.** Towards the Lord Jesus, personally, God Himself, personally, must ever have stood on terms of infinite love. Truly the Only Begotten was never more lovely to the Father than when He was obedient unto death, even the death of the Cross.

But we must look upon God here as the Judge of all the earth and we must look upon the Lord Jesus in His official capacity as the Surety of the Covenant and the Sacrifice for sin. The great Judge of all cannot smile upon Him who has become the Substitute for the guilty. Sin is loathed of God and if, in order to its removal, His own Son is made to bear it, yet, as sin, it is still loathsome and He who bears it cannot be in happy communion with God. This was the dread necessity of expiation, but in the *essence* of things the love of the great Father to His Son never ceased, nor ever knew a diminution. Restrained in its flow it must be, but lessened at its fountainhead it could not be. Therefore, wonder not at the question, "Why have You forsaken Me?"

190

C. Hoping to be guided by the Holy Spirit, I am coming to **THE ANSWER** concerning which I can only use the few minutes which remain to me. "My God, My God, why have You forsaken Me?" What is the outcome of this suffering? What was the reason for it? Our Savior could answer His own question. If for a moment His Manhood was perplexed, yet His mind soon came to clear apprehension for He said, "It is finished." And as I have already said, He then referred to the work which in His lonely agony He had been performing.

Why, then, did God forsake His Son? I cannot conceive any other answer than this, *He stood in our place.* There was no reason in Christ why the Father should forsake Him, He was *perfect* and His life was without spot. God never acts without reason and since there were no reasons in the Character and Person of the Lord Jesus why His Father should forsake Him, we must look elsewhere. I do not know how others answer the question. I can only answer it in this one way: *"All the griefs He felt were ours, / Ours were the woes He bore. Pang not His own, /His spotless soul/With bitter anguish bore. /We held Him as condemned of Heaven/An outcast from His God/While for our sins He groaned, He bled, / Beneath His Father's rod."*
He bore the sinner's sin and He had to be treated, therefore, as though He were a sinner, though sinner He could never be. With His own full consent, He suffered as though He had committed the transgressions which were laid on Him. Our sin and His taking it upon Himself is the answer to the question, "Why have You forsaken Me?"
In this case we now see that *His obedience was perfect.* He came into the world to obey the Father and He rendered that obedience to the very uttermost. The spirit of obedience could go no farther than for one who feels forsaken of God still to cling to Him in solemn, avowed allegiance, still declaring before a mocking multitude His confidence in the afflicting God! It is noble to cry, "My God, My God," when One is asking, "Why have You forsaken He?" How much farther can obedience go? I see nothing beyond it. The soldier at the gate of

Pompeii, remaining at his post as sentry when the shower of burning ashes was falling, was not more true to his trust than He who adheres to a forsaking God with loyalty of hope.

Our Lord's suffering in this particular form was appropriate and necessary. It would not have sufficed for our Lord merely to have been pained in body, nor even to have been grieved in mind in other ways; He must suffer in this particular way. He must feel forsaken of God because *this* is the necessary consequence of sin. For a man to be forsaken of God is the penalty which naturally and inevitably follows upon his breaking his relationship with God. What is death? What was the death that was threatened to Adam? "In the day that you eat thereof you shall surely die." Is death annihilation? Was Adam annihilated that day?

Assuredly not. He lived many a year afterwards. But in the day in which he ate of the forbidden fruit he died by being *separated* from God. The separation of the soul from God is *spiritual* death, just as the separation of the soul from the body is *natural* death. The sacrifice for sin must be put in the place of separation and must bow to the penalty of death. By this placing of the Great Sacrifice under forsaking and death, it would be seen by all creatures throughout the universe that God cannot have fellowship with sin. If even the Holy One, who stood the Just for the unjust, found God forsaking Him, what must the doom of the actual sinner be? Sin is evidently always, in every case, a dividing influence, putting even the Christ Himself, as a Sin-Bearer, in the place of distance.

This was necessary for another reason, there could have been no laying on of suffering for sin without the forsaking of the vicarious Sacrifice by the Lord God. So long as the smile of God rests on the man, the Law is not afflicting him. **The approving look of the great Judge cannot fall upon a man who is viewed as standing in the place of the guilty.** Christ not only suffered *from* sin, but *for* sin. If God will cheer and sustain Him, He is not suffering for sin. The Judge is not inflicting suffering for sin if He is manifestly encouraging the smitten One. There could have been no vicarious suffering on the part of Christ for human guilt if He had continued, consciously, to enjoy the full sunshine of the

Father's Presence. It was essential to being a Victim in our place that He should cry, "My God, My God, why have You forsaken Me?"

Beloved, see how marvelously, in the Person of Christ, the Lord our God has vindicated His Law? If to make His Law Glorious He had said, "These multitudes of men have broken My Law and therefore they shall perish," the Law would have been terribly magnified. But, instead, He says, "Here is My Only Begotten Son, My other Self, He takes on Himself the Nature of these rebellious creatures and He consents that I should lay on Him the load of their iniquity and visit in His Person the offenses which might have been punished in the persons of all these multitudes of men and I will have it so."

When Jesus bows His head to the stroke of the Law, when He submissively consents that His Father shall turn away His face from Him, then myriads of worlds are astonished at the perfect holiness and stern justice of the Lawgiver! There are, probably, worlds innumerable throughout the boundless creation of God and all these will see, in the death of God's dear Son, a declaration of His determination never to allow sin to be trifled with! If His own Son is brought before Him, bearing the sin of others upon Him, He will hide His face from Him as well as from the actually guilty. **In God infinite Love shines over all, but it does not eclipse His Absolute Justice any more than His Justice is permitted to destroy His Love. God has all perfections in Perfection and in Christ Jesus we see the reflection of them.**

Beloved, this is a wonderful theme. Oh, that I had a tongue worthy of this subject. But who could ever reach the height of this great argument? Once more, when inquiring, "Why did Jesus suffer to be forsaken of the Father?" we see the fact that *the Captain of our salvation was thus made perfect through suffering.* Every part of the road has been traversed by our Lord's own feet. Suppose, Beloved, the Lord Jesus had never been thus forsaken? Then one of His disciples might have been called to that sharp endurance and the Lord Jesus could not have sympathized with him in it.

He would turn to His Leader and Captain and say to Him, "Did You, my Lord, ever feel this darkness?" Then the Lord Jesus would answer, "No. This is a descent such as I never made." What a dreadful lack would the tried one have felt! For the servant to bear a grief his Master never knew would be sad, indeed. There would have been a wound for which there was no ointment, a pain for which there was no balm. But it is not so now. "In all their affliction He was afflicted." "He was in all points tempted like as we are, yet without sin." Whereas we greatly rejoice at this time and as often as we are cast down, underneath us is the deep experience of our forsaken Lord.

I have done when I have said three things. **The first is, you and I that are Believers in the Lord Jesus Christ and are resting in Him alone for salvation, *let us lean hard.* Let us bear all our weight on our Lord. He will bear the full weight of all our sin and care. As to my sin, I hear its harsh accusations no more when I hear Jesus cry, "Why have You forsaken Me?"** I know that I deserve the deepest Hell at the hand of God's vengeance but I am not afraid! **He will never forsake *me*, for He *forsook His Son on my behalf.*** I shall not suffer for my sin, for Jesus has suffered to the full in my place, yes, suffered so far as to cry, "My God, My God, why have You forsaken Me?" Behind this brazen wall of Substitution, a sinner is safe. These "munitions of rock" guard all Believers and they may rest secure. The rock is cleft for me, I hide in its rifts and no harm can reach me. You have a full Atonement, a great Sacrifice, a glorious vindication of the Law, you can rest at peace, all you that put your trust in Jesus.

Next, if ever, from now on, in our lives we should think that God has deserted us, *let us learn from our Lord's example how to behave ourselves. If God has left you, do not shut up your Bible; no, open it as your Lord did and find a text that will suit you.* If God has left you, or you think so, do not give up prayer. No, pray as your Lord did and be more earnest than ever. If you think God has forsaken you, do not give up your faith in Him, but, like your Lord, cry, "My God, my God," again and again! If you have had one anchor before, cast out two anchors now and double the hold of your faith. If you cannot call Jehovah, "Father," as was Christ's habit, yet call Him your "God."

Let the personal pronouns take their hold: "My God, my God." Let nothing drive you from your faith. Still hold on Jesus, sink or swim. As for me, if ever I am lost it shall be at the foot of the Cross. To this pass have I come, that if I never see the face of God with acceptance, yet I will believe that He will be faithful to His Son and true to the Covenant sealed by oaths and blood. He that believes in Jesus has everlasting life, there I cling, like the limpet to the rock. There is but one gate of Heaven and even if I may not enter it, I will cling to the posts of its door! What am I saying? I shall enter in for that gate was never shut against a soul that accepted Jesus! And Jesus says, "Him that comes to Me I will in no wise cast out."

The last of the three points is this, *let us abhor the sin which brought such agony upon our Beloved Lord.* What an accursed thing is sin which crucified the Lord Jesus! Do you laugh at it? Will you go and spend an evening to see a mimic performance of it? Do you roll sin under your tongue as a sweet morsel and then come to God's house on the Lord's-Day morning and think to worship Him? Worship Him? Worship Him with sin indulged in your breast? Worship Him with sin loved and pampered in your life? O Sirs, if I had a dear brother who had been murdered, what would you think of me if I valued the knife which had been crimsoned with his blood, if I made a friend of the murderer and daily consorted with the assassin who drove the dagger into my brother's heart?

Surely I, too, must be an accomplice in the crime. Sin murdered Christ; will you be a friend to it? Sin pierced the heart of the Incarnate God; can you love it? Oh that there was an abyss as deep as Christ's misery, that I might at once hurl this dagger of sin into its depths where it might never be brought to light again. Begone, O Sin! You are banished from the heart where Jesus reigns Begone, for you have crucified my Lord and made Him cry, "Why have You forsaken Me?"

EXHORTATION: O my Hearers, if you did but know yourselves and know the love of Christ, you would each one vow that you would harbor sin no longer. You would be indignant at sin and cry: "The dearest idol I have known, / Whatever that idol is, Lord, / I will tear it from its throne, / And worship only You."

May that be the issue of my morning's discourse and then I shall be well content. The Lord bless you! May the Christ who suffered for you bless you, and out of His darkness may your light arise. Amen.

6.   Exposition on Matthew 27:27–54

*Verses 27–30. **Then the soldiers of the governor took Jesus into the common hall and gathered unto Him the whole band of soldiers. And they stripped Him, and put on Him a scarlet robe. And when they had platted a crown of thorns, they put it upon His head, and a reed in His right hand, and they bowed the knee before Him and mocked Him, saying, Hail, King of the Jew.! And they spit upon Him, and took the reed, and smote Him on the head.***

These soldiers were men to whom the taking of human life was mere amusement, or, at best, a duty to be performed. If the ordinary Roman citizen found his greatest delight in the amphitheater where men fiercely fought with each other, and shed each other's blood, or were devoured by wild beasts, you may imagine what Roman soldiers, the roughest part of the whole population, would be like! And now that One was given up into their hands, charged with making Himself a king, you can conceive what a subject for jest it was to them and how they determined to make all the mockery they could of this pretended king! They were not touched by the gentleness of His demeanor, nor by His Sorrowful Countenance, but they proceeded to pour all possible scorn and insult upon His devoted head. Surely the world never saw a more horrible scene than this, the King of Kings derided and made nothing of, treated as a mimic monarch by the very vilest and most brutal of men.

*31. **And after that they had mocked Him, they took the robe off Him and put His own raiment on Him, and led Him away to crucify Him.***

Their action, in restoring to Him His own seamless robe, was ordained by God, whatever their motive may have been, so that nobody might say that some other person had been substituted for the Savior. He went forth wearing that well-known garment which was woven from the top throughout, which He had always worn. And all who looked upon Him said, "It is He—the Nazarene. We know His face, His dress, His Person." There was no possibility of mistaking Him for anybody else.

32. *And as they came out, they found a man of Cyrene, Simon by name: him they compelled to bear His Cross.*

It was too heavy for Him to carry alone, so they bade Simon help Him and, truly, I think that Simon was thereby highly honored. If this was Simon, who is called Niger, then there may be some truth in the common belief that he was a black man and, assuredly, the Black race has long had to carry a very heavy Cross, yet there may be a great destiny before it. All Christ's followers are called to be Cross-bearers: *"Shall Simon bear the Cross alone, /And all the rest go free? /No, there's a cross for everyone, /And there's a cross for me."* If we belong to Christ, we must be as willing to take up His Cross as He was to carry ours and die upon it.

33, 34. *And when they were come unto a place called Golgotha, that is to say a place of a skull, they gave Him vinegar to drink mingled with gall: and when He had tasted thereof, He would not drink.*

It was not because of its bitterness that our Lord refused it, for He did not decline to endure anything that would add to His grief. But this was a stupefying draught, a death potion, which was given to those who were executed, in order to somewhat mitigate their pains. But the Savior did not intend that His senses should be beclouded by any such draught as that, so, "when He had tasted thereof, He would not drink."

35. *And they crucified Him.*

A short sentence, but what an awful depth of meaning there is in it. "They crucified Him," driving their iron bolts through His hands and feet, and lifting Him up to hang upon the gallows which was reserved for felons and for slaves. "They crucified Him."

35. *And parted His garments, casting lots: that it might be fulfilled which was spoken by the Prophet, They parted My garments among them, and upon My vesture did you cast lots.*

It was the executioners' perquisite to have the garments of the man they put to death, so, in order that no single portion of the shame of the Cross might be spared to the Savior, these soldiers divided His garments among them and raffled for His seamless robe. It must have taken a hard heart to gamble at the foot of the Cross, but I suppose that, of all sins under Heaven, there is none that does so harden the heart as gambling. Beware of it.

36. *And sitting down they watched Him there.*

Some to gloat, in their fiendish malice, over His sufferings. Others to make sure that He did really die and, possibly, some few to pity Him in His agony. "Sitting down they watched Him there."

37–44. *And set up over His head the accusation written against Him, THIS IS JESUS THE KING OF THE JEWS.*

Then were there two thieves crucified with Him, one on the right hand, and another on the left. And they that passed by reviled Him, wagging their heads, and saying, You that destroy the Temple, and build it in three days, save Yourself. If You are the Son of God, come down from the Cross. Likewise, also the chief priest's mocking Him, with the scribes and elders, said, He saved others; Himself He cannot save. If

He is the King of Israel, let Him now come down from the Cross, and we will believe Him. He trusted in God: let Him deliver Him now, if He will have Him: for He said, I am the Son of God. The thieves also, which were crucified with Him, cast the same in His teeth. So that, as He looked all around, He met with nothing but ribaldry, jest and scorn. His disciples had all forsaken Him. One or two of them afterwards rallied a little and came and stood by the Cross, but, just then, He looked and there was none to pity, and none to help Him, even as it had been foretold.

45. *Now from the sixth hour there was darkness over all the land unto the ninth hour.*

From twelve o'clock at noon, according to the Roman and Jewish time, till three in the afternoon, there was a thick darkness, whether over all the world, or only over the land of Palestine, we cannot very well say. It was not an eclipse of the sun; it was a miracle especially worked by God. Some have supposed that dense clouds came rolling up obscuring everything, but, whatever it was, deep darkness came over all the land. Dore has, in his wonderful imagination, given us a sketch of Jerusalem during that darkness. The inhabitants are all trembling at what they had done and, as Judas goes down the street, they point at him as the man who sold his Master and brought all this evil upon the city. I should think that such darkness at midday must have made them fear that the last day had come, or that some great judgment would overtake them for their wicked slaughter of the innocent Jesus of Nazareth. Even the sun could no longer look upon its Maker surrounded by those who mocked Him, so it traveled on in tenfold night, as if in very shame that the great Sun of Righteousness should Himself be in such awful darkness.

46-48. *And about the ninth hour Jesus cried with a load voice, saying, Eli, Eli, lama Sabachthani, that is to say, My God, My God, why have You forsaken Me?*

Some of them that stood there, when they heard that, said, This Man calls for Elijah. And straightway one of them ran and took a sponge, and filled it with vinegar, and put it on a reed, and gave Him to drink. For He had also said, "I thirst," which John records, specially mentioning that He said this, "that the Scripture might be fulfilled."

49–51. The rest said, Let Him be, let us see whether Elijah will come to save Him. Jesus, when He had cried again with a loud voice, yielded up the ghost. And, behold, the veil of the Temple was rent in twain from the top to the bottom.

That rending of the great veil of the Temple was intended to symbolize the end of Judaism. The horror of the sanctuary that its Lord was put to death. The opening of the mysteries of Heaven. The clearing of the way of access between man and God.

51. And the earth did quake, and the rocks rent.

Well says our poet: *"Of feeling, all things show some sign /But this unfeeling heart of mine."*

52–54. And the graves were opened; and many bodies of the saints which slept, arose, and came out of the graves after His Resurrection, and went into the holy city, and appeared unto many. Now when the centurion, and they that were with Him, watching Jesus, saw the earthquake, and those things that were done, they feared greatly, saying, truly this was the Son of God.

E. Words of Suffering

1. His Shortest Cry

"After this, Jesus, knowing that all things
were now accomplished, that the Scripture
might be fulfilled, said, 'I thirst!'"
(John 19:28 NKJV).

FOCUS: The text is viewed at in four ways (as 'the Spirit of God instructs'): First, as the ensign of His true humanity. Second, as the token of His suffering substitution. Third, as a type of man's treatment of his Lord. Fourth, as the mystical expression of the desire of His heart. Lastly, "the cry of, 'I thirst,' is to us the pattern of our death with Him." To those that know the Lord Jesus Christ, we are crucified together with Him.

IT was most fitting that every word of our Lord upon the Cross should be gathered up and preserved. As not a bone of His shall be broken, so not a word shall be lost. The Holy Spirit took special care that each of the sacred utterances should be fittingly recorded. There were, as you know, seven of those last words and seven is the number of perfection and fullness, the number which blends the three of the infinite God with the four of complete creation. Our Lord, in His death-cries, as in all else, was perfection itself. **There is a fullness of meaning in each utterance which no man shall be able fully to bring forth and, when combined, they make up a vast deep of thought which no human line can fathom.**

Here, as everywhere else, we are constrained to say of our Lord, *"Never man spoke like this Man."* In all the anguish of His spirit, His last words prove Him to have remained fully self-possessed, true to His Forgiving Nature, true to His kingly office, true to His filial relationship, true to His God, true to His love of the written Word, true to His glorious work and true to His faith in His Father. As these seven sayings were so faithfully recorded, we do not wonder that they have frequently been the subject of devout meditation. **Fathers and confessors, preachers and Divines have delighted to dwell upon every syllable of these matchless cries.** These solemn sentences have shone like the seven golden candlesticks or the seven stars of the Apocalypse and have lighted multitudes of men to Him who spoke them.

Thoughtful men have drawn a wealth of meaning from them and in so doing have arranged them into different groups and placed them under several heads. I cannot give you more than a mere taste of this rich subject, but I have been most struck with two ways of regarding our Lord's last words. ***First, they teach and confirm many of the doctrines of our holy faith.*** *"Father, forgive them; for they know not what they do"* is the first. Here is the forgiveness of sin, free forgiveness in answer to the Savior's plea. *"Today shall you be with Me in Paradise."* Here is the safety of the Believer in the hour of his departure and his instant admission into the Presence of his Lord....

"Woman, behold your son!" This very plainly sets forth the true and proper humanity of Christ, who, to the end, recognized His human relationship to Mary, of whom He was born. Yet His language teaches us not to worship her, for He calls her, "woman," but to honor *Him,* who in His direst agony thought of her needs and griefs, as He also thinks of all His people, for these are His mother and sister and brother. *"Eloi, Eloi, lama Sabachthani?"* is the fourth cry, and it illustrates the penalty endured by our Substitute when He bore our sins and was forsaken of His God. The sharpness of that sentence no exposition can fully disclose to us, it is keen as the very edge and point of the sword which pierced His heart.

"I thirst," is the fifth cry, and its utterance teaches us the truth of Scripture, for all things were accomplished, that the Scripture might be fulfilled and, therefore, our Lord said, *"I thirst."* **Holy Scripture remains the basis of our faith, established by every Word and act of our Redeemer.** The last word but one is, *"It is finished."* There is the complete justification of the Believer, since the work by which he

is accepted is fully accomplished. The last of His last words is also taken from the Scriptures and shows where His mind was feeding. He cried, before He bowed the head which He had held erect amid all His conflict, as one who never yielded, *"Father, into Your hands I commend My spirit."* In that cry there is reconciliation to God. He who stood in our place has finished all His work and now His spirit comes back to the Father and He brings us with Him! Every word, therefore, teaches us some grand fundamental doctrine of our blessed faith. *"He that has ears to hear, let him hear."*

A second mode of treating these seven cries is to view them as setting forth the Person and offices of our Lord who uttered them. *"Father, forgive them; for they know not what they do,"* here we see the Mediator interceding, Jesus standing before the Father pleading for the guilty. *"Verily I say unto you, today shall you be with Me in Paradise,"* this is the Lord Jesus in kingly power, opening, with the key of David, a door which none can shut, admitting into the gates of Heaven the poor soul who had confessed Him on the tree. Hail, everlasting King in Heaven, You admit to Your Paradise whomever You will. Nor do You set a time for waiting, but instantly You set wide the gate of pearl! You have all power in Heaven as well as upon earth.

Then came, *"Woman, behold your son!"* Here we see the Son of Man in the gentleness of a son caring for His bereaved mother. In the former cry, as He opened Paradise, you saw the Son of God, now you see Him who was verily and truly born of a woman, made under the Law, and under the Law you see Him still, for He honors His mother and cares for her in the last article of death. Then comes the, *"My God, My God, why have You forsaken Me?"* Here we behold His human soul in anguish, His inmost heart overwhelmed by the withdrawing of Jehovah's face and made to cry out as if in perplexity and amazement.

"I thirst," is His human body tormented by grievous pain. Here you see how the mortal flesh had to share in the agony of the inward spirit. *"It is finished"* is the last word but one and there you see the perfected Savior, the Captain of our salvation, who has completed the undertaking upon which He had entered, finished transgression,

made an end of sin, and brought in everlasting righteousness. The last expiring word, in which *He commended His spirit to His Father,* is the note of acceptance for Himself and for us all. As *He commends His spirit into the Father's hand,* so does He bring all Believers near to God and from then on we are in the hands of the Father, who is greater than all and none shall pluck us from His hands. Is not this a fertile field of thought? May the Holy Spirit often lead us to glean here.

There are many other ways in which these words might be read and they would be found to be all full of instruction. **Like the steps of a ladder or the links of a golden chain, there is a mutual dependence and interlinking of each of the cries, so that one leads to another and that to a third.** Separately or in connection, our Master's words overflow with instruction to thoughtful minds. But of all, save one, I must say, "Of which we cannot now speak particularly." Our text is the shortest of all the words of Calvary. It stands as two words in our language, "I thirst," but in the Greek it is only one.

I cannot say that it is short and sweet, for, alas, it was bitterness, itself, to our Lord Jesus. **And yet out of its bitterness I trust there will come great sweetness to us. Though bitter to Him in the speaking, it will be sweet to us in the hearing, so sweet that all the bitterness of our trials shall be forgotten as we remember the vinegar and gall of which He drank.** We shall, **by the assistance of the Holy Spirit,** try to regard these words of our Savior in a five-fold light.

A. First, we shall look upon them as *THE ENSIGN OF HIS TRUE HUMANITY.*

Jesus said, "I thirst," and **this is the complaint of a man.** Our Lord is the Maker of the ocean and the waters that are above the firmament, it is His hand that stays or opens the bottles of Heaven and sends rain upon the evil and upon the good. "The sea is His and He made it," and all fountains and springs are of His digging. He pours out the streams that run among the hills, the torrents which rush down the mountains and the flowing rivers which enrich the plains. One could have said, "If

He were thirsty He would not tell *us*, for all the clouds and rains would be glad to refresh His brow and the brooks and streams would joyously flow at His feet." And yet, though He was Lord of all, He had so fully taken upon Himself the form of a Servant and was so perfectly made in the likeness of sinful flesh that He cried with fainting voice, "I thirst."

How truly Man He is! He is, indeed, *"bone of our bone and flesh of our flesh,"* for He bears our infirmities. **I invite you to meditate upon the true humanity of our Lord very reverently and very lovingly.** Jesus was proven to be really Man because He suffered the pains which belong to manhood. Angels cannot suffer thirst. A phantom, as some have called Him, could not suffer in this fashion. Jesus really suffered, not only the more refined pains of delicate and sensitive minds, but the rougher and common pangs of flesh and blood. Thirst is a commonplace misery; such as may happen to peasants or beggars. It is a real pain and not a thing of a fancy or a nightmare of dreamland. Thirst is no royal grief, but an evil of universal manhood, Jesus is Brother to the poorest and humblest of our race.

Our Lord, however, endured thirst to an extreme degree, for it was the thirst of death and more which was upon Him, it was the thirst of one whose death was not a common one, for, "*He tasted death for every man.*" That thirst was caused, perhaps, in part by the loss of blood and by the fever created by the irritation caused by His four grievous wounds. The nails were fastened in the most sensitive parts of the body and the wounds were widened as the weight of His body dragged the nails through His blessed flesh and tore His tender nerves. The extreme tension produced a burning feverishness. It was pain that dried His mouth and made it like an oven, till He declared, in the language of the 22nd Psalm, *"My tongue cleaves to My jaws."* It was a thirst such as none of us have ever known, for not yet has the death dew condensed upon our brows. We shall, perhaps, know it in our measure in our dying hour, but not yet, nor ever so terribly as He did.

Our Lord felt that grievous drought of dissolution by which all moisture seems dried up and the flesh returns to the dust of death. This those know who have commenced to tread the valley of the shadow of death. **Jesus, being a Man, escaped none of the ills which are allotted to man in death.** He is, indeed, *"Immanuel, God with us"* everywhere. Believing this, let us tenderly feel how very near akin to us our Lord Jesus has become. You have been ill and you have been parched with fever as He was. And then you, too, have gasped out, "I thirst." Your path runs hard by that of your Master. He said, "I thirst," in order that someone might bring Him drink, even as you have wished to have a cooling draught handed to you when you could not help yourself.

Can you help feeling how very near Jesus is to us when His lips must be moistened with a sponge and He must be so dependent upon others as to ask for a drink from their hands? Next time your fevered lips murmur, "I am very thirsty," you may say to yourself, "Those are sacred words, for my Lord spoke in that fashion." The words, "I thirst," are a common voice in death chambers. We can never forget the painful scenes of which we have been witness, when we have watched the dissolving of the human frame. Some of those whom we loved very dearly, we have seen quite unable to help themselves. The death sweat has been upon them and this has been one of the marks of their approaching dissolution that they have been parched with thirst and could only mutter between their half-closed lips, "Give me a drink."

Ah, beloved, **our Lord was so truly Man that all our griefs remind us of Him.** The next time we are thirsty we may gaze upon Him. And whenever we see a friend faint and thirsting while dying we may behold our Lord dimly, but truly, mirrored in his members. How near akin the thirsty Savior is to us. Let us love Him more and more. **How great the love which led Him to such a condescension as this.** Do not let us forget the infinite distance between the Lord of Glory on His Throne and the Crucified dried up with thirst. A river of the Water of Life, pure as crystal, proceeds today out of the Throne of God and of the Lamb, and yet once He condescended to say, "I thirst."

He is Lord of fountains and all deeps, but not a cup of cold water was placed to His lips. Oh, if He had at any time said, "I thirst," before His angelic guards, they would surely have emulated the courage of the men of David when they cut their way to the well of Bethlehem that was within the gate and drew water in jeopardy of their lives. Who among us would not willingly pour out his soul unto death if he might but give refreshment to the Lord? And yet He placed Himself, for our sakes, into a position of shame and suffering where none would wait upon Him. And when He cried, "I thirst," they gave Him vinegar to drink. Glorious stoop of our exalted Head. O Lord Jesus, we love You and we worship You. We would gladly lift Your name on high in grateful remembrance of the depths to which You did descend.

While thus we admire His condescension, let our thoughts also turn with delight to His sure sympathy, for if Jesus said, "I thirst," then **He knows all our frailties and woes**. The next time we are in pain or are suffering depression of spirit we will remember that our Lord understands it all, for He has had practical, personal experience of it. Neither in torture of body nor in sadness of heart are we deserted by our Lord. His line is parallel with ours. The arrow which has lately pierced you, my Brother, was first stained with His blood. The cup of which you are made to drink, though it is very bitter, bears the marks of His lips about its brim. He has traversed the mournful way before you and every footprint you leave in the soil is stamped side by side with His footprints. **Let the sympathy of Christ, then, be fully believed in and deeply appreciated, since He said, "I thirst."**

From now on, also, **let us cultivate the spirit of resignation, for we may well rejoice to carry a Cross which His shoulders have borne before us.** Beloved, if our Master said, "I thirst," do we expect to drink every day of streams from Lebanon? He was innocent and yet He thirsted, shall we marvel if guilty ones are now and then chastened? If He were so poor that His garments were stripped from Him and He was hung up upon the tree, penniless and friendless, hungering and thirsting, will you groan and murmur because you bear the yoke of poverty and need? There is bread upon your table, today, and there will be at least a cup of cold water to refresh you. You are not, therefore, so poor as He.

Complain not, then. Shall the servant be above his Master, or the disciple above his Lord? Let patience have her perfect work. You suffer. Perhaps, dear Sister, you carry about with you a gnawing disease which eats at your heart, but Jesus took our sicknesses and His cup was more bitter than yours. In your chamber let the gasp of your Lord as He said, "I thirst," go through your ears and as you hear it, let it touch your heart and cause you to gird up yourself and say, "Does He say, 'I thirst'? Then I will thirst with Him and not complain! I will suffer with Him and not murmur." The Redeemer's cry of, "I thirst," is a solemn lesson of patience to His afflicted.

Once again, as we think of this, **"I thirst," which proves our Lord's humanity**, let us resolve to shun no denials, but rather court them that we may be conformed to His image. May we not be half ashamed of our pleasures when He says, "I thirst"? May we not despise our loaded table while He is so neglected? Shall it ever be a hardship to be denied the satisfying draught when He said, "I thirst"? Shall carnal appetites be indulged and bodies pampered when Jesus cried, "I thirst"? What if the bread is dry? What if the medicine is nauseous? For His thirst there was no relief but gall and vinegar, dare we complain?

For His sake we may rejoice in self-denials and accept Him and a crust as all we desire between here and Heaven. A Christian living to indulge us would not willingly pour out his soul unto death if he might but give refreshment to us. And yet Jesus placed Himself, for our sakes, into a position of shame and suffering where none would wait upon Him, when He cried, "I thirst," they gave Him vinegar to drink. A Christian living to indulge the base appetites of a brute beast, to eat and to drink almost to gluttony and drunkenness, is utterly unworthy of the name. The conquest of the appetites, the entire subjugation of the flesh must be achieved, for before our great Exemplar said, "It is finished," wherein I think He reached the greatest height of all, He stood as only upon the next lower step to that elevation and said, "I thirst." The power to suffer for another, the capacity to be self-denying even to an extreme to accomplish some great work for God, this is a thing to be sought after and must be gained before our work is done. And in this Jesus is before us as our example and our strength.

Thus have I tried to spy out a measure of teaching, by using that one glass for the soul's eyes through which we look upon, "I thirst," as the ensign of **His true humanity.**

B. Secondly, we shall regard these words, "I thirst," as ***THE TOKEN OF HIS SUFFERING SUBSTITUTION.*** The great Surety says, "I thirst," because He is placed in the sinner's place and He must, therefore, undergo the penalty of sin for the ungodly. *"My God, My God, why have You forsaken Me?"* points to the anguish of His soul. *"I thirst"* expresses, in part, the torture of His body, they were both necessary because it is written of the God of Justice that He is *"able to destroy both soul and body in Hell."* And the pangs that are due to Law are of both kinds, touching both heart and flesh.

See, … where sin begins, and mark that there it ends. It began with the mouth of appetite, when it was sinfully gratified, and it ends when a kindred appetite is graciously denied. Our first parents plucked forbidden fruit and, by eating, slew the race. Appetite was the door of sin and, therefore, in that point our Lord was put to pain. With, "I thirst," the evil is destroyed and receives its expiation. I saw the other day the emblem of a serpent with its tail in its mouth and if I carry it a little beyond the artist's intention, the symbol may set forth appetite swallowing up itself. A carnal appetite of the body, the satisfaction of the desire for food, first brought us down under the first Adam. And now the pang of thirst, the denial of what the body craved, restores us to our place.

Nor is this all. **We know from experience that the present effect of sin in every man who indulges in it, is thirst of soul**. The mind of man is like the daughters of the horseleech, which cry forever, *"Give, give.* "Metaphorically understood, thirst is dissatisfaction, the craving of the mind for something which it has not, but which it pines for. Our Lord says, *"If any man thirst, let him come unto Me and drink,"* that thirst being the result of sin in every ungodly man at this moment. **Now Christ, standing in the place of the ungodly, suffers thirst as a type of His enduring the result of sin.**

More solemn, still, is the reflection that according to our Lord's own teaching, **thirst will also be the eternal result of sin,** for He says concerning the rich glutton, *"In Hell he lifts up his eyes, being in* *torment,"* and his prayer, which was denied him, was, *"Father Abraham, send Lazarus, that he may dip the tip of his finger in water and cool my tongue, for I am tormented in this flame."*

Now remember, if Jesus had not thirsted, every one of us would have thirsted forever afar off from God, with an impassable gulf between us and Heaven. Our sinful tongues, blistered by the fever of passion, must have burned forever had not His tongue been tormented with thirst in our place. I suppose that the, "I thirst," was uttered softly, so that perhaps only one and another who stood near the Cross heard it at all, in contrast with the louder cry of, "Lama Sabachthani" and the triumphant shout of, "It is finished!" But that soft, expiring sigh, "I thirst," has ended for us the thirst which otherwise, insatiably fierce, had preyed upon us throughout eternity.

Oh, wondrous substitution of the Just for the unjust, of God for man, of the perfect Christ for guilty us, Hell-deserving rebels. Let us magnify and bless our Redeemer's name. It seems to me very wonderful that this, "I thirst," should be, as it were, the clearance of it all. He had no sooner said, "I thirst," and sipped the vinegar, then He shouted, **"It is finished!" And all was over, the battle was fought and the victory won forever, and our great Deliverer's thirst was the sign of His having smitten the last foe.** The flood of His grief had passed the high-water mark and began to be relieved. The, "I thirst," was the bearing of the last pang, what if I say it was the expression of the fact that His pangs had, at last, begun to *cease* and their fury had spent themselves and left Him able to note His lesser pains?

The excitement of a great struggle makes men forget thirst and faintness. It is only when all is over that they come back to themselves and note the spending of their strength. The great agony of being forsaken by God was over and He felt faint when the strain was withdrawn. I like to think of our Lord's saying, "It is finished," directly after He had exclaimed, "I thirst" because these two voices come so naturally together. **Our glorious Samson had been fighting our foes.** Heaps upon heaps, He had slain His thousands, and now like Samson He was terribly thirsty. He sipped of the vinegar and He was refreshed and no sooner has He thrown off the thirst than He shouted like a conqueror, "It is finished," and quit the field, covered with renown.

Let us exult as we **see our Substitute going through with His work even to the bitter end** and then with a, "Consummatum est," returning to His Father! **O Souls, burdened with sin, rest here, and resting, live!**

C. We will now take the text in a third way and may the Spirit of God instruct us once again. The utterance of, "I thirst," brought out *A TYPE OF MAN'S TREATMENT OF HIS LORD.* It was a confirmation of the Scripture testimony with regard to **man's natural enmity to God**. According to modern thought man is a very fine and noble creature, struggling to become better. He is greatly to be commended and admired, for his sin is said to be a seeking after God and his superstition is a struggling after light. Great and worshipful being that he is, the Truth of God is to be altered for him. The Gospel is to be modulated to suit the tone of his various generations and all the arrangements of the universe are to be rendered subservient to his interests.

Justice must fly the field lest it be severe to so deserving a being. As for *punishment*, it must not be whispered to his polite ears. In fact, the tendency is to exalt man *above* God and give him the highest place! But such is not the truthful estimate of man according to the Scriptures, there, **man is a fallen creature with a carnal mind which cannot be reconciled to God**. He is a worse than brutish creature, rendering evil for good and treating his God with vile ingratitude. Alas, man is the slave and the dupe of Satan and a black-hearted traitor to his God. Did not the prophecies say that man would give to his Incarnate God gall to eat and vinegar to drink? It is done! He came to save and man denied Him hospitality.

At first there was no room for Him at the inn and at the last there was not one cool cup of water for Him to drink, when He thirsted they gave Him vinegar to drink. This is man's treatment of His Savior. **Universal manhood, left to itself, rejects, crucifies and mocks the**

Christ of God. This was the act, too, of man at his best, when he is moved to pity, for it seems clear that he who lifted up the wet sponge to the Redeemer's lips did it in compassion. I think that Roman soldier meant well, at least well for a rough warrior with his little light and knowledge. He ran and filled a sponge with vinegar, it was the best way he knew of putting a few drops of moisture to the lips of One who was suffering so much. But though he felt a degree of pity, it was such as one might show to a dog, he felt no reverence, but mocked as he relieved.

We read, "The soldiers also mocked Him, offering Him vinegar." When our Lord cried, "Eloi, Eloi," and afterwards said, "I thirst," the persons around the Cross said, "Let Him be, let us see whether Elijah will come to save Him," mocking Him and, according to Mark, he who gave the vinegar uttered much the same words. He pitied the Sufferer, but he thought so little of Him that he joined in the voices of scorn. **Even when man pities the sufferings of Christ and man would have ceased to be human if he did not, still he scorns Him**. The very cup which man gives to Jesus is at once scorn and pity, for, "the tender mercies of the wicked are cruel." See how man at his best mingles admiration of the Savior's Person with scorn of His claims, writing books to hold Him up as an example and at the same moment rejecting His Deity. Admitting that He was a wonderful Man, but denying His most sacred mission! Extolling His ethical teaching and then trampling on His blood, thus giving Him drink, but that drink, vinegar.

O my [Readers], **beware of praising Jesus and denying His atoning Sacrifice**. Beware of rendering Him homage and dishonoring His name at the same time. Alas, my Brothers and Sisters, I cannot say much on the score of man's cruelty to our Lord without touching myself and you. Have we not often given Him vinegar to drink? Did we not do so years ago before we knew Him? We used to melt when we heard about His sufferings, but we did not turn from our sins. We gave Him our tears and then grieved Him with our sins. We thought, sometimes, that we loved Him, as we heard the story of His death, but we did not change our lives for His sake, nor put our trust in Him, and so we gave Him vinegar to drink.

Nor does the grief end here, for have not the best works we have ever done, the best feelings we have ever felt and the best prayers we have ever offered been tart and sour with sin? Can they be compared to generous wine? Are they not more like sharp vinegar? I wonder He has ever received them, as one marvels why He received this vinegar, and yet He has received them and smiled upon us for presenting them. He knew once how to turn water into wine and in matchless love He has often turned our sour drink offerings into something sweet to Himself, though in themselves, I think, they have been the juice of sour grapes, sharp enough to set His teeth on edge. We may, therefore, come before Him, with all the rest of our race, when God subdues them to repentance by His love and look on Him whom we have pierced and mourn for Him as one that is in bitterness for his firstborn.

We may well remember our faults this day: *"We, whose proneness to forget /Your dear love, on Olivet /Bathed Your brow with bloody sweat. / We, whose sins, with awful power, /Like a cloud did over You lower, In that God-excluding hour. /We, who still, in thought and deed, /Often hold the bitter reed /To You, in Your time of need."*

I have touched this point very lightly because I want a little more time to dwell upon a fourth view of this scene. May the Holy Spirit help us to hear a fourth tuning of the dolorous music, "I thirst."

D. I think, beloved Friends that the cry of, "I thirst," was **THE MYSTICAL EXPRESSION OF THE DESIRE OF HIS HEART**: "I thirst." I cannot think that natural thirst was all He felt. He doubtless thirsted for water, but His soul was thirsty in a higher sense. Indeed, He seems only to have spoken that the Scriptures might be fulfilled as to the offering Him vinegar. **Always was He in harmony with Himself and His body was always expressive of His soul's cravings as well as of its own longings. "I thirst" meant that His heart was thirsting to save men.** This thirst had been on Him from the earliest of His earthly days. *"Know you not,"* He said, while yet a boy, *"that I must be about My Father's business?"*

Did He not tell His disciples, *"I have a baptism to be baptized with and how am I straitened till it is accomplished"*? He thirsted to pluck us from between the jaws of Hell, to pay our redemption price and set us free from the eternal condemnation which hung over us. And when on the Cross the work was almost done, His thirst was not relieved and could not be till He could say, "It is finished."

It is almost done, Christ of God! You have almost saved Your people! There remains but one thing more, that You should actually die and, therefore, Your strong desire to come to the end and complete Your labor. You were still straitened till the last pang was felt and the last word spoken to complete the full redemption and, therefore, Your cry, "I thirst." **Beloved, there is now upon our Master and there always has been, a thirst after the love of His people**. Do you not remember how that thirst of His was strong in the old days of the Prophet? Call to mind His complaint in the 5th chapter of Isaiah, *"Now will I sing to my Well-beloved a song of my Beloved touching His vineyard. My Well-beloved has a vineyard in a very fruitful hill: and He fenced it, and gathered out the stones thereof, and planted it with the choicest vine, and built a tower in the midst of it, and also made a winepress therein."*

What was He looking for from His vineyard and its winepress? What but for the juice of the vine that He might be refreshed? "And He looked that it should bring forth grapes, and it brought forth wild grapes, "vinegar, not wine, sourness not sweetness. So He was thirsting then. According to the sacred canticle of love, in the 5th chapter of the Song of Songs, we learn that when He drank in those olden times it was in the garden of His Church that He was refreshed. What does He say? *"I am come into My garden, My sister, My spouse: I have gathered My myrrh with My spice; I have eaten My honeycomb with My honey; I have drunk My wine with My milk; eat, O Friends; drink, yes, drink abundantly, O Beloved."*

In the same song He speaks of His Church, and says, *"The roof of your mouth is as the best wine for My Beloved, that goes down sweetly, causing the lips of those that are asleep to speak."* And yet again in the 8th chapter the bride says, *"I would cause You to drink of spiced wine of the juice of my pomegranate.*" **Yes, He loves to be with His people. They are the garden where He walks for refreshment. And their love, their graces, are the milk and wine of which He delights to drink. Christ was always thirsty to save men and to be loved of men.** And we see a type of His life-long desire when, being weary, He sat thus on the well and said to the woman of Samaria, *"Give Me a drink."* There was a deeper meaning in His words than she dreamed of, as a verse further down fully proves, when He said to His disciples, *"I have meat to eat that you know not of."* He derived *spiritual* refreshment from the winning of that woman's heart to Himself.

And now, Brothers and Sisters, **our blessed Lord has, at this time, a thirst for communion with each one of you who are His people, not because you can do Him good, but because He can do you good.** He thirsts to bless you and to receive your grateful love in return. He thirsts to see you looking with believing eyes to His fullness and holding out your emptiness that He may supply it. He says, *"Behold, I stand at the door and knock."* For what does He? It is that He may eat and drink with you, for He promises that if we open to Him, He will enter in and sup with us and we with Him. He is still thirsty, you see, for our poor love, and surely we cannot deny it to Him.

Come, let us pour out full flagons until His joy is fulfilled in us! And what makes Him love us so? Ah, that I cannot tell, except **His own great love. He must love, it is His Nature.** He must love His chosen whom He has once begun to love, for He is the same yesterday, today and forever. His great love makes Him thirst to have us much nearer than we are. He will never be satisfied till all His redeemed are beyond gunshot of the enemy. I will give you one of His thirsty prayers, *"Father, I will that they, also, whom You have given Me, be with Me where I am, that they may behold My Glory."* He wants you, Brother, He wants you, dear Sister, He longs to have you wholly to Himself.

Come to Him in prayer. Come to Him in fellowship. Come to Him by perfect consecration. Come to Him by surrendering your whole being to the sweet mysterious influences of His Spirit. Sit at His feet with Mary. Lean on His breast with John. Yes, come with the spouse in the song and say, "Let Him kiss me with the kisses of His mouth, for His love is better than wine." He calls for that, will you not give it to Him? Is your heart so frozen that not a cup of cold water can be melted for Jesus? Are you lukewarm? O Brothers and Sisters, if He says, "I thirst," and you bring Him a lukewarm heart, that is *worse* than vinegar, for He has said, "I will spit you out of My mouth."

He can receive vinegar, but not lukewarm love. Come, bring Him your warm heart and let Him drink from that purified chalice as much as He wills. **Let all your love be His**. I know He loves to receive from you because He delights even in a cup of cold water that you give to one of His disciples. How much more will He delight in the giving of your whole self to Him? Therefore, while He thirsts give Him a drink this very day.

E. Lastly, the cry of, "I thirst," is to us *THE PATTERN OF OUR DEATH WITH HIM*. Know you not, Beloved, for I speak to **those who know the Lord, that you are crucified together with Christ?** Well, then, what does this cry mean, "I thirst," but this, that we should thirst, too? We do not thirst after the old manner wherein we were bitterly afflicted, for He has said, "He that drinks of this water shall never thirst." But now we covet a *new* thirst, a refined and heavenly appetite, a craving for our Lord. O blessed Master, if we are, indeed, nailed up to the tree with You, give us to thirst after You with a thirst which only the cup of "the new Covenant in Your blood" can ever satisfy.

Certain philosophers have said that they love the pursuit of truth even better than the knowledge of truth. I differ from them greatly, but I will say this, that next to the actual enjoyment of my Lord's Presence, **I love to hunger and to thirst after Him**. [Samuel] Rutherford used words somewhat to this effect, "*I thirst for my Lord and this is joy, a joy which no man takes from me. Even if I may not come to Him, yet shall I be full of consolation, for it is Heaven to thirst after Him, and surely He will never deny a poor soul liberty to admire Him, and adore Him, and thirst* *after Him.*" As for myself, I would grow more and more greedy after my Divine Lord and when I have much of Him I would still cry for more and then for more and still more. **My heart shall not be content till He is All in All to me and I am altogether lost in Him.** O to be enlarged in soul so as to take deeper draughts of His sweet love, for our heart cannot have enough.

One would wish to be as the spouse, who, when she had already been feasting in the banqueting house and had found His fruit sweet to her taste, so that she was overjoyed, yet cried out, "Stay me with flagons, comfort me with apples, for I am sick of love." She craved full flagons of love though she was already overpowered by it! This is a kind of sweet whereof if a man has much he must have more and when he has more he is under a still greater necessity to receive more. His appetite is forever growing by that which it feeds upon, till he is filled with all the fullness of God. "I thirst," yes, this is my soul's word with her Lord. Borrowed from His lips it well suits my mouth: *"I thirst, but not as once I did, / The vain delights of earth to share. Your wounds, /Emmanuel, all forbid / That I should seek my pleasures there. /Dear fountain of delight unknown! No longer sink below the brim /But overflow, and pour me* down /A living and life-giving stream."

Jesus thirsted, then let us thirst in this dry and thirsty land where there is no water. **Even as the hart pants after the water brooks, our souls would thirst after You, O God.**

Beloved, **let us thirst for the souls of our fellow men.** I have already told you that such was our Lord's mystical desire. Let it be ours, also. Brother, **thirst to have your children saved.** Brother, thirst I pray, **to have your workpeople saved.** Sister, **thirst for the salvation of your class, thirst for the redemption of your family, thirst for the conversion of your husband.** We ought all to have a longing for conversions. Is it so with each one of you? If not, bestir yourselves at once. Fix your hearts upon some unsaved one and thirst until he is saved. It is the way whereby many shall be brought to Christ, when this blessed soul-thirst of true Christian charity shall be upon those who are, themselves, saved.

Remember how Paul said, *"I say the truth in Christ, I lie not, my conscience also bearing me witness in the Holy Spirit, that I have great heaviness and continual sorrow in my heart. For I could wish that I myself were accursed from Christ for my brethren, my kinsmen according to the flesh."* He would have sacrificed himself to save his countrymen, so heartily did he desire their eternal welfare. Let this mind be in you, also.

EXHORTATION: As for yourselves, thirst after perfection. Hunger and thirst after righteousness, for you shall be filled. Hate sin and heartily loathe it. Thirst to be holy as God is holy. Thirst to be like Christ. Thirst to bring glory to His sacred name by complete conformity to His will.

May the Holy Spirit work in you the complete pattern of Christ Crucified and to Him shall be praise forever and ever. Amen.

2.   The Savior's Thirst

"After this, Jesus, knowing that all things were now accomplished, that the Scripture might be fulfilled, said, 'I thirst!'"
(John 19:28 NKJV).

FOCUS: The text is regarded first, as our Savior's cry, and as only such. Second, we shall consider its relationship to ourselves. And third, and sorrowfully, its relation to ungodly man.

THE early Christians were known to think and talk far more of our Savior than we do. Some of them were, perhaps, not quite so clear upon justification by faith as they ought to have been, but **they were very clear about the merits of the precious blood.** And if they did not always speak very clearly about the Doctrines of Grace, they spoke with wonderful power and savor about the "five" wounds, about the nail marks and the spear wound. I could wish that our religion would go back somewhat more to **that personal apprehension of Christ** than it does. By all means let us have dogmatic teaching, setting forth those most precious Truths of God that are our consolation, **but better than all is the Person of Christ Himself, the Way, the Truth, and the Life. We should do well if we more often stood in meditation at the foot of the Cross and viewed His wounds, counted the precious drops as they fall and sought fellowship with Him in His sufferings.** Some of those early saints wrote long treatises on the solitary, we have not the leisure. I am afraid we have not the mental application they possessed. Nevertheless, let us explore the sacred mystery as best we can. At this time would we get away to Calvary and there stand and hear our Redeemer crying, "I thirst," as He bears for us the guilt of sin.

A. First, *CONSIDER THIS CRY OF OUR SAVIOR, "I thirst."*

Is it not clear proof that **He was certainly Man?** Certain heretics sprang up in the early Church who asserted that the body of our Lord was only a phantom, that as God, He was here, but as Man He only exhibited Himself to the outward sense and did not actually exist in flesh and blood. But He thirsted. Now, a spirit has not thirst. A spirit neither eats nor drinks, it is immaterial and knows not the needs that belong to this poor flesh and blood! We may, therefore, rest quite sure that, *"the Word was made flesh and dwelt among us, and we beheld His glory, the glory as of the Only-Begotten of the Father, full of Grace and truth."*

No better proof could we have of **the substantiality of His Manhood** than the cry, "I thirst." Herein, at all events, we can sympathize with Him. From the moment when He rose from the Communion Supper, saying, **"I will not drink henceforth of this fruit of the vine until that day when I drink it new with you in My Father's Kingdom,"** from that moment He had had no further refreshment, either of meat or of drink. Yet well He needed drink, for all through that long night in Gethsemane He sweated, we know what kind of sweat, as it were great drops of blood falling to the ground. Such toil as His might well have needed refreshment. Then He was hurried away to Caiaphas and afterwards to Pilate. He had to encounter the accusations of His enemies and a strong bridle He had to put upon Himself, that, like a sheep before her shearers, He might be dumb. There was a strain upon His system such as none of us ever have had to endure, or ever shall have, a strain such as we can never imagine and yet not one morsel of bread, nor one drop of water crossed those blessed and parched lips. Well might He cry, "I thirst," when, after so many hours of wrestling with the powers of darkness, He was now about to die.

You remember, also, the peculiar way in which our Lord was put to death. The piercing of the hands and the feet was sure to bring on fever. Those members, though far remote from the vital parts, are yet full of the most delicate and tender nerves and pain soon travels along them till the whole frame becomes hot with burning fever! Our Lord's own words in the 22nd Psalm will occur to you, *"My strength is dried up like a potsherd, and My tongue cleaves to My jaws; and You have brought Me into the dust of death."* Those of you who have been afflicted with fever far less serious than this, will recollect how it parched you like a potsherd and dried up all the juices of your system and all the moisture of your body like the parched fields of summer. You had, then, a thirst, indeed. But your Savior had a double cause for thirst, long fasting without food or drink and then the bitter pangs of death. Sympathize with Him then, **Beloved, and remember that all this was for you, and for you as His enemies, for you as if there were no others in the world**. Though He suffered for all His elect, yet especially for each one of His people were the nails driven, for each one did He thirst and for each one did He take a draught of the vinegar and the gall. Come, then, and kiss those blessed lips and bow before your Savior in reverent praise.

Further, my Brothers and Sisters, we are quite certain that our Lord, in saying, "I thirst," must have felt the extreme bitterness of thirst. He was no complainer. You never heard a word come from His lips when it might have been withheld. He must have been driven to dire extremity, indeed, when He thus proclaimed to friends and foes that He was thirsting for a drop of water. Some have said that this cry, "I thirst," coming, as it does, after the far more bitter and awful cry, "My God, My God, why have You forsaken Me?" was an evidence of a turn in the

Savior's conflict, that during all the first part of our Savior's suffering He was taken up with such anxious thought and with such internal anguish that He could not think of the thirst, which, grievous as it was, was but a minor pain in comparison with **what He felt when His Father in justice turned away His face from Him, and that now He begins to collect His thoughts for a while and is able to fight with His own personal bodily pains.** It may be so. Possibly that cry was an indication that the battle had turned and that victory was coming to the suffering Hero. But, ah, Brothers and Sisters, however there may have come a gleam of sunshine in this cry compared to the blacker darkness, you can never dream what a thirst that was that parched the Savior's mouth and lips. You will never feel such a thirst as He felt to its direst extent. Cold, hunger, nakedness and thirst may fall to your lot, but there was more of grief in His thirst than you can ever know. There was a bitterness here which my language cannot possibly bring out.

Another thought rises up to my mind, I will not mislead you here. I feel thankful to our Lord for saying, "I thirst!" Ah, Brothers and Sisters, sometimes when we are sorely afflicted, or have some little infirmity, perhaps not anything vital or mortal, though it pains us much, we complain, or at least we say, "I thirst." Now, are we wrong in so doing? Ought we to play the stoic? Ought we to be like the Indian at the stake who sings while he is roasting? Ought we to be like St. Lawrence [a deacon martyred in 258 AD during the persecution, in ancient Rome, under Emperor Valerian] on the gridiron? Is stoicism a part of Christianity? Oh, no! Jesus said, "I thirst," and herein He gave permission to all of you who are bowed down with your griefs and your sorrows to whisper them into the ears of those who watch by the bed, and to say, "I thirst." I daresay you have often felt ashamed of yourselves for this. You have said, "Now, if I had some huge trouble, or if the pangs I suffered were absolutely mortal, **I could lean upon the Beloved's arm.** But as for this ache, or this pain, it darts through my body and causes me much anguish, though it does not kill me." Well, but just as Jesus wept that He might let you weep on account of your sorrows and your griefs, so He says, "I thirst," that you might have permission patiently, as He did, to express your little complaints; that you might not think He sneers at you, or looks down upon you as though you were an alien; that you might know He sympathizes with you in it all.

He does not use language like that of Cassius when he laughed at Caesar because he was sick and said: *"And when the fit was on him I did mark /How he did shake, 'tis true this god did shake/ His coward lips did from their color fly! /And that same eye whose head does awe the world / Did lose its luster—I did hear him groan! /Yes, and that tongue of his that bade the Romans /Mark him, and write his speeches in their books, /Alas, it cried, 'Give me some drink, Titinius,'/As a sick girl."*

And why should it not? He was but a man. He was but "as a sick girl," and what is there in a sick girl to despise, after all? Jesus Christ said, "I thirst," and in this He says to every sick girl, and every sick child, and every sick one throughout the world, "The Master, who is now in Heaven, but who once suffered on earth, despises not the tears of the sufferers, but has pity on them on their beds of sickness."

Jesus said, "I thirst." As our Lord used these words, may I ask you for a minute to contemplate it with wonder? Who was this that said, "I thirst"? Know you not that it was He who balanced the clouds and who filled the channels of the mighty deep? He said, "I thirst," and yet in Him was a well of water springing up unto everlasting life! Yes, He who guided every river in its course and watered all the fields with grateful showers, **He it was, the King of kings, and Lord of lords**, before whom Hell trembles and the earth is filled with dismay! He whom Heaven adores and all eternity worships, He it was who said, "I thirst." Matchless condescension, from the Infinity of God to the weakness of a thirsting, dying Man! And this, again I must remind you, was for you. He that suffered for you was no common mortal, no ordinary man, such as you are, but the perfect and ever blessed God, high above all principalities and powers and every name that is named! He it was who, with this condescending lowness of estate, stooped and cried, as you have done, "I thirst."

Once more, in this cry of our Lord, "I thirst," I think I see a trace of the Atonement which He was then offering. The pangs of Christ upon the Cross are to be regarded as a substitution for the sins and sorrows of ungodly men: *"He bore that we might never bear /His Father's righteous ire."*

Now, Brothers and Sisters, a part of the punishment of the wicked in Hell is the deprivation of every form of comfort. Man refused to obey His Creator, the time will come when the Creator will refuse to succor man. Man refused to minister to God, the time will come when God's creatures will not minister to man! Remember those solemn words of the Master when He said that the rich man was without a drop of water to cool his tongue and was tormented in the flame. And yet the water was withheld from coming near the sinner who had died in willful rebellion against God. Oh, my dear Friends, f we had our due, we should have none of the comforts of life. The very air would refuse to yield us breath and bread, the staff of life, to yield us nourishment! Yes, we would find the whole Creation in arms against us because we are up in arms against God! The time shall come when those who stand up against the Most High shall find no comfort left them, and no hope of comfort, everything that can make existence tolerable shall be withdrawn and everything that can make it intolerable shall be poured upon them. For upon the wicked, God shall rain fire and brimstone, and a horrid tempest, this shall be the portion of their cup.

Behold, then, when **Emmanuel stood for us and suffered in our place**, He, too, must thirst! He must be deprived of every comfort, stripped naked to the last rag and hung up on the Cross as though earth rejected Him and Heaven would not receive Him! Midway between the two worlds He dies in the most abject poverty! And because of our sin, He cries, "I thirst." Beloved, never seek for companionship with any who would ignore the miseries of the Lord, for, depend upon it, in that proportion they lessen the glory of the Atonement. If it is but a light thing for the sinner to rebel against God, it was not a light thing for Christ to redeem him. It covered Christ with the greatest luster, for, after all, it stands out as one of His most resplendent works that He has redeemed us from going down into the Pit, having found a ransom for us. By so much the greater the love, by so much the greater is the salvation. Think not lightly of sin and its punishment, lest you come to think lightly of Christ and what He suffered to redeem you from your guilt! **The cry, "I thirst," is part of the substitutionary work which Christ performed when He thirsted, because, otherwise, sinners would have thirsted forever and have been denied all the pleasure, joy and peace of Heaven.**

The meditation upon this cry as proceeding from our Lord invites one more remark. Will it be straining the text too far if we say that underlying those words, "I thirst," there is something more them a mere thirst for drink? Once, when He sat upon the well of Samaria, He said to the poor harlot who met Him there, *"Give Me a drink,"* and He got a drink from her, a drink that the world knew nothing about when she gave her heart to Him, obedient to His Gospel. **Christ is always thirsting after the salvation of precious souls and that cry on the Cross that thrilled all who listened to it was the outburst of the great heart of Jesus Christ as He saw the multitude, and He cried unto His God, "I thirst."** He thirsted to redeem mankind. He thirsted to accomplish the work of our salvation. This very day He still thirsts in that respect, as He is still willing to receive those who come to Him, still resolved that such as come shall never be cast out and still desirous that they may come! Oh, poor Souls, you do not thirst for Christ, but you little know how **He thirsts for you.** There is love in His heart towards those who have no love to Him! Christ would not have you die. Christ would not have you cast into Hell! Give yourselves up, then, to the gentle sway of Him who for your souls' good, said, "I thirst." Oh, I wish that all we who love Christ knew more of this hungering and thirsting after the redemption of our follow men. The Lord teach us to sympathize with them! If He wept for sinners, may our cheeks never be dry. He was in anguish for their souls, and we will not restrain our anguish because they will not be saved, but ignorantly, carelessly, or resolutely despise the Gospel of Christ.

Thus much upon this point, so far as it concerns our Lord, Himself. Turn not away your eyes, but look and listen as He cries, "I thirst." Very briefly, now let us notice:

B. *OUR RELATIONSHIP AND OUR BEARING TOWARDS THIS CRY.*

I shall address myself on this head to the people of God. And the first remark is this, ..., because Jesus Christ said, "I thirst," you and I are delivered from that terrible thirst which once devoured us. We were awakened by the Holy Spirit, some of us, years ago, to perceive our danger. We had not known before what sin was, what a destroying fever it was. We had cherished it in our bosom, but when we began to discover our desperate position, **we were compelled to thirst and cry for mercy.** With some of us, our thirst was very great, we could scarcely sleep, and as for our meals, we left them untouched often in the agony of our despair. I do remember how my soul chose strangling rather than life. It seemed so hard to live under the frown of God, awakened to a sense of sin, but unable to get rid of the sin! Now at this moment that thirst has gone, for we have received the adoption, the salvation, the forgiveness. You came to Jesus as you were with all your thirst and you stooped down and drank of the crystal stream. And now you rejoice with unspeakable joy because your thirst is gone! Oh, clap your hands for very joy at the remembrance of it. Be humble that you should need His thirst to save you from thirst, but oh, be glad to think that the work is done and that you shall never thirst again as you did then, for, "he that drinks," says Christ, "of the water that I shall give him shall never thirst, for it shall be in him a well of water springing up unto everlasting life." Your insatiable desires are stayed. The horseleech within you that cried, "Give, give," at last is satisfied. The cravings of conscience that had been awakened by the love of God are satisfied. Now, oh, joy, your sorrow is over. Your peace, like a river has come, and your righteousness is like the waves of the sea. Live happily, live joyously. **Tell others what Christ has done for you.** Eat not your morsel alone, but publish to the world that through the thirst of a dying Savior you have ceased to thirst.

And as you have done with that first thirst of bitter agony, now seek to be filled with another thirst, a thirst after more of Christ! Oh, that sweet wine of His love is very thirst-creating, those who have once tasted it need more of it! Thirst after a closer walk with Him. Thirst to know more of Him. Thirst to be more like He. Thirst to understand more the mystery of His sufferings and to be more full of anticipation of His blessed Advent: *"Nearer, my God, to Thee; nearer to Thee."*

Be this your cry. Open your mouth wide, for He will fill it. Enlarge your desires, for He will satisfy them all. Be eager after more of Christ! Hunger and thirst after more of righteousness. All your desires shall be supplied you. Do not, therefore, stint yourself by narrowing them. Oh, that you could ask more at His hands, for: *"All your capacious powers can ask, /In Christ do richly meet."*

Were your imagination to stretch her wings and soar ever so far beyond the narrow bounds of space, she would weary long before she reached the fullness of God which dwells bodily in our Lord Jesus Christ.

Let me also invite you to cultivate another thirst, a thirst like that which we read our Lord thirsted with, for **the conversion of our souls**. Give us but a score of men that hunger and thirst for the conversion of others and we shall see good work done. But oh, we are so cold, callous and sleeping, though men are perishing every day. Behold the mass of people gathered in this Tabernacle. We can never all meet again. Some of us will probably be in eternity before another Sabbath shall have dawned, and of those who shall have departed this life, some will, perhaps, have gone down to the Pit. And yet we have no tears for them. Oh, God, strike our hearts with a rod more powerful than that of Moses and fill our eyes with sympathetic tears. Think what it is that your own child could be lost, that your own relative could perish. Oh, wake yourselves up to passionate prayer, to longing desire and to constant effort, and never, from this moment on, cease to thirst with a passionate desire, which, like that of your Lord, shall fill you and compel you practically to say, in the industrious application of a spiritual life, "I thirst!" My last point is a very heavy one. I could wish it has not to be delivered. It is addressed:

C. *TO UNGODLY MEN AND WOMEN.*

If the Lord Jesus Christ thirsted when He only carried the sins of others, what thirst will be upon you when God shall punish you for your own sins? Either **Christ must thirst for you**, or you mush thirst forever.... There is but one alternative, Justice must be vindicated through a Substitute, or it must be glorified in your everlasting destruction. Think what it will be to have your sweet cup and your flowing bowl all put away from you, and not a drop of water to cool your tongue, to have your dainty meat and your [attractive] festivals forever abolished, no light for your eyes, no joy for any one of the senses of your body and your souls made to suffer unutterable woe.

EXHORTATION: I shall not stay to picture, even in Christ's own words, the agony of lost spirits. But I bid you keep this on your minds. If Christ, who was God's Son, suffered so bitterly for sins that were not His own, how bitterly must you, who are not God's sons, but God's enemies, suffer for sins that are your own? And you must so suffer unless Christ, the Substitute, stands for you. He was no Substitute for all, but only for His own people. You say to me, "Did He stand for me?" I can tell you if you can answer this question, "Do you trust Jesus Christ? Will you now trust Him?" If so, a simple childlike faith in Jesus will bring you salvation.

Now, remember, if you believe, all your sins are laid upon Christ and, therefore, they can never be laid upon you. If you believe, Christ was punished in your place and you can never be punished, because he was punished for you! <u>Substitution, this is the groundwork of our confidence.</u> Because He was accursed, we cannot be accursed, for, if we believe in Him, all that He suffered was for us, and we stand absolved before the Judgment Seat of Christ. The Lord give you this simple faith in the Redeemer this very night. And then He will see in you of the travail of His soul and the thirst of His great heart will be satisfied! The Lord bless you. Amen.

F. Words of Victory

1. "It Is Finished"

"So when Jesus had received the sour wine, He said, 'It is finished!' And bowing His head, He gave up His spirit" (John 19:30 NKJV).

FOCUS: **"My discourse will, I have no doubt, more fully illustrate the remark with which I have commenced; let us proceed to it at once. First, let us hear the text and understand it; Second, let us hear and wonder at it; Third, let us hear it and proclaim it."**

I would have you attentively observe the singular clearness, power, and quickness of the Savior's mind in the last agonies of death. When pains and groans attend the last hour, they frequently have the effect of discomposing the mind, so that it is not possible for the dying man to collect his thoughts, or having collected them, to utter them so that they can be understood by others. In no case could we expect a remarkable exercise of memory or a profound judgment upon deep subjects from an expiring man. But **the Redeemer's last acts were full of wisdom and prudence, although His sufferings were excruciating beyond all measure.** Mark how clearly He perceived the significance of every type. How plainly He could read, with dying eye, those Divine symbols which the eyes of angels could only desire to look into. He saw the secrets which have bewildered sages and astonished seers, all fulfilled in His own body. Nor must we fail to observe the power and comprehensiveness by which He grasped the chain which binds the shadowy past with the sun-lit present. We must not forget the brilliance of that intelligence which threaded all the ceremonies and sacrifices on one string of thought, beheld all the prophecies as one great revelation, and all the Promises as the heralds of one Person, and then said of the whole, "It is finished!" "Finished in Me." **What quickness of mind was** that which enabled Him to traverse all the centuries of prophecy; to penetrate the eternity of the Covenant, and then to anticipate the eternal glories. And all this when He is mocked by multitudes of enemies, and when His hands and feet are nailed to the Cross. What force of mind the Savior must have possessed, to soar above those Alps of Agony, which touched the very clouds. In what a singular mental condition must He have been during the period of His Crucifixion, to be able to review the whole roll of Inspiration.

Now, this remark may not seem to be of any great value, but I think its value lies in certain inferences that may be drawn from it. We have sometimes heard it said, "How could Christ, in so short a time, bear suffering which should be equivalent to the torments, the eternal torments of Hell?" Our reply is, we are not capable of judging what the Son of God might do even in a moment, much less what He might do, and what He might suffer in His life, and in His death. It has been frequently affirmed by persons who have been rescued from drowning, that the mind of a drowning man is singularly active. One who, after being sometime in the water, was at last painfully restored, said that the whole of his history seemed to come before his mind while he was sinking, and that if anyone had asked him how long he had been in the water, he would have said twenty years, whereas, he had only been there for a moment or two.

The intellect of mortal man is such that, if God wills it, when it is in certain states, it can think out centuries of thought at once; it can go through in one instant what we would have supposed would have taken years upon years of time for it to know or feel. We think, therefore, that from the Savior's singular clearness and quickness of intellect upon the Cross, it is very possible that He did in the space of two or three hours endure, not only the agony which might have been contained in centuries, but even an equivalent for that which might be comprehended in everlasting punishment. At any rate, it is not for us to say that it could not be so. When the Deity is arrayed in Manhood, then Manhood becomes Omnipotent to suffer; and just as the feet of Christ were once Almighty to tread the seas, so now His whole body became Almighty to dive into the great waters, to endure an immersion in "unknown agonies." Do not, I pray, let us attempt to measure Christ's sufferings by the finite one of our own ignorant reason, but let us know and believe that what He endured there was accepted by God as an equivalent for all our pains, and therefore, it could not have been a trifle, but must have been all that Hart conceived it to be, when he says He bore: *"All that Incarnate God could bear, /With strength enough, but none to spare."*

A. *LET US HEAR THE TEXT AND UNDERSTAND IT.*

The Son of God has been made Man. He has had a life of perfect virtue, and of total self-denial. He has been all that life despised and rejected of men, a Man of Sorrows and acquainted with grief. His enemies have been legion; His friends have been few, and those few faithless. He is at last delivered over into the hands of them who hate Him. He is arrested while in the act of prayer; He is arraigned before both the spiritual and temporal courts. He is robed in mockery, and then unrobed in shame. He is set upon His throne in scorn, and then tied to the pillar in cruelty. He is declared innocent, and yet, He is delivered up by the judge who ought to have preserved Him from His persecutors. He is dragged through the streets of that Jerusalem which had killed the Prophets, and would now crimson itself with the blood of the Prophets' Master.

He is brought to the Cross; He is nailed fast to the cruel wood. The sun burns Him. His cruel wounds increase the fever. God forsakes Him. "My God, My God, why have You forsaken Me?" contains the concentrated anguish of the world. While He hangs there in mortal conflict with sin and Satan, His heart is broken, His limbs are dislocated. Heaven fails Him, for the sun is veiled in darkness. Earth forsakes Him, for "His disciples forsook Him and fled." He looks everywhere, and there is none to help; He casts His eyes around, and there is no man that can share His toil. He treads the winepress alone; and of all the people, there is none with Him. On, on, He goes, steadily determined to drink the last dreg of that cup which must not pass from Him if His Father's will be done. At last, He cries, "It is finished!" and He gives up His spirit. **Hear it, Christians, hear this shout of triumph as it rings today with all the freshness and force which it had 1,800 years ago! Hear it from the Sacred Word, and from the Savior's lips, and may the Spirit of God open your ears that you may hear as the learned, and understand what you hear.**

1. **What meant the Savior, then, by this: "It is finished!"?** *He meant, first of all, that all the types, promises, and prophecies were now fully accomplished in Him.* Those who are acquainted with the original will find that the words, "It is finished," occur twice within three verses. In the 28th verse, we have the word in the Greek; it is translated in our version *"accomplished,"* but there it stands: *"After this, Jesus knowing that all things were now finished, that the Scripture might be fulfilled, said, 'I thirst.'"* And then, He afterwards said, "It is finished!" This leads us to see His meaning very clearly, that all the Scripture was now fulfilled, that when He said, "**It is finished!" the whole Book, from the first to the last, in both the Law and the Prophets, was finished in Him!** There is not a single jewel of Promise, from that first emerald which fell on the threshold of Eden, to that last sapphire of Malachi which was not set in the breastplate of the true High Priest. No, there is not a type, from the red heifer downward to the turtle dove, from the hyssop upwards to Solomon's Temple itself, which was not fulfilled in Him; and not a prophecy, whether spoken on Chebar's bank, or on the shores of Jordan; not a dream of wise men, whether they had received it in Babylon, or in Samaria, or in Judea, which was not now fully worked out in Christ Jesus. And, Brothers and Sisters, what a wonderful thing it is, **that a mass of promises, and prophecies, and types, apparently so heterogeneous, should all be accomplished in one Person.** Take away Christ for one moment, and I will

give the Old Testament to any wise man living, and say to him, "Take this. This is a problem; go home and construct in your imagination an ideal character who shall exactly fit all that which is herein foreshadowed. Remember, he must be a Prophet like unto Moses, and yet a champion like Joshua; he must be an Aaron and a Melchizedek; he must be David and Solomon, Noah and Jonah, Judah and Joseph. No, he must not only be the lamb that was slain, and the scapegoat that was not slain, the turtledove that was dipped in blood, and the priest who slew the bird, but he must be the Altar, the Tabernacle, the Mercy Seat and the Showbread.

"No, to puzzle this wise man further, we remind him of prophecies so apparently contradictory, that one would think they never could meet in one man! Such as these, *"All kings shall fall down before Him, and all nations shall serve Him;"* and yet, *"He is despised and rejected of men."* He must begin by showing a man born of a virgin mother: *"A virgin shall conceive and bear a Son."* **He must be a man without spot or blemish, but yet one upon whom the Lord does cause to meet the iniquities of us all. He must be a glorious one, a Son of David, but yet, a root out of a dry ground. Now, I say it boldly, if all the greatest intellects of all the ages could set themselves to work out this problem, to invent another key to the types and prophecies, they could not do it.** I see you, you wise men, you are poring over these hieroglyphs; one suggests one key, and it opens two or three of the figures, but you cannot proceed, for the next one puts you at a perplexity! Another learned man suggests another clue, but that fails most where it is most needed, and another, and another, and thus, these wondrous hieroglyphs, traced of old by Moses in the wilderness, must be left unexplained, till one comes forward and proclaims, "The Cross of Christ and the Son of God Incarnate" Then, the whole is clear, so that he who runs may read, and a child may understand. Blessed Savior. In You, we see everything fulfilled which God spoke of in old by the Prophets. In You, we discover everything carried out in substance which

God had set before us in the dim mist of sacrificial smoke. Glory be unto Your name. "It is finished," everything is summed up in YOU.

2. But the words have richer meaning. Not only were all types, and prophecies, and promises thus finished in Christ, **but all the typical sacrifices of the old Jewish Law were now abolished, as well as explained**. They were finished, finished in Him. Will you imagine for a minute the saints in Heaven looking down upon what was done on earth, Abel and his friends who had long ago before the Flood been sitting in the glories above? They watch while God lights star after star in Heaven. Promise after Promise flashes light upon the thick darkness of earth. They see Abraham come, and they look down and wonder while they see God revealing Christ to Abraham in the person of Isaac. They gaze just as the angels do, desiring to look into the mystery. From the times of Noah, Abraham, Isaac, and Jacob, they see altars smoking, recognitions of the fact that man is guilty, and the spirits before the Throne say, "Lord, when will sacrifices finish? When will blood no more be shed?" The offering of bloody sacrifices soon increases. It is now carried on by men ordained for the purpose. Aaron and the high priests, and the Levites every morning and every evening offer a lamb, while great sacrifices are offered on special occasions. Bullocks groan, rams bleed, the necks of doves are wrung, and all the while the saints are crying, *"O Lord, how long? When shall the sacrifice cease?"* Year after year, **the high priest** goes within the veil and sprinkles the Mercy Seat with blood; the next year sees him do the same, and the next, and again, and again, and again! **David** offers tens of hundreds, **Solomon** slaughters tens of thousands, **Hezekiah** offers rivers of oil, **Josiah** gives thousands of the fat of fed beasts, and the spirits of the just say, "Will it never be complete? Will the sacrifice never be finished? Must there always be a remembrance of sin? Will not the last High Priest soon come? Will not the order and line of Aaron

soon lay aside its labor, because the whole is finished?" Not yet, not yet, you spirits of the just, for after the captivity, the slaughter of victims still remains. But lo, He comes. Gaze more intently than before, He comes who is to close the line of priests! Lo, there He stands, clothed, not now with linen ephod, not with ringing bells, nor with sparkling jewels on His breastplate, but arrayed in human flesh He stands, His Cross, His altar, His body and His soul, the Victim, Himself the Priest, and lo, before His God, He offers up His own soul within the veil of thick darkness which has covered Him from the sight of men. Presenting His own blood, He enters within the veil, sprinkles it there, and coming forth from the midst of the darkness, He looks down on the astonished earth, and upward to expectant Heaven, and cries, "It is finished! It is finished!" that for which you looked so long, is fully achieved and perfected forever.

3. The Savior meant, we doubt not, that in this moment, **His perfect obedience was finished. It was necessary, in order that man might be saved, that the Law of God should be kept, for no man can see God's face except he is perfect in righteousness. Christ undertook to keep God's Law for His people, to its every mandate, and preserve its every statute intact.** Throughout the first years of His life, He privately obeyed, honoring His father and His mother; during the next three years, He publicly obeyed God, spending and being spent in His service, till if you would know what a man would be whose life was wholly conformed to the Law of God, you may see him in Christ: *"My dear Redeemer and my Lord, /I read my duty in Your Word, /But in Your life the Law appears / Drawn out in living characters."*

It needed nothing to complete the perfect virtue of life but the entire obedience of death. **He who would serve God must be willing not only to give all his soul and his strength while he lives, but he must stand prepared to resign his life when it shall be for God's Glory.**

Our perfect Substitute put the last stroke upon His work by dying, and therefore, He claims to be absolved from further debt, for "It is finished!" Yes, glorious Lamb of God, it is finished! You have been tempted in all points like as we are, yet have You sinned in none. It *was* finished, for the last arrow out of Satan's quiver had been shot at You; the last blasphemous insinuation, the last wicked temptation had spent its fury on You; the prince of this world had surveyed You from head to foot, within and without, but he had found nothing in You. Now, your trial is over, You have finished the work which Your Father gave You to do, and so finished it that Hell itself cannot accuse You of a flaw. And now, looking upon Your entire obedience, You say, "It is finished," and we Your people believe most joyously that it is even so.

... This is more than you or I could have said if Adam had never fallen! If we had been in the Garden of Eden today, we could never have boasted a finished righteousness, since a creature can never finish its obedience. As long as a creature lives, it is bound to obey, and as long as a free agent exists on earth it would be in danger of violating the vow of its obedience. If Adam had been in Paradise from the first day until now, he might fall tomorrow. Left to himself, there would be no reason why that king of Nature could not yet be uncrowned. But Christ the Creator, who finished Creation, has perfected Redemption. God can ask no more. The Law has received all it claims; the largest extent of justice cannot demand another hour's obedience. It is done. It is complete. The last throw of the shuttle is over, and the robe is woven from the top throughout. Let us rejoice, then, in this that the Master meant by His dying cry, that His perfect righteousness, wherewith He covers us, was finished.

4. But next, the Savior meant *that the satisfaction which He rendered to the Justice of God was finished.* The debt was now, to the last farthing, all discharged. The Atonement and Propitiation were made once for all, and forever, by the one Offering made in Jesus' body on the Tree. There was the cup; Hell was in it; the Savior drank it, not a sip, and then a pause;

not a draught, and then a ceasing; but He drained it till there is not a dreg left for any of His people. The great ten-thronged whip of the Law was worn out upon His back; there is no lash left with which to smite one for whom Jesus died. The great bombardment of God's Justice has exhausted all its ammunition; there is nothing left to be hurled against a child of God! Sheathed is your sword, O Justice! Silenced is your thunder, O Law! There remains nothing now of all the griefs, and pains, and agonies which chosen sinners ought to have suffered for their sins, for Christ has endured all for His Own Beloved, and "It is finished." Brothers and Sisters, *it is more than the damned in Hell can ever say.* If you and I had been compelled to make satisfaction to God's Justice by being sent to Hell, we never could have said, "It is finished." Christ has paid the debt which all the torments of eternity could not have paid. Lost souls, you suffer today as you have suffered for ages past, but God's Justice is not satisfied, His Law is not fully magnified. And when time shall fail, and eternity shall have been flying on, still forever, the uttermost farthing never having been paid, the punishment for sin must fall upon unpardoned sinners! But Christ has done what all the flames of the pit of Hell could not do in all eternity; He has magnified the Law and made it honorable, and now, from the Cross he cries: "It is finished!"

5. Once again, when He said, "It is finished," *Jesus had totally destroyed the power of Satan, of sin, and of death.* The Champion had entered the lists to do battle for our soul's redemption against all our foes. He met Sin. Horrible, terrible, all-but omnipotent Sin nailed Him to the Cross; but in that deed, Christ nailed Sin also to the tree. There, they both did hang together, Sin and Sin's Destroyer. Sin destroyed Christ, and, by that destruction, Christ destroyed Sin! Next, came the second enemy, Satan. He assaulted Christ with all his hosts. Calling up his warriors from every corner and quarter of the universe, he said, *"Awake, arise, or be forever fallen! Here is our great Enemy*

236

who has sworn to bruise my head; now, let us bruise His heel!"
They shot their hellish darts into His heart; they poured their
boiling cauldrons on His brain; they emptied their venom into
His veins; they spat their insinuations into His face; they hissed
their devilish fears into His ears. He stood alone, the Lion of the
tribe of Judah, hounded by all the dogs of Hell. Our Champion
quailed not, but used His holy weapons, striking right and
left with all the Power of God-supported Manhood! On came
the hosts; volley after volley was discharged against Him. No
mimic thunders were these, but such as might shake the very
gates of Hell. The Conqueror steadily advanced, overturning
their ranks, dashing in pieces His enemies, breaking the bow,
and cutting the spear in sunder, and burning the chariots in the
fire, while He cried, "In the name of God will I destroy you!"
At last, foot to foot, He met the champion of Hell, and now
our David fought with Goliath. Not long was the struggle; thick
was the darkness which gathered round them both; but He,
who is the Son of God as well as the Son of Mary, knew how
to smite the fiend, and He did smite him with Divine fury, till,
having despoiled him of his armor, having quenched his fiery
darts, and broken his head, He cried, "It is finished" and sent
the fiend, bleeding and howling, down to Hell. We can imagine
him pursued by the eternal Savior, who exclaims: *"Traitor! /
My bolt shall find and pierce you through, /Though under Hell's
profoundest wave /You dive to seek a sheltering grave."*

His thunderbolt overtook the fiend, and grasping him with both
His hands, the Savior drew around him the great chain. The angels
brought the royal chariot from on high, to whose wheels the captive
fiend was bound. Lash the mighty steeds up the everlasting hills. Spirits
made perfect come forth to meet Him. Sing to the Conqueror who
drags death and Hell behind Him, and leads captivity captive. *"Lift up
your heads, O you gates, and be you lifted up, you everlasting doors, that the
King of Glory may come in."* But stay; before He enters, let Him be rid of

this His burden. Lo, He takes the fiend, and hurls him down through illimitable night, broken, bruised, with his power destroyed, bereft of his crown, to lie forever howling in the Pit of Hell. Thus, when the Savior cried, "It is finished," He had defeated Sin and Satan; nor less had he vanquished Death. Death had come against Him, as Christmas Evans puts it, with his fiery dart, which he struck right through the Savior, till the point fixed in the Cross, and when he tried to pull it out again, he left the sting behind. What more could he do? He was disarmed. Then Christ set some of his prisoners free; for many of the saints arose and were seen of many, then He said to him, *"Death, I take from you your keys; you must live for a little while to be the warden of those beds in which My saints shall sleep, but give Me your keys."* And lo, the Savior stands today with the keys of death hanging at His belt, and He waits until the hour shall come of which no man knows; when the trumpet of the archangel shall ring like the silver trumpets of Jubilee, and then, He shall say, *"Let My captives go free."* Then, shall the tombs be opened in virtue of Christ's death, and the very bodies of the saints shall live again in an eternity of glory: *"'It is finished!'/Hear the dying Savior cry."*

B. Second, *LET US HEAR AND WONDER.*

Let us perceive what mighty things were effected and secured by these words, "It is finished." Thus, He *ratified the Covenant.* **That Covenant was signed and sealed before, and in all things it was ordered well, but when Christ said, "It is finished," then the Covenant was made doubly sure; when the blood of Christ's heart bespattered the Divine roll, then it could never be reversed, nor could one of its ordinances be broken, nor one of its stipulations fail.** You know of the Everlasting Covenant, God covenants on His part that He would give Christ to see of the travail of His soul; that all who were given to Him should have new hearts and right spirits; that they should be washed from sin, and should enter into life through Him. Christ's side of the Covenant was this, "Father, I will do Your will; I will pay the ransom to the last jot and tittle; I will give You perfect obedience and complete satisfaction." Now, if this second part of the Covenant had never been fulfilled, the first part would have been invalid, but when Jesus said, "It is finished," then there was nothing left to be performed on His part, and now, the Covenant is all on one side. **It is God's, "I will," and "They shall."** *"A new heart will I give you, and a right spirit will I put within you." "I will sprinkle clean water upon you, and you shall be clean." "From all your iniquities will I cleanse you." "I will lead you by a way that you know not." "I will surely bring them in."* **The Covenant that day was ratified. When Christ said, "It is finished,"** *His Father was honored, and Divine Justice was fully displayed.* The Father always did love His people. Do not think that Christ died to make God the Father loving. He always had loved them from before the foundation of the world, but, "It is finished," took away the barriers which were in the Father's way. He would, as a God of Love, and now He could as a God of Justice, bless poor sinners. From that day, the Father is well pleased to receive sinners to His bosom. When Christ said, "It is finished," *He Himself was glorified.* Then, on His head descended the all-glorious crown. Then, did the Father give to Him honors, which He had not before. He had honor as God, but as Man, He was despised and rejected; now, as God and Man, Christ was made to sit down forever on His Father's Throne, crowned with honor and majesty.

Then, too, by "It is finished," *the Spirit was procured for us: "'Tis by the merit of His death /Who hung upon the tree, /The Spirit is sent down to breathe /On such dry bones as we."*

Then, the Spirit which Christ had aforetime promised, perceived a new and living way by which He could come to dwell in the hearts of men, and men might come up to dwell with Him above. That day, too, when Christ said: "It is finished," *the words had effect on Heaven.* Then, the walls of chrysolite stood fast; then, the jasper light of the pearly-gated city shone like the light of seven days. Before, the saints had been saved as it were on credit. They had entered Heaven, God having faith in His Son Jesus. Had not Christ finished His work, surely they must have left their shining spheres, and suffered in their own persons for their own sins. I might represent Heaven, if my imagination might be allowed a moment, as being ready to totter if Christ had not finished His work; its stones would have been unloosed; massive and stupendous though its bastions are, yet, they would have fallen as earthly cities reel under the throes of earthquakes. But Christ said, **"It is finished," and Oath, and Covenant, and blood set fast the dwelling place of the Redeemed, made their mansions safely and eternally their own, and bade their feet stand immovably upon the Rock.** No, more, that word, "It is finished!" took effect in the gloomy caverns and depths of hell. Then, Satan bit his iron bands in a rage, howling, *"I am defeated by the very Man whom I thought to overcome; my hopes are blasted; never shall an elect one come into my prison, never a blood-bought one be found in my abode."* Lost souls mourned that day, for they said, "'It is finished!' And if Christ Himself, the Substitute, could not be permitted to go free till He had finished all His punishment, then, we shall never be free!" It was their double death-knell, for they said, "Alas for us! Justice, which would not allow the Savior to escape, will never allow us to be at liberty. It is finished with Him, and therefore, it shall *never* be finished for us."

That day, too, the earth had a gleam of sunlight cast over her which she had never known before! Then, her hilltops began to glisten with the rising of the sun, and though her valleys still are clothed with darkness, and men wander here and there, and grope in the noon-day as in the night, yet, that sun is rising, climbing still its heavenly steeps, never to set, and soon shall its rays penetrate through the thick mists and clouds, and every eye shall see Him, and every heart be made glad with His light. **The words "It is finished!" consolidated Heaven, shook Hell, comforted earth; delighted the Father, glorified the Son, brought down the Spirit, and confirmed the Everlasting Covenant to all the chosen seed.**

C. And now, I come to my last point, very briefly. "It is finished!" *LET US PUBLISH IT.*

Children of God, you who by faith received Christ as your All-in-All, tell it every day of your lives that "It is finished!" Go and tell it to those who are torturing themselves thinking through obedience and mortification to offer satisfaction.... Cease, cease, poor wretch, from all these pains, for "It is finished!" In all parts of the earth, there are those who think that the misery of the body and the soul may be atonement for sin. Rush to them, stop them in their madness, and say to them, "Why do you this? 'It is finished!'" All the pains that God asks, Christ has suffered! All the satisfaction by way of agony in the flesh that the Law demands, Christ has already endured! "It is finished!" And when you have done this, go next to the ignorant adherents of Rome, when you see the priests with their backs to the people, offering every day the pretended "sacrifice of the mass," and lifting up the "host on high," a sacrifice, they say, "an unbloody sacrifice for the quick and the dead." Cry to them, "Cease, false priest, cease; for 'It is finished!' Cease, false worshipper, cease to bow, for 'It is finished!'" God neither asks nor accepts any other sacrifice than that which Christ offered once for all upon the Cross! Go next to the foolish among your own countrymen who call themselves Protestants, but who are really Papists after all, who think by their gifts and their gold, by their prayers and their vows, by their church, and their chapel attendance, by their baptisms and their confirmations, to make themselves fit for God! And say to them, "Stop, 'it is finished.' God needs not this of you! He has received enough. Why will you pin your rags to the fine linen of Christ's Righteousness? Why will you add your counterfeit farthing to the costly ransom which Christ has paid into the treasure-house of God? **Cease from your pains, your works, your performances, for 'It is finished!' Christ has done it all."**

... "It is finished." **Why improve on what is finished? Why add to that which is complete?** The Bible is finished, he that adds to it never had his name in the Book of Life, and will never see the Holy City, Christ's Atonement is finished, and he who adds to that must expect the same doom! And when you shall have told it thus to the ears of men of every nation and of every tribe, tell it to all poor despairing souls. You find them on their knees, crying, "O God, what can I do to make recompense for my offenses?" Tell them, "It is finished;" the recompense is already made. "O God!" they say, "How can I ever get a righteousness in which You can accept such a worm as I am." Tell them, "It is finished;" their righteousness is already worked out; they have no need to trouble themselves about adding to it, if "It is finished." Go to the poor despairing wretch, who has given himself up, not merely for death, but for damnation, he who says, "I cannot escape from sin, and I cannot be saved from its punishment." Say to him, "Sinner, the way of Salvation is finished once and for all." And if you meet some professed Christians in doubts and fears, tell them, "It is finished." Why, we have hundreds and thousands who are converted who do not know that "It is finished!" They never know that they are safe! They do not know that "It is finished." They think they have faith today, but perhaps they may become unbelieving tomorrow. They do not know that "It is finished!" They hope God will accept them, if they do some things, forgetting that the way of acceptance is finished.

God as much accepts a sinner who only believed in Christ five minutes ago, as He will a saint who has known and loved Him eighty years, for He does not accept men because of anything *they do* or feel, but simply and only for what *Christ did* and *that is finished.* Oh, poor Hearts, some of you do love the Savior in a measure, but blindly. You are thinking that you must be this, and attain to that, and then you may be assured that you are saved. Oh, you may be assured of it today, if you believe in Christ, you are saved. "But I feel imperfections." Yes, but what of that? God does not regard your imperfections, but He covers them with Christ's Righteousness. He sees them to remove them, but not to lay them to your charge. "Yes, but I cannot be what I would be." But what if you cannot? **God does not look at *you*, as what you are in *yourself*, but as what you are in *Christ*.**

Come with me, poor Soul, and you and I will stand together this morning, while the storm gathers, for we are not afraid. How sharp that lightning flash! But yet, we tremble not. How terrible that peal of thunder! And yet, we are not alarmed, and why? Is there anything in us why we should escape? No, but we are standing beneath the Cross, that precious Cross, which like some noble lightning rod in the storm, takes to itself all the death from the lighting, and all the fury from the storm. **We are safe. Loud may you roar, O thundering Law, and terribly may you flash, O avenging Justice. We can look up with calm delight to all the tumult of the elements, for we are safe beneath the Cross.**

Come with me again. **There is a royal banquet spread; the King Himself sits at the table, and angels are the servitors. Let us enter.** And we do enter, and we sit down and eat and drink; but how dare we do this? Our righteousness are as filthy rags; how dare we venture to come here? Oh, because the filthy rags are not ours any longer! We have renounced our own righteousness, and therefore, we have renounced the filthy rags, and now, today, we wear the royal garments of the Savior, and are from head to foot arrayed in white, without spot or wrinkle or any such thing! We stand in the clear sunlight, black, but comely; loathsome in ourselves, but glorious in Him! Condemned in Adam, but accepted in the Beloved. We are neither afraid nor ashamed to be with the angels of God, to talk with the glorified, no, nor even alarmed to speak with God Himself and call Him our Friend.

And now, last of all, I publish this to *sinners.* I know not where you are this morning, but may God find you; you who have been a drunkard, swearer, thief; you who have been a blackguard of the blackest kind; you who have dived into the very kennel, and rolled yourself in the mire, if today you feel that sin is hateful to you, believe in Him who has said, "It is finished!" Let me link your hand in mine; let us come together, both of us, and say, "Here are two poor naked souls, good Lord; we cannot clothe ourselves." And He will give us a robe, for "*It is finished!*" "But, Lord, is it long enough for such sinners and broad enough for such offenders?" "Yes," He says, "*It is finished!*" "But we need washing, Lord! Is there anything that can take away black spots as hideous as ours?" "Yes," He says, "here is the bath of blood." "But must we not add our tears to it?" "No," He says, "no, it is finished, there is enough." "And now, Lord, You have washed us, and You have clothed us, but we desire to be completely clean *within,* so that we may never sin any more. Lord, is there a way by which this can be done?" "Yes" He says, "there is the bath of water which flows from the wounded side of

Christ." "And, Lord, is there enough there to wash away my guiltiness as well as my guilt?" "Yes," He says, "It is finished!" **"Jesus Christ is made unto you sanctification as well as redemption."** Child of God, *will you have Christ's finished righteousness this morning, and will you rejoice in it more than you have ever done before?*

And oh, poor Sinner, **will you have Christ or nothing?** "Ah," says one, "I am willing enough, but I am not worthy." He does not need any worthiness! All He asks is *willingness,* for you know how He puts it, *"Whoever will, let him come."* If He has *given you willingness,* you may believe in Christ's finished work this morning. "Ah," says one, "but you cannot mean *me."* But I do, for it says, "Ho, *everyone* who thirsts." Do you thirst for Christ? Do you wish to be saved by Him? *"Everyone* who thirsts," not only that young woman yonder, not simply that gray-headed old rebel yonder who has long despised the Savior, but this mass below, and you in these double tiers of gallery, "Everyone who thirsts, come you to the waters, and he that has no money come." O that I could "compel" you to come! Great God, won't You make the sinner willing to be saved, for he wills to be damned, and will not come unless You change his will. Eternal Spirit, source of light, and life, and Grace, come down and bring the strangers home. "It is finished!" Sinner, there is nothing for God to do. "It is finished!" There is nothing for you to do. "It is finished," "Christ need not bleed." It is finished. "You need not weep." "It is finished." God the Holy Spirit need not tarry because of your unworthiness, nor need you tarry because of your helplessness. "It is finished!" Every stumbling block is rolled out of the road; every gate is opened; the bars of brass are broken; the gates of iron are burst asunder. "It is finished!" Come and welcome, come and welcome! The table is laid; the fatlings are killed; the oxen are ready. Lo, here stands the messenger! Come from the highways and from the hedges; come from the dens and from the alleys of London.

EXHORTATION: Come, you vilest of the vile; you who hate yourselves today, come. Jesus bids you! Oh, will you tarry? Oh, Spirit of God, repeat the invitation, and make it an effectual call to many a heart, for Jesus' sake! Amen.

2.   Christ's Dying Word for His Church

"It is finished"
(John 19:30 NKJV).

FOCUS: Spurgeon said that "there are four ways in which (he) wishes to look at" the text. "First, (he) will speak of this dying saying of our Lord to His glory. Second, (he) will use the text to the Church's comfort. Third, (he) will try to handle the subject to every believer's joy. And fourth, (he) will seek to show how our Lord's Words ought to lead to our own awakening."

IN the original Greek of John's Gospel there is only one word for this utterance of our Lord. To translate it into English, we have to use three words, but when it was spoken, it was only one, an ocean of meaning in a drop of language, a mere drop, for that is all that we can call one word! "It is finished." Yet it would need all the other words that ever were spoken, or ever can be spoken, to explain this one word. It is altogether immeasurable. It is high, I cannot attain to it. It is deep, I cannot fathom it. "Finished." I can half imagine the tone in which our Lord uttered this word, with a holy glorying, a sense of relief, the bursting out of a heart that had long been shut up within walls of anguish. "Finished." It was a Conqueror's cry, it was uttered with a loud voice. There is nothing of anguish about it, there is no wailing in it. **It is the cry of One who has completed a tremendous labor and is about to die and before He utters His death-prayer, "Father, into Your hands I commend My spirit," He shouts His life's last hymn in that one word, "Finished."**

May God the Holy Spirit help me to handle aright this text that is at once so small and yet so great. **First**, then, I will endeavor to speak of this dying saying of Christ *TO HIS GLORY*. Let us begin with that. Jesus said, "It is finished." **Let us glory in Him that it is finished.** You and I may well do this when we remember how very few things *we* have finished. We begin many things and, sometimes, we begin well.

We commence running like champions who must win the race, but soon we slacken our pace and we fall exhausted on the course. The race commenced is never completed. In fact, I am afraid that we have never finished *anything* perfectly. You know what we say of some pieces of work, "Well, the man has done it, but there is no, 'finish,' about it." No, and you must begin with, "finish," and go on with, "finish," if you are, at last, able to say broadly as the Savior said without any qualification, "It is finished."

What was it that was finished? His lifework and His atoning Sacrifice on our behalf. He had interposed between our souls and Divine Justice and He had stood in our place to obey and suffer on our behalf. He began this work early in life, even while He was a Child. He persevered in holy obedience thirty-three years. That obedience cost Him many a pang and groan. Now it is about to cost Him His life and, as He gives away His life to finish the work of obedience to the Father, and of redemption for us, He says, "It is finished." It was a wonderful work, even to contemplate, only Infinite Love would have thought of devising such a plan. It was a wonderful work to carry on for so long, only boundless patience would have continued at hand now that it requires the offering of Himself and the yielding up of His earthly life, only a Divine Savior, very God of very God, would or could have consummated it by the surrender of His breath. What a work it was. Yet it was finished while you and I have lots of little things lying about that we have never finished. We have begun to do something for Jesus that would bring Him a little honor and glory, but we have never finished it. We did mean to glorify Christ, have not some of you intended, oh, so much? Yet it has never come to anything. But Christ's work, which cost Him heart and soul, body and spirit, cost Him everything, even His death on the Cross. He pushed through all that till it was accomplished and He could say, "It is finished."

To whom did our Savior say, "It is finished"? He said it to all whom it might concern, but it seems to me that He chiefly said it to His Father, for, immediately after, apparently in a lower tone of voice, He said, "Father, into Your hands I commend My spirit."

Beloved, it is one thing for me to say to you, "I have finished my work," possibly, if I were dying, you might say that I had finished my work, but for the Savior to say that to God, to hang in the Presence of Him whose eyes are as a flame of fire, **the great Reader and Searcher of all hearts**. For Jesus, I say, to look the dread Father in the face and say, as He bowed His head, "Father, it is finished; I have finished the work which You gave Me to do," oh, who but He could venture to make such a declaration as that? We can find a thousand flaws in our best works! And when we lie dying, we shall still have to lament our shortcomings and excesses. But there is nothing of imperfection about Him who stood as Substitute for us and, unto the Father, Himself, He can say, concerning *all* His work, "It is finished." Therefore, glorify Him tonight. Oh, **glorify Him in your hearts, …, that even in the Presence of the Great Judge of all, your Surety and your Substitute is able to claim perfection for all His service.**

Just think also, for a minute or two, now that you have remembered what Jesus finished, and to whom He said that He had finished it, *how truly He had finished it.* From the beginning to the end of Christ's life there is nothing omitted, no single act of service ever left undone! Neither is there any action of His slurred over, or performed in a careless manner. **"It is finished," refers as much to His Childhood as to His death. The whole of the service that He was to render to God, when He came here in human form, was finished in every single part and portion of it.** I take up a piece of a cabinet-maker's work and it bears a good appearance. I open the lid and am satisfied with the workmanship. But there is something about the hinge that is not properly finished. Or, perhaps, if I turn it over and look at the bottom of the box, I shall see that there is a piece that has been scratched, or that one part has not been well planned or properly polished.

But if you examine the Master's work right through, if you begin at Bethlehem and go on to Golgotha and look minutely at every portion of it, the private as well as the public, the silent as well as the spoken part, you will find that **it is finished, completed, perfected**. We may say of it that, among all works, there is none like it. It is a multitude of perfections joined together to make up one absolute perfection. Therefore, let us glorify the name of our blessed Lord. Crown Him! Crown Him, for He has done His work well. Come, you saints, speak much to His honor and in your hearts keep on singing to the praise of Him who did so thoroughly, so perfectly, all the work which His Father gave Him to do.

In the first place, then, we use our Lord's words to His Glory. Much might be said upon such a theme, but time will not permit it.

B. **Second**, we will use the text *TO THE CHURCH'S COMFORT.*

I am persuaded that it was so intended to be used, for none of the Words of our Lord on the Cross are addressed to His Church but this one. I cannot believe that when He was dying He left His people, for whom He died, without a word. "Father, forgive them; for they know not what they do," is for sinners, not for saints. "I thirst," is for Himself, and so is that bitter cry, "My God, My God, why have You forsaken Me?" "Woman, behold your son!" is for Mary. "Today shall you be with Me in Paradise," is for the penitent thief. "Into Your hands I commend My spirit," is for the Father. Jesus must have had *something* to say, in the hour of death, for His Church and, surely, this is His dying word for her! He tells her, shouting it in her ear that has become dull and heavy with despair, "It is finished." "It is finished, O My redeemed one, My bride, My well-beloved for whom I came to lay down My life. It is finished, the work is done!": *"Love's redeeming work is done. /Fought the fight, the battle won."*

"Christ loved the Church and gave Himself for it." John, in the Revelation, speaks of the Redeemer's work as already accomplished and, therefore, He sings, "Unto Him that loved us, and washed us from our sins in His own blood, and has made us kings and priests unto God and His Father; to Him be glory and dominion forever and ever. Amen." This Truth of God is full of comfort to His people.

And, first, as it concerns Christ, do you not feel greatly comforted to think that He is no longer to be humiliated? *His suffering and shame*

248

are finished. I often sing, with sacred exultation and pleasure, those lines of Dr. [Isaac] Watts: *"No more the bloody spear! /The Cross and nails no more, /For Hell itself shakes at His name /And all the heavens adore, /There His full glories shine /With uncreated rays, /And bless His saints' and angels' eyes /To everlasting days."*

I also like that expression in another of our hymns: *"Now both the Surety and sinner are free."*

Not only are they free for whom Christ became a Surety, but He, Himself, is forever free from all the obligations and consequences of His Suretyship. Men will never spit in His face again. The Roman soldiers will never scourge Him again! Judas, where are you? Behold the Christ sitting upon His Great White Throne, the glorious King who was once the Man of Sorrows. Now, Judas, come and betray Him with a kiss! What, man, dare you not do it? Come, Pilate, and wash your hands in pretended innocence and say, now, that you are guiltless of His blood. Come, you Scribes and Pharisees, and accuse Him and oh, you Jewish mob and Gentile rabble, newly risen from the grave, shout now, "Away with Him! Crucify Him!" But look! They flee from Him! They cry to the mountains and rocks, "Fall on us and hide us from the face of Him that sits on the Throne!" Yet that is the face that was more marred than any man's, the face of Him whom they once despised and rejected. Are you not glad to think that they cannot despise Him now, that they cannot entreat Him now? And Jesus says of it, "It is finished." *"'Tis past—that agonizing hour /Of torture and of shame"*

We derive further comfort and joy as we think that not only are Christ's pangs and sufferings finished, *but His Father's will and Word have had a perfect completion.* Certain things were written that were to be done and these are done. Whatever the Father required has been rendered. "It is finished." My Father will never say to me, "I cannot save you by the death of My Son, for I am dissatisfied with His work." Oh, no, Beloved, God is well pleased with Christ and with us in Him. There is nothing which was arranged in the eternal mind to be done! No, not a jot or tittle, Christ has done it all! As His eyes, those eyes that often wept for us, reads down the ancient writing, Christ is able to say,

"I have finished the work which My Father gave Me to do. Therefore, be comforted, O My people, for My Father is well pleased with Me and well pleased with you in Me."

I like, sometimes, when I am in prayer, to say to the great Father, "Father, look on Your Son. Is He not all loveliness? Are there not in Him unutterable beauties? Do You not delight in Him? If You have looked on me and grown sick of me, as well You may, now refresh Yourself by looking on Your Well-Beloved. Delight Yourself in Him: *"Him, and then the sinner sees, /Look through Jesus 'wounds on me."* The perfect satisfaction of the Father with Christ's work for His people so that Christ could say, "It is finished," is a ground of solid comfort to His Church forevermore.

Dear Friends, once more, take comfort from this, "It is finished," **for** *the redemption of Christ's Church is perfected!* There is not another penny to be paid for her full release. There is no mortgage upon Christ's inheritance. **Those whom He bought with blood are forever clear of all charges, paid for to the utmost.** There was a handwriting of ordinances against us, but Christ has taken it away, He has nailed it to His Cross. "It is finished," finished forever. All those overwhelming debts which would have sunk us to the lowest Hell have been discharged and they who believe in Christ may appear with boldness even before the Throne of God, itself. "It is finished." What comfort there is in this glorious Truth of God: *"Lamb of God! Your death has given /Pardon, peace, and hope of Heaven! / 'It is finished,' let us raise /Songs of thankfulness and praise!"*

And I think that we may say to the Church of God that when Jesus said, "It is finished," *her ultimate triumph was secured.* "Finished!" By that one Word He declared that He had broken the head of the old dragon. By His death Jesus has routed the hosts of darkness and crushed the rising hopes of Hell. We have a stern battle yet to fight, nobody can tell what may await the Church of God in years to come, it would be idle for us to attempt to prophesy. But it looks as if there are to be sterner times and darker days than we have ever yet known, but what of that? Our Lord has defeated the foe and we have to fight with one who is already vanquished. The old serpent has been crushed, his head is bruised, and we have, now, to trample on him. We have this sure Word of promise to encourage us, "The God of peace shall bruise Satan under your feet shortly." Surely, "It is finished," sounds like the trumpet of victory. Let us have faith to claim that victory through the blood of the Lamb. And let every Christian, here, let the whole Church of God, as one mighty army take comfort from this dying Word of the now risen and ever-living Savior, "It is finished." His Church may rest perfectly satisfied that His work for her is fully accomplished.

C. No, **third**, I want to use this expression, "It is finished," *TO EVERY BELIEVER'S JOY.*

When our Lord said, "It is finished," there was something to make every Believer in Him glad. What did that utterance mean? You and I have believed in Jesus of Nazareth. We believe Him to be the Messiah, sent of God. Now, if you will turn to the Old Testament, you will find that the marks of the Messiah are very many and very complicated. And if you will then turn to the life and death of Christ, you will see in Him *every mark of the Messiah plainly exhibited.* Until He had said, "It is finished," and until He had actually died, there was some doubt that there might be some one prophecy unfulfilled, but now that He hangs upon the Cross, every mark, every sign and every token of His Messiahship has been fulfilled and He says, "It is finished." **The life and death of Christ and the types of the Old Testament fit each other like hand and glove.** It would be quite impossible for any person to write the life of a man, by way of fiction, and then in another book to write out a series of types, personal and sacrificial, and to make the character of the man fit all the types, even if he had permission to make both books, he could not do it. If he were allowed to make both the lock and the key, he could not do it, but here we have the lock made beforehand. In all the Books of the Old Testament, from the prophecy in the Garden of Eden right down to Malachi, the last of the Prophets, there were certain marks and tokens of the Christ. All these were so very singular that it did not appear as if they could all meet in one Person. But they did all meet in One, every one of them, whether it concerned some minute point or some prominent characteristic! When the Lord Jesus Christ had ended His life, He could say, "It is finished; My life has tallied with all that was said of it from the first Word of prophecy even to the last." Now, that ought greatly to encourage your faith. **You are not following cunningly-devised fables, but you are following One who must be the Messiah of God since He so exactly fits all the Prophecies and all the Types that were given before concerning Him**.

"It is finished." Let every Believer be comforted in another respect, that **every *honor which the Law of God could require has been rendered to it***. You and I have broken that Law, as all the race of mankind has broken it. We have tried to thrust God from His Throne. We have dishonored His Law. We have broken His Commandments willfully and wickedly. But there has come One who is, Himself, God, the Law-Giver, and He has taken human Nature, and in that Nature He has kept the Law perfectly. And, inasmuch as the Law had been broken by man, He has in the Nature of man borne the sentence due for all man's transgressions. The Godhead, being linked with the Manhood, gave supreme virtue to all that the Manhood suffered. And Christ, in life and in death, has magnified the Law and made it honorable. And God's Law at this day is raised to even greater honor than it had before man broke it. **The death of the Son of God, the Sacrifice of the Lord Jesus Christ, has vindicated the great moral principle of God's government and made His Throne to stand out gloriously before the eyes of men and angels forever and ever**. If Hell were filled with men, it would not be such a vindication of Divine Justice as when God spared not His Own Son, but delivered Him up for us all, and made Him to die, the Just for the unjust, to bring us to God. Now **let every Believer rejoice in the great fact that, by the death of Christ, the Law of God is abundantly honored**. You can be saved without impugning the holiness of God! You are saved without putting any stain upon the Divine statute-book. The Law is kept and mercy triumphs, too.

And, Beloved, here is included, of necessity, another comforting Truth. Christ might well say, "It is finished," **for *every solace conscience can need is now given.*** When your conscience is disturbed and troubled, if it knows that God is perfectly honored and His Law vindicated, then it becomes easy. Men are always starting some new theory of the Atonement and one has said, lately, that the Atonement was simply meant as an easement to the conscience of men. It is not so, my Brothers and Sisters, there would be no easing of the conscience by anything that was meant for that, alone. Conscience can only be satisfied if God is satisfied. Until I see how the Law is vindicated, my troubled conscience can never find rest. Dear Heart, are your eyes red with weeping? Look to Him who hangs on the tree. Is your heart heavy, even to despair? Look to Him who hangs on the tree and believe in Him! Take Him to be your soul's atoning Lamb, suffering in your place. **Accept Him as your Representative, dying your death that you may live His life, bearing your sin that you may be made the righteousness of God in Him. This is the best quietus in the world for every fear that conscience can raise, let every Believer know that it is so.**

Once more, there is joy to every Believer when he remembers that, as Christ said, "It is finished," every *guarantee was given of the eternal salvation of all the redeemed.* <u>It appears to me that if Christ finished the work for us, He will finish the work *in* us.</u> If He has undertaken so supreme a labor as the redemption of our souls by blood and that is finished, then the great, but yet minor labor of renewing our natures and transforming us even unto perfection, shall be finished, too. If, when we were sinners, Christ loved us so as to die for us, now that He has redeemed us, and has already reconciled us to Himself, and made us His friends and His disciples, will He not finish the work that is necessary to make us fit to stand among the golden lamps of Heaven and to sing His praises in the country where nothing that defiles can ever enter? *"The work which His goodness began, /The arm of His strength will complete! /His promises is yes and Amen, /And never was forfeited yet! /Things future, nor things that are now, /Not all things below and above, /Can make Him His purpose forego, /O server my soul from His love!"*

I believe it, my Brothers and Sisters. He who has said, "It is finished," will never leave anything undone! It shall never be said of Him, "This Man began, but was not able to finish." **If He has bought me with His blood and called me by His Grace, and <u>I am resting on His promise and power</u>, I shall be with Him where He is, and I shall behold His Glory, as surely as He is Christ the Lord and I believe in Him! What comfort this Truth of God brings to every child of God.**

Are there any of you, here, who are trying to do something to make a righteousness of your own? How dare you attempt such a work when Jesus says, "It is finished"! Are you trying to put a few of your own merits together, a few odds and ends, fig leaves and filthy rags of your own righteousness? Jesus says, "It is finished." Why do you want to add anything of your own to what He has completed? Do you say that you are not fit to be saved? What? Have you to bring some of your fitness to eke out Christ's work? "Oh," you say, "I hope to come to Christ one of these days when I get better." What? What? What? What? Are you to make yourself better and *then* is Christ to do the rest of the work?

You remind me of the railways to our country towns! You know that, often, the station is half-a-mile or a mile out of the town, so that you cannot get to the station without having an omnibus to take you there. But my Lord Jesus Christ comes right to the town of Mansoul! His railway runs close to your feet and there is the carriage door wide open—step in. You have not even to go over a bridge, or under a subway, there stands the carriage just before you. This royal railroad carries souls all the way from Hell's dark door, where they lie in sin, up to Heaven's great gate of pearl where they dwell in perfect righteousness forever! Cast yourself on Christ! Take Him to be everything you need, for He says of the whole work of salvation, "It is finished."

I recollect the saying of a Scotchwoman who had applied to be admitted to the communion of the Church. Being thought to be very ignorant and little instructed in the things of God, she was put back by the elders. The minister also had seen her and thought that, at least for a while, she should wait. I wish I could speak Scotch, so as to give you her answer, but I am afraid that I would make a mistake if I tried it. It is a fine language, doubtless, for those who can speak it. She said something like this, "Aweel, Sir; aweel, Sir, but I ken ae thing. As the lintbell opens to the sun, so my heart opens to the name of Jesus." You have, perhaps, seen the flax flower shut itself up when the sun has gone and, if so, you know that whenever the sun has come back, the flower opens itself at once. "So," said the poor woman, "I know one thing that as the flower opens to the sun, so **my heart opens to the name of Jesus.**" Do you know that, Friends? Do you know that one thing? Then I do not care if you do not know much else. If that one thing is known by you, and if it is really so, you may be far from perfect in your own estimation, but you are a saved soul.

One said to me, when she came to join the Church, and I asked her whether she was perfect, "Perfect? Oh, dear no, Sir! I wish that I could be." "Ah, yes!" I replied, "that would just please you, would it not?" "Yes, it would, indeed," she answered. "Well, then," I said, "that shows that your heart is perfect and that you love perfect things; you are pining after perfection, there is a something in you, and, 'I' in you, that sins not, but that seeks after that which is holy. And yet you do that which you would not, and you groan because you do, and the apostle is like you when he says, 'It is no more I, the real I, that do it, but sin that dwells in me.'" May the Lord put that "I" into many of you, …, that "I" which will hate sin, that "I" which will find its Heaven in being perfectly free from sin, that "I" which will delight itself in the Almighty, that "I" which will sun itself in the smile of Christ, that "I" which will strike down every evil within as soon as ever it shows its head! So will you sing that familiar prayer of [Augustus] Toplady's that we have often sung: **"Let the water and the blood /From Your riven side which flowed, /Be of sin the double cure, /Cleanse me from its guilt and power.!"**

D. I close by saying, in the **fourth** place, that we shall use this text, "It is finished, *TO OUR OWN AWAKENING.*

Somebody once wickedly said, "Well, if Christ has finished it, there is nothing for me to do, now, but to fold my hands and go to sleep." That is the speech of a devil, not of a Christian! There is no Grace in the heart when the mouth can talk like that. On the contrary, **the true child of God says, "Has Christ finished His work for me? Then tell me what work I can do for Him."** You remember the two questions of Saul of Tarsus. The first enquiry, after He had been struck down, was, *"Who are You, Lord?"* And the next was, *"Lord, what will You have me to do?"* If Christ has finished the work for you which you could not do, now go and finish the work for Him which you are privileged and permitted to do. Seek to: *"Rescue the perishing, /Care for the dying, /Snatch them in pity from sin and the grave. /Weep over the erring one, /Lift up the fallen, /Tell them of Jesus, the Mighty to save."*

My inference from this saying of Christ, "It is finished," is this: Has He finished His work for me? Then I must get to work for Him and *I must persevere until I finish my work, too,* not to save myself, for that is all done, but because I am saved. Now I must work for Him with all my might and if there comes discouragements, if there comes sufferings, if there comes a sense of weakness and exhaustion, yet let me not give way to it, but, inasmuch as He pressed on till He could say, "It is finished," let me press on till I, too, shall be able to say, "I have finished the work which You gave me to do." You know how men who go fishing look out for the fish. I have heard of a man going to Keston Ponds [in Greater London] on Saturday to fish and staying all day Sunday, Monday, Tuesday and Wednesday! There was another man fishing there and the other man had only been there two days. He said, "I have been here two days and I have only had one bite." "Why," replied the other, "I have been here ever since last Saturday and I have not had a bite yet! But I mean to keep on." "Well," answered the other, "I cannot keep on without catching *something.*" "Oh!" said number one, "but I have such a longing to catch some fish that I shall stay here till I do." I believe that fellow would ultimately catch some fish if there were any to be caught! He is the kind of fisherman to do it and we need to have men who feel that they must win souls for Christ, and that they will persevere till they do. It must be so with us, Brothers and Sisters, we cannot let men go down to Hell if there is any way of saving them.

The next inference is that *we can finish our work, for Christ finished His.* You can put a lot of "finish" into your work and you can hold on to the end and complete the work by Divine Grace. And that Grace is waiting for you that Grace is promised to you. Seek it, find it, get it. Do not act as some do, ah, even some who are before me now. They served God, once, and then they ran away from Him. They have come back, God bless them and help them to be more useful. But future earnest service will never make up for that sad gap in their earlier career. It is best to keep on, and on, and on, from the commencement to the close. May the Lord help us to persevere to the end, till we can truly say of our lifework, "It is finished."

One word of caution I must give you. *Let us not think that our work is finished till we die.* "Well," says one, "I was just going to say of my work, 'It is finished.'" Were you? Were you? I remember that when **John Newton** wrote a book about Grace in the blade, and Grace in the ear, and Grace in the full corn in the ear, a very talkative body said to him, "I have been reading your valuable book, Mr. Newton. It is a splendid work and when I came to that part, 'The full corn in the ear,' I thought how wonderfully you had described *me*." "Oh," replied Mr. Newton, "but you could not have read the book rightly, for it is one of the marks of the full corn in the ear that it hangs its head very low." So it is and when a man, in a careless, boastful spirit, says of his work, "It is finished," I am inclined to ask, "Brother, was it ever begun? If your work for Christ is finished, I should think that you never realized what it ought to be." As long as there is breath in our bodies, let us serve Christ. As long as we can think, as long as we can speak, as long as we can work, let us serve Him! Let us even serve Him with our last gasp and, if it is possible, let us try to set some work going that will glorify Him when we are dead and gone! Let us scatter some seed that may spring up when we are sleeping beneath the hillock in the cemetery. Ah, Beloved, we shall never have finished our work for Christ until we bow our heads and give up the ghost.

The oldest friend here has a little something to do for the Master. Someone said to me, the other day, "I cannot think why old Mrs. So-and-So is spared, she is quite a burden to her friends." "Ah," I replied, "she has something yet to do for her Lord, she has another word to speak for Him." Sister, look up your work and get it done! And you, Brother, see what remains of your lifework yet incomplete. Wind off the ends, get all the little corners finished. Who knows how long it may be before you and I may have to give in our account? Some are called away very suddenly, they are apparently in good health one day and they are gone the next. I should not like to leave a half-finished life behind me. The Lord Jesus Christ said, "It is finished," and your heart should say, "Lord, and I will finish, too, not to mix my work with Yours, but because You have finished Yours, I will, by Your Grace, finish mine."

EXHORTATION: Now may the Lord give us the joy of His Presence at His Table. May the bread and wine speak to you much better than I can. May every heir of Heaven see Christ, tonight, and rejoice in His finished work, for His dear name's sake. Amen.

3. Christ's Finished Work

By Octavius Winslow
"It is finished"
(John 19:30 NKJV).

FOCUS: "[Jesus Christ] was the God-Man, Mediator, who, as the Son, and yet the Servant of the Father, relinquished His Throne for a Cross, that He might accomplish the Redemption, work out the Salvation of His Church, the people given to Him of God, and who, on the eve of that Redemption and with all the certainty of

an actual Atonement, could thus breathe His intercessory petition to Heaven, 'I have *finished* the work which You gave Me to do.'"

THERE never existed but one Being who in Truth could affirm of His work, "It is finished!" Incompleteness and defect trace the vastest, elaborate, and accomplished products of human genius and power. That brilliant volume of history, at a period of thrilling interest, falls from the death-struck hand of its author, fragmentary and incomplete. That magnificent work of art fades before the glazed eye of the painter and the sculptor, at a moment when the pencil is pointed, and the chisel upraised to impart the last and perfecting touch. That splendid edifice, the conception of a master mind, with all its architectural skill and beauty, is but a monument of human forethought and power, blinded and cramped in its range. Thus, contemplate man's noblest achievements, the intellectual and the physical, the touch of human imperfection and incompleteness mars and traces all. The great truth, then, stands out like a constellation flaming in its own solitary orbit, that there never was but *one* Man who could gaze with complacency upon His work and, with His expiring breath, exclaim, "It is finished!"

We summon you ... around the Cross of Calvary, to listen to the words now breathing from the quivering lips of our dying Lord, "It is finished!" And believing, as I do most firmly and solemnly, that no Scriptural Doctrine, no revealed Truth, will ever be able to confound the infidelity of the present day, we meet to explode the many errors and heresies, fearful and fatal, which are inseparable from this age of licentious thought, unchecked utterance and freedom of opinion. We summon you this evening to **proclaim the one remedy, the simple, full, unreserved exhibition of the *ATONEMENT*, the *SACRIFICIAL*, and *FINISHED WORK* of the Lord Jesus Christ.**

I am the more anxious and earnest on this important and impressive occasion to bend upon it your especial, devout, and solemn attention. Oh, that our modern theological controversialists, the men who are desirous of contending earnestly for the faith once delivered to the saints, who are putting on their armor and furbishing their weapons for the approaching conflict, might learn the secret of their might, wherein their great strength lies. It is not in accumulating around the Cross the stores of ancient and modern love; it is not in a strife of arms, dazzling and distinguished by profound intellectualism, learning, and eloquence, but in a simple, bold, uncompromising presentation of the Atoning and Finished Sacrifice of Christ, the lifting up, in its naked simplicity and solitary, unapproachable grandeur, of the Cross of the Incarnate God, the instrument of the sinner's Salvation, the foundation of the Believer's hope, the symbol of pardon, reconciliation, and hope to the soul; in a word, the grand weapon by which error shall bow to Truth, and sin give place to righteousness; and the kingdoms of this world long in rebellion against God, crushed and enthralled, shall yield to Messiah's specter, spring from the dust, burst their bonds, and exalt in the undisputed supremacy and benign reign of Jesus.

And believing, too, as I firmly do, that so large an amount of corroding doubts, and gloomy fears, and painful forebodings, which so essentially and so widely impede the religious progress, invade and cloud the spiritual joy and hope of the Lord's people, is mainly traceable to imperfect, crude, and dim views and apprehensions of Christ's complete work, of the Savior's finished Salvation which He has worked for His Church, not distinctly seeing that all is done, the great debt paid, the mighty bond cancelled, the full Atonement made, sin all and freely forgiven, I am still the more desirous of placing this great, this cardinal and precious Truth prominently and broadly, as the Lord the Spirit shall help me, before the present assembly, trusting and believing that, in answer to prayer, there will be tonight the Presence and Power of the Holy Spirit descending, invisible and noiseless, upon your souls, sealing upon your hearts this grand, this essential, this saving Truth, the **FINISHED WORK OF CHRIST**. "It is finished."

Let us consider these memorable words:

A. As ***THE CRY OF A SUFFERER***. And what a Sufferer! Contemplate for a moment *the Divine dignity* of the Sufferer. Here was no ordinary Sufferer, my Brothers and Sisters. We approach the scene of the Crucifixion, and we behold three individuals alike suspended upon three different crosses, two on either side and One in the center. They all suffer, all languish, all die. But the sufferings and death of One is attended by circumstances so strange, and events so unparalleled, by prodigies so miraculous and sublime, that we are led to exclaim in wondering awe, "Who is this?" And the voice of Prophecy replies, *"This is He of whom I spoke, 'Awake, O sword, against My Shepherd and against the Man who is My Fellow, says the Lord of Hosts; smite the Shepherd, and the sheep shall be scattered.'"* My dear Hearers, if throughout the life of Christ, I could fasten upon no other event confirming the Doctrine of the Godhead of Christ, I would be willing and satisfied to predicate my argument in vindication of His essential dignity upon the closing scene of the Cross, the last moments of His parting life. If His life were destitute of fact, His death alone would supply the evidence that He who died upon Calvary was none other than the Son of God. Hold fast the Doctrine of Christ's essential Deity, for upon it, as upon a rock, reposes the entire and stupendous fabric of the ATONEMENT.

The sufferings of Christ were *expiatory* and *vicarious*. You are aware that by many this fact is denied. The only solution of the mystery of Christ's death offered by the school to which I refer, is that which presents our Lord as a model of patience and resignation in suffering, a saint in virtue, a hero in endurance. And thus, the Cross of Christ is deprived of its magnificence and robbed of its Glory. But our Lord suffered as an expiatory Offering, as a vicarious Victim. All suffering is, *in a sense,* vicarious, not in the fullest meaning of the term, as conveying the idea of *substitution,* but simply and only in the sense that all suffering is the effect and consequence of sin. The man who violates the laws of his physical nature, who puts the empoisoned cup of intemperance to his lips to steal away his brains, who wastes his substance in riotous living, who herds among the unclean, and sacrifices to his baser passions health, property, character, shall suffer as a consequence of his lawlessness, folly and sin. He cannot trample upon the laws of his physical and mental constitution with impunity, he shall *suffer*. These sufferings shall not expiate his transgression, but they shall follow in its wake a sure and dire consequence. **Our Lord's sufferings were also the result and consequence of *sin*, sin not His own, but His people's; and in the fullest and most emphatic meaning of the terms, were expiatory and vicarious, sufferings, not only the fruit of sin, but more than that, suffering expiatory of sin, sufferings, substitutionary and vicarious, sacrificial and atoning.** There are theologians who dispute this statement, who deny this Doctrine. But I challenge them to explain these sufferings of our Lord satisfactorily upon any other hypothesis than this. I bring them back to the idea, that all human suffering is the effect of sin, our Lord suffered the death of the Cross. Was not that death in some way connected with sin? Most assuredly! Had there been no sin, there had been no suffering. This granted, we advance a step further, and claim for that death of Christ, a substitutionary character, an atoning nature, a sin expiatory result. And so the revealed Truth of God stands out in all its magnitude and Glory; and this is the only clue to the mystery, *"He was wounded for our transgressions, He was bruised for our iniquities." "Who, His own self, bore our sins in His own body on the tree." "Christ also has loved us and has given Himself for us an offering and a sacrifice to God, for a sweet smelling savor." "The blood of Jesus Christ, His Son, cleanses us from all sin."*

Behold the Almighty Sufferer. There stood the Son of God, bearing the sin and enduring the curse of His Church, putting away the one, and entirely exhausting the other, by the Sacrifice of Himself. To all the demands of God's moral government, to all the claims of Law and justice, Jesus now, on behalf of the people for whom He stood as Surety, gave a full, honorable, and accepted satisfaction. Come, poor sin-burdened, heart-broken penitent, and sit beneath the shadow of this Tree of Life, and its bending fruit of pardon, peace, joy and hope shall be sweet to your believing taste! But the sufferings of Christ were *unparalleled and intense*. Never since the universe was formed was there such a Sufferer as Jesus. He was the Prince of Sufferers. No sorrow ever broke the heart like that which tore His in two. Truly could He challenge the universe of sufferers, and ask, "Is it nothing to you, all you who pass by? Behold and see if there is any sorrow like unto My sorrow." No, Lord! Your sufferings had no parallel no sorrows were ever like unto Yours.

I do not go with the Greek Church, as you know. I differ from it both ecclesiastically and doctrinally. But I admire and love what is good, find it where I may. And I perfectly assent to the remark of my beloved Brother, made in the vestry before the service, "That there's some good in all Christian communions and creeds, and that it is our wisdom to accept what is good and leave what is evil." Now, that is a sublime sentence in the liturgy of the Greek Church, which I have often pondered with emotion, "Your unknown agonies." Yes, the agonies of our sin-suffering, sin atoning Lord were unknown. They were in their intensity known only to His Own Holy Soul. No angel could ever fathom their depth; no finite mind shall ever be able to gauge the breadth, to scale the height, to conceive even of the agony of His soul when He exclaimed, "My God, My God, why have You forsaken Me? I can bear the abandonment of My disciples, one has denied Me, another has betrayed Me, all have forsaken Me, but O My God, My God, why have *You* forsaken Me?" We may form some idea of their character, else how can we with Paul have fellowship with Him in His sufferings?

First, there was the *physical* element; our blessed Lord suffered *bodily*. Men of science and of sanctified intellect have endeavored to analyze and describe the physical agonies which Christ endured, when His heart was broken with grief; but physiology in its noblest triumphs has never been able to fully portray what the Savior endured when, like the rending rocks around His Cross. ***"The heart was torn asunder, / Never once defiled by sin."***

Then there was *mental agony*. The mental grief He endured, who can conceive. His mind was a human mind, and all the more sensitive because it was a sinless mind. The human sympathy of Christ infinitely transcends the most exquisite sympathy that glows in *our* bosom, because it was the sympathy of a pure and sinless Humanity.

The is selfishness in our sympathy. We love to sympathize with the sufferer because we love the sufferer, and we are paying an homage to our love to the creature when we take the hand and dry the tears, and speak the words of consolation. But the sympathy of Christ was all the more exquisite, and all the more tender, and all the more human, because it was all the freer from sin. The perfect sinlessness of Christ's sympathy did not in the slightest degree affect the perfect humanity of His sympathy. He was more human than you and I are, because His Humanity was entirely free from sin. We are not all human. We possess a part of a demoniacal nature. Sin has impaired all those glorious virtues and excellences which our humanity in its primitive condition possessed, and ours is a distorted, paralyzed, altered humanity. Let your humanity be restored to its original righteousness, to its primitive purity; let it be elevated, renewed, sanctified, ennobled, as your humanity will be if you are believers in Christ, and as you gradually recede from sin you will approach the perfect. As sin is eliminated and purged away from your nature, your crushed, your bruised, your bowed humanity will rise in its original purity, and majesty, and glory, and you will be all the more human because you approach all the more to the purity of the Divine.

But the *soul-suffering* of our Lord was more intense than all. This was inconceivable, indescribable. Listen to the cry in Gethsemane, "My soul is exceedingly sorrowful, even unto death." The billows of God's Wrath began now to penetrate His Nature, the storm to break in upon His Soul. Oh, that was a terrible moment. It was only now that He began to succumb to the woe. Before this He had maintained a comparatively calm and uncomplaining Demeanor. The tempest until now was *outside*. When a vessel, coursing its way over the ocean, is arrested by a storm, the fierce winds blowing, the ocean broken into billows, seething, raging, roaring, as long as his gallant boat plows its way, and keeps its course, the mariner treads its deck undaunted by fear, confident in the strength and firmness of his vessel to outride and outlive the tempest. But let the cry be heard, "A leak! A leak! A plank is sprung; the waters are coming in!" And in a moment, despair enters and enthrones itself upon the brow, and the hearts of the stern sons of the sea die within them. Beloved, that was the moment of our Lord's deep, unknown agony, when He could exclaim, *"Save Me, O God, for the waters are come into My soul. I sink in deep mire, where there is no standing. I am come into deep waters, where the floods overflow Me. All Your waves and Your billows are gone over Me!"* All this, O child of God, was for *your* soul. It pleased the Lord to crucify Him and put Him to grief for you. By His stripes you are healed. Your healing flows from His wounds, your joy from His sorrow, your glory from His abasement, your riches from His poverty; your hope beams through the darkness which enshrouds His Holy Soul. Oh, was ever love like Christ's Love? In what else can we resolve all this mystery of unknown agony of intense, unparalleled suffering, but in the *"Love of Christ which passes knowledge."* **"Christ also loved the Church and gave Himself for it."** O mystery of suffering! O deeper mystery of love! But these sufferings now are over. Hear him cry, "It is finished!"

Have you ever stood by the dying bed of one you have loved and have marked the throb, the throe of agony, the maddening convulsion, the terrible shaking of the earthly tabernacle as pin after pin, and beam after beam has fallen a shattered wreck; and as you caught the last breath that floated from the pale, quivering lips and closed those eyes in death, has not your heart in the depth of its grief felt something like a thrill of joy and gladness that the sufferings of the loved one now were over? Rejoice then, rejoice that the sufferings of Jesus are finished that the storm and the tempest will no more beat around Him. The sun of God's Love shall no more darken over Him, for He took the cup, pressed it to His lips, exhausted the last bitter drop, and then shouted out in words that made Heaven reverberate with its melody, and Hell to ring with its mightiness, "It is finished!" Child of sorrow, child of suffering, rejoice that the sufferings of your Lord are over, and that in all the suffering, and all the trial, and all the sorrow through which He leads you Home to Himself, has not one drop of the curse to embitter it; has not one particle of the sufferings He endured. He took your cup of grief, your cup of the curse, pressed it to His pressed it to His lips, drank

265

it to its dregs, then filled it with His sweet, pardoning, sympathizing Love, and gave it back for you to drink, and to drink forever.

B. Second, and more briefly, "It is finished" is not only the cry of a Sufferer, it is *THE LANGUAGE OF A SAVIOR.*

Our Lord's mission to our world was simply and singularly to save. He came for no other objective than to save man, to give His life a ransom for many; to provide, to execute an expedient devised in the Eternal Council, and purpose, and Love of the Triune God, for securing the full Redemption of His Church, an expedient that should harmonize and unite all the moral attributes and perfections of His being, and then lower from the battlement of Heaven to sin's fathomless depths the golden chain of mercy, pardoning Mercy, to which, if in faith you take hold, it will lift you up to the Throne from where it came.

It is the fashion of the present day to ignore the Saviorship of Jesus, and to represent His Person, and His life, and His death in any and every form, rather than acknowledge that He died on the Cross in the Character of a Savior, and that faith in the merits of His obedience and in the efficacy of His death, constitute the only basis on which a lost sinner can build his hope of Heaven.

I ask you, my beloved Hearers, **what is the grand objective of modern heresy but to undermine the Cross of Christ, to ignore the Sacrifice of His death, to blot out the glorious Atonement, and to reduce the splendid paraphernalia of Calvary, with all its moral and sublime results, to a mere nonentity?** His death, His obedience was the obedience of the Law-Maker in the form of the Law-Fulfiller to a Law which man had broken and violated; and that perfect and complete obedience of that broken Law is the righteousness that justifies the ungodly, and places him who believes spotless before God. Hold fast that Truth, the imputed righteousness of the Lord our righteousness worked out and complete in His perfect obedience to the precepts of a broken Law.

His death on Calvary was an Atonement to Divine Justice; the shedding of His blood was for the remission of man's sins;

the paying out of His soul to death was the perfect honor given to the moral government of Jehovah. And when He went out of the streets of Jerusalem staggering beneath the beam on which He was to be impaled; when, with lowly footsteps, He ascended that sacred hill, Calvary; when there, like a lamb led to the slaughter, He gave Himself up uncomplainingly, unreservedly into the hands of His executioners. When they stretched Him on that tree, transfixed His limbs to those beams, lifted it and let it fall into the place excavated for it to stand; when there the Son of God poured out His Holy Soul unto death; ... my Brothers and Sisters, it **was to harmonize Justice and Mercy, Holiness and Truth,** to blend in one vast bow of hope all these Divine Attributes, that they might span the moral Heaven, and encircle our lost humanity! It was then He gave up His Soul unto death, and offered up that Sacrifice for sin, which man, in his madness, folly, and infidelity, dares in this, our day, to ignore and to deny.

Yes, it is the language of a Savior. **Those words speak hope to the hopeless, pardon to the guilty, acceptance to the lost; they tell you, O poor sin-smitten, burdened sinner, that there is hope. There is pardon even for *you*.** He has finished all that Justice asked, that the Law demanded; He has finished the mission His Father had confided to His hands; He has finished the grand oblation that was to restore to God's moral government the Glory it had lost in man's apostasy. He has finished all the ancient types, predictions and shadows; He has torn the veil in two, and opened the bright pathway for the sinner to retrace his steps back to Paradise, back to God, and once more feel the warm embrace of his Father's forgiving Love. And yet this is the work, this is the Atonement, this is the Sacrifice which modern essayists dare with scorn and unbelief to trample beneath their feet.

Oh, it is the language of a Savior which bids you come. **Poor broken-hearted Sinner, with all your burden of sin, believe and be saved.** It bids you come without money and without price; it tells you the blood He poured from His broken heart can wash out and cancel the deepest stain that is on your soul; it tells you there is room in that bosom which He laid bare to the lightening-stroke of God's Wrath; it tells you, dry your tears, embrace the Cross, trust in the finished work of Christ; fling to the heavens all your own righteousness, wrap yourself up by faith in the righteousness of Christ, and all the choirs of Heaven shall tune their harps of gold, and make the heavens reverberate with their songs of praise over your submission in faith to the Atonement of the Son of God.

C. **Last** and only one word or two on this, it is *THE SHOUT OF A CONQUEROR.*

Christ was a Man of war; our glorious Joshua was He. He had come to gird on the sword, to invest Himself with the armor, and to go out and battle with Satan, with sin and with Hell. It was a terrible conflict, it was a fearful battle, but He girded Himself for the mighty and the solemn work, and He completed it, He finished it. He met His foes on the battlefield, confronted all His enemies, and on the Cross He destroyed, He divested death of its sting, triumphed over Satan, the grave, and Hell, and as He expired, He exclaimed, "It is finished!" Oh what a sublime conflict was that, my Brothers and Sisters, when **the Captain of our Salvation** met single-handedly and overcame the powers of darkness, fought the fight, won the victory, and died, saying, "It is finished!"

With two or three brief inferences from the subject I will close.

1. *What a spring of comfort flows from it to the true Believer amid his innumerable failures, flaws, and imperfections.* What service do you perform, what duty do you discharge of which you can say, "It is finished"? Alas, not one! Your service is imperfect, your obedience is incomplete, your love is fluctuating, yes, upon it all are the visible marks of human defilement and defect. But here is the work which God most delights in, "finished." *"You are complete in Him."* Turn, then, your eyes of faith out of *yourself,* and off of all your own doings, and deal more immediately, closely, and obediently with the

finished work of Immanuel. Come away from your fickle love, from your weak faith, from your little fruitfulness, from your uneven walk, from all your shortcomings and imperfections, and let your eyes of faith repose where God's eyes of satisfied Love reposes, on the finished work of Jesus. God beholds you only in Christ, it is not upon *you* He looks, but on His Beloved Son, and upon you in Him, "Wherein He has made us accepted in the Beloved."

2. *If Christ's Atoning work is finished, what folly and what sin to attempt to supplement it.* What vast numbers are doing this? Away with your tears, your confessions, your duties, your charities, even your repentance and faith, if these things dare to take their place side by side with the finished work of Christ! See that you attempt to add *nothing* to it. In a similar strain of exhortation let me:

3. *Warn you of the utter worthlessness and fallacy of all grounds of faith, and of all human hope that comes in conflict with the finished work of Christ.* My dear Hearers, you have nothing to do in the great matter of your Salvation, but to accept in faith the one Offering made once and for all by God manifest in your nature. *Cast your deadly doings at the foot of the Cross; cease from your own works; cease from your own righteousness; cease from resting in your confessions, in your tears, in your prayers, in your going to your church or your chapel. Oh, cease from all this, and in simple faith accept, take hold of the Divine work of the Lord Jesus Christ. God needs no more sacrifices; God asks no other atonement; God looks for nothing on your part to Propitiate His regard, or present you with acceptance; He is satisfied with the Divine work of Christ, with His obedience and with His blood-shedding.* And if tonight, sin-burdened and distressed one, you will renounce all your own doings, and rest in the finished work of Christ, the one eternal Redemption He has offered, God will expand His arms of Love and embrace you, take you into

a covenant, filial relation to Himself; and from that moment your path to eternity will be like the sun, growing brighter and brighter unto the perfect day. All is done. Christ has done all. Christ has suffered all, all He asks of you is in faith to receive His Glorious Sacrifice. Believe in Him, and be saved.

4. ***Beware of the errors of the day, the tendency of which is to veil the Light and Glory of Christ's finished work, to mislead, misguide, and misdirect souls on their way to the Judgment Seat.*** The fact is too patent to ignore, and it would be affectation to veil it, that there exists at the present moment, a theological school in our land, which by the press is endeavoring to circulate doctrines and statements which go to undermine the Divine Inspiration and Authority of the Bible, and to cast the pall of darkness, and of death over the splendors of the Cross. I warn you of these terrorists, and against their errors. Deceitful men, false to your Master, and unfaithful to His Truth. You may attempt to veil the luster of the Cross, you may sepulcher Incarnate Truth, roll upon it your stone, seal it, and set your watch, but the Truth of God shall leap from the dark chamber in which you attempt to entomb it, and shall walk this earth again, a thing of life, light and beauty. Rejoice, O Christian, that all these attempts to subvert the Truth as it is in Jesus, God will laugh to scorn, and finally His Gospel shall fully and universally prevail: *"Truth crushed to earth, shall rise again! /The eternal years of God are hers; /But error wounded writhes in pain, /And dies amid her worshippers!*

And now, from my heart, **I ask the blessing of the Triune God upon my beloved Brother, the grand substance of whose ministry I believe from my very soul is to exalt the finished work of Jesus.** And I pray that this noble edifice, reared in the name, and consecrated to the glory of the Triune God, may for many years echo and re-echo with his voice of melody and of power in expounding to you the glorious Doctrines and precepts of Christ's one finished Atonement. And God grant that none of you may be found rejecting to your everlasting woe the Doctrine of the Cross. You may attempt to laugh it to scorn; you may make your excuses for its rejection; but the hour is coming, yes, the hour is near, when death confronting you, the veil falling upon all earthly scenes, rising upon all eternal realities, you will discover the unbelief and slander that could trifle with the Atonement, dispute it in life, and in health, fail you in your solemn hour, and you will find yourself on the brink of eternity, without a plank, without a lifeboat, without a star of hope to cheer the dark spirit's travel to the Court of God! Reject it; deny it at your peril; your blood be upon your own heads.

EXHORTATION: And may God grant in His Grace, that before long you who have believed in Him, confessed Him, and loved Him here on earth, may cluster around His Throne, gaze upon His unclouded face, unite in the anthem of the blessed, and from those lips which once uttered that glorious sentence, "It is finished," receive the "Well done, good and faithful servant;" "Come, you blessed of My Father, inherit the Kingdom prepared for you from the foundations of the world." And to God the Father, God the Son, and God the Holy Spirit, we will all unite in one eternal ascription of praise. Amen.

4.   The Water and the Blood

"But one of the soldiers pierced His side with a spear,
and immediately blood and water came out"
(John 19:34 NKJV).

FOCUS: In this wound of Christ, caused by the soldier, [Spurgeon] discerns four obvious meanings. It has many more, but these four will be enough to occupy our attention .... First, it was the mark of Prophecy. Second, it was the emblem of shame. Third, the lance wound was the seal of death upon our Lord Jesus Christ. Lastly, this heart wound of Christ is always to be called the source of purity.

271

IT is with much fear and trembling that I usually stand upon this platform, not that I shrink before the face of the multitude however large, but the weight of the subject which I have continually to bring before your minds fills my own soul with awe. And yet it is with more than usual anxiety I approach my subject this evening, because although it is full of tender interest and touching pathos, I feel that without the unction of the Holy Spirit, it would be insipid and unprofitable. And yet, on the other hand, with that Divine anointing, it is one of the richest topics that can possibly engage our meditation.

Readers of old theology will have remarked **how constantly the fathers were accustomed to dwell upon the wounds of Jesus slain.** And this fifth wound which penetrated His heart was peculiarly attractive to them. They said a great many things about it. Some indeed that were fanciful, but other remarks that were truly excellent and well deserve to be treasured up. I would it were more the practice of Believers nowadays than it is to study the very Person of Christ, as well as the Doctrines of the Gospel, and to learn the Divine lessons which are discoverable in the wounds of Jesus as well as the sacred admonitions bequeathed to us by the words of His mouth. One of these old Divines says that Jesus Christ was typified by our first father, Adam. As Adam fell asleep, and out of his side Eve was taken, so Jesus slept upon the Cross, the sleep of death, and from His side, where the spear was thrust, His Church was taken. He who redeemed us unto God by His blood, formed us as a peculiar people for Himself. The Church is one with Him, she came out of His side, and as He looks upon her, He can say, "You are bone of My bone, and flesh of My flesh. With My blood have I redeemed you." Others have been pleased to compare Christ to the Rock in the wilderness, which was smitten, and this spear-thrust is the great cleft in the Rock. You may remember how [Augustus] Toplady puts it: *"Rock of Ages, cleft for me! /Let me hide myself in Thee."* And he clearly has this in view, for the next lines are: *"Let the water and the blood /From Your riven side which flowed, /Be of sin the double cure, /Cleanse me from its guilt and power."*

I do not consider this allusion fanciful, nor can I think it distorts the type. Moses hidden in the cleft of the rock, that he might see God's Glory, had not a standing place one-half so glorious as you and I have when, **sheltered in the wounds of the Savior slain**, we see the glorious Justice and the Infinite Love of God reconciled **in the Person of the dying Lamb**. In the course of reading, I have met with some remarkable expressions in regard to this great wound of Christ. Some have called it, "a gate of Heaven." Why should I object to the title? Do we not enter into Heaven through the wounds of Jesus? It is, of course, a metaphorical expression, yet quite allowable. If the teaching is that there is no other way of access to God except through the torn veil of Christ's body, and that veil was torn in two, indeed, when the soldier with the spear pierced His side, we may, without straining the thought, call that wound one of the gates of Heaven. Another calls it "a celestial window, a window of Paradise," and we have versified that idea in one of our own familiar sonnets: *"Look through Jesus' wounds on me: / Him, and then the sinners see."*

Another writer, carried away by the consideration of this spear-thrust, calls it **"a palace of refuge."** A palace! Surely, never kings had such a one! Solomon's palace of ivory was nothing like it. And what a refuge it is! When the poor heart, like the dove hunted by the hawk, needs a shelter, if it can fly to Jesus' wounds, it is sheltered from all its sins. Well does our song put it: *"Come guilty souls, and flee away /Like doves to Jesus' wounds! /This is the welcome Gospel Day, /Wherein free Grace abounds."*

I forget the name of the writer, who, in speaking upon his Master's wounds, seems to get so exalted and carried away by the subject that He calls this wound *"the sacred wellhead of the rivers of golden sand which cover all the earth,"* two rivers, one of water and the other of blood. Two quickening rivers that carry life through the realms of death. Two purifying rivers cleansing the Augean [extremely difficult task] stable of this filthy world. Two mighty rivers which bear the elect vessels onwards towards the sea of everlasting bliss, not one of them suffering shipwreck on the voyage, for this mighty river is too deep to have quicksands, too broad for the mariner to be cast away upon a rock-bound shore. I like the thought, and so let it be, the sacred wellhead of that river of more than golden sand, the streams whereof make glad the multitudes of God's chosen throughout the earth.

A. **IT WAS THE MARK OF PROPHECY.** In order that it might be fully known that Jesus Christ was the Messiah that was to come, **the Prophets had given many marks, all of which must be found in the Person of the Man who should be the Great Deliverer.** Among the rest was this one that John quotes, "A bone of Him shall not be broken." This description concerned the paschal lamb, of which it was expressly said by the Lord, through Moses, that they were never to break a single bone of it. Its joints were to be separated after it had been roasted with fire, but not a bone was to be snapped. Now, if Jesus Christ is the Lamb of God's Passover, it is necessary that He should never have a broken bone. And yet it looked as if His bones would be broken. The rough soldier brought up a great iron crowbar and, with an awful blow, smashed the legs of the poor thief who hung on one side of our Lord, but half-dead, in order to hasten his dissolution. It was a strange thing that he passed by Christ, who was in the middle. I know not what it was that made him do so, whether some flash of majesty beamed from that dead face, or whether some singular instinct checked his arm. But he went and administered the dreadful blow to the thief on the other side. And now he came to Christ and perhaps raised the iron rod, when he saw that He was already dead! His head was hanging down upon His bosom and the man saw clearly that there was no need to administer the deathblow to Him. It was a strange thing that his hands should be so restrained. The soldiers of that day were wanton enough. They were just as likely as not to have broken the bones even though the man were dead, but Divine Prophecy must have it so and, therefore, not a bone of Jesus can be broken.

And then the Prophet Zechariah had said concerning the Messiah, "*They shall look upon Him whom they have pierced, and they shall mourn for Him as one mourns for his only son."* Now up till that moment our Lord had not been pierced, except as to His hands and feet, and this would scarcely have been a carrying out of the word, "pierced." Somebody would have said, "Well, but He never was pierced so as to cause His death, there was no such piercing as the text indicates." But now that the soldier, moved by the mysterious impulse, lifts his lance and thrusts it deep into the side of Christ, now did Prophecy set its mark upon Christ, now did history identify Him, the Man without broken bones yet the Man whose side was pierced! Him for whom Israel should one day mourn! Him whom His enemies should one day confess to be their King. … Has it ever struck you with admiring wonder that Jesus Christ should answer to Prophecies so complicated and types so manifold, should answer even with coincidences the most minute to them all? It would be almost impossible to count the types of Christ which are given in the Old Testament. It would, perhaps, be easy to count the prophecies, but very difficult for anybody to form a character in which all these should be blended and fulfilled. It has been said that if you were to give all these types and all these prophecies to the wisest of men of all ages, and say to them, "You are required to compile a biography of a man who shall answer to all these," they must certainly give up in despair! You can find men who will make a key to fit any lock, by diligence of labor, no matter how complicated the mechanism may be, the thing may at last be done. But I will defy all the wisdom that ever was in humanity to form a key that will fit the exceedingly complex words of all the types of the Old Testament and all its prophecies. How palpable then the evidence is. Our Lord Jesus Christ answers to them all. Just as the stamp in the wax answers to the seal that stamped it, the Providence that transpired corresponds with the predictions that forestalled His course. He went as it was written of Him. There He is and **He fulfils types that look the most opposite and prophecies which seem to run counter to one another.**

If anybody thinks that the stories told by the four Evangelists are spurious, I would suggest to him to go and write a fifth, to try to write another that would as much correspond with the Old Testament and with the other four, as those four do with the Old Testament and with each other! And when that task was done, I would then give him another problem to solve before he could have reasonable ground for suspicion that Jesus of Nazareth was not the Messiah. Account for the incredulity of the Jews in the presence of those evidences that have produced conviction among the Gentiles upon any other hypotheses than that which ratifies their own Scripture. If the Old Testament is the Word of God, it seems marvelous to us that men do not receive Jesus as being the Shiloh that was to come, the promised Messiah, the Prince of the kings of the earth. Jewish unbelief amazes us. Yet I suppose if we judged aright, our own lack of faith in Jesus, notwithstanding the rational credit we give to His mission as a popular creed, is still more amazing. If that is gross unbelief which rejects Christ, while acknowledging the Old Testament, what shall I say of you who refuse allegiance to Him and yet profess to believe both the Old and the New? If they that receive the first yet stumble at the second, what shall I say of those who receive both and yet, over the head of this double belief professed, give not their hearts to the Crucified Son of God, and put not their trust in the merit of His precious blood, but still continue afar off from Him by wicked works?

Some time ago, when in Italy, at a town on the Italian side of the Alps, I saw one Sunday afternoon, in a quiet walk alone, a sight which struck me very much and which remains fixed upon my memory. There was outside the town a mountain and the way up the sides of which were different representations of the progress of our Lord, from the Garden where Judas betrayed Him to the place of His Resurrection. The figures were as large as life, carved in either stone or wood, and painted to imitate nature. When I got to the very summit of the hill, there was a church. There was no one in it and I pushed open the door and went in. All was still. It was a large building and all around it were images of the prophets and the apostles. There stood Isaiah, Jeremiah, Ezekiel and all the rest, one knew the usual portraits of them. And up in the dome, at the very top of the church, was a large and striking image of the Savior. Now, what struck me about the church was this—that the images of those prophets and apostles who stood there had their fingers all pointed upwards, so that, when I went in, I could not help looking up to the top to see what they were pointing at. All round the church there were the words, in Latin, *"Moses and the Prophets spoke concerning Him."* And there stood **Moses and the Prophets**, carved in stone, and all pointing to Him. Isaiah had a little scroll in his hand on which was written, *"The Lord has made to meet on Him the iniquity of us all."* Jeremiah had a scroll in his hand, on which was written, *"Behold, and see if there is any sorrow like unto My sorrow, which is done unto Me."* I think the church just represented the Truth in that case. It is even so. All the Prophets stand as a complete circle of distinct testifiers and, with uplifted fingers, they all concur with John the Baptist when he said, *"Behold the Lamb of God, which takes away the sin of the world."* They all point to Christ. If you read the life of Christ and then read what they said of Him, you will be persuaded that this is He which was to come.

B. But to pass on, we may look upon the spear-thrust in the side of Christ as *THE ESCUTCHEON [EMBLEM] OF SHAME.* While our Lord lived, He was the subject of every form of scorn. He was scourged as none but a felon might be according to the Roman Law. He was spat upon and mocked, as even a felon ought not to have been. That crown of thorns, that reed scepter and that old scarlet cloak who could have invented a more shameful insignia for One who was greater than all the kings on the earth but who was brought exceedingly low? And our Lord's death, itself, was a great portion of His shame. It was a shame for Him to die, and ignominy for Him to die the death of hanging on the Cross. Heraldry has so emblazoned the symbol that we do not ordinarily apprehend the real shame to which Christ was exposed. Were I to preach to you tonight that a certain man who was hanged was very God, people would begin to say, "Why do you preach of one who died on the gallows as a felon?" Literally and truly, that is just how Jesus Christ died, according to the customs of His times. Crucifixion was to the Romans what hanging is to us, only it was worse. It was more shameful, for crucifixion was reserved for the very worst of crimes.

Not all murderers were so punished, but only the worst and vilest crimes with murder to aggravate them received this opprobrious doom. People hang crosses round their necks and wear them as ornaments, I wonder whether they would make ornaments of gallows? Yet it means that. It is just the same thing and this is the shame of Christ. **This is the very shame in which Paul rejoiced and gloried, that Jesus Christ was not ashamed to be ashamed. That He was willing to be made ashamed and a curse for us. That He was content to be treated with all the scorn that human malignity and inhuman cruelty could heap upon Him.**

But, Beloved, when Christ was dead, they might certainly have ceased from their scorn. But no, the brutal Roman soldiers were not very nice as to what they did with living bodies. They would not, therefore, be particular as to what they did with dead bodies! Therefore, this soldier, in a mere freak of wanton brutality, thrust his lance into the Savior's heart. It was the last kick of the old enemy. It was, as it were, the last of the spit from the foul mouth of human slander and hatred. It was the last thrust that human malice could give to the Lord of Life and Glory! I see in this the mark, the crowning emblem of the shame which He endured.

Well, and what then? Why, **it should teach us, dear Friends, what a shameful thing sin must be.** For, though Christ was no sinner, yet when **our sins were laid upon Him, look how God treated Him and permitted Him to be treated as an outcast, to be covered with the utmost shame.** Ah Sin, what a shameful thing you must be. Blush, Christian, that you should be guilty of it. Blush again, that you do not blush more often! Be ashamed that you are not ashamed of sin, and be offended that your heart should be so stolid over a thing so detestable.

Another thought springs up, namely, that if Christ was put to so much shame for us, how glad we ought to be if we are sometimes allowed to be put to shame for Him. Oh, there are some people who cannot bear shame; they can endure anything else but ridicule and laughter. As John Bunyan says, "of all villains, Shame is the most shameless for he will go and make sport and fun of the Christian's virtues and mock at that which he ought to admire." Well, child of God, supposing today you have your face spat upon for Christ? [It would be] scarcely worthwhile to wipe it off! Ah, if you had to live a dying life, to be thrown in a dungeon, or to live upon the rack, as long as it was done for Him who bore all this for you, the thought might sweeten the wormwood and turn the gall into honey, that you were thus honored to have fellowship with Him in His sufferings. I leave that view of this wound of Christ with you, praying that it may nerve your hearts with a glorious courage as you see Jesus thus shamefully wounded for you.

C. This lance wound was *THE SEAL OF DEATH UPON OUR LORD JESUS CHRIST.* His enemies were so determined to put Him to death that they dragged His life out of its principal organ and then they pierced it, namely, the heart. It was not possible that Jesus Christ could have lived another moment longer, even had He been alive at that time, but when the heart was touched, death must come. Those who understand anatomy tell us that the pericardium around the heart was pierced and they say that from that there flowed the blood and the water. But I am extremely doubtful whether the pericardium in any state whatever could have yielded a sufficient quantity of lymph, for though there is water there, there is only a small quantity. In the state in which our Savior was, blood and water might have been found naturally in His heart, but only in a very small and infinitesimal quantity. The fountain that flowed from there was miraculous, not natural but supernatural, or if natural, yet so exalted and so increased in quantity as to become in itself supernatural.

Certainly, however, the piercing of His heart was the indication to all mankind that "He was dead already." Now, little as that may seem in the eyes of those of you who do not love Him, it is a most important thing to those who trust Him, for remember, if Jesus Christ had not died, you and I would have perished! It was of no use for our expiation that He sweat great drops of blood unless He had perfected the Sacrifice.

The Law required if, if Christ had not laid down His life, the Law would have required ours. In due time, our souls would have been cast into the Second Death on account of sin if Jesus had not died, actually and truly died. But we are quite sure about it now, for His heart was pierced. Indeed, I may say that **this is the one keystone of the whole Gospel system, for if Jesus did not die then, we have no Resurrection.** If He died not then, He did not rise and if we have no evidence of Resurrection, the whole of our religion becomes a lie! But, Brothers and Sisters, He did die. His soul left His body. That corpse that was taken by Joseph of Arimathaea was as lifeless as any that was ever committed to the sepulcher. And He did rise again, in proof to us that we who die and those we have parted with on the confines of this mortal life who are, alas, all truly dead, shall certainly rise again and in their flesh shall see God. This is a simple Truth of God for you to hear, perhaps, but never did angel have such weighty news to tell as I have told you tonight, that God was made flesh, the very God that made Heaven and earth took upon Himself our nature and as such He died, literally died for us. The God-Man, the Mediator, Jesus of Nazareth, the Son of God and the Son of Mary, died, was crucified and had His heart pierced for us. And if we depend upon this, we may rest secure. If He died, then we need not die. If He died for us, then we cannot die the Second Death. If Jesus was punished in our place, the sting of death is taken away, the Law is satisfied and every soul that believes in Him shall have eternal life.

D. But I cannot tarry longer upon that and, therefore, I come to the fourth point. ***THIS HEART WOUND OF CHRIST IS ALSO TO BE CALLED THE SOURCE OF PURITY.*** The text tells us that there issued from it a double flood of blood and water. We are not at a loss to explain this because the apostle John, in his Epistle, has told us that our Lord "*came by water and blood*; not by water only, but by water and blood," and he explains it by the connection that Christ came into the world by blood to take away the guilt of sin, and by water to take away the power of sin, by blood to remove the punishment, by water to remove the filth.

Now, ..., let us say that **there is no blood and no water that can wash away sin anywhere but in Christ**. All the blood of bulls could not take away sin, though offered by **Aaron**, himself, the father of the Levitical priesthood. And all the water in the world, though consecrated by bishops, cardinals and popes, cannot take away a single spot of iniquity. The only blood that can cleanse us from God's wrath is the blood of Jesus Christ, Himself, and the only water that can wash out of us the damning stain of sin is the water which came from Jesus Christ's heart. If you want to be thus doubly washed, go to the Son of God for the washing. Go nowhere else, I pray you, for every other trust is but a delusion and a lie. Jesus Christ can put away the guilt of every sin. Though you have been a drunk, an adulterer, a whoremonger, a thief, a murderer, yet the blood of Jesus Christ can wash you from the accumulated filth of years and the water from Christ's side can take away your propensities to sin, change your nature and make you holy instead of filthy can make you pure in heart instead of polluted in spirit! Nothing else can do it. No lie was ever more extraordinary than the lie that baptismal water can regenerate the soul. I marvel more and more that I should find myself living in an age of such idiots and have almost come to think that [Thomas] Carlyle was right when he spoke of our nation as "Consisting of twenty million people, mostly fools." So it seems to be, or else such a dogma as this would have been kicked out of the universe years since, and banished once and forever to the limbo of lunacy as an outrage on common sense. Is God the Holy Spirit confined to water, as that the priest's dropping it on the child's brow can work regeneration in the child's soul? Believe it not, it is a foul lie! But hold you to this, that which alone can work regeneration is the water from the side of Christ and when faith can get that, and trust that, the matter is done. Faith relies upon the sacred double flood. Then the heart is renewed, the man is changed, the soul is saved by Jesus Christ.

Remember, too, that the water and the blood flowed from the same place and flowed together. And, therefore, if a man would be saved; He must have the two. Tens of thousands would like to escape from Hell, but they have no wish to escape from sin. Are there not multitudes who are very anxious to get rid of the punishment, but are not at all concerned to be delivered from the habit of iniquity? Oh, yes, the drunk would gladly be forgiven, but he would like to keep to his tippling. Yes, the lecherous man would gladly have his constitution restored and his iniquity blotted out, but he must go to his dens of infamy again. Such is not the religion of Christ. The religion of Christ demands of us that if we take Christ, we should take Him for the double purpose, pardon for past sins and to deliver from sins to come. I think it was Celsus [author of *True Discourse*], the ancient philosopher, who jeered at the great Christian advocates, saying, "Your Master, Christ, receives all the filth of the universe into His Church. He tells you to go about to find out thieves, drunks, harlots and such like, and to tell them to come to Him. Your religion is nothing better than a hospital into which you thrust lepers." "Yes," said he who argued with him, "you have spoken well. We do receive them as into a hospital, but we heal them, Sir, we heal them. And while into the one door the spiritually and morally blind, cripples, and maimed come in as they are, the Great Physician touches them with His Grace and cleanses them with the water and the blood, and they are not what they were any longer."

Now, am I addressing one man who feels that he is saved by faith, and yet he is sinning as he used to do? Give up that belief, Sir, or it will ruin you. I pray you do not indulge in it, for it is a delusion of Satan! Do I address one man who has a hope that perhaps he can so trust Christ as to be saved, and yet continue to live in his own wicked way? If anyone has told you that, he has told you a lie. Rest assured that you are mistaken. Christ never came to be the minister of sin. **He came to save us, not in our sins, but from our sins.** He will forgive us all manner of iniquities, but not if we love the iniquity and continue in it. If you hug sin to your bosom, the viper will sting you, and no power, either human or Divine, can extract the poison unless the viper, itself, is taken away. You must have both the water and the blood, and I pray that you may have both.

Now, Christians, I have done when I have put to you one question. Answer it and answer it truthfully. It is this, ... **have you got such a**

hold of Christ as you should have in His double capacity as your Pardoner and your Sanctifier? I know you plead the blood for your remission. I know that is all your hope. I know that the blood of Christ is your comfort and your hope, but have you got the water quite as fully? You have a bad temper, perhaps. Well, it is a pitiable circumstance, but surely, if Christ can forgive a bad temper, He can remove a bad temper, too. Did you ever bring your bad temper to Christ to have it washed away with the water? You should have done so, for He can do it. Perhaps you have got an envious spirit, a murmuring spirit? Naturally so, you are generally depressed and downhearted. Did you ever believe in the power of Christ to kill envy and to lift you up above murmuring? You should do so. **You believe that Christ can forgive this sin. Well, that is through the power of the blood, but do you think that the water is less potent than the blood that Christ can forgive what He cannot subdue? Oh, think not so! Think as well of the Spirit and His sanctifying power as of Christ and His justifying righteousness.**

"Well," says one, "I have a besetting sin which I do not think I shall ever quite overcome," My dear Brother, why not? It strikes me that the Christian ought to get his greatest victories from his weakest points, and if you have a besetting sin, I think you ought to be distinguished by its opposite virtue. I do not know that it was so, but I always have a notion that Moses was, by his natural constitution, a thoroughly quick-tempered man. I think so from the fact that when he saw the Egyptian smiting the Israelite, he did not stop a minute, but he slew him at once and hid him in the sand. That looks to me to be the breaking out of the real Moses. But what did he become by the Grace of God? Why, after his spirit was subdued, he became the meekest of men and often was quiet where you and I would have spoken! Now, why should it not be so with us? It strikes me that the worst-tempered man who becomes a Christian ought to make this a strong point and to strive to become the best-tempered. There are some Christians who naturally have a little weakness in their hand and cannot open it well. If they get a little money in it, they are very apt to get their joints tied together very tightly! But, when Divine Grace comes in, I think they should try to defeat the devil by being more than ordinarily generous, so that, whereas other Christians might be content to give less, they say to Satan, *"O my enemy, you have held me in bondage in this way, but in wherever else you may get the upper hand of me, you never shall in this, for I will take care that whenever you tell me not to give a shilling, I will give two in order to let you see that you are no master of mine and that I have got rid of the foul sin of stinginess."* Do let us, each one, act upon this great Truth of God, **that as Christ has the power to forgive us our sin, so He also has the power to cleanse it away.**

EXHORTATION: Let us get closer to Christ. Let us be bedewed [sprinkled] more often than we have been before with the water and with the blood. Let us live in the spirit of this double purification and be it ours to find this blessed stream lead us right up to the heart of Christ, from which it flowed, that we may understand the everlasting love which dwells there deep in its eternal fountains and may rejoice and be glad in it all our days.

G.   Words of Contentment

1.   The Last Words of Christ on the Cross

"And when Jesus had cried out with a loud voice,
He said, 'Father, into Your hands I commit My
spirit.' Having said this, He breathed His last"
(Luke 23:46 NKJV).

"Into Your hand I commit my spirit;
You have redeemed me, O LORD God of truth"
(Psalm 31:5 NKJV).

"And they stoned Stephen as he was calling on God
and saying, 'Lord Jesus, receive my spirit'"
(Acts 7:59 NKJV).

FOCUS: There three texts that are much alike. First, we will consider our Savior's words just before His death, "Father, into Your hands I commend My Spirit." Second, our Savior quotes David, the Psalmist. "This Psalm is not so much concerning the Believer's death as concerning life." The third text is used "to explain to us the use of our Savior's dying words for ourselves."

THIS morning, dear Friends, I spoke upon the first recorded words of our Lord Jesus [Refer to 'The First Recorded Words of Jesus' in Part I, Sermon # 1666] when He said to His mother and to Joseph, *"How is it that you sought Me? Did you not know that I must be about My Father's business?"* Now, by the help of the blessed Spirit, we will consider the last words of our Lord Jesus before He gave up the ghost. And with them we will examine two other passages in which similar expressions are used.

The words, *"Father, into Your hands I commend My spirit,"* if we judge them to be the last which our Savior uttered before His death, ought to be coupled with those other words, *"It is finished,"* which some have thought were actually the last He used. I think it was not so, but, anyway, these utterances must have followed each other very quickly and we may blend them together. And then we shall see how very similar they are to His first words as we explained them this morning. There is the cry, "It is finished," which you may read in connection with our Authorized Version, *"Did you not know that I must be about My Father's business?"* That business was all finished: He had been about it all His life and now that He had come to the end of His days, there was nothing left undone, and He could say to His Father, "I have finished the work which You gave Me to do."

Then if you take the other utterance of our Lord on the Cross, *"Father, into your hands I commend My spirit,"* see how well it agrees with the other reading of our morning text, *"Did you not know that I must be in My Father's house?"* Jesus is putting Himself into the Father's hands because He had always desired to be there, in the Father's house with the Father. And now He is committing His spirit, as a sacred trust, into the Father's hands that He may depart to be with the Father, to abide in His house, and go no more out forever.

Christ's life is all of a piece, just as the alpha and the omega are letters of the same alphabet. You do not find Him one thing at the first, another thing afterwards, and a third thing still later, He is *"Jesus Christ, the same yesterday, and today, and forever."* There is a wondrous similarity about everything that Christ said and did. You never need write the name, "Jesus," under any of His sayings as you have to put the names of human writers under their sayings, for there is no mistaking any sentence that He has uttered.

If there is anything recorded as having been done by Christ, a believing child can judge whether it is authentic or not. Those miserable false gospels that were brought out did very little, if any mischief, because nobody with any true spiritual discernment was ever duped into believing them to be genuine! It is possible to manufacture a spurious coin which will, for a time, pass for a good one, but it is not possible to make even a passable imitation of what Jesus Christ has said and done. Everything about Christ is like Himself, there is a Christ-likeness about it which cannot be mistaken. This morning, for instance, when I preached about the Holy Child Jesus, I am sure you must have felt that there was never another child as He was. And **in His death He was as unique as in His birth, childhood and life.** There was never another who died as He did and there was never another who lived altogether as He did. Our Lord Jesus Christ stands by Himself. Some of us try to imitate Him, but how feebly do we follow in His steps. The Christ of God still stands by Himself and He has no rival.

A. I invite you **first** to consider *OUR SAVIOR'S WORDS JUST BEFORE HIS DEATH.* **"Father, into Your hands I commend My spirit."**

Here observe, first, how Christ lives and passes away in the atmosphere of the Word of God. *Christ was a grand original thinker and He might always have given us words of His own.* He never lacked suitable language, for, "never man spoke like this Man." Yet you must have noticed how continually He quoted Scripture, the great majority of His expressions may be traced to the Old Testament. Even where they are not exact quotations, His words drop into Scriptural shape and form. You can see that the Bible has been His one Book. He is evidently familiar with it from the first page to the last and not with its letter, only, but with the innermost soul of its most secret sense and, therefore, when dying, it seemed but natural for Him to use a passage from a Psalm of David as His expiring words. In His death, He was not driven beyond the power of quiet thought, He was not unconscious, He did not die of weakness. He was strong even while He was dying. It is true that He said, "I thirst," but, after He had been a little refreshed, He cried with a loud voice, as only a strong man could, "It is finished!" And now, before He bows His head in the silence of death, He utters His final words, "Father, into Your hands I commend My spirit." Our Lord might, I say again, have made an original speech as His dying declaration. His mind was clear, calm, and undisturbed, in fact, He was perfectly happy, for He had said, "It is finished!" So His sufferings were over and He was already beginning to enjoy a taste of the sweets of victory. **Yet, with all that clearness of mind, freshness of intellect and fluency of words that might have been possible to Him, He did not invent a new sentence, but He went to the Book of Psalms and took from the Holy Spirit this expression," Into Your hands I commend My spirit."**

How instructive to us is this great Truth of God *that the Incarnate Word lived on the Inspired Word.* It was food to Him, as it is to us and, Brothers and Sisters, **if Christ thus lived upon the Word of God, should not you and I do the same?** He, in some respects, did not need this Book as much as we do. The Spirit of God rested upon Him without measure, yet He loved the Scripture and He went to it, studied it and used its expressions continually. Oh, that you and I might get into the very heart of the Word of God and get that Word into ourselves. As I have seen the silkworm eat into the leaf and consume it, so ought we to do with the Word of the Lord, not crawl over its surface, but eat right into it till we have taken it into our inmost parts. It is idle to merely let the eyes glance over the Words, or to remember the poetical expressions, or the historic facts, but it is blessed to eat into the very soul of the Bible until, at last, you come to talk in Scriptural language and your very style is fashioned upon Scripture models and, what is still better, your spirit is flavored with the words of the Lord.

I would quote **John Bunyan** as an instance of what I mean. **Read anything of his and you will see that it is almost like reading the Bible itself. He had studied our Authorized Version, which will never be bettered, as I judge, till Christ shall come.** He had read it till his very soul was saturated with Scripture and though his writings are charmingly full of poetry, yet he cannot give us his *Pilgrim's Progress,* that sweetest of all prose poems, without continually making us feel and say, "Why, this man is a living Bible!" Prick him anywhere, his blood is Bibline, the very essence of the Bible flows from him. He cannot speak without quoting a text, for his very soul is full of the Word of God. I commend His example to you, Beloved and, still more, the example of our Lord Jesus. **If the Spirit of God is in you, He will make you love the Word of God and, if any of you imagine that the Spirit of God will lead you to dispense with the Bible, you are under the influence of another spirit which is not the Spirit of God at all.** I trust that the Holy Spirit will endear to you every page of this Divine Record so that you will feed upon it and, afterwards, speak it out to others. I think it is well worthy of your constant remembrance that, even in death, our blessed Master showed the ruling passion of His spirit so that His last words were a quotation from Scripture.

Now notice, secondly, that *our Lord, in the moment of His death, recognized a personal God. "Father, into Your hands I commend My spirit."* God is to some men an unknown God. "There may be a God," so they say, but they get no nearer the truth than that. "All things are God," says another. "We cannot be sure that there is a God," say others, "and, therefore, it is no use our pretending to believe in Him and so to be, possibly, influenced by a supposition." Some people say, "Oh, certainly, there is a God, but He is very far off. He does not come near to us and we cannot imagine that He will interfere in our affairs." Ah, but our blessed Lord Jesus Christ believed in no such impersonal, pantheistic, dreamy, far-off God, but in One to whom He said, "Father, into Your hands I commend My spirit." His language shows that **He realized the Personality of God** as much as I would recognize the personality of a banker if I said to him, "Sir, I commit that money into your hands." I know that I should not say such a thing as that to a mere dummy, or to an abstract something or nothing, but I would say it to a living man and I would say it only to a living man.

So, Beloved, **men do not commit their souls into the keeping of impalpable nothings**. They do not, in death, smile as they resign themselves to the infinite unknown, the cloudy "Father of everything," who may be nothing or everything. No, no, we only trust what we know. And so Jesus knew the Father, and knew Him to be a real Person having hands, and into those hands He commended His departing spirit. I am not now speaking materially, mark you, as though God had hands like ours, but He is an actual Being, who has powers of action, who is able to deal with men as He pleases and who is willing to take possession of their spirits and to protect them forever and ever. Jesus speaks like one who believed that and I pray that, both in life and in death, you and I may always deal with God in the same way. We have far too much fiction in religion, and a religion of fiction will bring only fictitious comfort in the dying hour. Come to solid facts! Is God as real to you as you are to yourself? Come now, do you speak with Him, "as a man speaks unto his friend"? Can you trust Him and rely upon Him as you trust and rely upon the partner of your bosom? If your God is unreal, your religion is unreal! If your God is a dream, your hope will be a dream and woe be unto you when you shall wake up out of it. It was not so that Jesus trusted. "Father," He said, "into Your hands I commend My spirit."

But, thirdly, here is a still better point. *Observe how Jesus Christ here brings out the Fatherhood of God.* The Psalm from which He quoted did not say, "Father." David did not get as far as that in words, though in spirit he often did. But Jesus had the right to alter the

Psalmist's words. He can improve on Scripture, though you and I cannot. He did not say, "O God, into Your hands I commend My spirit." He said, "Father." Oh, that sweet word! That was the gem of our thought, this morning that Jesus said, "Did you not know that I must be at My Father's, that I must be in My Father's house!" Oh, yes, the Holy Child knew that He was especially and, in a peculiar sense, the Son of the Highest, and therefore He said, "My Father." And, in dying, His expiring heart was buoyed up and comforted with the thought that God was His Father. It was because He said that God was His Father that they put Him to death, yet He still stood to it even in His dying hour and said, "Father, into Your hands I commend My spirit."

What a blessed thing it is for us, also, … to die conscious that we are children of God! Oh, how sweet, in life and in death, to feel in our soul the spirit of adoption whereby we cry, "Abba, Father"! In such a case as that: **"It is not death to die."**

Quoting the Savior's words, "It is finished," and relying upon His Father and our Father, we may go even into the jaws of death without the "quivering lips" of which we sang just now. Joyful, with all the strength we have, our lips may confidently sing, challenging death and the grave to silence our ever-rising and swelling music! O my Father, my Father, if I am in your hands, I may die without fear.

There is another thought, however, which is perhaps the best one of all. From this passage we learn that **our Divine Lord cheerfully rendered up His soul to His Father when the time had come for Him to die.** "Father, into Your hands I commend My spirit." None of us can, with strict propriety, use these words. When we come to die, we may perhaps utter them and God will accept them, **these were the very death-words of Polycarp, Bernard, Luther, Melanchthon, Jerome of Prague, John Huss and an almost endless list of saints, "Into Your hands I commend my spirit."** The Old Testament rendering of the passage, or else our Lord's version of it, has been turned into a Latin prayer and commonly used among Romanists almost as a charm, they have repeated the Latin words when dying, or, if they were unable to do so, the priest repeated the words for them, attaching a sort of magical power to that particular formula. But, in the sense in which our Savior uttered these words, we cannot, any of us, fully use them. We can commit or commend our spirit to God, but yet, ... remember that unless the Lord comes first, **we must die, and dying is not an act on our part.** We have to be passive in the process because it is no longer in our power to retain our life. I suppose that if a man could have such control of his life, it might be questionable when he would surrender it because suicide is a crime and no man can be required to kill himself. God does not demand such action as that at any man's hands and, in a certain sense, that is what would happen whenever a man yielded himself to death.

But there was no necessity for our blessed Lord and Master to die except the necessity which He had taken upon Himself in becoming the Substitute for His people. There was no necessity for His death even at the last moment upon the Cross, for, as I have reminded you, He cried with a loud voice when natural weakness would have compelled Him to whisper or to sigh. But His life was strong within Him, if He had willed to do so, He could have unloosed the nails and come down into the midst of the crowd that stood mocking Him. **He died of His own free will, "the Just for the unjust, that He might bring us to God."** A man may righteously surrender his life for the good of his country and for the safety of others. There have frequently been opportunities for men to do this and there have been brave fellows who have worthily done it. But all those men would have had to die at some time or other. They were only slightly anticipating the payment of the debt of nature. But, in our Lord's case, He was rendering up to the Father the sprit which He might have kept if He had chosen to do so. "No man takes it from Me," He said concerning His life. "I lay it down of Myself."

And there is here a cheerful willingness to yield up His spirit into His Father's hands! It is rather remarkable that none of the Evangelists describe our Lord as dying. He did die, but they all speak of Him as giving up the ghost, surrendering to God His spirit. You and I passively die, but He actively yielded up His spirit to His Father. In His case, death was an act and He performed that act from the glorious motive of redeeming us from death and Hell. So, in this sense, Christ stands alone in His death.

But ... if we cannot render up our spirit as He did, yet, when our life is taken from us, let us be perfectly ready to give it up. May God bring us into such a state of mind and heart that there shall be no struggling to keep our life, but a sweet willingness to let it be just as God would have it, a yielding up of everything into His hands, feeling sure that, in the world of spirits, our soul shall be quite safe in the Father's hands and that, until the Resurrection Day, the life-germ of the body will be securely in His keeping, and certain that when the trumpet shall sound, spirit, soul and body, that trinity of our manhood, shall be reunited in the absolute perfection of our being to behold the King in His beauty in the land that is very far off. When God calls us to die, it will be a sweet way of dying if we can, like our Lord, pass away with a text of Scripture upon our lips, with a personal God ready to receive us, with that God recognized distinctly as our Father and so die joyously, resigning our will entirely to the sweet will of the ever-blessed One, and saying, "It is the Lord." "My Father." "Let Him do as seems good to Him."

B. My **second** text is in the 31st Psalm, at the 5th verse. And it is evidently the passage which our Savior had in His mind just then *"Into Your hands I commit my spirit: You have redeemed me, O Lord God of Truth."* It seems to me that **THESE ARE WORDS TO BE USED IN LIFE**, for this Psalm is not so much concerning the Believer's death as concerning his life.

Is it not very amazing, dear Friends, that the words which Jesus uttered on the Cross you may still continue to use? You may catch up their echo and not only when you come to die, but tonight, tomorrow morning and as long as you are alive, you may still repeat the text the Master quoted, and say, "Into Your hands I commit my spirit." That is to say, first, let us cheerfully entrust our souls to God and feel that they are quite safe in His hands. Our spirit is the noblest part of our being; our body is only the husk, our spirit is the living kernel, so let us put it into God's keeping. Some of you have never yet done that, so I invite you to do it now. **It is the act of faith which saves the soul**, that act which a man performs when he says, **"I trust myself to God as He reveals Himself in Christ Jesus. I cannot keep myself, but He can keep me and, by the precious blood of Christ He can cleanse me. So I just take my spirit and give it over into the great Father's hands."** You never really live till you do that! All that comes before that act of full surrender is death. **But when you have once trusted Christ, then you have truly begun to live**. And every day, as long as you live, take care that you repeat this process and cheerfully leave yourselves in God's hands without any reserve. That is to say, give yourself up to God, your body, to be healthy or to be sick, to be long-lived or to be suddenly cut off. Your soul and spirit, give them, also, up to God, to be made happy or to be made sad, just as He pleases. Give Your whole self-up to Him and say to Him, "My Father, make me rich or make me poor, give me sight or make me blind. Let me have all my senses or take them away. Make me famous or leave me to be obscure. I give myself up to You, into Your hands I commit my spirit. I will no longer exercise my own choice, but You shall choose My inheritance for me. My times are in Your hands."

Now, dear children of God, are you always doing this? Have you ever done it? I am afraid that there are some, even among Christ's professing followers, who kick against God's will and even when they say to God, "Your will be done," they spoil it by adding, in their own mind, "and my will, too." **They pray, "Lord, make my will Your will,"** **instead of saying, "Make Your will my will."** Let us each one pray this prayer every day, "Into Your hands I commit my spirit." I like, at family prayer, to put myself and all that I have into God's hands in the morning, and then, at night, to just look between His hands and see how safe I have been. And then to say to Him, "Lord, shut me up again tonight! Take care of me all through the night watches. 'Into Your hands I commit my spirit.'"

Notice … that our second text has these words at the end of it, *"You have redeemed me, O Lord God of Truth."* Is not that a good reason for giving yourself up entirely to God? Christ has redeemed you and, therefore, you belong to Him. If I am a redeemed man and I ask God to take care of me, I am but asking the King to take care of one of His own jewels, a jewel that cost Him the blood of His heart.

And I may still more especially expect that He will do so, because of the title which is here given to Him, "You have redeemed me, O Lord God of Truth." Would He be the God of Truth if He began with redemption and ended with destruction, if He began by giving His Son to die for us and then kept back other mercies which we daily need to bring us to Heaven? No, the gift of His Son is the pledge that He will save His people from their sins and bring them home to Glory and He will do it. So, every day, go to Him with this declaration, "Into Your hands I commit my spirit." No, not only every day, but all through the day! Does a horse run away with you? Then you cannot do better than say, "Father, into Your hands I commit my spirit." And if the horse does not run away with you, you cannot do better than say the same words! Have you to go into a house where there is fever? I mean, is it your duty to go there? Then go saying, "Father, into Your hands I commit my spirit." I would advise you to do this every time you walk down the street, or even while you sit in your own house.

Dr. [John] Gill, my famous predecessor, spent very much time in his study and, one day, somebody said to him, "Well, at any rate, the studious man is safe from most of the accidents of life." It so happened that one morning, when the good man left his familiar armchair for a little while, there came a gale of wind that blew down a stack of chimneys which crashed through the roof and fell right into the place where he would have been sitting if the Providence of God had not just then drawn him away! And he said, *"I see that we need Divine Providence to care for us in our studies just as much as in the streets." "Father, into Your hands I commit my spirit."* I have often noticed that if any of our friends get into accidents and troubles, it is usually when they are away for a holiday. It is a curious thing, but I have often remarked about it. They go out for their health and come home sick. They leave us with all their limbs whole and return to us crippled. Therefore, we must pray God to take special care of friends in the country or by the sea, and we must commit ourselves to His hands wherever we may be. If we had to go into a leper colony, we would certainly ask God to protect us from the deadly leprosy. But we ought to equally seek the Lord's protection while dwelling in the healthiest place or in our own homes.

David said to the Lord, "Into Your hands I commit my spirit." But let me beg you to add that word which our Lord inserted, "Father." David is often a good guide for us, but David's Lord is far better. And if we follow Him, we shall improve upon David. So, let us each say, "Father, Father, into Your hands I commit my spirit." That is a sweet way of living every day, committing everything to our Heavenly Father's hands, for those hands can do His child no unkindness. "Father, I might not be able to trust Your angels, but I can trust You." **The Psalmist does not say, "Into the hand of Providence I commit my spirit." Do you notice how men try to get rid of God by saying, "Providence did this," and, "Providence did that," and, "Providence did the other"? If you ask them, "What is Providence?" they will probably reply, "Well, Providence is Providence." That is all they can say.**

There is many a man who talks very confidently about reverencing nature, obeying the laws of nature, noting the powers of nature and so on. Step up to that eloquent lecturer and say to him, "Will you kindly explain to me what nature is?" He answers, "Why, nature, well, it is, nature." Just so, Sir, but, what is nature? And he says, "Well, well, it is nature." And that is all you will get out of him. Now, I believe in nature and I believe in Providence, but at the back of everything, **I believe in God**, and in the God who has hands not in an idol that has no hands and can do nothing, but in the God to whom I can say, "'Father, into Your hands I commit my spirit.' I rejoice that I am able to put myself there, for I feel absolutely safe in trusting myself to Your keeping." So live, Beloved, and you shall live safely, happily and you shall have hope in your life, and hope in your death.

C. My **third** text will not detain us many minutes. It is intended to explain to us *THE USE OF OUR SAVIOR'S DYING WORDS FOR OURSELVES.*

Turn to the account of the death of Stephen, in the 7th chapter of Acts, at the 59th verse, and you will see, there, how far a man of God may dare to go in his last moments in quoting from David and from the Lord Jesus Christ. "And they stoned Stephen, as he was calling upon God and saying, Lord Jesus, receive my spirit." So here is a text for us to use when we come to die, "Lord Jesus, receive my spirit." I have explained to you that, strictly, we can hardly talk of yielding up our spirit, but we may speak of Christ receiving it and say with Stephen, "Lord Jesus, receive my spirit."

What does this prayer mean? I must just hurriedly give you two or three thoughts concerning it and so close my discourse. I think this prayer means that, if we can die as Stephen did, we shall die with a certainty of immortality. Stephen prayed, "Lord Jesus, receive my spirit." He did not say, "I am afraid my poor spirit is going to die." No, the spirit is something which still exists after death, something which Christ can receive and, therefore, Stephen asks Him to receive it! You and I are not going upstairs to die as if we were only like cats and dogs, we go up there to die like immortal beings who fall asleep on earth and open our eyes in Heaven. Then, at the sound of the archangel's trumpet, our very body is to rise to dwell, again, with our spirit, we have not any question about this matter! I think I have told you what an infidel once said to a Christian man, "Some of you Christians have great fear in dying because you believe that there is another state to follow this one. I have not the slightest fear, for I believe that I shall be annihilated and, therefore, all fear of death is gone from me." "Yes," said the Christian, "and in that respect you seem to me to be on equal terms with that bull grazing over there, which, like yourself, is free from any fear of death. Pray, Sir, let me ask you a simple question. Have you any hope?" "Hope, Sir? Hope, Sir? No, I have no hope! Of course I have no hope, Sir." "Ah, then!" replied the other, "despite the fears that sometimes come over feeble Believers, they have a hope which they would not and could not give up." And that hope is that our spirit, even that spirit which we commit into Jesus Christ's hands, shall be "forever with the Lord."

The next thought is that, to a man who can die as Stephen did, there is a certainty that Christ is near, so near that the man speaks to Him and says, "Lord Jesus, receive my spirit." In Stephen's case, the Lord Jesus was so near that the martyr could see Him, for he said, "Behold, I see the heavens opened, and the Son of Man standing at the right hand of God." Many dying saints have borne a similar testimony. It is no strange thing for us to hear them say, before they die, that they could see within the pearly gates and they have told us this with such evident truthfulness, and with such rapture, or sometimes so calmly, in such a businesslike tone of voice, we were sure that they were neither deceived nor speaking falsehood. They spoke what they knew to be true, for Jesus was there with them! Yes, Beloved, before you can call your children around your deathbed, Jesus will already be there! And into His hands you may commit your spirit.

Moreover, **there is a certainty that we are quite safe in His hands**. Wherever else we are insecure, if we ask Him to receive our spirit, and He receives it, who can hurt us? Who can pluck us out of His hands? Awaken, Death and hail! Come forth, all you powers of darkness. What can you do when once a spirit is in the hands of the Omnipotent Redeemer? We will be safe there! Then there is the other certainty, that He is quite willing to take us into His hands. Let us put ourselves into His hands now, and then we need not be ashamed to repeat the operation every day and we may be sure that we shall not be rejected at the last. I have often told you of the good old woman who was dying and to whom someone said, "Are you not afraid to die?" "Oh, no," she replied, "there is nothing at all to fear. I have dipped my foot in the river of death every morning before I have had my breakfast, and I am not afraid to die now." You remember that dear saint who died in the night, and who had left written on a piece of paper by her bedside these lines which, before she fell asleep, she felt strong enough to pencil down? *"Since Jesus is mine, I'll not fear undressing, /But gladly put off these* *garments of clay /To die in the Lord, is a Covenant blessing, /Since Jesus to Glory thro' death led the way."*

It was well that she could say it, and may we be able to say the same whenever the Master calls us to go up higher. I want, dear Friends, that we should, all of us, have as much willingness to depart as if it were a matter of will with us! Blessed be God it is not left to our choice; it is not left to our will when we shall die. God has appointed that day and ten thousand devils cannot consign us to the grave before our time! We shall not die till God decrees it: *"Plagues and death around me fly, /Till He please I cannot die! /Not a single shaft can hit/ Till the God of love sees fit."*

But let us be just as willing to depart as if it were really a matter of choice, for, wisely, carefully, coolly consider that if it were left to us, we should none of us be wise if we did not choose to go! Apart from the coming of our Lord, the most miserable thing that I know of would be a suspicion that we might not die. Do you know what quaint old Rowland Hill used to say when he found himself getting very old? He said, "Surely they must be forgetting me up there." And every now and then, when some dear old saint was dying, he would say, "When you get to Heaven, give my love to John Berridge [minister, revivalist, 1716–1793], and John Bunyan and ever so many more of the good Johns, and tell them I hope they will see poor old Rowley up there before long." Well, there was common sense in that wishing to get Home, longing to be with God. To be with Christ is far better than to be here.

Sobriety itself would make us choose to die. Well, then, do not let us run back and become utterly unwilling and struggle and strive and fret and fume over it. When I hear of Believers who do not like to talk about death, I am afraid concerning them. It is greatly wise to be familiar with our resting place. When I went, recently, to the cemetery at Norwood [West Norwood Cemetery, London, Borough of Lambeth], to lay the body of our dear Brother [W.] Perkins there for a little while, I felt that it was a healthy thing for me to stand at the grave's brink and to walk amid that forest of memorials of the dead, for this is where I, too, must go [*Spurgeon delivered this sermon in 1882, and was laid to rest in West Norwood Cemetery in 1892.*] You living men, come and view the ground where you must shortly lie and, as it must be so, let us who are Believers welcome it.

EXHORTATION: But, what if you are not Believers? Ah, that is another matter altogether. If you have not believed in Christ, you may well be afraid even to rest on the seat where you are sitting. I wonder that the earth itself does not say, "O God, I will not hold this wretched sinner up any longer. Let me open my mouth and swallow him!" All nature must hate the man who hates God! Surely, all things must loathe to minister to the life of a man who does not live unto God.

Oh, that you would seek the Lord and trust Christ and find eternal life. If you have done so, do not be afraid to go forth to live, or to die, just as God pleases. Amen.

2. His Last Cry from the Cross

"And when Jesus had cried out with a loud voice,
He said, 'Father, into Your hands I commit My
spirit.' Having said this, He breathed His last"
(Luke 23:46 NKJV).

FOCUS: From the text, first, let us learn the doctrine of this last cry from the cross; second, let us practice the duty, and third, let us enjoy the privilege.

THESE were the dying words of our Lord Jesus Christ, "Father, into Your hands I commend My spirit." It may be instructive if I remind you that the Words of Christ upon the Cross were seven. Calling each of **His cries, or utterances, by the title of a Word, we speak of the seven last Words of the Lord Jesus Christ.** Let me rehearse them in your hearing. The **first,** when they nailed Him to the Cross, was, "Father, forgive them; for they know not what they do." Luke has preserved that Word. **Later,** when one of the two thieves said to Jesus,

"Lord, remember me when You come into Your Kingdom," Jesus said to him, "Verily I say unto you, today shall you be with Me in Paradise." This, also, Luke has carefully preserved. **Farther on**, our Lord, in His great agony, saw His mother, with breaking heart, standing by the Cross and looking up to Him with unutterable love and grief, and He said to her, "Woman, behold. your son!" and to the beloved Apostle, "Behold your mother!" and thus He provided a home for her when He, Himself, should be gone away. This utterance has only been preserved by John.

The fourth and central Word of the seven was, "Eloi, Eloi, Lama, Sabachthani?" which is, being interpreted, "My God, My God, why have You forsaken Me?" This was the culmination of His grief, the central point of all His agony. That most awful word that ever fell from the lips of man, expressing the quintessence of exceeding agony, is well put fourth, as though it had need of three words before it, and three words after it, as its bodyguard. It tells of a good Man, a son of God, *the* Son of God, forsaken of His God. That central Word of the seven is found in Matthew and in Mark, but not in Luke or John.

But **the fifth Word** has been preserved by John, that is, "I thirst," the shortest, but not quite the sharpest of all the Master's Words, though under a bodily aspect, perhaps the sharpest of them all. John has also treasured up **another very precious saying of Jesus Christ on the** Cross that is the wondrous Word, "It is finished." This was the last word but one, "It is finished," the gathering up of all His lifework, for He had loft nothing undone, no thread was left raveling, the whole fabric of Redemption had been woven, like His garment, from the top throughout, and it was finished to perfection! After He had said, "It is finished," He uttered **the last Word of all**, "Father, into Your hands I commend My spirit," which I have taken for a text, tonight, but to which I will not come immediately.

There has been a great deal said about these seven cries from the Cross by many writers and though I have read what many of them have written, I cannot add anything to what they have said, since they have delighted to dwell upon these seven last cries, and here the most ancient writers, of what would be called the Romish school, are not

300

to be excelled, even by Protestants, in their intense devotion to every letter of our Savior's dying Words. And they sometimes strike out new meanings, richer and rarer than any that have occurred to the far cooler minds of modern critics, who are, as a rule, greatly blessed with moles' eyes, able to see where there is nothing to be seen, but never able to see when there is anything worth seeing! Modern criticism, like modern theology, if it were put in the Garden of Eden, would not see a flower. It is like the sirocco that blasts and burns. It is without either dew or unction, in fact, it is the very opposite of these precious things, and proves itself to be unblessed of God and unblessed to men.

Now concerning these seven cries from the Cross, many authors have drawn from them, **lessons concerning seven duties.** Listen. When our Lord said, "Father, forgive them," in effect, He said to us, *"Forgive your enemies."* Even when they despitefully use you and put you to terrible pain, be ready to pardon them. Be like the sandalwood tree which perfumes the axe that fells it. Be all gentleness, kindness and love, and be this your prayer, "Father, forgive them."

The next duty is taken from the second cry, namely, **that of penitence and faith in Christ,** for He said to the dying thief, "Today shall you be with Me in Paradise." Have you, like he, confessed your sin? Have you his faith and his prayerfulness? Then you shall be accepted even as he was! Learn, then, from the second cry, the duty of penitence and faith.

When our Lord, in **the third cry,** said to His mother, "Woman, behold your son!" **He taught us the duty of filial love.** No Christian must ever be short of love to his mother, his father, or to any of those who are endeared to him by relationships which God has appointed for us to observe. Oh, by the dying love of Christ to His mother, let no man here unman himself by forgetting his mother! She bore you, bear her in her old age and lovingly cherish her even to the last.

Jesus Christ's **fourth cry teaches us the duty of clinging to God and trusting in God,** "My God, my God." See how, with both hands, He takes hold of Him, "My God, My God, why have You forsaken Me?" He cannot bear to be left of God. All else causes Him but little pain compared with the anguish of being forsaken of His God. So learn to cling to God, to grip Him with a double-handed faith, and if you do ever think that He has forsaken you, cry after Him, and say, "Show me why You contend with me, for I cannot bear to be without You."

The fifth cry, "I thirst," **teaches us to set a high value upon the fulfillment of God's Word.** "After this, Jesus knowing that all things were now accomplished, that the scripture might be fulfilled, said, I thirst." Take good heed, in all your grief and weakness, to still preserve the Word of your God, and to obey the precept. Learn the doctrine and delight in the promise. As your Lord, in His great anguish said, "I thirst," because it was written that so He would speak, have regard unto the Word of the Lord even in little things.

That sixth cry, "It is finished," teaches us perfect obedience. Go through with your keeping of God's Commandments. Leave out no Command, keep on obeying till you can say, "It is finished." Work your lifework, obey your Master, suffer or serve according to His will, but rest not till you can say with your Lord, "It is finished." "I have finished the work which You gave Me to do."

And that last Word, *"Father, into Your hands I commend My spirit,"* **teaches us resignation.** Yield all things. Yield up even your spirit to God at His bidding. Stand still and make a full surrender to the Lord, and let this be your watch word from the first even to the last, "Into Your hands, my Father, I commend my spirit." I think that this study of Christ's last Words should interest you, therefore let me linger a little longer upon it. Those seven cries from the Cross also teach us something about *the attributes and offices of our Master.*

They are seven windows of agate and gates of carbuncle through which you may see Him and approach Him.

First, would you see Him as Intercessor? Then He cries, "Father, forgive them; for they know not what they do." **Would you look at Him as King?** Then hear His second Word, "Verily I say unto you, Today shall you be with Me in Paradise." **Would you mark Him as a tender Guardian?** Hear Him say to Mary, "Woman, behold your son!" And to John, "Behold your mother!" **Would you peer into the dark**

abyss of the agonies of His soul? Hear Him cry, "My God, My God, why have You forsaken Me?" **Would you understand the reality and the intensity of His bodily sufferings?** Then hear Him say, "I thirst," for there is something exquisite in the torture of thirst when brought on by the fever of bleeding wounds. Men on the battlefield who have lost much blood, are devoured with thirst, and tell you that it is the worst pang of all. "I thirst," says Jesus. See the Sufferer in the body and understand how He can sympathize with you who suffer, since He suffered so much on the Cross. **Would you see Him as the Finisher of your salvation?** Then hear His cry, *"Consummatum est,"* "It is finished." Oh, glorious note! Here you see the blessed Finisher of your faith. **And would you then take one more gaze and understand how voluntary was His suffering?** Then hear Him say, not as one who is robbed of life, but as one who takes His soul and hands it over to the keeping of another, "Father, into Your hands I commend My spirit."

Is there not much to be learned from these cries from the Cross? Surely **these seven notes make a wondrous scale of music if we do but know how to listen to them!** Let me run up the scale, again. Here, **first, you have Christ's fellowship with men,** "Father, forgive them." He stands side by side with sinners and tries to make an apology for them, "They know not what they do." Here is, **next, His kingly power.** He sets open Heaven's gate to the dying thief and bids him enter. "Today shall you be with Me in Paradise." **Thirdly, behold His human relationship.** How near of kin He is to us! "Woman, behold your son!" Remember how He says, *"Whoever shall do the will of My Father who is in Heaven, the same is My brother, and sister, and mother."* He is bone of our bone and flesh of our flesh. He belongs to the Human family. He is more of a Man than any man. As surely as He is very God of very God, He is also very Man of very man, taking into Himself the Nature, not of the Jew only, but of the Gentile, too. Belonging to His own nationality, but rising above all, He is the Man of men, the Son of Man.

See, **next, His taking our sin.** You say, "Which note is that" Well, they are all to that effect, but this one, chiefly, "My God, My God, why have You forsaken Me?" It was because **He bore our sins in His**

own body on the tree that He was forsaken of God. "He has made Him to be sin for us. who knew no sin," and hence the bitter cry, "Eloi, Eloi, Lama Sabachthani?" Behold Him, in **that fifth cry**, "I thirst," taking not only our sin, but also our infirmity, and all the suffering of our bodily nature. **Then, if you would see His fullness as well as His weakness, if you would see His All-Sufficiency as well as His sorrow, hear Him cry, "It is finished."** What a wonderful fullness there is in that note. Redemption is all accomplished! It is all complete! It is all perfect! There is nothing left, not a drop of bitterness in the cup of gall, Jesus has drained it dry! There is not a farthing to be added to the ransom price, <u>Jesus has paid it all.</u> Behold His fullness in the cry, "It is finished." And **then, if you would see how He has reconciled us to Himself, behold Him, the Man who was made a curse for us, returning with a blessing to His Father and taking us with Him, as He draws us all up by that last dear word, "Father, into Your hands I commend My spirit."** "Now both the Surety and sinner are free." Christ goes back to the Father, for, "It is finished," and you and I come to the Father through His perfect work.

I have only practiced two or three tunes that can be played upon this harp, but it is a wonderful instrument. If it is not a harp of ten strings, it is, at any rate, an instrument of seven strings, and neither time nor eternity shall ever be able to fetch all the music out of them! **Those seven dying words of the ever-living Christ will make melody for us in Glory through all the ages of eternity.**

I SHALL NOW ASK YOUR ATTENTION FOR A LITTLE TIME TO THE TEXT ITSELF: "*Father, into Your hands I commend My spirit.*"

Do you see our Lord? He is dying and, as yet, His face is toward man. **His last Word to man is the cry, "It is finished."** Hear, all you sons of men, He speaks to you, "It is finished." Could you have a choicer Word with which He should say, "Adieu," to you in the hour of death? He tells you not to fear that His work is imperfect, not to tremble lest it should prove insufficient. He speaks to you and declares with His dying utterance, "It is finished." Now He has done with you and He turns His face the other way. His day's work is done, His more than Herculean toil is accomplished, and the great Champion is going back to His Father's Throne, and He speaks, but not to you. His last Word is addressed to His Father, "Father, into Your hands I commend My spirit." **These are His First Words in going Home to His Father, as, "It is finished," is His last Word as, for a while, He quits our company.** Think of these words and may they be your first words, too, when you return to your Father! May you speak thus to your Divine Father in the hour of death.

The words were much hackneyed in Romish times, but they are not spoilt even for that. They used to be said in the Latin by dying men, "*In manus tuas, Domine, commendo spiritum meum.*" [**Into thy hands, O Lord, I commend my spirit.** "] Every dying man used to try to say those words in Latin and if he did not, somebody tried to say them for him. They were made into a kind of spell of witchcraft, and so they lost that sweetness to our ears in the Latin, but in the English they shall always stand as the very essence of music for a dying saint, "Father, into Your hands I commend my spirit."

It is very noteworthy that the last Words that our Lord used were quoted from the Scriptures. This sentence is taken, as I daresay most of you know, from the 31st Psalm, and the fifth verse. Let me read it to you. **What a proof it is of how full Christ was of the Bible! He was not one of those who think little of the Word of God. He was saturated with it. He was as full of Scripture as the fleece of Gideon was full of dew. He could not speak, even in His death, without uttering Scripture.** This is how David put it, "*Into your hand I commit my spirit: You have redeemed me, O Lord God of Truth.*" Now, Beloved, the Savior altered this passage, or else it would not quite have suited Him. Do you see, first, He was obliged, in order to fit it to His own case, to add something to it? What did He add to it? Why, that word, "Father"! David said, "*Into Your hand I commit my spirit,*" but Jesus said, "*Father, into Your hands I commend My spirit.*" Blessed advance! He knew more than David did, for He was more the Son of God than David could be. He was the Son of God in a very high and special sense by *eternal* filiation and so He begins the prayer with, "Father."

But then He takes something away from it. It was necessary that He should do so, for David said, *"Into Your hand I commit my spirit: You have redeemed me."* Our blessed Master was not redeemed, for **He was the Redeemer,** and He could have said, *"Into Your hand I commit My spirit, for I have redeemed My people."* But that He did not choose to say. He simply took that part which suited Himself and used it as His own, *"Father, into Your hands I commend My spirit."* Oh, my Brothers and Sisters, **you will not do better, after all, than to quote Scripture, especially in prayer.** There are no prayers so good as those that are full of the Word of God! May all our speech be flavored with texts! I wish that it were more so. They laughed at our Puritan forefathers because the very names of their children were fetched out of passages of Scripture, but I, for my part, had much rather be laughed at for talking much of Scripture than for talking much of trashy novels, novels with which (I am ashamed to say it) many a sermon nowadays is larded, yes, larded with novels that are not fit for decent men to read and which are coated over till one hardly knows whether he is hearing about a historical event, or only a piece of fiction, from which abomination, good Lord, deliver us.

So, then, you see how well the Savior used Scripture, and how, from His first battle with the devil in the wilderness till His last struggle with death on the Cross, His weapon was always, "It is written."

A. *LET US LEARN THE DOCTRINE* **of our Lord's last cry from the Cross**.

What is the Doctrine of this last Word of our Lord Jesus Christ? **God is His Father and God is our Father.** He who, Himself, said, "Father," did not say for Himself, "Our Father," for the Father is Christ's Father in a higher sense than He is ours. But yet He is not more truly the Father of Christ than He is our Father if we have believed in Jesus! "You are all the children of God by faith in Christ Jesus." Jesus said to Mary Magdalene, *"I ascend unto My Father and your Father; and to My God, and your God."* Believe the Doctrine of the Fatherhood of God to

His people. As I have warned you before, **abhor the doctrine of the universal fatherhood of God,** for it is a lie and a deep deception. **It stabs at the heart, first, of the Doctrine of the Adoption which is taught in Scripture**, for how can God adopt men if they are already all His children? In the second place, **it stabs at the heart of the Doctrine of Regeneration,** which is certainly taught in the Word of God. Now it is by regeneration and faith that we become the children of God, but how can that be if we are already the children of God? *"As many as received Him, to them gave He power to become the sons of God, even to them that believe on His name: which were born, not of blood, nor of the will of the flesh, nor of the will of man, but of God."* How can God give to men the power to become His sons if they have it already? Believe not that lie of the devil, but believe this Truth of God, that Christ and all who are, by living faith in Christ, may rejoice in the Fatherhood of God.

Next learn this Doctrine, that *in this fact lies our chief comfort*. In our hour of trouble, in our time of warfare, let us say, "Father." You notice that the first cry from the Cross is like the last, the highest note is like the lowest. Jesus begins with, "Father, forgive them," and He finishes with, "Father, into Your hands I commend My spirit." To help you in a stern duty like forgiveness, cry, "Father." To help you in sore suffering and death, cry, "Father." **Your main strength lies in your truly being a child of God.**

Learn the next Doctrine, that dying is going Home to our Father. I said to an old friend, not long ago, "Old Mr. So- and-so has gone Home." I meant that He was dead. He said, "Yes, where else would he go?" I thought that was a wise question. Where else would we go? When we grow gray, and our day's work is done, where should we go but home? So, when Christ has said, "It is finished," His next Word, of course, is, "Father." He has finished His earthly course and now He will go Home to Heaven. Just as a child runs to its mother's bosom when it is tired and wants to fall asleep, so Christ says, "Father," before He falls asleep in death.

Learn another Doctrine, that if God is our Father, and we regard ourselves as going Home when we die, because we go to Him, *then*

He will receive us. There is no hint that we can commit our spirit to God and yet that God will not have us. Remember how Stephen, beneath a shower of stones, cried, **"Lord Jesus, receive my spirit"?** Let us, however we may die, make this our last emotion if not our last expression, "Father, receive my spirit." Shall not our heavenly Father receive His children? If you, being evil, receive your children at nightfall, when they come home to sleep, shall not your Father, who is in Heaven, receive you when your day's work is done? **That is the doctrine we are to learn from this last cry from the Cross, the Fatherhood of God and all that comes of it to Believers.**

B. *LET US PRACTICE THE DUTY.*

That duty seems to me to be, first, *resignation.* Whenever anything distresses and alarms you, resign yourself to God. Say, "Father, into Your hands I commend my spirit." Sing, with Faber: *"I bow me to Your will, O God, /And all Your ways adore. /And every day I live I'll seek /To please you more and more."*

Learn, next, the duty of *prayer.* When you are in the very anguish of pain. When you are surrounded by bitter griefs of mind as well as of body, still pray. Drop not the, "Our Father." Let not your cries be addressed to the air. Let not your moans be to your physician, or your nurse, but cry, "Father." Does not a child so cry when it has lost its way? If it is in the dark at night, and it starts up in a lone room, does it not cry out, "Father!" And is not a father's heart touched by that cry? Is there anybody here who has never cried to God? Is there one here who has never said, "Father"? Then, my Father, put Your love into their hearts and make them say, tonight, *"I will arise and go to my Father."* You shall truly be known to be the sons of God if that cry is in your heart and on your lips.

The next duty is the *committal of ourselves to God by faith.* Give yourselves up to God. Trust yourselves with God. Every morning, when you get up, take yourself and put yourself into God's custody, lock yourself up, as it were, in **the box of Divine Protection,** and every night, when you have unlocked the box, before you fall asleep, lock it again and give the key into the hand of Him who is able to keep you when the image of death is on your face. Before you sleep, commit yourself to God. I mean, do that when there is nothing to frighten you, when everything is going smoothly, when the wind blows softly from the south and the boat is speeding towards its desired haven, still make not yourself quiet with your own quieting. **He who carves for himself will cut his fingers and get an empty plate. He who leaves God to carve for him shall often have fat things full of marrow placed before him. If you can trust, God will reward your trusting in a way that you know not as yet.**

And then practice one other duty, **that of *the personal and continual realization of God's Presence.*** *"Father, into Your hands I commend My spirit." "You are here; I know that You are. I realize that You are here in the time of sorrow, and of danger; and I put myself into Your hands. Just as I would give myself to the protection of a policeman, or a soldier, if anyone attacked me, so do I commit myself to You, You unseen Guardian of the night, You unwearied Keeper of the day! You shall cover my head in the day of battle. Beneath Your wings will I trust, as a chick hides beneath the hen."*

See, then, your duty. **It is to resign yourself to God, pray to God, commit yourself to God and rest in a sense of the Presence of God. May the Spirit of God help you in the practice of such priceless duties as these.**

C. Lastly, *LET US ENJOY THE PRIVILEGE.*

First, let us enjoy the high privilege of *resting in God in all times of danger and pain.* The doctor has just told you that you will have to undergo an operation. Say, "Father, into Your hands I commend my spirit." There is every probability that that weakness of yours, or that disease of yours, will increase upon you and that, by-and-by, you will have to take to your bed and lie there, perhaps, for many a day. Then say, "Father, into Your hands I commend my spirit." Do not fret, for that will not help you. Do not fear the future, for that will not aid you. Give yourself up (it is your *privilege* to do so) to the keeping of those dear hands that were pierced for you, to the love of that dear heart which was set a broach with the spear to purchase your redemption.

It is wonderful what rest of spirit God can give to a man or a woman in the very worst condition. Oh, how some of the martyrs have sung at the stake! How they have rejoiced when on the rack. Bonner's coal-hole, across the water there, at Fulham [Southwest London], where he shut up the martyrs, was a wretched place to lie on a cold winter's night, but they said, "They did rouse them in the straw, as they lay in the coal-hole, with the sweetest singing out of Heaven! And when Donner said, 'Fie on them that they should make such a noise!' they told him that he, too, would make such a noise if he was as happy as they were." When you have commended your spirit to God, then you have sweet rest in time of danger and pain.

The next privilege is that of a *brave confidence, in the time of death, or in the fear of death*. I was led to think over this text by using it a great many times last Thursday night. Perhaps none of you will ever forget last Thursday night. I do not think that I ever shall, if I live to be as old as Methuselah. From this place till I reached my home, it seemed one continued sheet of fire, and the further I went, the more vivid became the lightning flashes. But when I came, at last, to turn up Leigham Court Road [Lambeth, London], then the lightning seemed to come in very bars from the sky and, at last, as I reached the top of the hill, and a crash came of the most startling kind, down poured a torrent of hail, hailstones that I will not attempt to describe, for you might think that I exaggerated. And then I felt, and my friend with me, that we could hardly expect to reach home alive. We were there at the very center and summit of the storm. All around us, on every side, and all within us, as it were, seemed nothing but the electric fluid, and God's right arm seemed bared for war. I felt then, "Well, now, I am very likely going Home," and I commended my spirit to God. And from that moment, though I cannot say that I took much pleasure in the peals of thunder, and the flashes of lightning, yet I felt quite as calm as I do

310

here at this present moment, perhaps a little *calmer* than I do in the presence of so many people, happy at the thought that, within a single moment, I might understand more than all I could ever learn on earth and see in an instant more than I could hope to see if I lived here for a century! I could only say to my friend, "Let us commit ourselves to God. We know that we are doing our duty in going on as we are going, and all is well with us."

So we could only rejoice together in the prospect of being soon with God. We were not taken Home in the chariot of fire, we are still spared a little longer to go on with life's work, but I realize the sweetness of being able to have done with it all, to have no wish, no will, no word, scarcely a prayer, but just to take one's heart up and hand it over to the great Keeper, saying, *"Father, take care of me. So let me live, so let me die. I have, henceforth, no desire about anything. Let it be as You please. Into Your hands I commend my spirit."*

This privilege is not only that of having rest in danger, and confidence in the prospect of death, it is also full of consummate joy. Beloved, if we know how to commit ourselves into the hands of God, what a place it is for us to be in. What a place to be in, in the hands of God! There are the myriads of stars. There is the universe, itself. God's hand upholds its everlasting pillars and they do not fall. If we got into the hands of God, we get where all things rest and we get home and happiness. We have got out of the nothingness of the creature into the All-Sufficiency of the Creator. Oh, get you there. Hasten to get there, beloved Friends, and live, henceforth, in the hands of God.

"It is finished." **You have not finished, but Christ has. It is all done**. What you have to do will only be to work out what He has already finished for you, and show it to the sons of men in your lives. And because it is all finished, therefore say, "Now, Father, I return to You. My life, henceforth, shall be to be in You. **My joy shall be to shrink to nothing in the Presence of the All-in-All, to die into the eternal life, to sink my ego into Jehovah, to let my manhood, my creature hood lives only for its Creator and manifest only the Creator's Glory.**

EXHORTATION: O Beloved, begin tomorrow morning and end tonight with, "Father, into Your hands I commend my spirit." The Lord be with you all! Oh, if you have never prayed, God help you to begin to pray now, for Jesus' sake! Amen.

3.   Exposition on Luke 23:2–49

Luke 23:27. And *there followed Him a great company of people, and of women, which also bewailed and lamented Him.*

Their best Friend, the Healer of their sick, the Lover of their children, was about to be put to death, so they might well bewail and lament.

28–30. *But Jesus turning unto them said, Daughters of Jerusalem, weep not for Me, but weep for yourselves, and for your children. For, behold, the days are coming, in the which they shall say, Blessed are the barren, and the wombs that never bore, and the paps which never gave suck. Then shall they begin to say to the mountains, fall on us; and to the hills, Cover us.*

Our Savior spoke of the terrible siege of Jerusalem, the most tragic of all human transactions. I think I do not exaggerate when I say that history contains nothing equal to it. It stands alone in the unutterable agony of men, women and children in that dreadful time of suffering.

31. *For if they do these things in a green tree, what shall be done in the dry?*

If the Christ of God is put to death even while the Jewish capital seems vigorous and flourishing, what shall be done when it is all dry and dead, and the Roman legions are round about the doomed city?

32. *And there were also two other malefactors, led with Him to be put to death.*

Every item of scorn was added to our Savior's death and yet the Scriptures were thus literally fulfilled, for, "He was numbered with the transgressors."

33, 34. *And when they were come to the place which is called Calvary, there they crucified Him, and the malefactors, one on the right hand, and the other on the left. Then said Jesus, Father, forgive them; for they know not what they do. And they parted His raiment, and cast lots.*

Do you hear the hammer fall? "Then said Jesus, Father, forgive them, for they know not what they do." Do you see the bleeding hands and feet of Jesus? This is all that is extracted by that fearful pressure, nothing but words of pardoning love, a prayer for those who are killing Him, "Father, forgive them; for they know not what they do."

35. *And the people stood beholding. And the rulers also with them derided Him, saying, He saved others; let Him save Himself, if He is Christ, the chosen of God.*

You know how mockery puts salt and vinegar into a wound. A man does not at any time like to be reviled, but when he is full of physical and mental anguish and his heart is heavy within him, then ridicule is peculiarly full of acid to him.

36, 37. *And the soldiers also mocked Him, coming to Him, and offering Him vinegar, and saying, If You are the King of the Jews, save Yourself.*

These rough soldiers knew how to put their jests in the cruelest shape and to press home their scoffs upon their suffering Victim.

38. *And a superscription also was written over Him in letters of Greek, and Latin, and Hebrew.*

These were the three languages that could be understood by all the people round about.

38. *THIS IS THE KING OF THE JEWS.*

And so He is, and so He shall be. He has never quit the throne. The Son of David is still King of the Jews, though they continue to reject Him. But the day shall come when they shall recognize and receive the Messiah. "Then shall they look upon Him whom they have pierced, and they shall mourn for Him, as one mourns for His only son, and shall be in bitterness for Him, as one that is in bitterness for His first-born."

39. *And one of the malefactors which were hanged railed on Him, saying, if you are Christ, save Yourself and us.*

Matthew and Mark speak of both the thieves as railing at Jesus. We must take their expressions as being literally correct and, if so, both the malefactors *at first* cast reproaches in Christ's teeth.

40, 41. *But the other answering rebuked him, saying, do not you fear God, seeing you are in the same condemnation? And we indeed justly; for we receive the due reward of our deeds: but this Man has done nothing amiss.*

Not only has He done nothing worthy of death, but He has done nothing improper, nothing out of place. "This man has done nothing amiss." The thief bears testimony to the perfect Character of this wondrous Man, whom he, nevertheless, recognized to be Divine, as we shall see in the next verse.

42–47. *And He said unto Jesus, Lord, remember me when You come into Your Kingdom. And Jesus said unto him, Verily I say unto you, today shall you be with Me in Paradise. And it was* *about the sixth hour, and there was a darkness over all the earth until the ninth hour. And the sun was darkened, and the veil of the Temple was rent in the midst. And when Jesus had cried with a loud voice, He said, Father, into Your hands I commend My spirit: and having said this, He gave up the ghost. Now when the centurion saw what was done, He glorified God, saying, certainly this was a righteous Man.*

He was set there at the head of the guard, to watch the execution, and he could not help saying, as he observed the wonderful signs in Heaven and earth, "Certainly this was a righteous Man."

48. And all the people that came together to that sight, beholding the things which were done, smote their breasts, and returned.

What a change must have come over that ribald crowd! They had shouted, "Crucify Him!" They had stood there and mocked Him and now they are overcome with the sight, and they strike their breasts. Ah, dear Friends, their grief did not come to much! Men may strike their breasts, but unless *God* smites their *hearts*, all the outward signs of a gracious work will come to nothing at all.

49. And all His acquaintance, and the women that followed Him from Galilee, stood afar off, beholding these things.

Let "these things" be before your mind's eye this evening and think much of your crucified Lord, all you who are of His acquaintance, and who are numbered among His followers.

4.   Exposition on Matthew 27:50–54

Matthew 27:50. *Jesus, when He had cried again with a load voice, yielded up the ghost.*

Christ's strength was not exhausted. His last Word was uttered with a loud voice, like the shout of a conquering warrior! And what a Word it was, "It is finished"! Thousands of sermons have been preached upon that little sentence, but who can tell all the meaning that lies compacted within it? It is a kind of infinite expression for breadth, depth, length and height altogether immeasurable! Christ's life being finished, perfected, completed, He yielded up the ghost, willingly dying, laying down His life as He said He would, "I lay down My life for My sheep. I lay it down of Myself. I have power to lay it down, and I have power to take it again."

51–53. *And, behold, the veil of the Temple was rent in two from the top to the bottom; and the earth did quake, and the rocks rent; and the graves were opened; and many bodies of the saints which slept arose, and came out of the graves after His resurrection, and went into the holy city, and appeared unto many.*

Christ's death was the end of Judaism. The veil of the Temple was torn in two from the top to the bottom. As if shocked at the sacrilegious murder of her Lord, the Temple rent her garments, like one stricken with horror at some stupendous crime! The body of Christ being rent; the veil of the Temple was torn in two from the top to bottom. Now was there an entrance made into the holiest of all, by the blood of Jesus, and a way of access to God was opened for every sinner who trusted in Christ's atoning Sacrifice.

See what marvels accompanied and followed the death of Christ! The earth did quake, and the rocks rent; and the graves were opened. Thus did the material world pay homage to Him whom man had rejected, while Nature's convulsions foretold what will happen when

Christ's voice once more shakes not the earth, only, but also Heaven. These first miracles worked in connection with the death of Christ were typical of spiritual wonders that will be continued till He comes again, rocky hearts are rent, graves of sin are opened, those who have been dead in trespasses and sins, and buried in sepulchers of lust and evil, are quickened and come out from among the dead, and go unto the holy city, the New Jerusalem.

54. *Now when the centurion, and they that were with him, watching Jesus, saw the earthquake, and those things that were done, they feared greatly, saying, truly this was the Son of God.*

These Roman soldiers had never witnessed such scenes in connection with an execution, before, and they could only come to one conclusion about the illustrious Prisoner whom they had put to death, "Truly this was the Son of God." It was strange that those men should confess what the chief priests and scribes and elders denied, yet since their day it has often happened that the most abandoned and profane have acknowledged Jesus as the Son of God while their religious rulers have denied His Divinity.

PART III

FROM THE CROSS TO HIS GLORIOUS APPEARANCE

A. On the Cross after Death

"Therefore, because it was the Preparation Day, that the bodies should not remain on the cross on the Sabbath (for that Sabbath was a high day), the Jews asked Pilate that their legs might be broken, and that they might be taken away. Then the soldiers came and broke the legs of the first and of the other who was crucified with Him. But when they came to Jesus and saw that He was already dead, they did not break His legs. But one of the soldiers pierced His side with a spear, and immediately blood and water came out. And he who has seen has testified, and his testimony is true; and he knows that he is telling the truth, so that you may believe. For these things were done that the Scripture should be fulfilled, 'Not one of His bones shall be broken.' And again another Scripture says, 'They shall look on Him whom they pierced'"
(John 19:31–37 NKJV).

FOCUS: Spurgeon: "The task before me ... is to draw out of this well of wonders. I shall ask you to look at the events before us in three lights: first, let us see the fulfillment of Scripture; second, the identification of our Lord as the Messiah, and third, the instruction which He intends."

CRIMINALS who were crucified by the Romans were allowed to rot upon the cross. That cruel nation can hardly be so severely

319

condemned as our own people who, up to a late period, allowed the bodies of those condemned to die to hang in chains upon gallows in conspicuous places. The horrible practice is now abandoned, but it was retained to a time almost, if not quite, within living memory. I wonder whether any aged person here remembers such a horrible spectacle. Among the Romans it was usual, for there are classical allusions to this horror showing the bodies of persons crucified were usually left to be devoured by ravenous birds. Probably out of deference to the customs of the Jews, the authorities in Palestine would, sooner or later, allow of the interment of the crucified, but they would by no means hasten it, since they would not feel such a disgust at the sight as an Israelite would.

The Mosaic Law, which you will find in the Book of Deuteronomy, runs as follows, *"If you hang him on a tree, his body shall not remain all night upon the tree, but you shall surely bury him that day"* (21:22, 23). This alone would lead the Jews to desire the burial of the executed, but there was a further reason. Lest the land should be defiled upon the holy Sabbath of the Passover, the chief priests were importunate that the bodies of the crucified should be buried and, therefore, that their deaths should be hastened by the breaking of their legs. Their consciences were not wounded by the murder of Jesus, but they were greatly moved by the fear of ceremonial pollution. Religious scruples may live in a dead conscience. Alas, this is not the only proof of that fact: we could find many in our own day.

The Jews hurried to Pilate and sought, as a blessing, the merciless act of having the legs of the crucified dashed to pieces with an iron bar. That act was sometimes performed upon the condemned as an additional punishment, but in this instance it was meant to be a finishing stroke, hastening death by the terrible pain which it would cause and the shock to the system which it would occasion. Ferocious hate of our Lord made His enemies forgetful of everything like humanity, doubtless the more of pain and shame which they could cause to Him, the better would they be pleased. Not, however, out of cruelty, but out of regard to the ceremonials of their religion, they, *"besought Pilate that their legs might be broken and that they might be taken away."* I have already told you that this breaking of the bones of the crucified was a Roman custom. We have evidence of this, since there is a Latin word, *crucifragium*, to express this barbarous act. Pilate had no hesitation in granting the desire of the Jews, what would he care about the dead body since he had already delivered up the living Man?

Soldiers go at once to perform the hideous operation and they commence with the two malefactors. It is a striking fact that the penitent thief, although he was to be in Paradise with his Lord that day, was not, therefore, delivered from the excruciating agony occasioned by the breaking of his legs. We are saved from *eternal misery*, not from *temporary pain.*

Our Savior, by our salvation, gives no pledge to us that we shall be screened from suffering in this life. It is true, as the Proverb has it, *"All things come alike to all: there is one event to the righteous and to the wicked; to the clean and to the unclean."* Accidents and diseases afflict the godly as well as the ungodly. Penitent or impenitent, we share the common lot of men and are born to troubles as the sparks fly upward. You must not expect, because you are pardoned, even if you have the assurance of it from Christ's own lips, that, therefore, you shall escape tribulation. No, but from His gracious mouth you have the forewarning assurance that trial shall befall you, for Jesus said, *"These things I have spoken unto you, that in Me you might have peace. In the world you shall have tribulation."* Suffering is not averted, but it is turned into a blessing. The penitent thief entered Paradise that very day, but it was not without suffering. Say, rather, that the terrible stroke was the actual *means* of the prompt fulfillment of his Lord's promise to him. By that blow, he died that day, otherwise he might have lingered long. How much we may, any of us, receive by the way of suffering it were hard to guess, perhaps the promise that we shall be with our Lord in Paradise will be fulfilled that way.

At this point it seemed more than probable that our blessed Lord must undergo the breaking of His bones, but *"He was dead already."* It had pleased Him, in the infinite willingness with which He went to His Sacrifice, to yield up His life and His spirit had, therefore, departed. Yet one might have feared that the coarse soldiers would have performed their orders to the letter. Look, they do not. Had they conceived a dread of One around whom such prodigies had gathered? Were they, like their centurion, impressed with awe of this remarkable Person? At any rate, perceiving that He was dead already, they did not use their hammer. Happy are we to see them cease from such loathsome brutality. But we may not be *too* glad, for another outrage will take its place. To make sure that He was dead, one of the four soldiers pierced His side with a spear, probably thrusting His lance quite through the heart. **Here we see how our gracious God ordained, in His Providence, that there should be sure evidence that Jesus was dead and that, therefore, the Sacrifice was slain.**

Paul declares this to be the Gospel, that the Lord Jesus died according to the Scriptures. Strange to say, there have been heretics who have ventured to assert that Jesus did not actually die. They stand refuted by this spear-thrust. If our Lord did not die, then no Sacrifice has been presented, the Resurrection is not a fact and there is no foundation of hope for men. Our Lord assuredly died and was buried, the Roman soldiers were keen judges in such matters and they saw that, "he was dead already" and, moreover, their spears were not used in vain when they meant to make death a certainty.

When the side of Christ was pierced, there flowed from it blood and water upon which a great deal has been said by those who think it proper to dilate upon such tender themes. It was supposed by some that by death the blood was divided, the clots parting from the water in which they float and that in a perfectly natural way. But it is not true that blood would flow from a dead body if it were pierced. Only under certain very special conditions would blood gush forth. The flowing of this blood from the side of our Lord cannot be considered as a common occurrence, it was a fact entirely by itself. We cannot argue from any known fact in this case, for we are here in a new region. Granted, that blood would not flow from an ordinary dead body, yet remember that our Lord's body was unique, since it saw no corruption. Whatever change might come over a body liable to decay, we may not ascribe any such change to His frame and, therefore, there is no arguing from facts about common bodies so as to conclude from them anything concerning our blessed Lord's body. Whether, in His case, blood and water flowed naturally from His holy and incorruptible body, or whether it was a miracle, it was evidently a most notable and remarkable thing and John, as an eyewitness, was evidently astonished at it, so astonished at it that he recorded a solemn affirmation in order that we might not doubt his testimony. He was certain of what he saw and he took care to report it with a special note in order that we might believe, as if he felt that if this fact was truly believed, there was a certain convincing power which would induce many to believe on **our Lord Jesus as the appointed Savior.** I could enter into many details, but I prefer to cast a veil over this tender mystery. It is scarcely reverent to be discoursing anatomy when the body of our adorable Lord is before us. Let us close our eyes in worship rather than open them with irreverent curiosity.

A. I ask you to notice *THE FULFILLMENT OF SCRIPTURE*.

Two things are predicted, not a bone of Him must be broken and He must be pierced. These were the Scriptures which now remained to be accomplished. Last Lord's-Day morning we were, all of us, delighted as we saw the fulfillment of Scripture [Refer to Sermon on *Jesus Declining the Legions, No. 1955*] in the capture of our Lord and His refusal to deliver Himself from His enemies. The theme of the fulfillment of Scripture is worth pursuing yet further in an age when Holy Scripture is treated with so much slight and is spoken of as having no Inspiration in it, or, at least, no Divine Authority by which its Infallibility is secured. You and I favor no such error. On the contrary, we conceive it to be to the last degree, mischievous. **"If the foundations are removed, what can the righteous do?"** We are pleased to notice how the Lord Jesus Christ and those who wrote concerning Him treated the Holy Scriptures with an intensely reverent regard. The prophecies that went before of Christ must be fulfilled and holy souls found great delight in dwelling upon the fact that they were so.

I want you to notice, concerning this case, that *it was amazingly complicated*. It was negative and positive, the Savior's bones must not be broken *and*, He must be pierced. In the type of the Passover lamb, it was expressly enacted that not a bone of it should be broken, therefore not a bone of Jesus must be broken. At the same time, according to Zechariah 12:10, the Lord must be *pierced*. He must not only be pierced with the nails and so fulfill the prophecy, *"They pierced My hands and My feet,"* but He must be conspicuously *pierced* so that He can be emphatically regarded as a Pierced One. How were these prophecies and a multitude more, to be accomplished? Only God, Himself, could have brought to pass the fulfillment of prophecies which were of all kinds and appeared to be confusing and even in contradiction to each other.

It would be an impossible task for the human intellect to construct so many prophecies, types, foreshadowing and then to *imagine* a person in whom they should all be embodied. **But what would be impossible to men has been literally carried out in the case of our Lord. There are prophecies about Him and about everything connected with Him, from His hair to His garments, from His birth to His tomb, and yet they have *all* been carried out to the letter.** That which lies immediately before us was a complicated case, for if reverence to the Savior would spare His bones, would it not also spare His flesh? If a coarse brutality pierced His side, why did it not break His legs? How can men be kept from one act of violence, and that an act authorized by the *authority* and yet perpetrate another violence which had not been suggested to them? But, let the case be as complicated as it were possible for it to have been, Infinite Wisdom knew how to work it out in all points, and He did so. **The Christ is the *exact substance* of the foreshadowing of the Messianic prophecies.**

Next, we may say of the fulfillment of these two prophecies, that *it was especially improbable*. It did not seem at all likely that when the order was given to break the legs of the crucified, Roman soldiers would abstain from the deed. How could the body of Christ be preserved after such an order had been issued? Those four soldiers are evidently determined to carry out the governor's orders. They have commenced their dreadful task and they have broken the legs of two of the executed three. The crosses were arranged so that Jesus was hanging in the midst; He is the second of the three. We naturally suppose that they would proceed in order from the first cross to the second. But they seem to pass by the second cross and proceed from the first to the third. What was the reason of this singular procedure? The supposition is, and I think a very likely one, that the center cross stood somewhat back and that thus the two thieves formed a sort of first rank. Jesus would thus be all the more emphatically, "in the midst."

If He was placed a little back, it would certainly have been easier for the penitent thief to have read the inscription over His head and to have looked to our Lord and held a conversation with Him. Had they been placed exactly in a line, this might not have been so natural. But the suggested position seems to suit the circumstances. If it were so, I can understand how the soldiers would be taking the crosses in order when they performed their horrible office upon the two malefactors and came last to Jesus, who was in the midst. In any case, such was the order which they followed. The marvel is that they did not, in due course, proceed to deal the horrible blow in the case of our Lord. Roman soldiers are apt to fulfill their commissions very literally, they are not often moved with much desire to avoid barbarities. Can you see them intent upon their errand? Will they not even now mangle that sacred body? Commend me for roughness to the ordinary Roman soldier, he was so used to deeds of slaughter, so accustomed to an empire which had been established with blood and iron, that the idea of pity never crossed his soul, except to be mocked as a womanly feeling unworthy of a brave man! Yet behold and wonder. The order is given to break their legs, two out of the three have suffered, and yet no soldier may crush a bone of that sacred body. They see that He is dead already and they do not break His legs.

As yet you have only seen one of the prophecies fulfilled. He must be pierced as well. And what was that which came into that Roman soldier's mind when, in a hasty moment, he resolved to make sure that the apparent death of Jesus was a real one? Why did he open that sacred side with his lance? He knew nothing of the prophecy. He had no dreams of Eve being taken from the side of the man and the Church from the side of Jesus. He had never heard that ancient notion of the side of Jesus being like the door of the ark, through which an entrance to safety is opened. Why, then, does he fulfill the prediction of the Prophet? **There was no accident or chance here!** Where are there such things? The hand of the Lord is here and we desire to praise and bless that Omniscient and Omnipotent Providence which thus fulfilled the Word of Revelation. God has respect unto His own Word and while He takes care that no bone of His Son shall be broken, He also secures that no text of Holy Scripture shall be broken. **That our Lord's bones should remain unbroken and yet that He should be pierced seemed a very unlikely thing, but it was carried out. When next you meet with an unlikely promise, believe it firmly. When next you see things working contrary to the Truth of God, believe God and believe nothing else.** Let God be true and every man a liar. Though men and devils should give God the lie, hold on to what God has spoken, for Heaven and earth shall pass away, but not one jot or tittle of His Word shall fall to the ground.

Note again, dear Friends, concerning this fulfillment of Scripture, that *it was altogether indispensable.* If they had broken Christ's bones, then that Word of John the Baptist, *"Behold the Lamb of God,"* had seemed to have a slur cast upon it. Men would have objected, "But the bones of the Lamb of God were not broken." It was especially commanded twice over, not only in the first ordaining of the Passover in Egypt, but in the allowance of a second to those who were defiled at the time of the first Passover. In Numbers, as well as in Exodus, we read that not a bone of the lamb must be broken. How, then, if our Lord's bones had been broken, could we have said, **"Christ our Passover is sacrificed for us,"** when there would have been this fatal flaw? Jesus must remain intact upon the Cross and He must also be pierced, otherwise that famous passage in Zechariah, which is here alluded to, "They shall look on Me whom they have pierced," could not have been true of Him. *Both* prophecies must be carried out and *they were* so in a conspicuous manner.

But why need I say that **this fulfillment was *indispensable*?** Beloved, the keeping of every Word of God is indispensable. It is indispensable to the Truth of God that He should always be true, for if one Word of His can fall to the ground, then all may fall and His veracity is gone. If it can be demonstrated that one prophecy was a mistake, then all the rest may be mistakes. If one part of the Scripture is untrue, all may be untrue and we have no sure ground to go on. Faith loves not slippery places. **Faith seeks the sure Word of Prophecy and sets her foot firmly upon certainties.** Unless all the Word of God is sure and pure, *"as silver tried in a furnace of earth, purified seven times,"* then we have nothing to go upon and are virtually left without a Revelation from God.

If I am to take the Bible and say, "Some of this is true and some of it is questionable," I am no better off than if I had no Bible. A man who is at sea with a chart which is only accurate in certain places is not much better off than if he had no chart at all. I see not how it can ever be safe to be *"converted and become as little children"* if there is no Infallible Teacher for us to follow. Beloved, it is indispensable to the honor of God and to our confidence in His Word, that every line of Holy Scripture should be true! It was evidently indispensable in the case now before us and this is only one in- stance of a rule which is without exception.

But now let me remind you that although the problem was complicated and its working out was improbable, *yet it was fulfilled in the most natural manner.* Nothing can be less constrained than the action of the soldiers. They have broken the legs of two, but the other is dead and so they do not break His legs. Yet, to make sure that they will be safe in omitting the blow, they pierce His side. There was no compulsion put upon them, they did this of their own proper thought. No angel came from Heaven to stand with his broad wings in front of the Cross, so as to protect the Savior. No awful protection of mystery was hung over the sacred body of the Lord so that intruders might be driven back with fear. No, the quaternion [a set, a group] of soldiers did whatever they wished to do. **They acted of their own free will and yet, at the same time, they fulfilled the eternal counsel of God.**

Shall we never be able to drive into men's minds the Truth of God that *predestination* and free agency are both *facts*?

Men sin as freely as birds fly in the air and they are altogether responsible for their sin and yet *everything* is ordained and foreseen of God. The fore-ordination of God in no degree interferes with the responsibility of man. I have often been asked by persons to reconcile the two Truths of God. My only reply is, They need no reconciliation, for they never fell out. Why should I try to reconcile two friends? Prove to me that the two Truths do not agree. In that request I have set you a task as difficult as that which you propose to me. These two facts are parallel lines; I cannot make them unite but you cannot make them cross each other. Permit me, also, to add that I have long ago given up the idea of making all my beliefs into a system. I believe, but I cannot explain. I fall before the majesty of Revelation and adore the Infinite Lord. I do not understand all that God reveals, but I believe it. How can I expect to understand all the mysteries of Revelation, when even the arithmetic of Scripture surpasses My comprehension, since I am taught that in the Godhead the Three are One, while in the undivided One I see most manifestly Three?

Need I measure the sea? Is it not enough that I am borne up by its waves? I thank God for waters deep enough for my faith to swim in. Understanding would compel me to keep to the shallows, but faith takes me to the main ocean. I think it more to my soul's benefit to *believe* than to understand, for faith brings me nearer to God than reason ever did. The faith which is limited by our narrow faculties is a faith unworthy of a child of God, for as a child of God he should begin to deal with infinite sublimities, like those in which his great Father is at home. These are only to be grasped by faith. To return to my subject, albeit the matter must be as Scripture foreshadowed, yet no constraint nor inducement was put forth. But, **as free agents, the soldiers performed the very things which were written in the Prophets concerning Christ.**

Dear Friends, suffer one more observation upon this fulfillment of Scripture, *it was marvelously complete.* Observe that in these transactions a seal was set upon that part of Scripture which has been most exposed to skeptical derision, for the seal was set, first of all, upon the *types*. Irreverent readers of Scripture have refused to accept the types. They say, *"How do you know that the Passover was a type of Christ?"* In other cases, more serious persons object to detailed interpretations and decline to see a meaning in the smaller particulars. Such persons would not attach *spiritual* importance to the law, "Not a bone of it shall be broken," but would dismiss it as a petty regulation of an obsolete religious rite.

But observe, Beloved, the Holy Spirit does nothing of the kind, for He fixes upon a minor particular of the type and declares that this must be fulfilled. Moreover, **the Providence of God intervenes** so that it shall be carried out. Therefore, be not scared away from the study of the types by the ridicule of the worldly-wise. There is a general timidity coming over the minds of many about Holy Scripture, a timidity to which, thank God, I am an utter stranger! It would be a happy circumstance if the childlike reverence of the early fathers could be restored to the Church and the present irreverent criticism could be repented of and cast away. We may delight ourselves in the types as in a very Paradise of Revelation. Here we see our best Beloved's beauties mirrored in 10,000 delightful ways. There is a world of holy teaching in the books of the Old Testament and in their types and symbols. To give up this patrimony of the saints and to accept criticism instead of it would be like selling one's birthright for a mess of pottage. I see in our Lord's unbroken bones a setting of the seal of God upon the *types* of Scripture.

Let us go further. I see, next, the seal of God set upon **unfulfilled prophecy**, for the passage in Zechariah is not yet completely fulfilled. It runs thus, *"They shall look upon Me whom they have pierced."* Jehovah is the speaker and He speaks of *"the house of David and the inhabitants of Jerusalem."* They are to look on Jehovah whom they have pierced and to mourn for Him. Although this prophecy is not yet fulfilled on the largest scale, yet it is so far certified, for Jesus is pierced, the rest of it, therefore, stands good and Israel shall one day mourn because of her insulted King. The prophecy was fulfilled in part when Peter stood up and preached to the eleven, when a great company of the priests believed and when multitudes of the seed of Abraham became preachers of Christ Crucified. Still it awaits a larger fulfillment and we may rest quite sure that the day shall come when all Israel shall be saved. As the piercing of their Lord is true, so shall the piercing of their hearts be true and they shall mourn and inwardly bleed with bitter sorrow for Him whom they despised and abhorred. The point to mark here is that a seal is set in this case to a prophecy which yet awaits its largest fulfillment and, therefore, we may regard this as a pattern and may lay stress upon prophecy, rejoice in it and receive it without doubt, come what may.

I have said this much upon the fulfillment of the Word concerning our Lord. Let us learn, therefore, **a lesson of reverence and confidence in reference to Holy Scripture.**

B. But now, secondly, and briefly, ***THE IDENTIFICATION OF OUR LORD AS THE MESSIAH*** was greatly strengthened by that which befell His body after death. It was necessary that He should conclusively be proven to be the Christ spoken of in the Old Testament. Certain marks and tokens are given and those marks and tokens must be found in Him, they were so found.

The first mark was this: ***God's Lamb must have a measure of preservation.*** If Christ is what He professes to be, He is the Lamb of God. Now, God's lamb could only be dealt with in God's way. There is the lamb. Kill it, sprinkle its blood, roast it with fire, but break not its bones. It is God's lamb and not yours, therefore thus far shall you come, but no further. Not a bone of it shall be broken. Roast it, divide it among yourselves and eat it, but break no bone of it. The Lord claims it as His own and this is His reserve. So, in effect, the Lord says concerning the Lord Jesus, *"There is My Son. Bind Him, scourge Him, spit on Him, crucify Him, but He is the Lamb of My Passover and you must not break a bone of Him."* The Lord's right to Him is declared by the reservation which is made concerning His bones. Do you not see, here, how He is identified as being, "the Lamb of God, which takes away the sin of the world"? It is a mark of identity upon which faith fixes her eyes and she studies that mark until she sees much more in it than we can, this morning, speak about, for we have other things to dwell upon.

The next mark of identity must be that *Jehovah our Lord should be pierced by Israel.* So Zechariah said and so must it be fulfilled. Not merely must His hands and feet be nailed, but most conspicuously must He, Himself, be *pierced.* *"They shall look upon Me whom they have pierced, and they shall mourn for Him."* Pierced He must be! His wounds are the marks and tokens of His being the real Christ. When they shall see the sign of the Son of Man in the last days, then shall all the tribes of the earth mourn and is not that sign His appearing as a Lamb that has been slain? The wound in His side was a sure mark of His identity to His own disciples, for He said to Thomas, *"Reach here your hand and thrust it into My side: and be not faithless, but believing."* It shall be the convincing token to all Israel, *"They shall look upon Me whom they have pierced, and they shall mourn for Him, as one that mourns for his only son."* To us, the opened way to His heart is in His flesh, the token that this is the Incarnate God of Love, whose heart can be reached by all who seek His Grace.

But I have not finished this identification, for observe, that when that side was pierced, "and immediately blood and water came out." You that have your Bibles will have opened them already at Zechariah 12, will you kindly read on till you come to the first verse of the 13th Chapter, which ought not to have been divided from the 12th chapter? What do you find there? *"In that day there shall be a fountain opened to the house of David and to the inhabitants of Jerusalem for sin and for uncleanness."* They pierced Him and in that day they began to mourn for Him. But more, in that day there was a fountain opened! And what was that fountain but this gush of water and of blood from the split side of our redeeming Lord? The *prophecies* follow quickly, one upon another, they relate to the same Person, to the same day and we are pleased to see that the *facts* also follow quickly upon one another, for when the soldier with the spear pierced the side of Jesus, *"immediately blood and water came out."* Jehovah was pierced and men repented and beheld the cleansing fountain within a brief space. The men who saw the sacred fountain opened rejoiced to see in it the attestation of the finished Sacrifice and the token of its cleansing effect.

The identification is more complete if we add one more remark. Take all the types of the Old Testament together and you will gather this, that *the purification of sin was typically set forth by blood and water.* Blood was always conspicuous. You have no remission of sin without it. But water was also exceedingly prominent. The priests, before sacrificing, must wash and the victim, itself, must be washed with water. Impure things must be washed with running water. Behold how our Lord Jesus came by water and by blood, not by water, only, but by water *and* blood. John, who saw the marvelous stream, never forgot the sight, for though he wrote his Epistles, I suppose, far on in life, the recollection of that wondrous scene was fresh with him. Though I suppose he did not write his Gospel until he was a very old man, yet when he came to this passage it impressed him as much as ever and he uttered affirmations which he was not at all accustomed to use! **"He who has seen has testified, and his record is true: and he knows that he is telling the truth"** In solemn form he thus, after a manner, gave his affidavit before God's people that he did *really* behold this extraordinary sight.

In Jesus we see One who has come to atone and to sanctify. He is that High Priest who cleanses the leprosy of sin by blood and water. This is one part of the sure identification of the great Purifier of God's people, that He came both by water and by blood and poured out both from His pierced side. I leave these identifications to you. They are striking to my own mind, but they are only part of the wonderful system of marks and tokens by which it is seen that God attests the Man Christ Jesus as being in very deed the true Messiah.

C. I must close by noticing, thirdly, *THE INSTRUCTION INTENDED FOR US* in all these things.

The first instruction intended for us must be only hinted at, like all the rest. *See what Christ is to us.* He is the Paschal Lamb, not a bone of which was broken. You believe it. Come, then, and act upon your belief by feeding upon Christ! Keep the feast in your own souls this day. That sprinkled blood of His has brought you safety, the Destroying Angel cannot touch you or your house. The Lamb, Himself, has become your food. Feed on Him. Remove your spiritual hunger by receiving Jesus into your heart. This is the food of which, if a man eats, he shall live forever. Be filled with all the fullness of God as you now receive the Lord Jesus as God and Man. **"You are complete in Him." You are "perfect in Jesus Christ." Can you say of Him, "He is all my salvation and all my desire"? "Christ is all and in all." Do not merely learn this lesson as a doctrine, but enjoy it as a personal experience. Jesus our Passover is slain, let Him be eaten! Let us feast on Him and then be ready to journey through the wilderness in the strength of this Divine food, until we come to the promised rest.**

What next do we learn from this lesson but this? See *man's treatment of Christ.* They have spit on Him; they have cried, "Crucify Him, crucify Him." They have nailed Him to the Cross. They have mocked His agonies and He is dead, but man's malice is not yet glutted. The last act of man to Christ must be to pierce Him through! That cruel wound was the concentration of man's ill-treatment of Jesus. His experience at the hands of our race is summed up in the fact that they pierced Him to the heart. That is what men have done to Christ, they have so despised and rejected Him that He dies, pierced to the heart. Oh, the depravity of our nature. **Some doubt whether it is total depravity.** It deserves a worse adjective than that! There is no word in the human language which can express the venom of the enmity of man to his God and Savior; he would wound Him mortally if He could. Do not expect that men will love either Christ or you, if you are like He? Do not expect that Jesus will find room for Himself in the inn, much less that He will be set on the throne by guilty, unrenewed men. Oh, no! Even when He is dead, they must insult His corpse with a spear thrust. One soldier did it, but he expressed the sentiment of the age. This is what the world of sinners did for Him who came into the world to save it.

Now, learn, in the next place, **what Jesus did for men**. Beloved, that was a sweet expression in our hymn just now: *"Even after death His heart /For us its tribute poured."*

In His life He had bled for us, drop by drop the bloody sweat had fallen to the ground. Then the cruel scourges drew purple streams from Him. And as a little store of life-blood was left near His heart, He poured it all out before He went His way. It is a materialistic expression, but there is something more in it than mere sentiment that there remains among the substance of this globe a sacred relic of the Lord Jesus in the form of that blood and water. As no atom of matter ever perishes, that matter remains on earth even now. His body has gone into Glory, but the blood and water are left behind.

I see much more in this fact than I will now attempt to tell. O world, the Christ has marked you with His blood and He means to have you! Blood and water from the heart of God's own Son have fallen down upon this dark and defiled planet and thus Jesus has sealed it as His own and, as such, it *must* be transformed into a new Heaven and a new earth wherein dwells righteousness! Our dear Lord, when He had given us all He had, and even resigned His life on our behalf, then parted with a priceless stream from the fountain of His heart, "and immediately blood and water came out." Oh, the kindness of the heart of Christ, that did not only, for a blow, return a kiss, but for a spear thrust returned streams of life and healing. But I must hurry on. I can also see in this passage *the safety of the saints*. It is marvelous how full of eyes the things of Jesus are, for His unbroken bones look backward to the Paschal lamb, but they also look forward throughout all the history of the Church to that day when He shall gather all His saints in one body and none shall be missing. Not a bone of His mystical body shall be broken! There is a text in the Psalms which says of the righteous man and all righteous men are conformed unto the image of Christ, "He keeps all His bones: not one of them is broken." I rejoice in the safety of Christ's elect! He shall not permit a bone of His redeemed body to be broken: *"For all the chosen seed /Shall meet around the Throne, /Shall bless the conduct of His Grace, /And make His glories known."*

A perfect Christ there shall be in the day of His appearing, when all the members of His body shall be joined to their glorious Head, who shall be crowned forever. Not *one* living member of Christ shall be absent, "Not a bone of Him shall be broken." There shall be no lame, maimed Christ, no half-worked redemption. The purpose for which He came to accomplish shall be perfectly achieved to the glory of His name.

I have not quite done, for I must add another lesson. *We see here the salvation of sinners.* Jesus Christ's side is pierced to give to sinners the double cure of sin, the taking away of its guilt and power and, better than this, sinners are to have their hearts broken by a sight of the Crucified. By this means they are also to obtain faith. *"They shall look upon Me whom they have pierced, and they shall mourn for Him."* Beloved, **our Lord Jesus came not only to save sinners, but to seek them.** His death not only saves those who have faith, but it creates faith in those who have it not. The Cross produces the faith and repentance which it demands. If you cannot come to Christ *with* faith and repentance, come to Christ *for* faith and repentance, for He can give them to you. He is pierced on purpose that you may be pricked to the heart. His blood, which freely flows, is shed for many for the remission of sins. What you have to do is just look and, as you look, those blessed feelings which are the marks of conversion and regeneration shall be worked in you by a sight of Him.

EXHORTATION: Oh, blessed lesson. Put it into practice this morning. Oh, that in this great house many may now have done with self and look to the crucified Savior and find eternal life in Him. For this is the main end of John's writing this record. And this is the chief design of our preaching upon it, we long that you may believe. Come, you guilty. Come and trust the Son of God who died for you. Come, you foul and polluted. Come and wash in this sacred stream poured out for you. There is life in a look at the Crucified One. There is life at this moment for every one of you who will look to Him. God grant you may look and live, for Jesus Christ's sake. Amen.

B. The First Appearance of the Risen Lord to the Eleven

"Now as they said these things, Jesus Himself stood in the midst of them, and said to them, 'Peace to you.' But they were terrified and frightened, and supposed they had seen a spirit. And He said to them, 'Why are you troubled? And why do doubts arise in your hearts? Behold My hands and My feet, that it is I Myself. Handle Me and see, for a spirit does not have flesh and bones as you see I have'"
"When He had said this, He showed them His hands and His feet. But while they still did not believe for joy, and marveled, He said to them, 'Have you any food here?' So they gave Him a piece of a broiled fish and some honeycomb. And He took it and ate in their presence"
"Then He said to them, 'These are the words which I spoke to you while I was still with you, that all things must be fulfilled which were written in the Law of Moses and the Prophets and the Psalms concerning Me'"
(Luke 24:36–44 NKJV).

FOCUS: **"In this wonderful manifestation of our Lord to His apostles, ...[this] incident teaches us first, the certainty of the resurrection of our Lord; second, the character of our risen Master and ... it gives us certain hints as to, third, the nature of our own resurrection when it shall be granted us. May we be counted worthy to attain to the resurrection from among the dead."**

THIS, beloved Friends, is **one of the most memorable of our Lord's many visits to His disciples after He had risen from the dead.** Each one of these appearances had its own peculiarity. I cannot, at this time, give you even an outline of the special colorings which distinguished each of the many manifestations of our risen Lord. The instance now before us may be considered to be the fullest and most deliberate of all the manifestations, abounding beyond every other in "infallible proofs." Remember that it occurred on the same day in which our Lord had risen from the dead and it was the close of a long day of gracious appearings. It was the summing up of a series of interviews, all of which were proofs of the Lord's Resurrection. There was the empty tomb and the grave clothes left there, the place where the Lord lay was accessible to all who chose to inspect it, for the great stone which had been sealed and guarded was rolled away. This, in itself, was most impressive evidence. Moreover, the holy women had been there and had seen a vision of angels who said that Jesus was alive. Magdalene had enjoyed a special interview. Peter and John had been into the empty tomb and had seen for themselves. The report was current that *"the Lord was risen, indeed, and had appeared unto Simon."* It was a special thing that He should appear unto Simon for the disciples painfully knew how Simon had denied his Master and His appearance unto Simon seemed to have struck them as peculiarly characteristic, it was so like the manner of our Lord.

They met together in their bewilderment, the eleven of them gathered, as I suppose, for a social meal, for Mark tells us that the Lord appeared unto them *"as they sat at meat."* It must have been very late in the day, but they were loath to part and so kept together till midnight. While they were sitting at meat, two Brothers came in who, even after the sun had set, had hastened back from Emmaus. These newcomers related how One who seemed a stranger had joined Himself to them as they were walking from Jerusalem, had talked with them in such a way that their hearts had been made to burn and had made Himself known unto them in the breaking of bread at the journey's end. They declared that it was the Lord who had thus appeared to them and, though they had intended to spend the night at Emmaus, they had hurried back to tell the marvelous news to the eleven! Hence the witnesses accumulated with great rapidity, it became more and more clear that Jesus had really risen from the dead! But as yet the doubters were not convinced, for Mark says, *"After that He appeared in another form unto two of them, as they walked and went into the country. And they went and told it unto the residue: neither believed they them."*

Everything was working up to one point, the most unbelieving of them were being driven into a corner. They must doubt the truthfulness of Magdalene and the other saintly women. They must question the veracity of Simon. They must reject the two newly-arrived Brothers and charge them with telling idle tales, or else they must believe that Jesus was still alive, though they had seen Him die upon the Cross. At that moment the chief confirmation of all presented itself, *"for Jesus, Himself, stood in the midst of them."* The doors were shut, but, despite every obstacle, their Lord was present in the center of the assembly. In the Presence of One whose loving smile warmed their hearts, their unbelief was destined to thaw and disappear. Jesus revealed Himself in all the warmth of His vitality and love, and made them understand that it was none other than Himself and that the Scriptures had told them it should be so. They were slow of heart to believe all that the Prophets had spoken concerning Him, but He brought them to it by His familiar communion with them. Oh, that in a like way He would put an end to all *our* doubts and fears.

Though you and I were not at that interview, yet we may derive much profit from it while we look at it in detail, anxiously desiring that we may in spirit see, look upon and handle the Word of Life manifested in the flesh. Oh, to learn all that Jesus would teach us as we now, in spirit, take our places at that midnight meeting of the chosen ones.

A. First, then, let us see here *THE CERTAINTY OF OUR LORD'S RESURRECTION.* We have often asserted and we affirm it yet again, that no fact in history is better attested than the Resurrection of Jesus Christ from the dead. The common mass of facts accepted by all men as historical are not one-tenth as certainly assured to us as this fact is. It must not be denied by any who are willing to pay the slightest respect to the testimony of their fellow men, that Jesus, who died upon the Cross and was buried in the tomb of Joseph of Arimathea, did literally rise again from the dead.

Observe, that when this Person appeared in the room, the first token that it was Jesus was His speech, ***they were to have the evidence*** *of hearing,* He used the same speech. No sooner did He appear than He *spoke.* He was never dumb and it was natural that the great Teacher and Friend should at once salute His followers, from whom He had been so painfully parted. His first words must have called to their minds those cheering notes with which He had closed His last address. They must have recognized that charming voice. I suppose its tone and rhythm to have been rich with a music most sweet and heavenly. A perfect voice would naturally be given to a perfect Man. The very sound of it would, through their ears, have charmed conviction into their minds with a glow of joy had they not been frozen up in unbelief. **"Never man spoke like this Man."**

They might have known Him by His speech, alone. There were tones of voice as well as forms of language which were peculiar to Jesus of Nazareth. What our Lord said was just like He, it was all of a piece with His former discourse. Among the last sounds which lingered in their ears was that word, *"Peace I leave with you, My peace I give unto you: not as the world gives, give I unto you,"* and now it must surely be the same Person who introduces Himself with the cheering salutation, *"Peace be unto you."* About the Lord there were the air and style of one who had peace, Himself, and loved to communicate it to others. The tone in which He spoke peace tended to create it! He was a peacemaker and a peace give and by this sign they were driven to discern their Leader.

Do you not think that they were almost persuaded to believe that it was Jesus when He proceeded to chide them in a manner more tender than any other chiding could have been? How gentle the words when He said, *"Why are you troubled? And why do thoughts arise in your hearts?"* Our Lord's chidings were comforts in disguise. His upbraiding was consolation in an unusual shape. Did not His upbraiding on this occasion bring to their minds His question upon the sea of Galilee when He said to them, *"Why are you fearful, O you of little faith?"* Did they not also remember when He came to them walking on the water and they were afraid that He was a spirit and cried out for fear and He said to them, *"It is I. Be not afraid"*? Surely they remembered enough of these things to have made sure that it was their Lord had not their spirits been sunken in sorrow. Our Lord had never been unwisely silent as to their faults. He had never passed over their errors with that false and indulgent affection which gratifies its own ease by tolerating sin. No, He had pointed out their faults with the fidelity of true love. And now that He thus admonished them, they ought to have perceived that it was none other than He. Alas, unbelief is slow to die.

When Jesus came at last **to talk to them about Moses, the Prophets and the Psalms**, He was upon a favorite topic. Then the eleven might have nudged each other and whispered, *"It is the Lord!"* Jesus had, in His latter hours, been continually pointing out the Scriptures which were being fulfilled in Himself and, at this interview, He repeated His former teaching. This is assuredly none other than He who always spoke His Father's mind and will and constantly did honor to the Holy Spirit by whom the sacred Books were inspired! Thus in His tones and topics our Lord gave clear indications that it was He who had suddenly appeared in that little assembly.

I want you to notice that this evidence was all the better because they, themselves, evidently remained the same men as they had been. *"They were terrified and frightened, and supposed that they had seen a spirit."* And thus they did exactly what they had done long before when He came to them walking on the waters. In the interval between His death and His appearing, no change had come over them! Nothing had happened to them to elevate them, as yet, out of their littleness of mind. The Holy Spirit was not yet given and, therefore, all that they had heard at the Last Supper and seen in Gethsemane and at the Cross had not yet exercised its full influence upon them. They were still childish and unbelieving. The same men, then, are looking at the same Person and they are in their ordinary condition, this argues strongly for the correctness of their identification of their well-beloved Lord. They are not carried away by enthusiasm, nor wafted aloft by fanaticism, they are not even, as yet, borne up by the Holy Spirit into an unusual state of mind, they are as slow of heart and as fearful as ever they were. If *they* are convinced that Jesus has risen from the dead, depend upon it, it must be so! If they go forth to tell the tidings of His Resurrection and to yield up their lives for it, you may be sure that their witness is true, for they are not the sort of men to be deceived.

In our day [April 1887] there has been a buzz about certain miracles of faith, but the statements usually come from persons whose impartiality is questionable, credulous persons who saw what they evidently *wished* to see. I know several good people who would not willfully deceive who, nevertheless, upon some points are exceedingly unreliable because their enthusiasm is prepared to be imposed upon. Any hawker of wonders would expect them to be buyers, they have a taste for the marvelous. As witnesses, the evidence of such people has no value in it as compared with that of these eleven men who evidently were the reverse of credulous or excitable. In the apostles' case, the facts were tested to the utmost and the truth was not admitted till it was forced upon them. I am not excusing the unbelief of the disciples, but I claim that their witness has all the more weight in it because it was the result of such cool investigation. These apostles were, in a special manner, to be witnesses of the Resurrection and it makes assurance *doubly sure* to us when we see them arrive at their conclusion with such deliberate steps. These were men like ourselves, only perhaps a little less likely to be deceived: they needed to be convinced by overwhelming witness and they were so. And afterwards they always declared boldly that their crucified Lord had, indeed, risen from the dead.

Thus far in the narrative they had received the evidence of their ears and that is by no means weak evidence. But now **they are to have the evidence of sight**, for the Savior said to them, *"Behold My hands and My feet, that it is I, Myself."* "And when He had thus spoken, He showed them His hands and His feet." John says, *"His side,"* also, which *he* especially noted because he had seen the piercing of that side and the blood and water flow out. They were to see and identify that blessed body which had suffered death. The nail prints were visible, both in His hands which were open before them, and also in His feet which their condescending Lord deigned to expose to their deliberate gaze. There was the mark of the gash in His side and this the Lord Jesus graciously bared to them, as afterwards He did more fully to Thomas, when He said, *"Reach here your hand and thrust it into My side."* **These were the marks of the Lord Jesus by which His identity could be verified.**

Beyond this, **there was the general contour of His Countenance and the fashion of the whole Man by which they could discern Him.** His body, though it was now, in a sense, glorified, was so far veiled as to its new condition that it retained its former likeness. They must have perceived that the Lord was no longer subject to the pains and infirmities of our ordinary mortality, otherwise His wounds had not been healed so soon, but there remained sure marks by which they knew that it was Jesus and no other. He looked like a lamb that had been slain, the signs of the Son of Man were in His hands and feet and side. Their sight of the Lord was not a hasty glimpse, but a steady inspection, for John, in his first Epistle writes, "Which we have seen and looked upon." This implies a lengthened looking and such the Lord Jesus invited His friends to take. They could not have been mistaken when they were afforded such a view of those marks by which His identity was established. The same Christ that died, had risen from the dead! The same Jesus that had hung upon the Cross, now stood in the midst of those who knew Him best! It was the same body and they identified it, although a great change had doubtless come over it since it was taken down from the tree.

Furthermore, that they might be quite sure, *the Lord invited them to receive the evidence of touch or feeling.* He called them to a form of examination from which, I doubt not, many of them shrank. He said, "Handle Me. Handle Me and see; for a spirit has not flesh and bones, as you see I have." Writers have remarked upon the use of the word, "bones," instead of, "blood," in this case. But I do not think that any inference can be safely drawn from there. It would have been barely possible for the disciples to have discovered, by handling, that the Lord had *blood*, but they could, by handling, perceive that He had bones and, therefore, the expression is natural enough, without our imputing to it a meaning which it may never have been intended to convey! The Savior had a reason, no doubt, other than some have imagined, for the use of the terms, "a spirit has not flesh *and bones* as you see I have." The

Savior had not assumed a phantom body, there were bones in it as well as flesh, it was, to the fullest, as substantial as ever. He had not put on an appearance, as angels do when they visit the sons of men. No, His body was solid substance which could be handled. *"Handle Me and see that it is I."* He bade them see that it was flesh and bone, such as no spirit has. There were the substantial elements of a human frame in that body of Christ which stood in the midst of the eleven. Jesus cried, "Handle Me and see."

Thus our Lord was establishing to the apostles, not only His identity, but also His substantial corporeal existence, He would make them see that He was a Man of flesh and bones, not a ghost, airy and unsubstantial. This should correct a certain form of teaching upon the Resurrection which is all too common. I was present some years ago at the funeral of a man of God for whom I had much respect. In the chapel a certain excellent Doctor of Divinity gave us an address, before the interment, in which he informed us as to the condition of his departed friend. He said that he was not in the coffin, indeed, there was nothing of him there. This I was sorry to hear, for if so, I was ignorantly mourning over a body which had no relation to my friend. The preacher went on to describe the way in which the man of God had ascended to Heaven at the moment of death, his spirit fashioning for itself a body as it passed through the air.

I believed in my friend's being in Heaven, but not in his being there in a *body*. I knew that my friend's body was in the coffin and I believed that it would be laid in the tomb and I expected that it would rise again from the grave at the coming of the Lord. I did not believe that my friend would weave for himself a filmy frame, making a second body, nor do I believe it now, though I heard it so affirmed. I believe in the resurrection of the dead. I look to see the very body which was buried, raised again. It is true that as the seed develops into the flower, so the buried body is merely the germ out of which will come the spiritual body, but, still, it will not be a second body, but the *same* body, as to identity. I shall enter into no dispute about the atoms of the body, nor deny that the particles of our flesh, in the process of their decay, may be taken up by plants and absorbed into the bodies of animals and all that. I do not care one jot about identity of atoms. There may not be a solitary ounce of the same matter, but yet identity can be preserved and it must be preserved if I read my Bible right.

My body today is the same as that which I inhabited twenty years ago and yet all its particles are different. Even so, the body put into the grave and the body that rises from it are not two bodies, but one body. The saints are not, at the coming of their Lord, to remain disembodied spirits, nor to wear freshly created bodies, but their entire manhood is to be restored and to enjoy endless bliss. Well said the Patriarch of old, *"in my flesh shall I see God." "He which raised up the Lord Jesus shall raise up us, also, by Jesus."* I cannot see how the doctrine of Christ goes beyond the doctrine of Plato and others if it is not a doctrine which respects this body. The immortality of the soul was accepted and known as a Truth of God before the faith of Christ was preached, for it is dimly discoverable by the light of nature. But the **resurrection** of the body is a Revelation peculiar to the Christian dispensation, at which the wise men of the world very naturally mocked, but which it ill becomes Christian men to spirit away.

The body which is buried shall rise again. It is true it is sown a natural body and shall be raised a spiritual body, but it will be truly a *body* and the same *it* which was sown shall be raised. It is true it is sown in weakness and raised in power, but the same *it* is thus raised. It is true that it is sown in weakness to be raised in power and sown a corruptible body, to be raised in incorruption, but in each case it is the *same body*, though so gloriously changed.

It will be of a material substance, also, for our Savior's body was material, since He said, *"Handle Me and see that it is I, for a spirit has not flesh and bones, as you see I have."* Still further to confirm the faith of the disciples and to show them that their Lord had a real body and not the mere form of one, **He gave them evidence which appealed to their common sense.** He said *"Have you any food here? And they gave Him a piece of a broiled fish and some honeycomb. And He took it and ate in their presence."* This was an exceedingly convincing proof of His Unquestionable Resurrection. In very deed and fact, and not in vision and phantom, the Man who had died upon the Cross stood among them.

Let us just think of this and rejoice. **This Resurrection of our Lord Jesus is a matter of certainty, for, if you spirit this away, you have done away with the Gospel altogether.** If He is not risen from the dead, then is our preaching vain and your faith is also vain. You are yet in your sins. Justification receives its seal in the Resurrection of Jesus Christ from the dead, not in His appearing as a phantom, but in His being loosed from death and raised to a glorious life. This is God's mark of the acceptance of the work of the great Substitute and of the justification of all for whom His atoning work was performed.

Note well that this is also our grand hope concerning those who are asleep. You have buried them forever if Christ was not raised from the dead. They have passed out of your sight and they shall never again have fellowship with you unless Jesus rose again from the dead. The apostle makes the resurrection of all who are in Christ to hinge upon the Resurrection of Christ. I do not feel it necessary, when I talk with the bereaved, to comfort them at all concerning those that are asleep in Christ, as to their souls, we know that they are forever with the Lord and are supremely blessed and, therefore, we need no further comfort. The only matter upon which we need consolation is that poor body which once we loved so well, but which now we must leave in the cold clay. The resurrection comes in as a final undoing of all that death has done. *"They shall come again from the land of the enemy."* Jesus says, *"Your dead men shall live, together with My dead body shall they arise."* If we question the Resurrection of Christ, then is the whole of our faith questioned and those who have fallen asleep in Christ have perished. And we are left just where others were before Christ brought this Divine Truth of God to light. Only as we are sure of the Resurrection of Jesus can we cry, *"O death, where is your sting? O grave, where is your victory?"*

B. Secondly, will you follow me while I very briefly set forth **OUR LORD'S CHARACTER WHEN RISEN FROM THE DEAD?**

What is He, now that He has conquered death and all that belongs to it? What is He, now that He shall hunger no more, neither thirst anymore? He is much the same as He used to be. Indeed, He is altogether what He was, for He is *"the same yesterday, today and forever."*

Notice, first, that in this appearance of Christ we are taught that *He is still anxious to create peace in the hearts of His people.* No sooner did He make Himself visible than He said, *"Peace be unto you."* Beloved, your risen Lord wants you to be happy! When He was here on earth, He said, *"Let not your hearts be troubled."* He says the same to you today. He takes no delight in the distresses of His people. He would have His joy to be in them, that their joy may be full. He bids you rejoice in Him always. He whispers to you, this morning, as you sit in the pew, *"Peace be unto you."* He has not lost His tender care over the least of the flock, He would have each one led by the still waters and made to lie down in green pastures.

Note, again, that *He has not lost His habit of chiding unbelief and encouraging faith,* for as soon as He has risen and speaks with His disciples, He asks them, *"Why are you troubled? And why do thoughts arise in your hearts?"* He loves you to believe in Him and be at rest. Find if you can, Beloved, one occasion in which Jesus inculcated doubt, or bade men dwell in uncertainty. The apostles of unbelief are everywhere, today, and they imagine that they are doing God a service by spreading what they call, "honest doubt." This is death to all joy. Poison to all peace. The Savior did not do so. He would have them take extraordinary measures to get rid of their doubt. *"Handle Me,"* He says. It was going a long way to say that, but He would sooner be handled than His people should doubt! Ordinarily it might not be proper for them to touch Him. Had He not said to the women, *"Touch Me not"?* But what may not be allowable, ordinarily, becomes proper when necessity demands it. The removal of their doubt as to our Lord's Resurrection necessitated that they should handle Him and, therefore, He bids them do so.

O Beloved, you that are troubled and vexed with thoughts and, therefore, get no comfort out of your religion because of your mistrust, your Lord would have you come very near to Him and put His Gospel to any test which will satisfy you. He cannot bear you to doubt! He appeals tenderly, saying, *"O you of little faith, why do you doubt?"* He would at this moment still encourage you to taste and see that the Lord is good. He would have you believe in the substantial reality of His religion and handle Him and see. Trust Him largely and simply, as a child trusts its mother and knows no fear. Notice, next, that when the Savior had risen from the dead and a measure of His Glory was upon Him, *He was still most condescendingly familiar with His people.* He showed them His hands and His feet and He said, *"Handle Me and see."* When He was on earth, before His passion, He was most free with His disciples, no pretense of dignity kept Him apart from them. He was their Master and Lord and yet He washed their feet. He was the Son of the Highest, but He was among them as One who *serves!* He said, *"Suffer little children to come unto Me."* He is the same today: *"His scared name a common word /On earth He loves to hear; /There is no majesty in Him /Which love may not come near."*

Though He reigns in the highest heavens, His delights are still with the sons of men! He will still permit us to sit at His feet, or even to lean our head upon His bosom. Jesus will listen as we pour out our griefs. He will regard our cry when we are not pleading about a sword in our bones, but only concerning a thorn in our flesh. Jesus is still the Brother born for adversity. He still manifests Himself to us as He does not unto the world. Is not this clear and also very pleasant to see, as we study this interview?

The next thing is that *the risen Lord was still wonderfully patient*, even as He had always been. He bore with their folly and infirmity, for, *"while they yet believed not for joy, and wondered,"* He did not chide them. He discerned between one unbelief and another and He judged that the unbelief which grew out of wonder was not so blamable as that former unbelief which denied credible evidence. Instead of rebuke, He gives confirmation. He says, *"Have you any food here?"* And He takes a piece of broiled fish and some honeycomb and eats it. Not that He needed food. His body could receive food, but it did not require it. Eating was His own sweet way of showing them that if He could, He would solve all their questions. He would do *anything* in His great patience that they might be cured of their mistrust. Just so today, Beloved, Jesus does not chide you, but He invites you to believe Him. He invites you, therefore, to sup with Him and eat bread at His table. *"He will not always chide, neither will He keep His anger forever,"* but in His great mercy He will use another tone and encourage you to trust Him. Can you hold back? Oh, please, do not do so.

Observe that our Savior, though He was risen from the dead and, therefore, in a measure, in His Glory, entered *into the fullest fellowship with His own.* Peter tells us that they did eat and drink with Him. I do not notice, in this narrative, that He drank with them, but He certainly ate of such food as they had, and this was a clear token of His fellowship with them. In all ages eating and drinking with one another has been the most expressive token of communion and so the Savior seems to say to us, today, *"I have eaten with you, My people, since I have quit the grave. I have eaten with you through the eleven who represented you. I have eaten and I will still eat with you, till we sit down together at the marriage supper of the Lamb. If any man opens unto Me, I will come into Him and will sup with Him and he with Me."* Yes, the Lord Jesus is still wonderfully near to us and He waits to grant us the highest forms of fellowship which can be known this side the gate of pearl! In this let our spirits quietly rejoice.

Let me call your attention to the fact that when Jesus had risen from the dead, *He was just as tender of Scripture as He was before His decease.* I have dwelt for two Sunday mornings [Refer to Sermons *Jesus Declining the Legions (# 1955)* and *On the Cross After Death (# 1956)*] upon the wonderful way in which our Lord always magnified the Scriptures. And here, as if to crown all, He told them that, *"all things must be fulfilled which were written in the Law of Moses, and in the Prophets, and in the Psalms concerning Me. And He opened their understanding that they might understand the Scriptures and said unto* them, *Thus it is written, and thus it behooved Christ to suffer, and to rise from the dead.*" Find Jesus where you may, He is the antagonist of those who would lessen the authority of Holy Scripture.

"It is written" is His weapon against Satan, His argument against wicked men. The learned at this hour scoff at the Book and accuse of Bibliolatry those of us who reverence the Divine Word. But in this they derive no assistance from the teaching or example of Jesus. Not a word derogatory of Scripture ever fell from the lips of Jesus Christ, He always manifested the most reverent regard for every jot and tittle of the Inspired Volume. Since our Savior, not only before His death, but after it, took care, thus, to commend the Scriptures to us, let us avoid with all our hearts all teaching in which Holy Scripture is put into the background! **Still the Bible and the Bible, alone, should be and shall be the religion of Protestants and we will not budge an inch from that standpoint, God helping us.**

Once again, our Savior, after He had risen from the dead, *showed that He was anxious for the salvation of men,* for it was at this interview that He breathed upon the apostles and bade them receive the Holy Spirit, to fit them to go forth and preach the Gospel to every creature. The missionary spirit is the spirit of Christ, not only the spirit of Him that died to save, but the spirit of Him who has finished His work and has gone to His rest. Let us cultivate that spirit, if we would be like the Jesus who has risen from the dead.

C. In the third place, to the light which is thrown by this incident upon *THE NATURE OF OUR OWN RESURRECTION.*

First, I gather from this text that our nature, *our whole humanity, will be perfected at the day of the appearing of our Lord and Savior Jesus Christ,* when the dead shall be raised incorruptible and we that may then be alive shall be changed. Jesus has redeemed not only our souls, but our bodies! **"Know you not that your bodies are the temples of the Holy Spirit?"** When the Lord shall deliver His captive people out of the land of the enemy, He will not leave a bone of one of them in the adversary's power. The dominion of death shall be utterly broken. Our entire nature shall be redeemed unto the living God in the day of our resurrection. After death, until that day, we shall be disembodied spirits, but in the adoption, to wit, the redemption of the body, we shall attain our full inheritance! We are looking forward to a complete restoration. At this time the body is dead because of sin and, therefore, it suffers pain and tends to decay, but the spirit is life because of righteousness. In our resurrection, however, the body shall also be quickened and the resurrection shall be to the body what regeneration has been to the soul. Thus shall our humanity be completely delivered from the consequences of the Fall. Perfect manhood is that which Jesus restores from sin and the grave and this shall be ours in the day of His appearing.

I gather next that in our resurrection our ***nature will be full of peace***. Jesus Christ would not have said, *"Peace be unto you,"* if there had not been a deep peace within Himself. He was calm and undisturbed. There was much peace about His whole life, but after His Resurrection, His peace becomes very conspicuous. There is no striving with scribes and Pharisees; there is no battling with anybody after our Lord is risen! A French author has written of our Lord's Forty Days on earth after the Resurrection under the title of, *"The Life of Jesus Christ in Glory."* Though rather misleading at first, the title is not so inaccurate as it appears, for His work was done and His warfare was accomplished, and our Lord's life here was the beginning of His Glory. Such shall be *our* life, we shall be flooded with eternal peace and shall never again be tossed about with trouble, sorrow, distress or persecution! An infinite serenity shall keep our body, soul and spirit throughout eternity.

When we rise again ***our nature will find its home amid the communion of saints***. When the Lord Jesus Christ had risen again, His first resort was the room where His disciples were gathered. His first evening was spent among the objects of His love. Even so, wherever we are, we shall seek and find communion with the saints. I joyfully expect to meet many of you in Heaven, to know you and commune with you. I would not like to float about in the future state without a personality in the midst of a company of undefined and unknown beings. That would be no Heaven to me. No, Brothers and Sisters, we shall soon perceive who our comrades are and we shall rejoice in them and in our Lord. There could be no communion among unknown entities. You cannot have fellowship with people whom you do not recognize and, therefore, it seems to me most clear that we shall, in the future state, have fellowship through recognition and our heavenly resurrection bodies shall help the recognition and share in the fellowship. As the risen Christ wends His way to the upper room of the eleven, so will you, by force of holy gravitation, find your way to the place where all the servants of God shall gather at the last. Then shall we be truly at home and go no more out forever.

Furthermore, I see that in that day *our bodies will admirably serve our spirits*. For look at our Lord's body. Now that He is risen from the dead, He desires to convince His disciples and His body becomes at once the means of His argument, the evidence of His statement! His flesh and bones were text and sermon for Him. "Handle Me," He says, "and see." Ah, Brothers and Sisters, whatever we may have to do in eternity, we shall not be hindered by our bodies as we now are. Flesh and blood hamper us, but "flesh and bones" shall help us! I need to speak, sometimes, but my head aches, or my throat is choked, or my legs refuse to bear me up, but it is not so in the resurrection from the dead. A thousand infirmities in this earthly life compass us about, but our risen body shall be helpful to our regenerated nature. It is only a natural body now, fit for our soul, but hereafter it shall be a *spiritual body*, adapted to all the desires and wishes of the Heaven-born spirit and no longer shall we have to cry out, *"The spirit, indeed, is willing, but the flesh is weak."* We shall find in the risen body a power such as the spirit shall wish to employ for the noblest purposes. Will not this be wonderful?

In that day, Beloved, when we shall rise again from the dead, *we shall remember the past*. Do you not notice how the risen Savior says, *"These are the words which I spoke unto you, while I was yet with you"* He had not forgotten His former state. I think Dr. [Isaac] Watts is right when he says that we shall, *"with transporting joys recount the labors of our feet."* [From the hymn: *'Lord! What a Wretched Land Is*

This -- There on a green and flowery mount /Our weary soul shall sit,/And with transporting joys recount /The Labors of our feet.] is rather a small subject and probably we shall far more delight to dwell on the labors of our Redeemer's hands and feet but still, we shall remember all the ways whereby the Lord our God led us and we shall talk to one another concerning them. In Heaven we shall remember our happy Sabbaths here below, when our hearts burned within us while Jesus, Himself, drew near. Since Jesus speaks after He has risen of the things that He said while He was with His disciples, we perceive that the river of death is not like the fabled [Greek] Lethe, which caused all who drank thereof to forget their past. We shall arise with a multitude of hallowed memories enriching our minds! Death will not be oblivion to us, for it was not so to Jesus. **Rather shall we meditate on mercies experienced and, by discoursing on them, we shall make known to principalities and powers the manifold wisdom of God.**

Observe that our Lord, after He had risen from the dead, *was still full of the spirit of service* and, therefore, He called others out to go and preach the Gospel and He gave them the Spirit of God to help them. When you and I are risen from the dead, we shall rise full of the spirit of service. What engagements we may have throughout eternity we are not told because we have enough to do to fulfill our engagements now, but assuredly we shall be honored with errands of mercy and tasks of love fitted for our heavenly being. and I doubt not it shall be one of our greatest delights, while seeing the Lord's face, to serve Him with all our perfected powers. He will use us in the grand economy of future manifestations of His Divine Glory. Possibly we may be to other dispensations what the angels have been to this. Be that as it may, we shall find a part of our bliss and joy in constantly serving Him who has raised us from the dead.

There I leave the subject, wishing that I could have handled it much better. **Think it over** when you are quiet at home and add this thought to it, **that you have a share in all that is contained in resurrection.** May the Holy Spirit give you a personal grip of this vital Truth of God! You, *yourself,* shall rise from the dead: therefore, be not afraid to die.

EXHORTATION: If any of my [Readers] have no share in our Lord's Resurrection, I am truly sorry for them. O my Friend, what you are losing. If you have no share in the living Lord, may God have mercy upon you. If you have no share in Christ's rising from the dead, then you will not be raised up in the likeness of His glorified body. If you do not attain to that resurrection from among the dead, then you must abide in death, with no prospect but that of a certain fearful looking for of judgment and of fiery indignation. Oh, look to Jesus, the Savior. Only as you LOOK TO HIM can there be a happy future for you. God help you to do so at once, for His dear name's sake. AMEN.

CONCLUSION

The first recorded words of Christ as the holy child speak of His Father's "work, worship, and truth." The Lord Jesus Christ came to do His Father's business, and His first words on the cross were words of forgiveness. It was from the Friend of sinners. His cries from the cross were reflective of the love of His Father and were words "of divine grace."

The last words of the Lord Jesus Christ on the cross come from the inspired scriptures which "were written for our learning, that we through the patience and comfort of the scriptures might have hope" (Romans 15:4). His last words of forgiveness, remembrance, and salvation, anguish, suffering, victory, of contentment (and resignation) are "instructive of the work of the church and offers suggestions to the unconverted" and strength to believers.

Christ's words of suffering and anguish ceased with words of "the triumphant shout of 'It is finished.'" The Savior's "work was finished and his bearing of desertion was a chief part of the work he had undertaken for our sake." He was crucified on the cross, and we were crucified with him.

The Lord Jesus Christ finished the work of the Father that He willingly decided for Himself in the Eternal Council of Heaven. In the words of Octavius Winslow: "[Jesus Christ] was the God-Man, Mediator, who, as the Son, and yet the Servant of the Father, relinquished His throne for a cross, that He might accomplish the redemption, work out the salvation of His church, the people given to him of God, and who, on the eve of that redemption and with all the certainty of an actual atonement, could thus breathe His intercessory petition to heaven, 'I have *finished* the work which you gave me to do.'"

This [devotional] book closes with two of Spurgeon's sermons under the title "From the Cross to His Glorious Appearance": "On the Cross

After Death" and "The First Appearance as the Risen Lord." The focus of the sermons is on "the wonderful manifestation of our Lord to his apostles. ... [It] teaches ... the certainty of the resurrection of our Lord, ... the character of our risen master and ... it gives us certain hints as to ... the nature of our own resurrection when it shall be granted us."

Let us confess saying, Lord the *condemnation* was
Yours, that the *justification* might be mine;
The *agony* Yours, that the *victory* might be mine;
The *pain* was Yours, and the *ease* mine;
The *stripes* were Yours, and the *healing balm* issuing from them mine;
The *vinegar and gall* were Yours, that the
honey and *sweet* might be mine;
The *curse* was Yours, that the *blessing* might be mine;
The *crown of thorns* was Yours, that the *crown of glory* might be mine;
The *death* was Yours, the *life* purchased by it mine;
You paid the *price* that I might enjoy the *inheritance*.
The Works of John Flavel, Volume 1 (The Banner
of Truth Trust, Reprinted, 2015), 101.

APPENDIX A

List of sermons, as used in this publication with original titles and numbers, and expositions available online from http://spurgeongems.org

1. Patience, Comfort, and Hope from the Scriptures [2573]
2. The First Recorded Words of Jesus [1666]
3. Unknown Depths and Heights [3068]
4. The First Cry from the Cross [897]
5. A Plea from the Cross [3558]
6. Exposition on Matthew 27:32–49 [3558]
7. Christ's Plea for Ignorant Sinners [2263]
8. Exposition on Luke 23:33–46 [2263]
9. The Believing Thief [2078]
10. Witnessing at the Cross [3363]
11. Exposition on John 19:25–28 [3311]
12. Cries from the Cross [2562]
13. Our Lord's Solemn Inquiry [3507]
14. The Saddest Cry from the Cross [2803]
15. The Three Hours of Darkness [1896]
16. "My God, My God, Why Have You Forsaken Me?" [2133]
17. Exposition on Matthew 27:27–54 [2803]
18. The Shortest of the Seven Cries [1409]
19. The Savior's Thirst [3385]
20. "It Is Finished!" [421]
21. Christ's Dying Word for His Church [2344]
22. Christ's Finished Work by Octavius Winslow [378]
23. The Water and the Blood [3311]

APPENDIX B

The following preface is taken from *The Chequebook of the Bank of Faith* by C. H. Spurgeon published in the Christian Heritage imprint by Christian Focus Publications, Fearn, Ross-shire, Scotland, www.christianfocus.com. The book is also available from Christian Book Distributors, www.christianbook.com (1-800-CHRISTIAN), in the United States.

A *promise* from God may very instructively be compared to a check payable to order. It is given to the believer with the view of bestowing upon him some good thing. It is not meant that he should read it over comfortably and then have done with it. No, he is to treat the promise as a reality, as a man treats a check.

He is to take the promise and endorse it with his own name by personally receiving it as true. He is by faith to accept it as his own. He sets to his seal that God is true and true to this particular word of promise. He goes further and believes that he has the blessing in having the sure promise of it, and therefore he puts his name to it to testify to the receipt of the blessing.

This done, he must believingly present the promise to the Lord, as a man presents a check at the counter of the bank. He must plead it by prayer, expecting to have it fulfilled. If has come to heaven's bank at the right date, he will receive the promised amount at once. If the date should happen to be further on, he must patiently wait till its arrival; but meanwhile he may count the promise as money, for the bank is sure to pay when the due time arrives.

Some fail to place the endorsement of faith upon the check, and so they get nothing; and others are slack in presenting it, and these also

359

receive nothing. This is not the fault of the promise but of those who do not act with it in a common-sense, business-like manner.

God has given no pledge that He will not redeem and encouraged no hope that He will not fulfill. To help my brethren to believe this, I have prepared this little volume. The sight of the promises themselves is good for the eyes of faith: the more we study the words of grace, the more grace shall we derive from the words. To the cheering scriptures, I have added testimonies of my own, the fruit of trial and experience. I believe all the promises of God, but many of them I have personally tried and proved. I have seen that they are true, for they have been fulfilled to me. This, I trust, may be cheering to the young, and not without solace to the older sort. One man's experience may be of utmost use to another; and this is why the man of God of old wrote, "I sought the Lord, and he heard me"; and again, "This poor man cried, and the Lord heard him."

I commenced these daily portions when I was wading in the surf of controversy. Since then I have been cast into "waters to swim in," which, but for God's upholding hand, would have proved waters to drown in. I have endured from many flails. Sharp bodily pain succeeded mental depression, and this was accompanied in the person of one dear as life. The waters rolled in continually, wave upon wave. I do not mention this to exact sympathy, but simply to let the reader see that I am no dry-land sailor. I have traversed those oceans which are not Pacific full many a time; I know the roll of the billows, and the rush of the winds. Never were the promises of Jehovah so precious to me as at this hour. Some of them I never understood till now; I had not reached the date at which they matured, for I was not myself mature enough to perceive their meaning.

How much more wonderful is the Bible to me now than it was a few months ago! In obeying the Lord, and bearing His reproach outside the camp, I have not received new promises; but the result to me is much the same as if I had done so, for the old ones have opened up to me with richer stores. Especially has the word of the Lord to his servant Jeremiah sounded exceedingly sweet in my ears. His lot it was to speak to those who would not hear, or hearing, would not believe. His was the sorrow that comes of disappointed love, and resolute loyalty; he would have turned his people from his errors, but he would not himself quit the way of the Lord. For him there were words of deep sustaining power, which kept his mind from falling where nature unaided must have sunk. There and such like golden sentences of grace I have loved more than my necessary food, and with them I have enriched these pages.

Oh, that I might comfort some on my Master's servants! I have written out of my heart with the view of comforting their hearts. I would say to them in their trials, "My brethren, God is good. He will not forsake you: he will bear you through. There is a promise prepared for your present emergencies; and if you will believe and plead it at the mercy-seat through Jesus Christ, you shall see that hand of the Lord stretched out to help you. Everything else will fail, but His word never will. He has been to me so faithful in countless instances that I must encourage you to trust Him. I should be ungrateful to God and unkind to you if I did not do so."

May the Holy Spirit, the Comforter, inspire the people of the Lord with fresh faith! I know that, without His divine power, all that I can say will be of no avail; but under His quickening influence, even the humblest testimony will confirm feeble knees, and strengthen weak hands. God is glorified when His servants trust Him implicitly. We cannot be too much of children with our heavenly Father. Our young ones ask no question about our will or our power, but having received a promise from their father, they rejoice in the prospect of its fulfillment, never doubting that it is sure as the sun. May many readers, whom I will never see, discover the duty and delight of such childlike trust in God while they are reading the little bit which I have prepared for each day in the year.

C. H. Spurgeon

INDEX

Title and Topical References:

Printed in the United States
By Bookmasters